# Adam Smith and *The Wealth of Nations* in Spain

Adam Smith's *An Inquiry into the Nature and Causes of the Wealth of Nations* was the product of the rich tradition of the Scottish Enlightenment but the book's fame immediately spread across the whole of Europe. This book looks at the long journey of Smith's ideas from Scotland to peninsular Spain, reconstructing in detail the reception, adaptation, interpretation and application of Smith's central concepts from 1777 up to 1840.

In light of methodological advances during the last two decades in the history of economic thought and the studies on the late Spanish Enlightenment and early Liberalism, the book tackles a series of significant issues and gaps in the historiography. In particular: this book sheds new light on the role of France as an intermediate step as the ideas spread from Britain southwards; the analysis draws not just on translations but also handwritten materials, book reviews, syntheses, summaries, plagiarism and rebuttals; a wide range of methods of dissemination are considered including the printing press and periodicals, parliamentary debates, academic chairs and societies; the role of individual translators and agents is given due prominence; the political interpretations of the *Wealth of Nations* and the ways in which the book was incorporated into the work of Spanish economists in the decades following publication are also considered.

This book marks a significant contribution to the literature on the reception of Smith's *Wealth of Nations,* studies of the Spanish Enlightenment and the history of economic thought more broadly.

**Jesús Astigarraga** holds a PhD in Economics and a PhD in History, and is a Full Professor at the University of Zaragoza, Spain.

**Juan Zabalza** holds a PhD in Economics and is an Associate Professor at the University of Alicante, Spain.

# Routledge Studies in the History of Economics

**John Locke and the Bank of England**
*Claude Roche*

**Poverty in Contemporary Economic Thought**
*Edited by Mats Lundahl, Daniel Rauhut, and Neelambar Hatti*

**Thomas Aquinas and the Civil Economy Tradition**
The Mediterranean Spirit of Capitalism
*Paolo Santori*

**The Macroeconomics of Malthus**
*John Pullen*

**Competition, Value and Distribution in Classical Economics**
Studies in Long-Period Analysis
*Heinz D. Kurz and Neri Salvadori*

**David Ricardo. An Intellectual Biography**
*Sergio Cremaschi*

**Humanity and Nature in Economic Thought**
Searching for the Organic Origins of the Economy
*Edited by Gábor Bíró*

**European and Chinese Histories of Economic Thought**
Theories and Images of Good Governance
*Edited by Iwo Amelung and Bertram Schefold*

**Adam Smith and *The Wealth of Nations* in Spain**
A History of Reception, Dissemination, Adaptation and Application, 1777–1840
*Edited by Jesús Astigarraga and Juan Zabalza*

For more information about this series, please visit www.routledge.com/series/ SE0341

"A powerful insight into Spanish economic thought in a turbulent age that lay the foundations of modern European culture. A path-breaking approach that creates new standards for next-generation historiography of economics."

*Marco E.L. Guidi, University of Pisa, Italy*

# Adam Smith and *The Wealth of Nations* in Spain

## A History of Reception, Dissemination, Adaptation and Application, 1777–1840

**Edited by**
**Jesús Astigarraga and Juan Zabalza**

Routledge
Taylor & Francis Group

LONDON AND NEW YORK

First published 2022
by Routledge
2 Park Square, Milton Park, Abingdon, Oxon OX14 4RN

and by Routledge
605 Third Avenue, New York, NY 10158

*Routledge is an imprint of the Taylor & Francis Group, an informa business*

*British Library Cataloguing-in-Publication Data*
A catalogue record for this book is available from the British Library

*Library of Congress Cataloging-in-Publication Data*
A catalog record has been requested for this book

ISBN: 978-0-367-71600-4 (hbk)
ISBN: 978-0-367-71601-1 (pbk)
ISBN: 978-1-003-15280-4 (ebk)

DOI: 10.4324/9781003152804

Typeset in Bembo
by Newgen Publishing UK

# Contents

*List of contributors*                                                    ix
*Preliminary note*                                                        xii
*List of abbreviations*                                                   xiv

1  Adam Smith's *The Wealth of Nations* in Spain: a state of the art      1
   JESÚS ASTIGARRAGA AND JUAN ZABALZA

**SECTION I**
**Translations**                                                          9

2  Smith, Campomanes and a networked translator: John
   Geddes and the early history of English print in Spain                 11
   JOHN STONE

3  Vicente Alcalá-Galiano: an interpretation of Smith between
   the public sphere and the state apparatus                              28
   JOSÉ MANUEL VALLES GARRIDO

4  A new analysis of Martínez de Irujo's *Compendio de la
   Riqueza de las Naciones* and the role of Marquis de Condorcet          41
   SIMONA PISANELLI

5  The first complete Spanish translation of Adam Smith's
   *The Wealth of Nations*: José Alonso Ortiz's *Riqueza de las
   naciones* (1794)                                                       57
   JOSÉ CARLOS DE HOYOS

6  José Alonso Ortiz, Adam Smith's translator: a new
   interpretation                                                         79
   JESÚS ASTIGARRAGA

## SECTION II
## Influences

101

7  Adam Smith's *The Wealth of Nations*: The first Spanish
readings, 1777–1800                                                    103
JESÚS ASTIGARRAGA

8  Nuancing Adam Smith: *The Wealth of Nations'* reception
and influences in Spain, 1800–1820                                     121
JESÚS ASTIGARRAGA, JOSÉ M. MENUDO AND JAVIER USOZ

9  "Readings" of Adam Smith's *The Wealth of Nations* by
Spanish economists, 1820–1840                                          138
JOSÉ M. MENUDO

## SECTION III
## Institutions

155

10  Adam Smith in the Spanish press, 1780–1808                         157
JESÚS ASTIGARRAGA

11  Adam Smith in the chairs on political economy in Spain,
1780–1823                                                             172
JAVIER SAN JULIÁN ARRUPE

12  Adam Smith and the Cortes of Cádiz (1810–1813):
more than enlightened liberalism                                      186
JAVIER USOZ

13  Adam Smith in the economic debates during the Liberal
Triennium (1820–1823), the Second Liberal Exile and
Hispanic America                                                      205
JUAN ZABALZA

14  Spanish translations of *The Wealth of Nations*: Beyond the
Enlightenment, 1792–2020                                              222
JUAN ZABALZA

*Sources and bibliography*                                            229
*Index*                                                               255

# Contributors

**Jesús Astigarraga** is a Full Professor at the University of Zaragoza (Spain). He holds a PhD in Economics (1991) and a PhD in History (2015). He is author or editor of several books, notably: *Los ilustrados vascos* (Crítica, 2003); *Luces y Republicanismo* (CEPC, 2011); *The Spanish Enlightenment Revisited* (Voltaire Foundation, 2015) and *A Unifiying Enlightenment. Institutions of Political Economy in Eighteenth-Century Spain* (Brill, 2021).

**José Carlos de Hoyos** is a Maître de Conferences (Senior Lecturer) at the University Lumière Lyon 2 (France), in the Department of Spanish and Portuguese (DEMHIL), and a member at the CeRLA Laboratory (Centre de Recherche en Linguistique Appliquée). He is a specialist in Hispanic linguistics in the field of the history of economic terminology. His latest book in the field is: *Léxico económico en la lengua española del siglo XIX. El 'Epítome' de Jean-Baptiste Say* (Cilengua, 2018).

**José M. Menudo** is an Associate Professor at Pablo de Olavide University in Seville (Spain). He has focused his research on History of Economic Thought during the eighteenth and nineteenth centuries and published his contributions in many journals like *History of Political Economy* and the *Journal of the History of Economic Thought*. He is the editor of *The Economic Thought of Sir James Steuart, First Economist of the Scottish Enlightenment* (Routledge Studies in the History of Economics, 2019).

**Simona Pisanelli** is a Senior Researcher at the University of Salento (Lecce, Italy). Her interest lies in the History of Economic Thought. Her main research topics are French and Scottish Enlightenment, the debate on slavery in the eighteenth and nineteenth centuries, and social and economic inequalities. Her latest works on the eighteenth century include *Condorcet et Adam Smith. Réformes économiques et progress social au siècle des Lumières* (Classiques Garnier, 2018); "James Steuart: Slavery and Commercial Society in his 'Principles of Political Economy'" in *The Economic Thought of Sir James Steuart*, edited by José Manuel Menudo (Routledge Studies in the History of Economics, 2019).

**Javier San Julián Arrupe** is an Associate Professor at the Department of Economics at the University of Barcelona (Spain). His research has focused on the international dissemination of economic ideas and the institutionalisation of economics in the nineteenth century. His latest contributions are: "An expansionary economist against fiscal discipline in mid-nineteenth-century Spain," in *Research in the History of Economic Thought and Methodology* (2020) and "The reception of Malthus in Spain and Spanish-speaking Latin America," in Gilbert Facarrello, Masashi Izumo and Hiromi Morishita eds. *Malthus Across Nations. The Reception of Thomas Malthus in Europe, America and Japan* (Edward Elgar, 2020).

**John Stone** is the Serra Hunter fellow in English Literature at the Universitat de Barcelona (Spain). His current research centres on library formation and manuscript culture at the Royal Scots College, Valladolid, between 1770 and 1808. More broadly, in recent years he has worked on English as a language of culture in eighteenth-century Spain, with a particular emphasis on personal and institutional libraries, books and networks, and instances of direct English-to-Spanish translation. He has published a scholarly edition of Samuel Johnson's Preface to Shakespeare in Catalan, as well as articles in the collections *Samuel Johnson in Context* (Cambridge UP, 2011), *Anniversary Essays on Johnson's Dictionary* (Cambridge UP, 2005), *Cultural Transfer through Translation* (Rodopi, 2010) and *The Eighteenth Century* (Ashgate Critical Essays on Early English Lexicographers, vol. 5, 2012), and in many journals.

**Javier Usoz** is an Associate Professor at the Department of Applied Economics at the University of Zaragoza (Spain). He has focused his research on the history of economic thought, the international circulation of the Spanish and European Enlightenment ideas, the relationships between political, social and economic ideas, and intellectual history. He has published in journals such as *Historia Agraria*, *Revista de Historia Económica*, CROMOHS or *Revista de Estudios Políticos*, and coedited *L'Économie Politique et la sphère publique dans les débats des Lumières* (Casa de Velázquez, 2013). He is now engaged in the re-edition of the writings of the Spanish economists Tomás de Anzano.

**José Manuel Valles Garrido** holds a PhD in History. Before retiring he was Associate Professor of Economic History at the University of Valladolid (Spain). He has focused his research on the fields of the circulation of economic and political ideas, the reforms of the Spanish monarchy during the Age of the Enlightenment, the Sociedad Económica de Segovia and the human and intellectual biography of the renowned enlightened Spaniard Vicente Alcalá-Galiano. He is the author of *Un científico Amigo del País en la España de la Ilustración: Vicente Alcalá-Galiano, 1757–1810* (Fundación Jorge Juan, 2004) and *Ciencia, Economía Política e Ilustración en Vicente Alcalá-Galiano* (CEPC, 2008).

**Juan Zabalza** holds a PhD in Economics and is an Associate Professor at the Department of Applied Economic Analysis at the University of Alicante

(Spain). His research has focused on economic doctrines, intellectual history and the relationships between economic theory and economic policy. His work has been published in leading journals such as *History of Political Economy, Journal of the History of Economic Thought, History of Economic Ideas, European Journal of the History of Economic Thought, History of the Economic Theories and Policies, Storia del Pensiero Economico, Il Pensiero Economico Italiano, Storia e Politica, Historia Agraria, Revista de Historia Económica, Revista de Historia Industrial* as well as in many Spanish and international monographs.

# Preliminary note

The making of this book is the result of a lengthy and planned research project. In fact, from the very beginning, the contributors have participated in a series of seminars, sessions in conferences and scientific meetings to design it and afterwards to evaluate the first outcomes of the research. In November 2018, the first workshop at the University of Zaragoza (Spain) was held to debate the goals, methodology, structure and organisation of the research project. On the other hand, the successive advances have been presented in the following scientific meetings: Sessions "Adam Smith's *Wealth of Nations* in Spain, 1780–1830 (I) and (II)," in *15th International Congress for Eighteenth-Century Studies* (Edimburgh, Great Britain, July 2019); the seminar *La influencia de Adam Smith en España (1780–1830): nuevas perspectivas* (Zaragoza, Spain, September 2019); session "Adam Smith in Spain, 1780–1823," at *7th Latin American Conference of the History of Economic Thought* (Curitiba, Brasil, November 2019). A further meeting that aimed at culminating the research project ("Adam Smith en España (1780–1840): recepciones, diseminaciones, adaptaciones," at *XIII Congreso Internacional de la Asociación Española de Historia Económica*—Bilbao, Spain, September 2020—that counted with the support of the Adam Smith International Society) was eventually cancelled as a result of the Covid-19 pandemics. However, the difficulties arising from the pandemics did not prevent the research project to culminate, as the edition of this book demonstrates.

The structure of this book is pretty simple. Besides an introductory chapter (Chapter 1) dealing with the "state of the art" and a final chapter (Chapter 14) tackling the translations into Spanish, Catalan and Galician of the *Wealth of Nations* (WN) beyond the Enlightenment, the book is divided into 12 additional chapters organised into three sections. The first contains five chapters ("Translations", Chapters 2–6) and covers the study of the most significant translations of the WN during the last quarter of the eighteenth century. The second ("Influences", Chapter 7–9) has three chapters and analyses the reception of the WN in the economic literature published in three successive chronological phases between 1780 and 1840. The third ("Institutions", Chapters 10–13) consists of four chapters dealing with institutional issues: the WN's impact in the press, the first chairs in political economy and commerce, and the parliamentary sessions held during the Cortes of Cádiz (1810–1813) and the Liberal Triennium (1820–1823) as well as among liberals condemned to exile after the restoration of absolutist power in 1823 and a glance to the arrival of the WN to Hispanic America. In addition, it is worth remarking that the quotations included here have been translated by their respective authors where there is no English version, the Spanish spelling has been updated and the online articles were accessed in May 2021.

Finally, the editors want to note that the book has been made possible thanks to the institutional and financial support received from the *Interdisciplinary Group of Intellectual and Institutional History* at the University of Zaragoza (GIHII, 2017–2019, H26_17R) and the researchs projects HAR2016–77344-R (2016–2020) and PID2020–115261RB-I00 (2021–2023) of the Spanish Ministry of Economy and Competitiveness. They would also like to thank Carolyn Black as a language adviser, Dolores Hernández, Librarian at the University of Zaragoza, and Xavier Gil, lecturer at the University of Barcelona, for the invaluable assistance they have given them during the production of the book.

# Abbreviations

## Archives and libraries

| | |
|---|---|
| AC | Archivo Campomanes (Madrid). |
| ADB | Arxiu Diocesà de Barcelona (Barcelona). |
| AGI | Archivo General de Indias (Sevilla). |
| AHN | Archivo Histórico Nacional (Madrid). |
| AMAE | Archivo del Ministerio de Asuntos Exteriores (Madrid). |
| AMH | Archivo del Ministerio de Hacienda (Madrid). |
| AMS | Archivo Municipal de Segovia (Segovia). |
| BBE | Biblioteca del Banco de España (Madrid). |
| BIEF | Biblioteca del Instituto de Estudios Fiscales (Madrid). |
| BNE | Biblioteca Nacional de España (Madrid). |
| FUE | Fundación Universitaria Española (Madrid). |
| MNM | Museo Naval de Madrid (Madrid) |
| RAH | Real Academia de la Historia (Madrid). |
| RSC | Royal Scots College (Valladolid). |
| RSESAP | Real Sociedad Económica Segoviana de Amigos del País (Segovia). |
| SCA | Scottish Catholic Archive (Aberdeen). |

## Journals

| | |
|---|---|
| CLE | *Correo literario de la Europa* (1781–1782, 1786–1787; ed. by Francisco Antonio Escartín). |
| CM | *Correo mercantil de España y sus Indias* (1792–1808; ed. by Diego María Gallard). |
| CMC | *Correo de Madrid o de los ciegos* (1786–1791; ed. by José Antonio Manegat). |
| DP | *Diario Pinciano* (1787–1788; ed. by José Mariano Beristain). |
| EC | *El Censor* (1781–1787; ed. by Luis García del Cañuelo and Luis Marcelino Pereira). |
| EDJ | *L'Esprit des journaux* (1772–1818; ed. by Jean-Louis Coster and Jean-Jacques Tutot). |

EMD      *Espíritu de los mejores diarios literarios que se publican en Europa* (1787–1791; ed. by Cristóbal Cladera).

GM      *Gaceta de Madrid* (1661–).

JEN      *Journal Encyclopédique* (1756–1794; ed. by Pierre Rousseau).

MHP      *Mercurio histórico y político* (1738–1830).

MI      *Miscelánea instructiva, curiosa y agradable* (1796–1800; ed. by Blas Román, Antonio Cruzado and Antonio Ulloa).

ML      *Memorial literario, instructivo y curioso de la Corte de Madrid* (1784–1808; ed. by Joaquín Ezquerra).

SAP      *Semanario de agricultura y artes dirigido a los párrocos* (1797–1808; ed. by Juan Antonio Melón).

VCLA,      *Variedades de ciencia, literatura y artes* (1803-1805; ed. By Manuel José Quintana).

## Publishing houses

BAE      Biblioteca de Autores Españoles.

BCA      Biblioteca de Ciencia y Artillería.

CEPC      Centro de Estudios Políticos y Constitucionales.

CNRS      Centre National de la Recherche Scientifique.

CSIC      Centro Superior de Investigaciones Científicas.

CUP      Cambridge University Press.

FCE      Fondo de Cultura Económica.

GG-CL      Galaxia Gutenberg-Círculo de Lectores.

IEF      Instituto de Estudios Fiscales.

IFC      Instituto Fernando el Católico.

IFE      Instituto Feijoo de Estudios del Siglo XVIII.

OUP      Oxford University Press.

PUF      Presses Universitaires de France.

PUG      Presses Universitaires de Grenoble.

PUZ      Prensas Universitarias de Zaragoza.

RACMP      Real Academia de Ciencias Morales y Políticas.

RAE      Real Academia Española.

UNED      Universidad Nacional de Educación a Distancia.

VF      Voltaire Foundation.

# 1 Adam Smith's *The Wealth of Nations* in Spain

## A state of the art

*Jesús Astigarraga and Juan Zabalza*

## Introduction

The publication of Adam Smith's *The Wealth of Nations* (WN) in London on 9 March 1776 represents a highpoint for political economy in the European Enlightenment. Although the book was essentially a mature result of the rich intellectual tradition of the Scottish Enlightenment, it immediately spread throughout the whole of Europe. The work crossed national borders in a variety of forms—straightforward translations, summaries and book reviews, but also plagiarisms and even rebuttals—and became a reference for intellectual elites and politicians at the dawn of the nineteenth century. The WN also penetrated peninsular Spain during the last two decades of the eighteenth century, the result of a long journey that started in the cosmopolitan, cultured and relatively developed Scotland, continued through continental Europe and ended in the impoverished, Catholic and economically and culturally backward Kingdom of Spain. The WN was to undertake a second journey during the new century, however, as Smith's ideas spread all over Spain and increasingly permeated Spanish economic culture, which undoubtedly became more diverse and plural during the first four decades of the nineteenth century. This book is about the WN's long journeys through space and time. It describes how Adam Smith, a distinguished University of Glasgow professor, became "Adan", "Smit", "Smiz" and even "Smitch" in the hands of enlightened and liberal Spaniards. It also aims to create a detailed reconstruction of the reception, dissemination, adaptation and application of Smith's economic ideas and policies to peninsular Spain from 1778 to 1840.

## The "Spanish Smith": three phases

The long journey outlined here begins with a survey of the prolegomena through which knowledge about the "Spanish Smith" has been gathered from numerous articles and book chapters since the 1950s. It essentially refers to the book's main theme, which is the reception of the WN in Spain; it is now known that the TMS aroused lesser interest in the period under study and was translated into Spanish only much later, in the twentieth century (Trincado

DOI: 10.4324/9781003152804-1

2014). This book's origins lie in the revival of Spanish Enlightenment studies in the 1950s, in particular the work done by Sarrailh, the French Hispanic studies specialist who effectively challenged the traditional way of viewing history of Spanish *Lumières*. Faced with the national approach, which was mired in zeal for Catholic orthodoxy and narrow nationalism, Sarrailh not only converted the Enlightenment into a key moment of openness and modernisation in Spain's history, but also highlighted political economy as one of the preferred languages that the enlightened "select minority" cultivated to foster the spread of ideas coming from Europe (Sarrailh 1957, 514–72). The first author to transfer this perspective to the history of economic thought field was R.S. Smith, in his 1957 analysis of the WN's reception in Spain and Hispanic America between 1760 and 1830 (Smith 1957a). His research may have been inspired by a range of factors; it was probably no accident that Lázaro Ros and Franco both published Spanish editions of the WN in 1956 and 1959 (Smith 1956; 1959), nor that Schumpeter had underlined the value of Campomanes and Jovellanos, the two main Spanish Enlightenment economists, to the applied economics field a few years earlier (Schumpeter 1954, 214–15), while Hutchison had paved the way for studies of the international transfer of economic ideas (Hutchison 1955). However, Sarrailh's book, which was translated into Spanish three years after publication, may have been the decisive factor in R.S. Smith's increasing tendency around that time to shift his attention away from the history of facts and institutions to economic ideas, always against the backdrop of the Spanish-speaking world (Goodwin et al. 1969; Almenar 2000b). He wrote a review of Sarrailh's book, significantly entitled "Economists and the Enlightenment, 1750–1800", and focusing on "the impossibility of maintaining, in any age, an iron curtain against migration of ideas" (Smith 1955, 348), while emphasising that this could be extended to the political economy field. His iconic 1957a research into Adam Smith was a magnificent example of this. R.S. Smith applied the methodology of the international transfer of economic ideas to the WN's reception in Spain and Hispanic America during this period through analysing the work's translations, adaptations and influences. According to Almenar (2000b, 345), the work of this professor of the Duke University was not only ground-breaking in Spain in terms of the study of the influence of economic thought from abroad and the reconstruction of the Classical period, but also helped to reign in the longstanding tradition marked by a nationalist and somewhat romantic view of Spanish economists, and in which an excessive interest in seeking forerunners flourished, even among enlightened Spaniards regarding Adam Smith (Colmeiro 1863, II, 356). At the same time, he shrewdly avoided Palyi's theory (1966 [1928]) that the WN had been read mainly through Say in countries such as Spain and Italy, as this "minimised the talents" of eighteenth-century economists in both countries (Smith 1957b, 1217).

R.S. Smith's work had an immediate impact in Spain, largely because in the year it was published a translation also appeared in the *Revista de Economía Política*, one of the most prestigious journals in Spain at the time (it was reprinted in another distinguished review, the *Hacienda Pública Española*, in 1970). His arguments were corroborated in a long introduction in which the translator appealed to the author to underline the enormous—and little known—wealth of economists in eighteenth-century Spain, and the notion that the identification between Spanish Liberalism and Smithianism had been exaggerated (Plaza 1957). This encouraged the beginning of a growing interest in the "Spanish Smith" and R.S. Smith's 1957a article emerged as a broader research agenda devoted to the reception of European economic ideas in Spain during the late Enlightenment and early liberal period, including the WN. To complement his article he wrote two notes on the history of Spanish translations of the WN, showing that 180 years had had to elapse before a complete translation became available, which was Lázaro Ros' 1956 version published, following Cannan (R.S. Smith 1961; 1967; A. Smith 1958). In a later study devoted to English economic thought in Spain between 1776 and 1848 he stressed that these ideas arrived in Spain in "trickles" and not in a "continuous torrent," nonetheless substantially broadening the list of Spanish economists that had been influenced by the WN, particularly during the first half of the nineteenth century and largely via French sources (Smith 1968a); the work was reissued in 1968 and translated into Spanish in 2000.

At the same time, R.S. Smith's work quickly became the main benchmark for Spanish research into Adam Smith. Herr, an American Hispanic studies specialist, followed Sarrailh's line about the importance of the political economy strand in the Spanish Enlightenment the following year, although he identified its principle Smithian influences more specifically (Herr 1959, 39–48, 46–47, 298–99). Although these were once again muddled in the haze of "naive and elementary" liberalism characterising Beltrán's handbook of the history of economic thought with additions on Spain (1961, 97–103), Elorza highlighted the importance of Smith's theories in the reconstruction of Spanish Enlightenment Liberalism a few years later. His framework differed from Sarrailh's, however: according to Elorza, the doctrinal and reformist foundations of the "enlightened minority" in Spain lacked the uniformity and homogeneity that Sarrailh had attributed to them. This heterogeneity did exist in Spanish interpretations of Smith, which in some cases was more aligned with the Ancien Régime. However, as the Enlightenment in Spain gathered speed from 1780 onwards, the WN not only contributed to the maturing of enlightened liberalism, but was a genuine representation of the upsurge of bourgeois thought towards the end of the century (Elorza 1970, 164–207; 2021, 218–25). With echoes of Elorza's book still fresh, Zapatero (1975) studied the image of Spain in the WN and Lasarte (1975) conclusively addressed another front opened by R.S. Smith: the Inquisition's censorship of the WN and its Spanish translations, which he documented with transcriptions of the most important documents.

The Spanish authors who championed the use of interpretative models of the international transfer of ideas during the 1970s were the first to qualify and look more closely into R.S. Smith's theories. Lluch's study of Catalan economists between 1760 and 1840 illustrated the existence of regional differences in the arrival of Enlightenment economic thought in Spain for the first time. The WN had a somewhat unorthodox reception in Catalonia due to the existence of a protectionism and prohibitionism-based tradition in the region, which included authors such as Dou and Jaumeandreu whose distance from Smith was a result of the longevity of the "mercantile system" and Say's strong influence (Lluch 1973 189–210, 259–332). For their part, Fernández and Schwartz (1978) deepened R.S. Smith's analysis to salvage the importance of Alonso Ortiz, author in 1794 of the first complete translation of the WN into Spanish, and his *Ensayo sobre el papel moneda y el crédito público* (1796) as a singular case of Smithian monetarism influence on economic literature in Spain. However, over and above their specific content, these works revealed the emergence of the first generation of historians of economic thought who were willing to tackle a research agenda with a Spanish focus. Subsequent studies devoted to economic translations (Reeder 1973; Cabrillo 1978; Llombart 2004; Martín 2018), "regional Enlightenments" and the WN's first readers in Spain (Campomanes, Foronda, Alcalá-Galiano, Jovellanos and Álvarez Estrada) helped to assess the true extent of this work's influence. At the same time, studies of sociability and cultural practices centred on economic and patriotic societies, university chairs and the press provided contextualisation with respect to the actors, texts and institutions that encouraged the emergence of political economy in Spain that had been lacking in R.S. Smith's work, and the WN's arrival was part of this process.

The atmosphere of academic effervescence with respect to the "Spanish Smith" reached its peak during the 1990s, and the current mainstream interpretation of the issue took shape during this decade. The first phase was structured around two works by Schwartz (1990) and Perdices (1991), which complemented each other but had only limited circulation to begin with. While Schwartz's earlier work essentially focused on the WN's initial reception and Alonso Ortiz's translation, Perdices extended the analysis to the first decades of the nineteenth century. The asymmetry between "knowledge" of Smith's work, which was early, and its "effective influence," which was drastically conditioned by censorship, an outdated institutional framework and the cautious attitude of Spanish economists, was emphasised. The outcome of this asymmetry was that awareness of the WN's importance was delayed, interest in its analytical innovations was sidelined and its applications to economic policy were full of rectifications, nuances and discrepancies that affected central issues, such as free trade. As there was no straightforward acceptance of Smith, the WN's influence was "fleeting"—Schwartz extended it to 1814, the symbolic beginning of the "Say era"—and, according to Perdices, was "not important" and "weak," more meaningful to enlightened thinkers than to liberals. In any event, it was soon to be diluted, due to the fact that the work's general principles were modified when they were applied to Spain, and also because the undisputed hegemony of authors such as Say and Bastiat meant that it was interpreted in an "eclectic" and narrow fashion.

Another line of interpretation aimed to assess Smith's influence on the way that Classical economists were received in Spain. According to Llombart, the

WN reached the country during the period of vigorous intellectual growth in the late eighteenth century and did not represent a break with the doctrinal and political ideology of the time. In addition to being somewhat belated, this reception was "plural" since it coexisted alongside other currents of thought, including conflicting ones, and "active" because it was not a mechanical reflection of foreign economic thought but came about while "thinking" about Spain's own problems (Llombart 1992, 295–305; 2000, 66–68). For their part, Lluch and Almenar (1992) sidestepped the fact that Classical school Spanish economists were less well-known than those of the Enlightenment in the 1990s, putting forward the first interpretation of this school's development in Spain between 1776 and 1870, which later Almenar's research completed and broadened (Almenar 2000a). Their first work, which had limited initial circulation, focused on the WN's unusual reception in Spain (Lluch and Almenar 1992, 140–42). While the work continued to be influential during the emergence of liberal society there, although its impact diminished after the 1820s, its sway was strongest between 1790 and 1808. In this period, however, there were hardly any genuinely Smithian economists: the WN was not only moulded to the censorship requirements of the Inquisition and the government, but was read with caution, with emphasis on its agrarian orientation, usefulness to the particular Spanish context and the inappropriateness of its principles to a backward country like Spain (Almenar 2000a, 18–19). It also contributed to the intensifying of criticism of the Ancien Régime in specific areas (the tax system, the grain trade, the guilds and agricultural property), but without breaking with pre-existing Spanish tradition, which goes some way towards explaining why some interpreters there used it to reaffirm the principles of the "mercantile system." In any event, this cautious and limited reception was not the result of intellectual inconsistency, but was rooted in Spain's social, economic and political peculiarities when Smith's work arrived in the country.

There were two further manifestations of the blossoming of studies on the "Spanish Smith" in the 1990s. The first was the growing interest in the first Spanish translators of the WN, such as Alonso Ortiz, and the quality of their work (Schwartz and Fernández 1999), Martínez de Irujo (Lluch and Argemí 1987; Lluch 1989) and Alcalá-Galiano (Hernández 1978, 1993; Valles 1992). The second was the publication of the first reprints of the "Spanish Smith"; Alcalá-Galiano, published by Valles (1992); Alonso Ortiz's *Ensayo*, published by Schwartz and Fernández (1999 [1796]), and, most notably, Alonso Ortiz's translation, published in a facsimile edition by Fuentes and Perdices (1996).

This decade of concentrated accumulation of material on the "Spanish Smith" culminated in the impressive magnum opus *Economía y economistas españolas* (1999–2004, 9 vols.). As well as being the most mature overview of the history of economic thought in Spain to date, it represented an attempt by its editor Enrique Fuentes—invoking Campomanes—to rescue Spanish economists from the "wreck" of their oblivion and ignorance (Fuentes 1999, 15). The work, especially volume IV on *La economía clásica* (2000), brought together some of the most noteworthy studies of the "Spanish Smith", some original (Almenar

2000; Fuentes 1999, 128–36), others foreign and widely circulated—Smith (1968a); Lasarte (1975)—and lastly, the most important works produced in the early 1990s, whose distribution until then had been limited—Schwartz (2000); Perdices (2000a); Lluch and Almenar (2000). All these works upheld the mainstream interpretation of the "Spanish Smith" and almost immediately became a basis for introducing the topic to an international audience—Perdices (2000b); Schwartz (2001); Reeder and Cardoso (2002).

When the two fertile research cycles in the 20 years after the publication of R.S. Smith's pioneering research and the 1990s came to an end, studies on Adam Smith in Spain declined considerably, to the point of being almost entirely abandoned. Research has been both scarce and frequently repetitive. It is true that there have been reprints— Smith [1819–1820]) and Martínez de Irujo (2012)—and new partial studies—López (1999), Cervera (2003), Sánchez (2005, 2018), Menudo (2005), Astigarraga (2010) and Llombart (2017)—but, on the whole, these have failed to question the mainstream interpretation established during the last decade of the twentieth century.

## About this book

This book is the first to be devoted entirely to the WN in the Spanish-speaking world, and one of its main aims is to revitalise studies of Adam Smith in Spain and Hispanic America. This firstly entails incorporating recent developments at international level concerning the author and his work, as well as others from the history of economic thought, on the one hand, and the late Enlightenment and early Spanish Liberalism, on the other. However, above and beyond this essential updating task—some of the core research on the "Spanish Smith" is already three decades old—the book aims to develop a fresh and comprehensive interpretation of the WN's reception in peninsular Spain between 1778 and 1840. The 14 chapters it contains are all new and unpublished, which ensures that it is not merely a repetition or rehash of familiar ingredients. The work's innovative spirit is also owed to the fact that it addresses a series of core issues, some of which were left off the research agenda in earlier phases and among which the most important are the following. Firstly, the book recreates the catalogue of the different Spanish versions of the WN, including formats of all kinds, both published texts and manuscripts, long treatises (translations—whether complete or otherwise—summaries and adaptations) and "smaller formats" (reviews, print articles and many others). Secondly, it analyses the different channels through which the WN reached peninsular Spain, paying particular attention to French sources, whose intermediation activity may have been essential, triggering a dual process of active reception. Thirdly, it addresses the WN's impact on Spanish political economy treatises up to 1840, going beyond the first phase of reception before 1808, which is generally better known. The many interpretations of the WN show that the influence of the five books making up this work was uneven; that is, whether its influence was due to its analytical or applied innovations, and therefore whether it was read more as a book about "politics" than "economics," as a recent historiographical trend argues—Winch (1978); Robertson (1983); Hont (2005). Fourthly, it incorporates recent developments in prosopography and cultural history regarding the Spanish Enlightenment and Liberalism in order to revisit the main "actors" involved in the WN's reception in Spain. Fifthly, and finally, it extends the analysis of the "Spanish Smith" to the institutional sphere for the first time, covering a range of epitexts and the WN's reception in: (1) the press; (2) university chairs in political economy and commerce; (3) parliamentary debates (the Cortes de Cádiz and the Liberal Triennium Cortes), and (4) the economic literature produced by exiled Spanish liberals, with a brief look at the arrival of the WN to the Hispanic America. In short, this book aims to offer a fresh and thorough interpretation of the WN's spheres of influence in peninsular Spain, as well as of the different "readings" it was subject to by Spanish economists from 1777 to 1840; an interpretation that aims to avoid the anachronisms and presentisms that abound in analyses of the WN and that aspires to restore the "Spanish Smith" to his own time.

# Section I

# Translations

# 2 Smith, Campomanes and a networked translator

## John Geddes and the early history of English print in Spain

*John Stone*

## Introduction

It was Schwartz who, in a 1990 working paper, first drew scholars' attention to a partial manuscript translation held by Madrid's *Fundación Universitaria Española* (FUE) of Smith's *The Wealth of Nations* (WN). The manuscript, part of the Campomanes fonds, is supported by correspondence between Campomanes and John Geddes, the rector or principal of the Royal Scots College (RSC), a Spanish foundation at the service of the Scottish Catholic church, then housed in Valladolid. Schwartz dates the translation, comprising the first five chapters of book I, in 1777–1778, on the basis of both Geddes's 25 April 1778 letter to Campomanes[1] and the positive dating of documents of parallel provenance. As Schwartz noted later in his paper, Geddes's successor as rector, Alexander Cameron, would convey a bundle of books, including a third edition of the WN sent by Smith himself, to Campomanes in 1785. The same fonds features, in the same hand and in a single quire, a translation of paragraphs 46–59 of book I, chapter X, on the English Poor Laws; and a translation of an unidentified pamphlet on Thomas Gilbert's Poor Relief Bills, dated at some point between Easter 1776 and 1782, when Gilbert's last draft was enacted.[2] In different hands are two other texts clearly reflecting allied or ancillary concerns: on a single sheet, a list of 21 English and French works on the relief of the poor, dated between 1751 and 1777, of which 15 are English;[3] and the Count of Fernán Núñez's 6 March 1783 letter of presentation to Campomanes on behalf of the prison reformer John Howard.[4] Cervera (2019, 146) has gone so far as to suggest that the translation originates in an exchange between Geddes and Campomanes concerning the Poor Laws, rather than a more generic interest in the WN.

To these bare facts, reflected in subsequent publications by San Julián (2013), Meikle (1995, 71), Perdices (2003, 348) and very recently Hamnett (2017, 15) among others, I wish to add gleanings from archival collections at the RSC itself and the Scottish Catholic Archive (SCA), now held and administered by the University of Aberdeen. Schwartz had speculated that Geddes intended a full translation and rather glibly put Geddes's failure to produce one down to Olavide's experience with the Holy Office in 1778; and he was right that

DOI: 10.4324/9781003152804-3

Geddes had produced more materials, for the RSC archive features a draft of Geddes's translation,[5] originally entitled "*Discusión de la naturaleza y de las causas de la riqueza de las naciones*." The draft—which is not complete—exists in various states, from rough to clean, and both overlaps with the copy known to Schwartz and features new material. Significantly, with a separate cover page, Geddes had translated chapter VII of book IV, "Of Colonies," though this translation breaks off in the middle of the 13th paragraph; also appearing, though absent from the Madrid copy, is chapter VI, book I, but here the foul papers trail off in mid sentence, succeeded by what I read as one of Geddes's young students picking up the quill and practising "My me". In total, then, Geddes translated eight of Smith's chapters in all or part, as well as part of the front matter.

This discovery raises a series of concatenated questions. In whose hand is the RSC manuscript written? Is it the same as that of the FUE manuscript discovered by Schwartz? That is, is Geddes the translator in both cases? What copy text did the translator use? What do the manuscripts tell us about the translator's working method? How ambitious was the translator's project? How much of it has been lost? Why was it cut short? Why did he undertake these and not other chapters? Was the translation known and available to Alonso Ortiz, whose licensed translation of the WN was first issued in 1794? And, of greater interest to me: Why was a Scot, a non-native speaker far from court circles, chosen as translator (or, at the very least, accepted as translator when his offer to translate was accepted)? And how did this minuscule Catholic diasporic institution figure in the networks of late Enlightenment Spain?

In this chapter, I will argue that Geddes was indeed the translator; that the copy text was a 1776 first edition of the WN; that Geddes set out to translate more than has survived, but was delayed in part by his own working method; and that Alonso did not use the FUE and RSC manuscripts. I will further argue that Geddes's unusual role as a non-native translator stems from his status as a supremely networked individual, equipped not merely with a linguist's skill, but by his own role as a node. Geddes is precisely what Ferguson had in mind when he took up the interplay over time between vertical hierarchies and horizontal networks in *The Square and the Tower*: dependent on two hierarchies—one Scottish, one Spanish—but at arm's length from both, he conveyed his autonomy and his skill at networking into a unique kind of resourcefulness; and he achieved greater access to contemporary British print culture than any other individual in Spain, with the exception of the ambassador and his household.

## The manuscript

The RSC manuscripts comprise 49 leaves of handwritten material,[6] in three sewn quires of irregular length, featuring complete or incomplete translations of six chapters, as well as Smith's "Introduction and Plan." The only chapter not taken from book I is book IV, chapter VII, of which only 11 sheets survive, a translation of the first 13 paragraphs of "Part First: Of the Motives for Establishing New Colonies." The "Introduction and Plan," and chapters I–III and 5 of book I in the RSC manuscripts are earlier drafts, complete (chapters 1–2) and incomplete (chapters 3 and 5) of the FUE translation; the material not appearing in the FUE manuscript,[7] and so first reported here, in addition to "Of Colonies," is chapter VI of book I. But the story does not end there, for both the fragmentary nature of the materials and mixture of foul papers and fair copies, as well as intermediate states, suggest a more ambitious project.

The first 19 leaves of the first quire are a general title page,[8] the "Introduction and Plan," and all but the last leaf of book I, chapter I: and these have the appearance of clean copy readied for circulation, with a running header, page numbers, marginal chapter references and catch words, as well as the numbered paragraphs seen in FUE.[9] They nonetheless bear interlinear and marginal additions and corrections—which are regularly reflected in the FUE manuscript—as though Geddes had imagined himself ready to circulate the manuscript when he began the copy, only to realise that he was not, and thus adopt a more hurried format, at the end of book I, chapter I. Changes in appearance from the first to the second half of the quire suggest as much,[10] the single correction in the margin of 8r (undoing the Englished synax of a simple noun phrase, from "mucho mayor número" to "número mucho mayor"), the mise-en-page of early folios mimic that of the printed source text. Line spacing and margins make the text easy to read; and the hand is regular. Here and there blanks have been left for words untranslated, e.g. in "hasta el blanquedor y planchador del lienzo; y desde el pastor de las ovejas, hasta el teñidor y del paño",[11] and "El pasto, el escogidor de la lana, el cardador, el tintorero, el hilador, el texidor."[12] By leaf 19, most of the paratext falls away and the margins shrink to a minimum. By the final quarter of the quire,[13] the text is riddled with cancels, corrections and additions; and its appearance is sometimes messy, blotted or smudged: vertical strokes in particular are often heavy, and the baselines for Geddes's script slightly irregular. The number of lines per page has also increased, from 21–23 to 28, making for a denser text. Yet the second quire,[14] returns to something very like the format of the first 18 leaves of the first quire.[15] The title page is neat and preserves both the long title and Smith's academic credentials: it looks rather like the cover of an offprint. What has survived of the chapter itself resembles the opening leaves of the first quire, but for the marginal chapter references: the chapter number and long titles are centred; the script is again large and neat, the baselines regular and the margins wide.

This breaks off with the first two words of the 14th paragraph, "Finding nothing" (WN IV,VIIa, 561), "No hallando [nada]" in the translation,[16] in the latter as catchwords. The "Of Colonies" translation shows lighter correction and no gaps for words pending translation: its fragmentary nature cannot be due to the translator's having given up here, but rather to the loss of further manuscript material. Who undertakes a clean copy of an incomplete text? The FUE manuscript shows the translator's aim of circulating entire chapters: the first RSC quire[17] should therefore be taken as evidence that this first, albeit partial, Spanish translation of the WN was to take in the whole of "Of Colonies," the work's second-longest chapter.

The third quire[18] is entirely fragmentary—it begins with a translation of "was said to have a great deal of other people's copper" (WN I, V, 56) and breaks off in midsentence at "Let us suppose too, that the coarse materials" (WN I, IV, 66), ranging across book I, chapters V–VI, neither of which is complete. It is the foulest and, presumably, the most preliminary of the materials, featuring untranslated English words (the underlined "shillings" and "pennies" of 3v) and lengthy cancels (in 4v, most of the sentence beginning "In the proportion between the different metals in the English coin" (WN I, V, 60). One further observation will justify, I hope, the hypothesis to follow concerning the translator's working method: the third quire[19] is headed "III" though the material translated is neither from book III nor from a third chapter, marking one quire in a sequence. It represents a first state of the translation, the roughest draft; most of the first quire[20] records a second draft, perhaps intended as definitive but subsequently corrected and recopied; and "Of Colonies" (which is without gaps) a final draft to which the finishing touches of format seen in FUE manuscripts[21]—ruled margins and, in them, page and paragraph markers—were never added. As much of this material is in the FUE manuscripts in its definitive form, scholars of translation history are afforded a rare—and for the language combination, probably unique—opportunity to study translation as process in the Enlightenment.

## The hand and the copy text

The anonymous author of the RSC Archives' handwritten index attributes the translation to Alexander Cameron (born 1767, in Valladolid, 1780–1793 and 1798–1833), the RSC's fourth rector after its refounding—not to John Geddes (born 1735, in Spain, 1770–1781), the first. (This Cameron was the nephew of the second rector, also an Alexander Cameron: they are sometimes discussed as Alexander Cameron II and Alexander Cameron I.) Settling this question very nearly settles the matter of the copy text: Geddes could only have worked from a first or second edition before leaving Spain; and attribution to Cameron would place the translation very late in Campomanes's career. (Campomanes's involvement with the RSC was decades' long: his grandson Joaquin was admitted in October 1784.[22]) Indeed, there is no record of Cameron being in contact with Campomanes (as contemporaneous rectors were); and Geddes reported the progress of his work to Campomanes in the 25 April 1778 letter mentioned above. That the attribution is groundless is confirmed by the hand in which the manuscript is written: comparison to samples of each man's correspondence[23] show that the manuscripts bear a far stronger resemblance to Geddes's script than to Cameron's: they share Geddes's very long left-sloping ascenders on the lower-case "d", relatively short descenders on the upper-case "Y" and "G" (Cameron's are distinctly long), and oddly vertical descenders on "z", in an otherwise sloping hand.

Geddes was undoubtedly the translator: but what did he translate? His tenure as rector took in the publication of both the first and the second editions of the WN (Smith 1776; 1778). The RSC could bring books from England and Scotland in a matter of months and, occasionally, weeks, particularly when conveyed by a new cohort of students, or new members of staff, among their personal affects,[24] and a cohort did arrive on 28 March 1778 (Taylor 1971, 322), a date neatly placed midway between the late February publication of the first edition (Sher 2002, 19) and Geddes's first letter to Campomanes mentioning the translation, dated 25 April 1778.[25] Thus, while circumstances point to a first edition as copy text, a second edition might have conceivably reached the RSC in time for Geddes to begin work and offer (as he does in the letter) a first opinion. Neither edition is preserved at the RSC itself: identifying the copy text will, accordingly, rely on collations of the first two editions and the text of the Geddes manuscript.

Todd, the Glasgow Edition's textual editor, described the changes to the second edition as "providing new information," "correcting matters of fact," "perfecting the idiom" and "documenting references in footnotes" (62). The most reliable indicator of the copy text is that of additions, as changes for the sake of clarity of style (Todd's perfection of the idiom) may simply entail a rearrangement of sentence elements or change of pronoun, conjunction and article. Take this example (Table 2.1), from the "Introduction and Plan," for

*Table 2.1* Comparison between the 1776 and 1778 editions of the WN, RSC manuscript and Alonso´s translation

| | | | |
|---|---|---|---|
| **In what has consisted** the revenue of the great body of the people, or what **is the nature** of those funds which, in different ages and nations, have supplied their annual consumption, **is treated of in** these four first: Books. The Fifth and last Book treats of the revenue of the sovereign, or commonwealth. | **To explain in what has consisted** the revenue of the great body of the people, or what **has been the nature** of those funds, which, in different ages and nations, have supplied their annual consumption, **is the object** of these Four first Books. The Fifth and last Book treats of the revenue of the sovereign, or commonwealth; | **Después de haber hablado**, en los quatro primeros libros, **de lo en que consiste** la entrada del gran cuerpo del Pueblo, **o de la naturaleza** de aquellos fondos, que suministran lo que en cada año consume; en el quinto y ultimo libro se trata de la entrada del Soberano o de la Republica. | En estos quatro primeros Libros **se trata de examinar** en qué consista la renta del gran cuerpo de la sociedad, **ó qual sea la naturaleza** de aquellos fondos que la han provisto de su mantenimiento anual en diferentes Naciones y siglos. El quinto y último trata de las rentas del Soberano ó de la República: |
| Smith (1776, I, 4) | Smith (1778, I, 4) | RSC (22/9/10, 5v–6r) | Alonso (Smith 1794, I, 4–5) |

Table elaborated by the author.

which I supply both editions, the Geddes translation and (for the sake of comparison) the Alonso translation in its first edition.

Two caveats are required before proceeding. Geddes is a non-native translator, some of whose departures from the source text are mistranslations. And students of eighteenth-century translation soon grow used to target-text punctuation dictated as much by the translator's notion of euphony as by the source text, for punctuation is both grammatical and cultural. Hence, the most useful changes in the passage are, in bold, a short addition, a change of tense and an equally short substitution. Alonso has clearly followed "To explain" in choosing "examinar"; but might Geddes have combined the notions of aim ("the object," in 1778) and explanation in writing "Después de haber hablado" [After have spoken]? After all, like Alonso, he shifts mention of the first four books to the beginning of the passage. Nor is the change of tense, from present to present perfect, of much use, for Geddes has simply elided the verb, and Alonso's subjunctive ("o sea") is more abstract than historical. In such passages, then, the evidence is inconclusive. What is needed, then, is information newly supplied between the first and second editions.

I shall take up two such examples, from "Of the Division of Labour" and "Of Colonies" (Table 2.2). In the former passage Smith both chose a more specific lexeme and added data. Smith's fussy insistence on "corn-lands" in 1778 means very little to Alonso, for whom elegant variation is more important; but the remark on duties is too substantive to have been omitted by Geddes on a whim. Here, then, is evidence that Geddes used a 1776 *Inquiry* (presumably, the first copy to reach Spain); and this is confirmed by Smith's addition to a list of Portuguese discoveries in "Of Colonies." Where 1776 reads "They discovered the Madeiras, the Canaries, the Azores, the Cape de Verd islands, the coast of Guinea, that **of Congo, Angola, and Loango**, and, finally, the Cape of Good Hope" (Smith 1776 II, 149), 1778 has "**that of Loango, Congo, Angola, and Benguela**" (Smith 1778 II, 151): and here Geddes likewise follows 1776 in both the sequence and number of references ("la de Congo, de Angola y de Loango"),[26] while Alonso adds the new term and follows the new sequence ("Loango, Congo, Angola y Benguela" (Smith 1794, III, 120).

## Geddes as translator / Geddes's translation: the process and the product

A Scots speaker from the Enzie, a district in the Country of Moray known for its recusant population, Geddes came to correspond in English, French, Spanish, Latin and Italian. Nine years in Rome, beginning at the age 14, equipped him with Italian; and it was both his affability[27] and his Italian that made him the Scottish Catholic bishops' choice as envoy and lobbyist at the Spanish court in 1770. His Madrid letters of April–June 1770 are mainly in Italian: he seems to have acquired Spanish by immersion,[28] and honed it through both voluminous correspondence and, during his extended visits to Madrid, gregarious

*Table 2.2* Comparison between the 1776 and 1778 editions of the WN, RSC manuscript and Alonso´s translation

| | | | |
|---|---|---|---|
| The **lands** of England, however, are better cultivated than those of France, and the **lands** of France are said to be much better cultivated than those of Poland. [....] The silks of France are better and cheaper than those of England, because the silk manufacture does not suit the climate of England. | The **corn-lands** of England, however, are better cultivated than those of France, and the **corn-lands** of France are said to be much better cultivated than those of Poland. [....] The silks of France are better and cheaper than those of England, because the silk manufacture, **at least under the present high duties upon the importation of raw silk**, does not **so well** suit the climate of **England as that of France.** | Con todo esto las **tierras** de Ynglaterra se cultivan mejor que las de Francia, y **las** de Francia, según lo que dice, mejor que las de Polonia. [....] Las sedas de Francia son de mejor calidad y mas baratas, que las de Ynglaterra; porque las fabricas de seda no son a propósito para el clima de Ynglaterra. | ... las **tierras** de Inglaterra están mejor cultivadas que las de Francia, y **las** de esta nación mejor que las de Polonia. [....] Las sedas de Francia son mejores y mas baratas que las de Inglaterra, porque las manufacturas de seda (**á lo menos en las presentes circunstancias de los altos impuestos que se pagan en la introducción de la seda en rama**) no fon **proporcionadas** al estado **de esta nación.** |
| Smith (1776, I, 9) | Smith (1778, I, 9) | RSC (22/9/10, 12r–12v) | Alonso (Smith 1794, I, 12) |

Table elaborated by the author.

sociability. His circle took in the royal librarian Francisco Cerdá y Rico, the poet Tomás de Iriarte, the royal tutor Vicente Blasco and the translator Ramón de Guevara, as well as noblemen, diplomats and bishops.

Geddes made a habit of inverse translation: his *Wealth of Nations* project, though the most ambitious of Geddes's undertakings as a translator, was not the first. While still in Scotland, he composed and then translated into Italian a short account of the clandestine Catholic seminary at Scalan,[29] perhaps for the benefit of Cardinals Alessandro Albani and Giuseppe Castelli, with whom he kept up a correspondence. In 1780 he would translate an account of the Gordon Riots as "Noticia del tumulto que ha habido en Londres";[30] and translated or composed a similar account of the February 1779 anti-Catholic riots in Edinburgh with an eye to publication in a Madrid periodical.[31] He also regularly translated Spanish texts into English, working with sources from poetry to pieces published in the Madrid periodical press.[32] Yet he was not a native speaker; and the early draft discussed above[33] shows Geddes following

Smith's syntax closely and using cognates when available. His strategy is one of faithfulness, of formal correspondence, but only such as would serve the purposes of a narrow readership able to tolerate loan-words from English. That is, he emphasises the source language and text, as he has no trouble decoding Smith's text, but is limited in his ability to encode. He falls back on cognates, but will supply a paraphrase sooner than rely on a cognate of which he is not certain, and omit an ancillary word sooner than mistranslate it. This can be seen in both his process—for which we have less evidence—and his product.

For the roughest draft material of Geddes's translation—the fragments of book I, chapters V and VI described above—there is no intermediate draft, and so the only comparison to be made is to the copy reported by Schwartz. In the two versions of the "Introduction and Plan" and book I, chapter I, on the other hand, we have evidence of the late stages of Geddes's process. With one significant exception, these materials show Geddes making sentence-level adjustments in the early part of his process, and word-level changes in the later part. Consider the closing sentences of book I, chapter V (Table 2.3).

Geddes is struggling with the pragmatics of "it is to be observed" early in the passage and Smith's ellipsis at the end: his phrasing, and so his syntax, change significantly from draft to draft. By way of contrast, nine out of ten changes in the famous "trifling manufacture" paragraph of book I, chapter I as recorded in the carefully copied and formatted first quire of the RSC and FUE manuscripts,[34] are lexical: new translations are supplied for "perhaps" (in the first sentence), "peculiar" (in the second), "though" (in the third), "consequently" (in the fourth), "very poor" and "necessary" (in the fifth), and "But" and "educated" (in the ninth). The tenth change, an expansion, appears in the closing words— "a proper division and combination of their different operations" (WN I, I, 15)—rendered first as "una prudente repartición y combinacion de sus varias operaciones"[35] and finally as "una prudente repartición del trabajo, y de una combinación de sus varias operaciones."[36] The exception to this pattern is the first sentence of the "Introduction and Plan," which shows both an inversion of sentence elements, and breaking up into two sentences in the older draft, and a new translation of "fund" as "caudal" rather than "fondo."

Geddes's approach and method underline the strangeness of the source text, expanding (for instance) a reference to "acres," itself a gloss of the Latin *jugera*, rather than supplying one or more Spanish equivalents.[37] Consider his treatment of the English coinage mentioned so frequently in chapters IV and V of book I, in comparison to Alonso's 1794 translation. Smith first mentions shillings in the following passage:

> The shilling too seems originally to have been the denomination of a weight. *When wheat is at twelve shillings the quarter,* says an antient statute of Henry III. *then wastel bread of a farthing shall weighe eleven shillings and four pence.*
>
> (WN I, IV, 42)

*Table 2.3* Comparison between the WN and the RSC and FUE manuscripts

| By the money price of goods, it is to be observed, I understand always the quantity of pure gold or silver for which they are sold, without any regard to the denomination of the coin. Six shillings and eight-pence, for example, in the time of Edward I., I consider as the same money-price with a pound sterling in the present times; because it contained, as nearly as we can judge, the same quantity of pure silver. | **Se debe observar que yo entiendo por el precio de generos** en modeda entiendo (sic) siempre la cantidad de o oro o plata pura por la cual se venden, sin parar en el nombre de la moneda. Yo considero, por ejemplo, seis shillings y ocho pennies en el tiempo de Eduardo I de Ynglaterra como por el mismo precio en moneda con una libra esterlina de estos tiempos porque ~~esta contiene porq~~ la cantidad de pura plata **de ambas partes, en cuanto podemos jusgar, es muy igual casi la misma.** | **Será a proposito el avisar que yo por el precio de géneros** en moneda entiendo siempre la cantidad de oro **puro**, o de plata pura, por la cual se venden, sin parar en el nombre de la moneda. Yo considero, por ejemplo, seis shillings y ocho pennies en el tiempo de Eduardo I de Ynglaterra como el mismo precio en moneda con una libra esterlina de estos tiempos, porque la cantidad de pura plata es la misma, **en quanto lo podemos jus[gar], en ambos casos.** |
| (WN I,V, 63–64) | RSC (22/9/11, 9r; early draft) | FUE (AC 32-13, 75; draft sent to Campomanes) |

Table elaborated by the author.

The paragraph is dense with the technical language of Roman, French, English and Scottish coinage—Tower weight, Troy weight, pennyweight, *livre*, *sou*—and Geddes uses the Spanish equivalents of French terms without a gloss. The English terms, however, are retained and glossed so extensively that the second sentence in the passage above reads:

> Parece que también el sueldo o <u>shilling</u> originalmente era una unidad de peso. Una Ley antigua de Henrique III de Ynglaterra dice así: "Cuando el trigo está a doce <u>shillings</u> el <u>Quarter</u>," (una medida) "entonces el pan usual del valor de un <u>farthing</u>" (la quarta parte de un <u>penny</u>) "deberá ser del peso de once <u>shillings</u> y quatro <u>pennies</u>."[38]

"Sueldo" is, elsewhere in the passage, the rendering of "sou," just as Geddes later uses "dinero" as a "gloss" for "penny", relying in both cases on Spanish readers' familiarity with French coinage or its Roman antecedents (*sou/denier, solidus/denarius*). But he does so without explaining English coinage as a system: and retains "shillings" and "pennies" throughout. By way of contrast, Alonso adds an almost Derridean footnote on the history of Spanish coinage and, in handling the same passage, opts for Spanish equivalence when viable:

> El Shelin también parece haber sido en Inglaterra denominación de cierto peso. *Cuando el trigo esté a doce shelines la quartera* (★) dice un antiguo estatuto de Enrique III, *el pan vendido por un farthing pesará once shelines, y quatro peniques.*
>
> (Smith 1794, I, 42)

Neither "chelín" nor "penique" would appear in a normative Spanish Royal Academy dictionary until the late nineteenth century, but both were in use by the 1770s (the former sometimes spelt "eschelin", "esquelín" or "chilin") and boast entries in Terreros y Pando's polyglot four-volume *Diccionario castellano con las voces de ciences y artes* (1786–1793). Why, then, would Geddes have retained the English words? It may be that he chose loans over equivalents to underline the foreignness of the text; but I think it more likely that he had not encountered, or did not recall, Spanish words that Campomanes himself had used (1761, 17–18).

It should be remembered that by the time the first volume of Alonso's *Investigación* appeared he had published ambitious translations—Macpherson's *Ossian* (1788) and Butler's *Lives of the Fathers, Martyrs and Other Principal Saints* (1789–1792). He knew the licensing process, to be sure: but he also knew his own preferences, which broadly align with the privileging of the target over the source language so widespread in the Enlightenment. He is less likely to opt for the cognate, less likely to paraphrase, and more systematic than Geddes in his renderings. Illustrative instances of all these traits may be found in the first paragraph of "Of Colonies": where Smith has ancient colonists on a "quest for a new habitation" (WN IV, VIIa, 556), and Geddes has "a buscar para si una nueva habitación,"[39] Alonso writes "en busca de establecimiento" (Smith 1794, III, 115); and where Smith has "warlike neighbours," "confinantes valerosos" in Geddes, Alonso dispenses with "neighbours" (Smith's "who surrounded them on all sides" says as much) and writes instead "Naciones guerreras." In the preceding sentence, Smith's "plain and distinct [interest]" becomes "[intereses] claros y distintos" in Alonso, but Geddes resorts to paraphrase in rendering the second adjective: "ni se pudo tan fácilmente percibir" ("nor could it be so easily perceived"), as though troubled by *distinto*'s polysemy. (All eighteenth-century editions of the Spanish Royal Academy dictionaries list four senses.) Where Smith has Roman slaves working under an "overseer" (WN IV, VIIa, 556), Geddes likewise resorts to paraphrase ("debajo de la inspección de uno que también era escalavo,"[40] "as supervised by one who was also a slave"), Alonso has "caporal o sobrestante" (Smith 1794, III, 117). Where Smith writes "the bounties of the candidates" (WN IV, VIIa, 557), Geddes resorts to "lo que les daban los candidatos" [that which the candidates gave to the citizens],[41] and Alonso, "sobornos y gratificaciones" ("bribes and emoluments;" Smith 1794, III, 117). These periphrastic expansions represent no translation strategy on Geddes's part: he is at a loss for words, and works around the problem of his loss with paraphrase.

Yet it in Smith's repeated use of "mother city" that Geddes shows himself to be the less confident translator, and Alonso the more programmatic. "Of

Colonies" features 44 uses of "mother" as a modifier, the head words being "country," "city," or (in one instance) "state." "Mother city" is used for the ancient Greek city-states in the first part of the chapter: "mother country" is in the same passages Greece, but later refers to European polities of early modernity. Alonso regularly renders these expressions as "Nación matriz," although the different cast of his sentences means that some of the translations are pronominal.[42] The Greek city states are, accordingly, mother countries rather than mother cities in the 1794 text: but not so in Geddes's manuscript translation. Where Smith has "The mother city, though she considered the colony as a child" (WN IV,VIIa 556)—the metaphor could hardly be more traditional, nor more obvious—Geddes begins with "la ciudad de donde salía la colonia" ("the city from whence the colony went out"),[43] only to adopt "Madre Ciudad" later in the same paragraph. Alonso's only departures from "matriz"—"la Metropoli" (see, for example, Smith 1794, II, 188)—show his recollection of the Greek root of the word. Curiously, Campomanes himself had used "nación matriz" in the third part of the *Apéndice a la Educación Popular* (Campomanes 1776, III, 278, n. 68).

If Geddes has a virtue as a translator it is his extreme reluctance to take liberties with the message content of Smith's work. Smith's mention of the Roman tribunes is slightly clarified by Geddes, but very nearly rewritten by Alonso (additions in both translations are in bold) (Table 2.4). Geddes is clumsy: "irritar" in the first sentence hardly works as a collocate, "embiar" was a dated variant for "enviar", and the crossed third-person plural referents of the last sentence would have benefitted from clitic doubling. His only expansion, "de la plebe", simply gives the office's full title. But Alonso has written a politics into Smith's economic historiography: "en fomentar la sedicion" ("to stir up sedition") and "justas o injustas quejas" ("just or unjust complaints") suggest a translator worried that the reader will walk away from the passage with a politics, and ensuring that he is not to be blamed for what they walk away with. Print culture and manuscript culture contrast, in this case, very nearly as much as do the native and the non-native translator: a manuscript-cultural agent, Geddes is at liberty to write what he pleases so long as his writing maintains or enhances his status in Camponanes's circle. Though appointed by the king of Spain, he was beholden to the clandestine hierarchy of the Scottish Catholic church, and it was his institution's rather than his own success that depended, albeit slightly, on an ability to satisfy members of the elite's requests for translations, as for books, and their appetite for his brand of sociability.

## Why John Geddes? Notes on a networked translator

Geddes's vast correspondence stands at the confluence of sociability and strategy: to enhance the status of the RSC, he supplemented his Spanish friends' meagre access to English print and to the intellectual life of Great Britain. As Goldie points out, of all the leaders of Scottish Catholicism in the period, it

*Table 2.4* Comparison between the WN, the RSC manuscript and Alonso's translation

| | | |
|---|---|---|
| The tribunes, when they had a mind to animate the people against the rich and the great, put them in mind of the antient division of lands, and represented that law which restricted this sort of private property as the fundamental law of the republick. The people became clamorous to get land, and the rich and the great, we may believe, were perfectly determined not to give them any part of theirs. To satisfy them in some measure, therefore, they frequently proposed to send out a new colony. | Los Tribunos **de la plebe**, quando querían irritar el pueblo contra los ricos y poderosos, les acordaban de la antigua division de las tierras y representaban la Ley, que ponía ciertos limites a esta suerte de posesión privada, como la Ley fundamental de la republica. El pueblo gritaba, que se les diesen tierras, y podemos creer, que los ricos y grandes estaban muy resueltos en el no concederles alguna parte de las suyas. Por tanto para darles alguna satisfaccion y **contentarles a lo menos en parte**, frecuentemente proponían el embiar (sic) fuera una colonia. | Siempre que los Tribunos penaban **en fomentar la sedicion,** y exasperar los animos contra los Ricos y los Poderosos, hacian presente al pueblo, y le traian á la memoria la antigua division de las tierras, representando aquella disposicion de la propiedad de los particulares como una ley fundamental **é inviolable** de la Republica. El Pueblo entonces clamaba por la division de las tierras, y el Rico y el Poderoso por otra parte resistia sus solicitudes: **no quedando les á veces otro recurso** para satisfacer **de algun modo sus justas ó injustas quexas** que proponer al pueblo el establecimiento de alguna nueva Colonia. |
| (WN IV,VIIa, 557) | RSC (22/9/10a, 5r–5v) | Alonso (Smith 1794, III, 118) |

Table elaborated by the author.

was Geddes "who had the closest personal links with the Protestant literati" (Goldie 1991, 22), and these links helped extend Spanish scholarly networks to Glasgow, Aberdeen and Edinburgh. This stands for lesser-known individuals such as Cerdá y Rico, just as it does Geddes's involvement with Campomanes, which began within weeks of his arrival in Madrid in April 1770, on a mission from the Scottish vicars apostolic to recover the endowments of the Scottish Catholic college founded in Madrid in the 1620s. Long Jesuit-run, and Scottish in not much more than name, the college had been merged with an Irish counterpart. Though Campomanes required that the Scots draw up and submit a series of memorials—as, I suspect, a test of Geddes's resource-fulness and accurate knowledge (Briody 2015, 38)—his August 1770 *dictamen* was instrumental in the restitution of the endowment to the use of Scotland's clandestine Catholic hierarchy, and its transfer to Valladolid in various stages between December 1770 and March 1771. Campomanes would regularly entertain Geddes on his visits to Madrid (Taylor 1971, 106; Briody 2015, 41), show him his library (Briody 2015, 49), and introduce him, in December 1776, to Floridablanca. Geddes described his patron as "truly humane and generous" (Briody 2015, 85): while Campomanes termed Geddes "un grande picarón"[44] (a tricky or naughy fellow). Their surviving correspondence, extending beyond Geddes's return to Scotland, attests to shared contacts, common scholarly interests and cosmopolitanism. Geddes takes particular delight in informing Campomanes, in December 1781,[45] that he had seen William Robertson, to whom Campomanes had written concerning the Edinburgh riots via Geddes and his bishop in Edinburgh, George Hay;[46] and that he had struck a friendship with the "Lord *Corregidor*" of Edinburgh, with whom he conversed in Spanish.[47] Indeed, it was through Geddes that Campomanes's scholarly network extended to Enlightenment Scotland. Geddes himself mentions that a Scottish correspondent had best write to Campomanes in English: "When I reflect that he understands English, it is better in that Language, than in Latin […]: nay there will be no harm in putting some article of news in it.[48]" The advantages to be had by the polyglot rather than bilingual cosmopolitan are speed and freedom from French censorship. When Campomanes published a work on the apprenticeship system, trades and craft industries in the mid 1770s—the *Apéndice a la educación popular* (Campomanes 1775–1777)—he arranged that the four-volume set be delivered in 1778 to the classicist William Ogilvie, of King's College, Aberdeen, with alternating English and Spanish inscriptions in Geddes's hand. (Ogilvie wrote to Geddes the following year to both convey his estimate of Campomanes—which was high—and list books in English that should be sent to the count.[49]) It is the language pairing that makes the gesture distinctive. There is nothing unusual, in the 1750s, 1760s and 1770s, in scholarly gifts being sent from Berlin to Paris, from Copenhagen to Frankfurt, from Amsterdam to London: each city was a centre of French-language publishing. The flow of Spanish print to Scotland, and English print (much of it Scottish) to Spain comes as more of a surprise. Yet this is not Anglophilia, but part of a broader European promotion of his work (Guasti 2013, 237–38).

Who else might have been called upon to undertake the translation?[50] This begs the to-date only anecdotally answered question of how common a reading knowledge of English was in Spain before the consolidation of a liberal exile community in London around 1810; and, by extension, whether is it possible to speak of Smith's early reception in Spain without speaking of the medium of translation. Spanish Enlightenment historiography has long emphasised French mediation: Geddes affords evidence of a counter-narrative, of the emergence of English as a language of intellectual life in Spain in the second half of the eighteenth century. He is one agent, not *the* agent of this development. Spaniards were learning English: witness Meléndez Vidal (Jovellanos 1984, 140–41), José Cadalso (Cadalso 1979, 39) and Francisco de Saavedra (Molina 1991, 15). Spaniards were translating from English, often in manuscript form: see, in the 1760s and 1770s, the work of Felipe de Samaniego (Cáceres 2004, 99), Julián de Arriaga,[51] Manuel José de Ayala (de Solano 1981, 21); and, at Campomanes's behest, Ramon de Guevara (Nava 1990) and the emigré Thomas Southwell.[52]

Military and scientific libraries were building up very considerable English stock, from those of the Academia de Guardias Marinas—the Academy of Midshipmen—[53] and its sister institution the Real Instituto y Observatorio de la Armada—the Royal Institute and Observatory of the Navy—(González and Quevedo 2011) to Cádiz's Real Colegio de Cirugía—Royal Surgery College— (Gestido 1993). Diasporic individuals of Scottish (Stone 2014) and Irish descent, such as engineer Brigadier Ricardo or Richard Ailmer (Galland-Seguela 2004), could boast English stock in their private libraries: and it is in the 1824 post-mortem inventory of the library of a nobleman of Irish descent, Fernando Cagigal y Mac Swing (1726–1824) married to another Hiberno-Spaniard, Bárbara Kindelán, that the *Inquiry* appears in a three-volume quarto edition.[54] Early copies have also been documented in the catalogues or inventories of the Catalan noblewoman  Concepción de Martín y de Magarola (1821)—though the library was largely inherited from her father, Fernando Martín de Miravall, Baron of Balsareny[55]—and the Duke and Duchess of Osuna, whose library was open to the public until 1808.[56]

It is in this context the Geddes stands out, for in the 1770s he imported and circulated English print on a grand scale. At the RSC itself Geddes assembled a remarkable Scottish Enlightenment library, thanks to a special dispensation from the Holy Office, a bookseller/agent in London, and various regular routes by which to transport books from Britain to Valladolid (he used outbound students, diplomatic mail—thanks to his friendship with Munro, the consul general— and shipments of cannon from Falkirk to Ferrol). By the meridian of Geddes's tenure, the college library was unique in Spain in English holdings: most titles were recent and the spectrum of subjects was broad. Students and masters at the RSC could turn to recent editions of works by Adam Ferguson, David Hume, Francis Hutcheson, James Beattie, Thomas Reid and John M'Farlan, as well as long runs of London and Edinburgh periodicals, some of which featured reviews of the WN.[57] Geddes's correspondence attests to his importing books on behalf of Spanish friends, many associated with the Real Academia de la Historia—the Royal Academy of History: Nicolás Laso,[58] Francisco Cerdá y Rico,[59] Ramón de Guevara,[60] the Count of Marmilla[61] and Tomás de Iriarte.[62] Indeed, it may be that a further draft of "Of Colonies" was readied for circulation and lost when forwarded to Ramón de Guevara, whose mention of "las notas de las colonias" among other materials in a letter to Geddes clearly refers to manuscript material.[63] For such Spaniards, Geddes removed reliance on the mediation of French translators and facilitated ready access to English print. Other factors, of prestige and mobility especially, favoured the emergence of English print as a feature of cultural life in Spain, but the process was surely quickened by the charismatic Geddes, in himself a mediator in whom for a decade two print cultures overlapped. Why, then, did Campomanes commission or accept the Smith translation from a Scottish priest? Geddes had access to works that loomed large in Smith's training (Hutcheson); to abundant British domestic policy discussion, in periodicals and longer works, touching on such matters as the apprenticeship system, the Poor Laws and the Laws of Settlement;

and to the early reception of the WN. Thus, his library, and the print he could secure through his network, ensured that he could read behind and around the treatise itself.

## Notes

1  FUE, AC, 37–35.
2  FUE, AC, 32–13.
3  FUE, AC, 32–13.
4  FUE, AC, 48–73.
5  RSC, 22/9/10, 22/9/10A and 22/9/11.
6  RSC, 22/9/10, 22/9/10A and 22/9/11.
7  FUE, AC, 31-8.
8  RSC, 22/9/10.
9  FUE, AC, 31–8.
10  RSC, 22/9/10, 7v–8r.
11  RSC, 22/9/10, 11r. The untranslated word is "dressers" from "How many different trades are employed in each branch of the linen and woollen manufactures, from the growers of the flax and the wool, to the bleachers and smoothers of the linen, or to the dyers and dressers of the cloth" (WN I, I, 16).
12  RSC, 22/9/10, 18v. The untranslated word is "scribbler" in the context of woollens in the sentence, "The shepherd, the sorter of the wool, the wool-comber or carder, the dyer, the scribbler, the spinner, the weaver, the fuller, the dresser, with many others, must all join their different arts in order to complete even this homely production" (WN I, I, 22).
13  RSC, 22/9/10, 22r and 24v.
14  RSC, 22/9/10A.
15  RSC, 22/9/10.
16  RSC, 22/9/10A, 12v.
17  RSC, 22/9/10A.
18  RSC, 22/9/11.
19  RSC, 22/9/11.
20  RSC, 22/9/10.
21  FUE, AC, 31–8 and 32–13.
22  See Campomanes's 1791 letter to Joaquín de Nava (SCA, CA 4/62/5), then at the RSC, one of the eight children of his daughter Manuela Rodríguez Campomanes. I suspect that the various doodles signed by "Pedro" in the college library were left by another grandson.
23  See, for example, SCA BL 4/159/1, Alexander Cameron to Thomas Bagnall, 1 December 1801; and RSC, 20/1, John Geddes to Manuel Quintano Bonifaz, 16 March 1771.
24  See Geddes to George Hay, 11 January 1779 (SCA, BL 3/312/1), in which Geddes requests books in boards as well laxatives, forks, spoons, magazines and antimony pills; and notes three means by which to convey them. I discuss these circuits in greater detail below.
25  Geddes also received books via newcomers at Valladolid's English College, as well as the British general consul in Madrid, Alexander Munro (RSC, 52/7/54, James Coghlan to John Geddes, 18 March 1779).

26  RSC, 22/9/10a, 8r.

27  Geddes has been called "the most charming personality" in the history of Scottish recusancy before emancipation; see McRoberts (1955, 46).

28  See, for example, SCA, CA 4/52/18, an Italian-language account of the history of the RSC apparently drafted for circulation during these months.

29  "Memorie Della Casa Di Scalan, 4 die Settembre [...] 1762" (SCA, CS/1/2).

30  RSC, 19/36.

31  Geddes to George Hay, 7 March 1779 (SCA, BL 3/312/4).

32  See, for example, "Miscellaneous Observations and Anecdotes" (SCA, B/2/4/2).

33  RSC, 22/9/11.

34  RSC, 22/9/10; and FUE, AC, 32–13.

35  RSC, 22/9/10, 10r.

36  FUE, AC, 32–13, 10.

37  There was no unified system of measurement for land area in old-regime Spain: terms were often specific to regions and might serve as units of labour or of capacity as well as measuring surfaces. Geddes's expansion on "jugera" reads "que hacen cerca de trescientos y cincuenta de aquellas medidas, que llamamos en Ingles Acres."

38  FUE, AC, 32–13, 43.

39  RSC, 22/9/10a, 2v.

40  RSC, 22/9/10a, 4v.

41  RSC, 22/9/10a, 5r.

42  The first instance of "mother country" (WN I,VIII, 87) is translated as "aquí" [here], (Smith 1794, I, 116).

43  RSC, 22/9/10a, 3r.

44  Jospeh Shepherd to Geddes, 2 December 1778 (RSC, 51/7/61).

45  Geddes to Campomnes, 21 June 1781 (FUE, AC, 35-45).

46  See Geddes to George Hay, 28 July 1778 (SCA, BL 3/312/16), which includes both Campomanes's letter to Robertson and an English translation by Geddes, whom Campomanes had consulted about the draft.

47  He meant, of course, the Lord Provost, at that time David Steuart, a bibliophile and hispanophile who had lived in Barcelona from 1768 to 1771.

48  Geddes to George Hay, 3 March 1777 (SCA, BL 2/292/2).

49  See William Ogilvie to John Geddes, 23 April 1779 (SCA, BL 3/322/12).

50  Other manuscript translations from the English may be found in the very FUE fonds that features Geddes's partial translation of the *Inquiry*, of which only one is signed, by the nobleman and northern grand tourist Ignacio de Asso.

51  AGI, *Estado*, 44–68.

52  FUE, AC, 14–21, 14–23 and 20–2.

53  MNM, 1181, 271–294. According to the long title of this document, the librarian was "el Maestro de Idiomas y traductor de Facultades Matemáticas D. Joseph Carbonel." The academy possessed Newton's work in the original language (i.e. Latin or English, as the case may be) and ten volumes of Boyle's in English. In neither case were the English texts complemented by French translations.

54  ADB, *Censura de Llibres*, Llig. 1, exp. 28. The other works in English in the marquise's library, by Addison, Dryden and Pope, suggest a collection formed in his youth.

55  Biblioteca de Catalunya MS 1555.

56  Biblioteca Nacional de España MSS/10978 V.21.

57  Specifically, a two-part review in the *Weekly Magazine or Edinburgh Amusement* and the two-page notice in the *Annual Register*.

58 Nicolás Laso Rodriguez to Geddes, 24 January 1774 (RSC, 51/2/24).

59 See Francisco Cerdá to Geddes (SCA, CA 4/55, 4/56 and 4/60).

60 Ramón de Guevara to Geddes, 19 June 1779 (RSC, 51/2/68). In fact, the author of the translation was Geddes's better-known cousin, the Biblical scholar Alexander Geddes.

61 Count of Marmilla (Pedro de Alcántara Fernández de Córdoba y Figueroa de la Cerda y Moncada) to Geddes (RSC, 51/2/54)

62 Tomás de Iriarte to Geddes, 24 June 1780 (RSC, 51/2/86). To his credit, Iriarte knew that he was critiquing his friend's cousin, and not his friend.

63 Ramón de Guevara to Geddes, 24 March 1779 (RSC, 57/2/64).

# 3 Vicente Alcalá-Galiano

## An interpretation of Smith between the public sphere and the state apparatus

*José Manuel Valles Garrido*

## Introduction

The role played by Vicente Alcalá-Galiano (Doña Mencía, Córdoba, 1757 – Cádiz, 1810) in the reception (and application) of Smithian thought in Spain is starting to be more apparent,[1] and provides valuable lessons for intellectual history. Alcalá-Galiano worked his way to the top of the political-administrative apparatus of the Spanish monarchy after completing his scientific training in the artillery academy and having promoted the Sociedad Económica de Amigos del País—the Economic Society of Friends of the Country—of Segovia, the Castillian city located near Madrid, between 1781 and 1788. The latter was one of the most active economic societies during Carlos III's reign (1759–1788). Therefore, Alcalá-Galiano's ideas were progressively accrued upon his condition of "friend of the country," first, and, then, as a "servant of the state," enabling us to appreciate different nuances concerning his view whether in the public sphere or the state apparatus.[2]

Regarding his intellectual biography, he moved through three institutional environments: first, the scientific militia—the military academies were by then training centres for public positions—; then, the enlightened societies (and among the economic societies, created mainly by the monarchy, the Economic Society of Segovia was closely linked to the seats of power); and, finally, the state apparatus. The institutional permeability between these environments allowed the circulation of individuals and the flow of ideas that adapted discursive and institutional requirements.

## The scientific militia

At the end of 1770, Vicente Alcalá-Galiano enrolled in the Real Colegio de Artillería—the Royal Academy of Artillery—of Segovia, where he taught mathematics from 1774, becoming lieutenant in 1780 and captain in 1784. From 1779 he came to be one of the first members of the Economic Society of Segovia. After completing his scientific training (and within the context of the economic societies concern for applied science), he promoted the spread of new scientific innovations.[3]

DOI: 10.4324/9781003152804-4

The Royal Academy of Artillery, established in 1764, was a top-level scientific and educational institution. The young cadets, who enrolled at the age of 13 or 14, received a complete education in mathematics and technical drawing, which prevailed on other subjects. Mathematics included infinitesimal calculus and experimental physics. For the matters related explicitly to artillery (metallurgy, explosive powders, etc.), a well-equipped laboratory was built, and the prestigious French chemist Louis J. Proust, was hired. The Academy trained its teachers—Alcalá-Galiano became one of them—and published handbooks of a high standard.[4] Hence the need to have a well-furnished library.

The library's *Catalogue* compiled in 1796 by Pietro Giannini demonstrates that the library included a wide selection of French and English scientific books.[5] There is not any work by Adam Smith; but it does include the *Encyclopédie* by Diderot (1751–1772), from which Vicente Alcalá-Galiano translated or paraphrased the well-known 1755 article by Rousseau entitled "Économie ou Oeconomie (morale et politique)";[6] and also the *Supplément au Dictionnaire raisonné* (1776–1777), which was not edited by Diderot, but by Panckoucke. However, there is no copy of Panckoucke's *Encyclopédie Méthodique*, who, as it is known, reproduced many excerpts of the WN as part of different entries in the volumes on "Economie Politique et Diplomatique" (notably, volumes III and IV, published in 1788).[7] Apparently, it was precisely after 1788 when Smith's work began to be widely disseminated in France.[8] As will be seen, 1788 was also a crucial year in Spain.

## The economic societies in the Enlightenment

The Economic Society of Segovia, established in 1780, was committed to political economy and social action, and granted government support thanks to the mandatory connection to the Sociedad Económica Matritense—the Economic Society of Madrid. The latter, founded in 1775 by the Court of Madrid, served as a model to the other societies. Furthermore, from the beginning, the government granted the Segovia Society the privilege of a tax on wool,[9] which provided the society with funds to finance its many reforms and publications.

Alcalá-Galiano, as secretary of the society between 1781 and 1789, was involved in almost every activity of the institution. He shaped his ideological line through many statements and reports that occupied a large share of the four first volumes of *Actas y Memorias* published by the Economic Society of Segovia in 1785, 1786, 1787 and 1793 (RSESAP 1785; 1786; 1787; 1793). His economic thought was based on Campomanes's initial plan for Spanish economic societies. But, subsequently, his readings began to diversify: Montesquieu, Rousseau on *Oeconomie* of the *Encyclopédie* or some Spanish economists such as Arriquíbar; when he started to focus on finance, he was highly influenced, first by Necker,[10] and, finally, by Smith.

Perhaps it was the financing of the Segovia Society with the tax on wool (which, at one point, was in danger, obliging the institution to call in its highest-level political contacts to recover it) that led Alcalá-Galiano to study taxation.

He began at a local level by analysing the database of the revenue administration of Segovia, which was a conscious exercise of actual "political arithmetic." Alcalá-Galiano reported certain injustices observed in the complex system of indirect taxes on consumption and trade called *rentas provinciales*—provincial revenues—and proposed new features that the Spanish government well and promptly received.[11]

Due to his powerful position within the society, he backed the tax reform of 1785, promoted by Minister Pedro de Lerena, Count of Lerena, that counted on the support of the secretary of state, Count of Floridablanca.[12] The reform concerned the *rentas provinciales* and attempted to reduce their burden and technically improve their collection. Besides, it also included establishing a new tax called the *frutos civiles*—civil fruits—on the income arising from property, that is, rents.

On 8 February 1786, Alcalá-Galiano defended the new tax system in the Economic Society of Segovia and proposed a competition, with a 1,500 *reales* prize, to the best report based on observations and data about the drawbacks of the former tax systems and the advantages of the new one (RSESAP 1786, 98). The society accepted the competition, which lasted two years.

Volume III of the *Actas y Memorias* of the Society (1787) was fully devoted to support Lerena's tax reform. The volume began with the legislative texts regulating the reform and included the following (RSESAP 1787, 1–80): *Ventajas políticas de España por los nuevos reglamentos de rentas provinciales, tanto en la menor, más uniforme y equitativa contribución del vasallo, como por el fomento que resulta a la agricultura, al comercio, y a las artes,* by Diego María Gallard (RSESAP 1787, 81–363); *Perjuicios del antiguo sistema de rentas provinciales; y utilidades y ventajas del que se establece por los nuevos reglamentos,* by Vicente Alcalá-Galiano and Vicente Mantecón de Arce (RSESAP 1787, 1–237),[13] dated 17 February 1787.

After both works that endorsed Lerena's tax reform of 1785, Alcalá-Galiano published in 1793 volume IV of the Society's *Actas y Memorias* — *Sobre la necesidad y justicia de los tributos, fondos de donde deben sacarse, y medios de recaudarlos*— (RSESAP 1793, 269–358), dated 18 March 1788, where he profusely used Smith's WN.

Months later, Alcalá-Galiano widely evaluated one of the reports presented to a competition organised by the Economic Society of Segovia (Alcalá-Galiano 1793 [1788]). That critical review was published in volume VI of *Memorias* of Larruga (1789b, 283–99). The authors of both works of 1787—the youngs Gallard, Alcalá-Galiano and Mantecón—were thoroughly imbued in the reformist ideal of their time and well informed about the new science of political economy. Mantecón was then a civil servant of the revenue administration in the province of Segovia, and it seems that he was never promoted to a high position. Alcalá-Galiano and Gallard, on the other hand, moved up rapidly to high ranks in the state apparatus: Alcalá-Galiano was an influential expert in the advisory team of Minister Lerena and his successors until 1799, and, after 1808, was General Treasurer; Gallard—in the same year his report on revenue was published—became an official in the Ministry of Finance and, in 1792, together with Larruga, promoted the *Correo Mercantil de España y sus Indias* (1792–1808), the first Spanish newspaper specialised in commerce. Later on, he directed the office of the Balance of Trade, the first official agency of statistics, and, subsequently, he held different positions in municipalities and consulates. Alcalá-Galiano did not cut off his ties with the Economic Society of Segovia once he joined Lerena's ministerial team, as he even chaired the society between 1794 and 1799.

The intellectual significance of the Economic Society of Segovia in the last two decades of the eighteenth century was the result of Alcalá-Galiano's efforts and the commitment of many other members. For example, Alcalá-Galiano was succeeded as secretary in 1789 by a fellow artilleryman, Juan Manuel Munárriz, a disciple of Louis J. Proust, who had translated Lavoisier's principal works into Spanish.[14] In 1790, he was responsible for the society's library and greatly contributed to enrich it, purchasing a vast number of works on political economy.[15]

Was Adam Smith read by the members of the Segovia Economic Society? We find the answer in the minutes of the meetings of the society. On 22 August 1792 there is a reference to two consignments of books bought for the society's library to Madrid and Valladolid. The latter was "the compendium of Smith's work,"[16] that is, the translation carried out by Martínez de Irujo of the compendium attributed to Condorcet (Smith 1792).[17]

Two years later—at a meeting of 15 October 1794—the Society agreed to subscribe "to the translation of Smith's work titled *The Wealth of the Nations*," the Spanish translation by Alonso Ortiz. In the same session, which Vicente Mantecón and Juan Manuel Munárriz attended, Alcalá-Galiano was elected as director, succeeding the recently deceased Duke of Almodóvar. Ambrosio López Momediano, canon of the cathedral of Segovia and undoubtedly one of the most active society members, was re-elected as vice-director, a position that he had held since 1788. In October 1791, Momediano had undertaken the society's prescriptive report on Proust's *Anales del Real Laboratorio de química de Segovia* (1791), which earned him honorary membership. Furthermore, Momediano helped Alcalá-Galiano evaluate the reports on revenues that aspired to win the society's award.

There is another surprising fact about Momediano from our point of view. Although the four thick volumes of *Actas y Memorias* published by the society— in 1785, 1786, 1787 and 1793—are well known, the small volume *Extracto de las actas de la Sociedad de Segovia* (RSESAP 1799) is hardly known. The *Extracto* lists the tasks carried out by the society. It accounts for the conflict presented to the magistrate of Segovia arising from the claim of a master glassmaker and tinsmith who had arrived from the Castillian city of Ávila where he had obtained the certificate allowing him to practise his profession. The craftsman demanded that anyone practising his business should have the formal qualification for performing the profession. Momediano was entrusted to render a decision that Munárriz transcribed: in this text, dated at the end of 1796, Momediano resolves the conflict favouring the freedom to work (RSESAP 1799, 47–51):[18]

the competence of craftsmen, more than the formality of a piece of paper or exam, was certified by the appreciation of their customers and was stirred up by the concurrence of their aptitudes; that is, by the market.

Furthermore, to dispel any doubt, Momediano included two literal quotes from Adam Smith in his verdict.[19] By comparing these works to the versions available until then, it is pretty clear that Momediano seems to have overturned the order of the citations—as the briefer text does not precede the longer one, as he claims, but the other way around. The source used was not Alonso (Smith 1794) or Roucher (Smith 1791 [1790]), where this brief text does not appear. We conclude that he drew them from Condorcet's compendium, not from the Spanish version by Martínez de Irujo (Smith 1792), but the original French published in the *Bibliothèque de l'Homme Public* (Smith 1790, III, 133–35). In short, leaving aside the particular case of Alcalá-Galiano, it is clear that the Segovia Society purchased the Spanish translations of 1792 and 1794. Still, it had already been referring to Smith in French since some time after 1790.

## Alcalá-Galiano in the state apparatus

Alcalá-Galiano carried out different tasks in the Ministry of Finance, which referred to foreign trade—French tariffs—and, aided by Covarrubias, compiled the legislation related to finance.[20] From very early on, he became a prominent civil servant, influencing Lerena and his successor Gardoqui, to the extent that, when the powerful financier Francisco Cabarrús was prosecuted, he accused Alcalá-Galiano of being the principal instigator of his disgrace.

In December 1795, Alcalá-Galiano was appointed as one of the general directors of the Office of Revenue. Later on, in 1799, after this position disappeared, he was downgraded to a discreet secondary political place in the Council of Finance.[21] In 1808, he regained prominence due to the "Mutiny of Aranjuez," the fall of Prime Minister Godoy and the appointment of his friend Miguel José de Azanza as Minister of Finance. He accepted the position of General Treasurer—from 1799 onwards, the highest position in the Ministry of Finance after the minister itself—and came along with Azanza to Bayonne, where, in the context of the abdications of Fernando VII and Carlos IV, the minister handed over to Napoleon a detailed report of the economy of the Spanish monarchy. Once in Bayonne, he became a member of the assembly that endorsed the Constitution of Bayonne proposed—or rather imposed—by Napoleon. Having returned to Madrid, he remained General Treasurer from July 1808 until February 1809, when he fled and joined the Central Board in Seville, while being ousted by José Bonaparte.

In Seville, Alcalá-Galiano opposed the decision, which finally would be taken by the Cortes of Cádiz in 1813, abolishing the *rentas provinciales* and replacing them with a direct tax. This fact allowed him to write an extensive *Informe* (Alcalá-Galiano 1810),[22] detailing his financial, economic and political ideas that now move away from his youthful enthusiasm for Mably and Rousseau. *Informe* was printed months after being written. Unfortunately, the

Regency Council repeatedly refused to authorise it, demonstrating that Alcalá-Galiano came to be an inconvenient political figure, despite his solid training and experience in public finances. After his death, in November 1810 in Cádiz, his brother Antonio published some of his later writings. He defended Alcalá-Galiano's view in the Cádiz parliamentary debates that abolished in 1813 the former revenue system.

## Alcalá-Galiano's interpretation of Smith

The WN circulated in Spain from 1777, when Campomanes, *Fiscal* of the Council of Castille, was interested in Smith's policy on poverty. The next critical moment in the circulation of Smith's work in the country was, without a doubt, Alcalá-Galiano's *Sobre la necesidad y justicia de los tributos, fondos de donde deben sacarse, y medios de recaudarlos* (Alcalá-Galiano 1793 [1788]).[23] This work was the first summary of Smith's economic ideas in Spain and was published before the WN was translated into Spanish.

Alcalá-Galiano drafted *Sobre la necesidad y justicia de los tributos* in Madrid, in March 1788, when he was a member of Lerena's advisory team. However, it was not published until 1793—in volume IV of the *Actas y Memorias* of the Economic Society of Segovia—although it may have circulated as a manuscript. In between, different works that had certain Smithian influence were published in 1789: the "Prólogo" to *Colección Alfabética de los Aranceles de Francia* (Alcalá-Galiano and Gallard 1789); the above-mentioned *Juicio de la memoria intitulada Abusos que reinan generalmente en la administración de las principales rentas*; and, finally, *Memoria sobre la naturaleza de las rentas públicas de España*, dated October 1789, a kind of Necker-style *compte rendu* signed by the Minister of Public Finances Lerena (1834 [c.1790]),[24] but which, curiously, quotes, when supporting the *frutos civiles* tax, the same text as Alcalá-Galiano did in his *Juicio de la memoria*.

Concerning *Sobre la necesidad y justicia de los tributos*, it looks clear Alcalá-Galiano's interest in the WN goes far beyond a mere quotation of Smith or an incidental paraphrase. Alcalá-Galiano's interpretation of Smith was not limited to book V of the WN but shows a profound understanding of all the work and its analytical premises (wages, consumption, rent, capital). Furthermore, he sought to support a specific economic policy regarding finance and trade through the rule of reason, a method that he took from the economists in vogue at the time in France. Taxes have to be excised from the "wealth" of the nation, which does not depend on the "fertility" or abundance of resources, as the Physiocrats claimed, but "on the annual labour of individuals" (Alcalá-Galiano 1793 [1788], 276). The growth of the wealth of a nation will depend on its ability to accumulate capital. Therefore, it is significant enough "not to excise [or charge] the funds advanced for subsequent products, but those that produce nothing" (Alcalá-Galiano 1793 [1788], 280).

Alcalá-Galiano discussed, also influenced by Smith, the three primary factors of production among which the product of the nation is distributed: wages (workers), interest (owners of "funds" of advances, that is, of capital) and land rent (land-owners). He mainly assesses the tax incidence on consumer goods, the tax object of *rentas provinciales*.

Then, consumption excises are proportionate to the level of accumulated wealth or capital. In a developing country, they are detrimental; still, in a rich country, a moderate tax on consumption that preserves the freedom of domestic trade is not only harmless but "an excellent and easy way of collecting a considerable amount." Alcalá-Galiano adapted such Smithian doctrine by substituting "poor nation" for "small population" and "rich nation" for "highly-populated city;" but also by distinguishing between two different environments in terms of capital concentration and levels of consumption, and by taking for granted that taxing luxury consumption would have a lower incidence on prices and national wealth. Furthermore, the higher the duty on consumption in the large cities, the higher the collection of taxes, which is in line with the high number of tax officers required (Alcalá-Galiano 1793 [1788], 289).[25]

While excising manufactured goods—like any other tax in the long run—consumption excises have the great advantage of preserving annual labour productivity; furthermore, they tax consumption very extensively. As they are only collected in large cities, they tax unproductive luxury consumption. When the high-income non-productive population consume these products, they are indirectly making part of their capital productive. To further clarify this idea, Alcalá-Galiano devotes three paragraphs to establishing the Smithian distinction between productive and unproductive labour (WN III, II).

Regarding the consumption excises, there is a formula to adjust "the wage of labour, the interests of the funds and the rent of land-owners to a uniform and fair contribution, which does not affect the funds advanced for accruing the national capital, but those consumed annually." The only requirement is to lighten the burden of these taxes on small populations to avoid the severe damage caused by the ecclesiastic tithes.[26]

After justifying the appropriateness of the consumption excises, which are the core of the *rentas provinciales*, Alcalá-Galiano substantiates the other object of the 1785 reform: the *frutos civiles*, that is, the tax on rents. In this respect, his analysis takes Smith's definition of land rent due to the monopoly of the land-owners (WN I, XI). Additionally, he strongly criticised—in a liberal line of thought—the Spanish economic context:

> The funds used for land do not generate higher interest for us than the rest of the funds as they mainly depend on the large land-owners and "dead hands", who maintained outside of trade a large amount of land. Therefore there is always less land to sell than capital to use on them. Sales of land are made at the monopoly price, thereby preventing an increase in agriculture.
> (Alcalá-Galiano 1793 [1788], 296)

The rent does not influence the price of manufactured goods but has a secondary role concerning wages and interests (WN I, VI). Therefore, the rent can be taxed without harming trade, farming or industry, and, consequently, is the least burdensome and the fairest of the whole tax system. Therefore, the Lerena´s contribution of *frutos civiles* has unquestionable Smithian foundations.

Implementing such a contribution in Spain was slow and challenging, as it found widespread administrative and social resistance. But, in the most educated circles of "public opinion," the contribution was bored out by a theoretical background reinforced by a carefully constructed argument that, in Alcala-Galiano´s work, found its best intellectual support in the WN. The taxes on land property were helpful for the common good, as they taxed "unproductive" incomes that are not advanced funds for subsequent productions. Alcalá-Galiano powerfully conveyed this analytical argument at a social level:

> Preserving the civil order is by far more advantageous to rich owners than the poor settlers. For every rich owner in a state, there must live a hundred poor people. And the latter, who are more ignorant and stronger due to their considerable number, would destroy the private and peaceful property of the powerful, which is the cause of their misery if public authorities did not contain them. To maintain this order, it is somewhat fair that the rich contribute the most as they are who benefit the most from it.[27]

In this respect, Alcalá-Galiano seems to be much closer to Necker than Smith in many passages. He mainly brings to mind chapters XXV and XXVI of the first part of *Sur la législation et le commerce des grains*,[28] which proposes an "iron law of wages" and explains the mechanism of exploitation by the capitalists.[29]

However, returning to Smith, Alcalá-Galiano addresses the four ways capital can be employed (WN II, V). That allocated in agriculture is the most productive, followed by industry, domestic trade and foreign trade. He accepts Smith's theory of free trade, even paraphrasing the Smithian passage of the "invisible hand" (Alcalá-Galiano 1793 [1788], 319–20); however, he remarks on the importance of foreign trade aiming at securing a favourable balance of trade.[30]

Alcalá-Galiano applied Smith's four taxation maxims to Lerena's tax reform, which were already a classic in fiscal doctrine (WN V, II, II). Furthermore, he also added three more maxims, advising against coercive methods (Alcalá-Galiano 1793 [1788], 323).[31] This reference to "laws and oppressions" also demonstrates his different view concerning domestic or foreign trade. Regarding the former, "laws and oppressions" are only admitted as a rare exception; concerning foreign trade, conversely, he believes they were appropriate to support domestic production.

Regarding the funds to be taxed—a crucial issue—Alcalá-Galiano establishes a general principle: "generally speaking, taxing the income of the owners of the assets of a nation is the least detrimental if taxes are levied from everywhere except for trade, agriculture and industry." He completes this statement by quoting an extensive excerpt in the WN about "Smith's profound policy" that suggests taxing the rent and the easily controlled assets as they are non-transportable and accrue a non-productive fund.[32] Therefore, the taxes on the rent, housing—or civil fruits—and consumption excises, both being the main objects of the 1785 reform, were the most appropriate. Finally, Alcalá-Galiano provides 15 "general maxims of political economy" which, as Llombart (2000a) pointed out, are a complete enlightened economic programme.

In short, Alcalá-Galiano's report is a reasoned opinion of the foundations of the fiscal ideas of Smith in book V of the WN, which is in line with the economic policy implemented by then in Spain. The young Lerena´s collaborator gave theoretical coherence to this economic plan, reinforced with a genuine civic enthusiasm forged during his membership of the Economic Society of Segovia. The government recruited officials—like Alcalá-Galiano—from the economic societies and military academies. These civil servants could undertake specialised tasks either temporarily or permanently as advisers, propagandists or civil servants. To a great extent, the Enlightenment provided the rational background needed for setting up the state apparatus.

The compilation of the tariffs of France that the government commissioned from Alcalá-Galiano in 1787 was published two years later as *Colección alfabética de los aranceles de Francia*,[33] in the context of an unfavourable balance of trade. Secretary of the State Floridablanca aimed a policy of foreign trade that pretended to gain an advantage in the Spanish balance of trade.[34] Zylberberg, undoubtedly, has better interpreted the unique combination of the compilation's political and intellectual dimensions. Although he wrongly points out that the author of the *Colección alfabética* was Juan Bautista Virio (Pradells 1990),[35] he correctly underlined the great interest in the Smithian "Prologue" of the "anonymous" compiler (Zylberger 1993, 251), who was none other than Alcalá-Galiano.

The "Prologue" begins by associating free trade with Physiocracy. Afterwards, Alcalá-Galiano takes from Smith—who describes Physiocracy as a purely speculative system at the beginning of chapter IX of book IV of the WN—the arguments that he needed to back a restrictive trade policy. Given the different wealth of the nations, customs duties are a means of defending developing countries from more powerful economic powers. Furthermore, to demonstrate this, he refers to his recent reading of Smith and compares two countries. The most "industrious" will have a series of "concomitant advantages": its "territorial tax"—tax on rent of land—will yield more; its funds or capital will be more abundant and, consequently, it will enjoy lower interest rates. Therefore, it will produce at a lower cost and be at a significant advantage in free competition.

Between extreme freedom—which Alcalá-Galiano identified with Physiocracy[36]—and extreme restriction—old-fashioned trade—the "good midpoint" that he proposes would consist of mild protectionism with moderate customs duties, as immoderate taxation would only stimulate smuggling. He attempts to show that this "good midpoint" can be backed by Smith's arguments condemning the "mercantile system" and advising against customs barriers, to which the Scottish economist devoted many pages in the WN.[37]

Alcalá-Galiano's adapted Smith's system by differentiating the role attributed to the different factors of production: land, labour and capital funds may change separately and generate relative advantages or disadvantages. They may be exacerbated by their consequences on the behaviour of the other factors as if it were a multiplying effect. Furthermore, as the political will of a wealthy country is to destroy the wealth of a poorer one, custom duties are justified for protecting its productions. This "correction" made to Smith enabled Alcalá-Galiano to theorise about the fiscal reforms of 1785 and the commercial orientation of Floridablanca's economic policy.

Alcalá-Galiano returned to Smith once again some years later. In his *Informe* of 1810, he points out that "he discovered" in 1789 the Physiocrats' fundamental error (Alcalá-Galiano 1810). We believe that he referred to the "Prologue" mentioned above. Moreover, he claims to have gone even further than Smith, who, according to him, did not dare to oppose the Physiocrats on foreign trade.

Therefore, "the famous Smith" was known in the circles of opinion connected to the political power, like certain economic media of the economic societies, through Alcalá-Galiano's writings from 1788 onwards. These works supported the reforms of taxation—mainly *Perjuicios del antiguo sistema de rentas provinciales*—and trade policy—in the "Prologue" to *Colección alfabética*. In this case, however, Alcalá-Galiano was not only influenced by Smith but also invoked his authority.

Concerning the content, it can be confirmed that, in the case of Alcalá-Galiano, they were not mere circumstantial quotations. On the contrary, however, they reveal that Smith's work was assimilated in all its analytical complexity and adapted to the needs of justifying and reinforcing Spanish economic policy.

## Notes

1  The pioneer studies of R.S. Smith (1957; 1968) hardly take the role played by Alcalá-Galiano into account; Elorza (1970) published a complete analysis of Alcalá-Galiano within the liberal currents of thought of the Spanish Enlightenment; and, particularly, Hernández (1978; 1993) underlined the importance of Alcalá-Galiano's economic thought. Fuentes (2000b) includes some of the above-mentioned studies, together with a broad summary by Schwartz (2000). Finally, my contributions aim at building a complete intellectual and political biography of Alcalá-Galiano; see, particularly, Valles (2008).

2  An excellent overall view in Astigarraga and Usoz (2013). More precise references to many of the points here raised in Astigarraga (2015).

3  Alcalá-Galiano translated pieces on agricultural meteorology (Toaldo) and electrotherapy (Mauduit de la Varenne). He also proposed—with the explicit support of the State Secretary, Count of Floridablanca—putting together a network of meteorological observers with a central node formed by himself and Giannini, both mathematics teachers at the Royal Academy of Segovia. He also disseminated the experiences of Tessier in Rambouillet regarding wheat diseases, seeking to create—counting on official support—a professional network between the economic societies. Furthermore, commissioned by Floridablanca, he translated a piece dealing with hospitals and home-based care in the large cities by the Physiocrat Dupont de Nemours.

4  On Giannini (1779–1803), see Navarro (2013).

5  The *Catalogue* is made up of approximately 2,500 volumes in French, Spanish, English and Italian. The books on mathematics, physics, astronomy and chemistry particularly stand out. There were more than a thousand volumes of publications of 24 learned societies and science academies from the rest of Europe, containing the most advanced developments in the science of the day; see García and Valles (1989).

6  Alcalá-Galiano based his speech titled *Sobre la economía política y los impuestos*, precisely on this work by Rousseau. His speech was given to the Economic Society of Segovia in 1783 and published in the first volume of *Actas y Memorias* of the RSESAP (1785, 223–67); see Valles (1992). It also includes other works such as *Sobre la necesidad y justicia de los tributos,* based on Smith´s WN.

7  The first volume on "Économie Politique et Diplomatique" (1784–1786) of the *Encyclopédie Méthodique* (1784) and the three volumes on "Finances" (1784–1787) lack any references to Smith and are, without doubt, more "Neckerian."

8  See, for example, Carpenter (2002).

9  Half a *real* for each *arroba* of washed wool sent outside the province abroad (Royal Decree of 6 August 1784); it was published in RSESAP (1786).

10  Astigarraga (2000; 2011) studies in depth the significance of the figure of Necker in Spain regarding politics and economic thought. In addition to other aspects highlighted by Astigarraga, Necker served as a theoretical curb against free trade, which he considered a radical Physiocratic abstraction. In this respect, Necker and forcibly Smith "served" the same political purpose.

11  See Alcalá-Galiano, *Sobre los nuevos impuestos* (RSESAP 1786, 181–200); also in the above-mentioned *Sobre la economía política y los impuestos*.

12  Although he was appointed as a war commissioner—serving the Ministry of Finance—on 11 November 1787, he possibly was consulted as an expert in some government circles. For example, he contributed to some sessions of the Economic Society of Madrid and he even might have been appointed as an advisor by Minister Lerena before enrolling as part of his team; see Moral (2015).

13  Vicente Mantecón was the archivist of the Segovia Society and official on the provincial revenues; he had assisted Alcalá-Galiano in *Sobre los nuevos impuestos*.

14  He also translated Chaptal and the Count of Carli; additionally, he translated Pastoret on Zoroastro, Confucio and Mahoma, although it did not pass the censorship in 1795.

15  He claimed to have commissioned certain works "in Valladolid so as to attract works from outside of the Kingdom"; he also attached a list of several works that he had purchased, among them: *Ventajas de la Francia y la Gran Bretaña* (1771) by Plumard de Dangeul or *Dialogos sobre el comercio del trigo* (1775) by Galiani; and, finally, he proposed the purchase of the volumes that were missing of the following works: *Memorias de la Sociedad de Madrid; Agricultura General,* by Valcárcel; *Lecciones de Comercio,* by Genovesi; *Historia Natural,* by Buffon; *Memorias,* by Larruga; *Diccionario de Agricultura,* by Rozier; *Economía de la Casa de Campo* by Liger, etc.

16  The other works ordered from Valladolid were: *Considérations sur le mécanisme des sociétés,* by Casaux; *Oeuvres,* by Necker; *Mélanges de philosophie et de l'économie politique,* by Grivel; *Essai politique sur le commerce,* by Melon; and *Observations sur le Commerce d'Amérique,* by Sheffield.

17  The advertisement in MHP (September 1792, 86–87) said: "This work, which is already well-known in Europe for being the greatest that has been written of its kind so far, displays the economic and political composition and organisation of

the states and the politics to maintain and strengthen them. It is beneficial for all public figures and particularly for spreading the true principles which should lead the society towards the general good of the monarchy."

18  It was not a Momediano personal point of view. The society upheld a line contrary to the guilds, seeking to liberalise their regulations ("Interim rules of 1789").

19  "Mechanical arts (says Smith addressing this issue in his famous book on the origin of the Wealth of the Nations), the most delicate mechanical arts contain no such mystery as to require a long course of instruction"; and later: "The property which every man has in his own labour, as it is the original foundation of all other property, so it is the most sacred and inviolable. The patrimony of a poor man lies in the strength and dexterity of his hands; and to hinder him from employing this strength and dexterity in what manner he thinks proper without injury to his neighbour is a plain violation of this most sacred property. It is a manifest encroachment upon the just liberty both of the workman and of those who might be disposed to employ him. As it hinders the one from working at what he thinks proper, so it hinders the others from employing whom they think proper. To judge whether he is fit to be employed, may surely be trusted to the discretion of the employers, whose interest it so much concerns. The affected anxiety of the lawgiver, lest they should employ an improper person, is evidently as impertinent as it is oppresive." Momediano´s report is dated in Segovia on 20 December 1796 (RSESAP 1799, 49–50); cfr. WN (I, X, 138–39).

20  The compilation of the laws needed to facilitate the functioning of the complex administrative system of the Ministry of Finance also had a self-explanatory function concerning the public sphere; a crucial function—as pointed out by Necker—particularly, during times of reform. The compilation commissioned by Lerena to José de Covarrubias at the end of 1789—which should have been carried out under the supervision of Alcalá-Galiano—was never published. The manuscript—six volumes on loose sheets, conserved in the IEF´s library (Covarrubias c.1790)—includes a "Preliminary Discourse" that, without referring to Smith, constitutes a summary of his fiscal doctrine. The next attempt to compile the fiscal laws in 1795–1796 comprised an update of the compilation carried out by Juan de Ripia; it was undertaken by Diego María Gallard (1795). See Chapter 7 in this book.

21  In 1801, he married a relative of Floridablanca. The marriage was more an effect than a cause of his promotion.

22  The abolition of *rentas provinciales* was debated in the Cortes of Cádiz. However, it goes beyond the scope of this work: In this respect, see López (1995) and Valles (2008, 437–52).

23  Obviously, we refer to its reception beyond the private realm; for example, it is known, from his inventory of books of 1782, that Meléndez Valdés, a distinguished Spanish jurist, had a WN´s French translation from 1778.

24  See Moral (1990).

25  On this point, the source is again Necker (1784, I, 193–202).

26  Smith considers the tithe to be an unequal tax (WN, V, II, I). Alonso Ortiz, WN´s Spanish translator, points out through a prudent note that inequality should not be confused with unfairness and tithes, although unequal in real terms, is fair (Smith 1794, IV, 210–11). By clarifying this point, he tried to safeguard himself from ecclesiastic censorship. In this respect, Alcalá-Galiano is not so careful and criticises the tithe "according to the system by which we are charged," without calling into question its principles (Alcalá-Galiano 1793 [1788], 295).

27   Alcalá-Galiano (1793 [1788], 302–03); cfr. WN (V, I, II).
28   It was published in Paris in 1775 and was available in Spanish since 1783, when it was translated by Miguel Gerónimo for his collection of *Memorias instructivas y curiosas* (1778–1791).
29   Grange (1974, 91–105) has contributed texts that show that Necker clearly conceived what Marx would later call "capital gain."
30   Alonso, Smith´s Spanish translator, shares Alcalá-Galiano's view (Smith 1794, 173–352). In fact, both were involved in creating the Office of the Balance of Trade promoted by Lerena.
31   He referred mainly to smuggling modern economic doctrines at the time underlined the adverse economic effects of suppressing smuggling. However, he was not in favour of doing away with confiscations and fines "as the *economists*"—that is, the Physiocrats—"would wish." On the reality of smuggling, beyond theoretical approaches, see Melón (2009).
32   The quotation corresponds to WN (V, II, I, 844) and is the same used by Alcalá-Galiano on the report of *Abusos* in *Juicio crítico*.
33   Volume I contains a "Prologue," an Index and a "Preliminary Observations" which describe the whole system of French custom duties; volume II includes the tariffs from A to I; volume III, from M to Z (Alcalá-Galiano and Gallard 1789, 1–436), and also a series of recent supplementary decrees (Alcalá-Galiano and Gallard 1789, 437–509), French weights and measures tables and their Spanish equivalents. The copy consulted belongs to the BNE.
34   Floridablanca, in chapter CCCIV of his *Instrucción Reservada* (1787), writes: "France seeks and will seek to gain advantages for its trade, direct us as a subordinate nation into all of its designs and wars and detain the increase in our prosperity" (Ruiz 1982, 241). This statement about a powerful and ally neighbouring France was highly expressive about the policy finally adopted.
35   Virio also published the tariffs of Great Britain in 1792 and compiled those of Austria, which remained unpublished.
36   On the diverse political "uses" of anti-Physiocracy in the European Enlightenment, see Kaplan and Reinert (2019).
37   This also motivated many of the translator Alonso Ortiz (Smith 1794) notes, arguing continuosly that free foreign trade was detrimental for poor countries, whose "emerging industry" required protection.

# 4 A new analysis of Martínez de Irujo's *Compendio de la Riqueza de las Naciones* and the role of Marquis de Condorcet

*Simona Pisanelli*

## Introduction: the state of the art

Research into the spread of Smith's *The Wealth of Nations* (WN) in Spain can hardly be considered innovative. On this issue, 20 years ago, Schwartz had already proposed not a new analysis but a survey, starting from R.S. Smith's paper,"La 'Riqueza de las Naciones' en España e Hispanoamerica" (1957b).The latter identified the main ways the economic work of Smith was disseminated in Spain:

1   The *Compendio de la obra inglesa intitulada Riqueza de las Naciones, hecho por el marqués de Condorcet, y traducido al castellano con varias adiciones del original*, by Carlos Martìnez de Irujo (Smith 1792);
2   The *Riqueza de las Naciones* of which José Alonso Ortiz did a complete translation two years later (1794).

Schwartz also recalled the main hindrances to the spread of the WN in Spain:

3   The *Expediente sobre la obra de Mr. Smith intitulada* Recherches sur la nature et les causes de la richesses des nations, *2 tomos, en 8.°, marquilla impresa en Londres, año de 1788*;
4   The edict of prohibition of 4 March 1792: "La obra titulada *Recherches sur la nature et les causes de la richesses des nations*, traduit de l'anglois de Mr. Smith, impresa en Londres, año de 1792, en dos tomos en octavo mayor. Se prohíbe la lectura porque, bajo un estilo capcioso y obscuro, favorece el tolerantismo en punto a religión y es inductiva al naturalismo" (Schwartz 2000, 179).

These four "cardinal points" characterise all the studies on the subject—from that of R.S. Smith to the most recent—especially going deeper into the comparison between Smith's original work and Ortiz's translation. On the other hand, Martínez de Irujo's translation is generally overlooked. R.S. Smith summarised the main aspects of his work in a few lines, highlighting the tricks

DOI: 10.4324/9781003152804-5

he used to avoid censorship (1, 2) and to provide a version more suited to the Spanish public compared to the French summary (3, 4).[1] Martínez de Irujo:

1   never mentions Smith;
2   deletes entire paragraphs on religious tolerance;
3   adds the digression about the Amsterdam bank;
4   adds a single footnote, debating Smith's statement that "the individual is more competent than the state to select the most advantageous employment of capital" (Smith 1957a, 109).

Starting from the helpful previous studies (especially Lasarte 1976; Schwartz 2000), this contribution aims to go deeper into the comparison between the summary of the WN published in the *Bibliothèque de l'homme* and the *Compendio* of Martínez de Irujo, first giving some biographical information on the latter.

Carlos Martínez de Irujo y Tacón was born on 3 November 1763 in Cartagena. His diplomatic career brought him to London as First Secretary of the Spanish Embassy. According to Eric Beerman, "in addition to his diplomatic skills, he must have had a literary bent, for while in London he translated into Spanish with comments, and published in Madrid, *Compendio*" (Beerman 1981, 447) Actually, Martínez de Irujo's role as a diplomat influenced his literary effort, forcing him to make changes to the original text of Smith's work. At the end of 1795, following the worsening of relations between Spain and Great Britain, the Spanish Minister Manuel Godoy sent Martínez de Irujo to the United States, where he remained for 12 years, moving between Philadelphia and Washington. He did not successfully conclude his diplomatic mission because "he left under a cloud of suspicion as he had been accused of buying up open lands in the West. By a Royal Order in 1809, he was relieved of duties and told to return to Spain" (Beerman 1981, 452). This did not prevent King Fernando VII from appointing him Secretary of State in 1819 (Beerman 1981, 453).

## *Compendio* vs *Bibliothèque*: deletions, modifications and additions

The first occasion on which Martínez de Irujo's *Compendio* significantly differs from the abridged version in the *Bibliothèque de l'homme* is the long *Discurso preliminar del traductor*. In it, the translator praises some aspects of the WN and rejects others. In contrast, the editors of the *Bibliothèque de l'homme* introduce Smith's work only in a few lines and recommend reading the whole book, since Smith "a déjà réduit" the knowledge that must constitute a science like political economy "à ses plus juste proportions":

En essayant de donner l'analyse d'un écrit aussi substantiel, nous sommes donc bien loin de prétendre qu'elle puisse dispenser nos lecteurs de lire l'ouvrage même; nous désirons au contraire, qu'elle leur inspire le désir de le connaître et de le méditer.

(Smith 1790, III, 108)[2]

Also according to Martínez de Irujo, "el autor reduce a sistema las verdades políticas antes aisladas o desconocidas," appreciating "el modo de presentar su enlace con toda la claridad y precisión de que son susceptibles" (Smith 1792, IX). Nevertheless, he points out that his *Compendio* "combines all the advantages" of Smith's "theories," eliminating some "improper applications" of them (Smith 1792, X). His additions are few and generally aimed at increasing the interest of the Spanish readers.

Now, we get to the heart of the comparison between the *Compendio* and the summary of the *Bibliothèque de l'homme*, starting from Schwartz's criticism:

> The lack of interest [of M. de Irujo] in economic analysis is evident in the summing up of the chapters on price and value, which are much briefer than those of the French version; all of this fits into just two pages out of the three hundred and two that make up the book.
>
> (Schwartz 2000, 180–81)

This criticism seems unjustified, since Martínez de Irujo follows the exact text of the *Bibliothèque*, which announces:

> Nous ne suivrons pas M. Smith dans les développements de ces différentes propositions, il faut les lire dans l'ouvrage même, et peut être encore une seule lecture ne suffira-t-elle pas à ceux qui voudront les approfondir. Nous passerons donc au chapitre dans lequel M. Smith traite du salaire et du bénéfice dans les différent emplois du travail et des fonds.
>
> (Smith 1790, III, 125)

There follow some very brief parts of the text that do not seem significant regarding the circulation of Smith's work.[3] Instead, it is worth dwelling on the suppression of Smith's criticisms or expressions that might appear outrageous to the Spanish nation.

The first occurrence of this kind appears in the *Conclusions of the Digression Concerning the Variations in the Value of Silver*, in which Smith explains that the underlying causes of two concomitant phenomena—"the increase of the quantity of gold and silver in Europe, and the increase of its manufactures and agriculture" (WN I, XI, 255)—are different.

Martínez de Irujo is not afraid to refer to the positive consequences in terms of progress of the productive organisation of agriculture and handicrafts due to "la ruina del sistema feudal" (Smith 1792, 63). Nevertheless, he rejects the negative judgment on Spain expressed by Smith, who considers it to be at the same level as Poland concerning: (1) the high level of poverty; and (2) the inability to replace the feudal system, already compromised, with systems of government suitable for the new production techniques and the general needs of the contemporary economic system. The fragment that Martínez de Irujo eliminates is translated in the *Bibliothèque* as follows: "L'Espagne et le Portugal, propriétaires de la richesse des mines, sont peut-être, après la Pologne, les deux états les plus pauvres de l'Europe; car en détruisant le gouvernement féodal, ils ne l'ont point remplacé par un meilleur gouvernement" (Smith 1790, III, 158). Smith harshly criticises the persistence of unsuitable regulations attributable to the feudal system in the chapter *Of the discouragement of agriculture in the ancient state of Europe after the fall of the Roman Empire*. He reconstructs the historical events that caused the fall of the Roman Empire, describing the passage from the conception of land as a "means only of subsistence and enjoyment" to the conception of a "means [...] of power and protection." While in the first case, all the children of the family share the land, in the second case "the law of primogeniture" establishes its inalienability (WN III, II, 382–83). Martínez de Irujo literally follows the French translation, stating that the requirement of inalienability "se ha mirado como necesario para perpetuar en una clase de ciudadanos el privilegio exclusivo de los empleos y dignidades principales del estado" (Smith 1792, 134), but—unlike the French translation—his text lacks Smith's conclusion:

> et comme par ce privilège les nobles ont usurpé sur le reste de la société un avantage dont l'injustice est criante, ils en ont obtenu un autre, non moins injuste, celui d'une richesse inamovible, de peur que l'inconsidération attachée à la pauvreté, ne finît par attacher aussi le ridicule à leur prétentions.
>
> (Smith 1790, III, 196)

Again, with the aim of smoothing "any harshness" (Elorza 1970, 93), Martínez de Irujo removes two critical statements sentences about the "expensive vanity" of the landlord, which—according to Smith—hinders the employment of resources in order to increase the general national wealth:

> *Tout pour soi, et rien pour autrui*, semble avoir été, dans tous les pays et dans tous les siècles, la vile maxime des maîtres du genre humain.
>
> (Smith 1790, III, 210)

> La vanité dispendieuse du propriétaire fit accepter cette condition; et de là naquirent les longs baux.
>
> (Smith 1790, III, 213)

These two gibes from Smith are placed towards the end of the third volume of the *Bibliothèque de l'homme* (1790), which closes with the summary of book III of the WN.

As mentioned in the introduction, ever since the paper by R.S. Smith (1957), the literature has referred to two important additions to the French text that

Martínez de Irujo introduced in his *Compendio*: the section entitled *Del Banco de Deposito de Amsterdam* (Smith 1792, 86–107) and a footnote (Smith 1792, 169):

> Compared to the original work, Martínez de Irujo brings the *Digression concerning banks of deposit, particularly concerning that of Amsterdam*, forward from book IV (*Of Systems of Political Oeconomy*) to book II (*Of the Nature, Accumulation, and Employment of Stock*), just after chapter II *Of money considered as a particular branch of the general stock of the society, or of the expence of maintaining the national capital.*

The French editors interrupt "ce chapitre sur l'argent et sur les banques […] très curieux et très instructif: on sent fort bien que nous n'avons pu que l'effleurer" (Smith 1790, III, 175), whereas Martínez de Irujo enhances it, stating that "aunque los límites de un extracto solo permiten tocarlos de paso, con todo no nos parece importuno hacer una digressión sobre el Banco de Depósito de Amsterdam, tan nombrado y conocido por toda Europa" (Smith 1792, 85).

The literature has already pinpointed the reasons for Martínez de Irujo's interest in the *Digression*: this part of the WN can be "very interesting for the Spanish readers who witnessed the origin of the Banco de San Carlos" (Fuentes and Perdices 1997, xlii; see also Schwartz 2000, 181), founded by Francisco Cabarrús, "a French-born financier", in June 1782:

> When an increase in taxes by one third and loans from the merchant guilds of Madrid and the bishops failed to supply enough money for the war, […] Cabarrús was authorised […] to found the first national bank of Spain, the Banco de San Carlos, with the task of redeeming the *vales*. To assure its financial strength, the bank was given a monopoly on issuing contracts to supply the army and navy and on exporting species and was to receive a commission for its services in both cases.
>
> (Herr 1959, 146)

The presence of such a *Digression* in the *Compendio* shows that Martínez de Irujo belonged to that "distinguished minority" (Lasarte 1976, 32) who had been able to consult the "original English" version (Smith 1957, 109; Elorza 1970, 93; Cervera 2003, 127).[4] Nevertheless, in addition to "English editions", also "French" versions "had long been on the [Spanish] market" (Lasarte 1976, 32). One cannot rule out the chance that Martínez de Irujo was able to access the version of Roucher (based on the 1786 edition)—"the very one condemned by the Holy Office" (Schwartz 2000, 179)—"readily available, despite increased inquisitorial vigilance in the wake of the Revolution" (Reeder and Cardoso 2002, 187).

The second main addition made by Martínez de Irujo is his footnote in which he comments on Smith's appreciation of free trade. In order to facilitate the reader, below we give the Smithian text translated in the *Compendio* (1), then the footnote of the translator (2) and, finally, some observations about what follows in the French version of *Bibliothèque* and disappears in the *Compendio* (3).

(1) ¿No es evidente que cada particular, considerado en su situacion individual, sabrá juzgar mejor que el hombre de estado o el legislador la especie de industria que ofrece la probabilidad de mayores ganancias a su capital?

(Smith 1792, 169)

Like most Spanish authors of the time who commented on the WN, Martínez de Irujo suggests the applicability of free trade only to countries that have already reached an appreciable level of spread of Enlightenment ideas (Schwarz 2000, 181–82).[5]

(2) Esta reflexión puede ser exacta en un país ilustrado en que los particulares por lo general conozcan el uso más ventajoso que pueden hacer de su dinero; pero hay otros en que los capitalistas necesitan que el gobierno los lleve, por decirlo así, de la mano para que den movimiento a sus fondos, y los empleen con utilidad. El deseo de ganar es un aliciente poderoso, pero requiere ciertos conocimientos que le dirijan. Este es a mi parecer el objeto de las *gratificaciones temporales* con que la Inglaterra favorece ciertos ramos, las cuales cesan cuando el Gobierno ve que los particulares han de hacer ya por su propio interés, lo que emprendieron por el estímulo del premio.

(Smith 1792, 169, note; *my italics*)

Two observations can be made here. Martínez de Irujo's final judgement on Great Britain seems to justify a mild form of protectionism, limited to "nascent industries." More generally, the question is whether the Spanish are sufficiently enlightened to decide what and how much to produce without being subject to strict governmental instructions.

The fact that Martínez de Irujo eliminates the next passage of the WN would suggest a lack of confidence in Spain's degree of development:

(3) L'administrateur public, qui voudrait prendre sur lui le soin de diriger l'emploi du capital de chaque particulier, non-seulement se chargerait d'un soin très inutile, mais il affecterait encore une autorité, qui, à coup sûr, n'inspirerait de confiance à personne, et ne serait jamais en de plus mauvaises mains que dans celles d'un homme assez fou et assez présomptueux pour se croire en état de l'exercer.

(Smith 1790, IV, 10)

This cut is almost certainly induced by the need to overcome the Inquisition's judgment on the *Compendio*, since in his *Observations on the commerce of Spain with her American colonies in time of war* (1799), Martínez de Irujo shows complete appreciation for the Smithian approach:

[R]eason and the celebrated Adam Smith, who is, without dispute, the apostle of political economy, demonstrate that Government, in measures directed to the general good, must limit itself to the removal of obstacles; private interest, always active, discerning, and industrious, will do the rest. The same author adds, *and in my opinion with reason*, that governments must not give an exclusive protection to any particular branch; or direct, by any predilection, the employment of the capitals of individuals. The fetters once broken, and the road open and free, the individual knows, and always will know better than government, the most productive use to which he can apply either his capital or his labour.

(Martínez de Irujo 1800, 16; *my italics*)[6]

After referring to the additions made by Martínez de Irujo to the text of the *Bibliothèque*, one should pay attention to the more serious textual deletions, which are to be found in books IV and V of the WN. These heavy cuts in favour of the Spanish public (or, better, the Holy Office) can be easily placed under two topics:

(1)  "juicios detractorios" towards Spanish colonial policy;
(2)  "afirmaciones heréticas" of Smith on religion.

(1) As for the first point, it is well known that Smith dwells at length on the organisation of the colonial system in book IV of the WN, criticising the way in which Spain (and Portugal) managed the colonies on more than one occasion. Although confined to a small number of pages of the *Compendio* (Smith 1792, 200–07), the changes related to this issue have a significant impact and, sometimes, are very surprising.

Straight after introducing the different reasons and principles that have pushed the European powers to set the colonies up, Smith harshly attacks Spain:

It was the sacred thirst of gold that carried Oieda, Nicuessa, and Vasco Nugnes de Balboa, to the isthmus of Darien, that carried Cortez to Mexico, and Almagro and Pizarro to Chili and Peru. When those adventurers arrived upon any unknown coast, their first enquiry was always if there was any gold to be found there; and according to the information which they received concerning this particular, they determined either to quit the country or to settle in it.

(WN IV, VII, 562)

In the French text, the meaning of such harsh criticism remains unchanged:

C'est la soif sacrilège de l'or, qui a conduit les Espagnols dans le nouveau monde.

(Smith 1790, IV, 26)

Otherwise, in Martínez de Irujo's text, it becomes:

> El oro y la plata fueron los atractivos poderosos que contribuyeron a fixar en las costas americanas a los descubridores y conquistadores europeos.
>
> (Smith 1792, 200)

Therefore, the direct reference to Spanish and their "soif sacrilège" disappears. In the same way, the Spanish translator deletes another long fragment concerning Spain's policy of conquest:

> Un projet de conquête occasionna donc tous les établissements des Espagnols dans ces pays nouvellement découverts. Le motif de la conquête fut l'espoir de trouver des mines abondantes d'or et d'argent, et par une suite d'accidents au-dessus de la prévoyance humaine, ce projet réussit beaucoup mieux qu'on n'avait raisonnablement lieu de s'y attendre.
>
> (Smith 1790, IV, 27)

The matter of the colonies is naturally linked to the exploitation of slaves on colonial plantations. As is well known, and as correctly emphasised by both French and Spanish translators, Smith disagrees with the institution of slavery, but his fight against it is limited to "consideraciones dirigidas al interés personal" (Smith 1792, 204).[7]

Here we find the most striking case of *traduttore traditore*.[8] Since Smith charges Spain with pursuing enrichment by deplorable means, Martínez de Irujo attempts to reduce the damage to Spain's image by writing that Smith,

> echa en cara a los ingleses el que traten a sus esclavos con más crueldad que *nosostros*, y atribuye esta diversidad caracteristica a la diferencia de gobiernos.
>
> (Smith 1792, 204; *my italics*)

Shrewdly, Martínez de Irujo ascribes Smith's positive opinion of the French to the Spanish, translating literally from the French of the *Bibliothèque*:

> il reproche en quelque sorte aux anglais de traiter leurs esclaves plus cruellement que *nous*; et il attribue cette diversité caractéristique à la différence de gouvernement.
>
> (Smith 1790, IV, 31; *my italics*)

Regarding such a difference, Smith points out that:

> *The administration of the French colonies, however, has always been conducted with more gentleness and moderation than that of the Spanish and Portuguese.* This superiority of conduct is suitable both to the character of the French nation, and to what forms the character of every nation, the nature of their

government, which [...] is legal and free *in comparison with those of Spain and Portugal.*

(WN IV,VII, 586; my italics)

It is useful to remind that Smith also criticises the British government, as is evident from the following quote:

> Celle de l'Angleterre, quoique la meilleure, n'est après tout qu'un peu moins malhonnête et moins oppressive que les autres.
>
> (Smith 1790, IV, 34)

Once again, Martínez de Irujo's translation is misleading, since the change in the text does not seem justified:

> El método de la Inglaterra, aunque malo, es menos opresivo que los demás.
> (Smith 1792, 207)

(2) As far as the theme of religion is concerned, in the WN it is closely linked to that of education. As is well known, Smith "believed that more educated citizens can better understand their own interests, and those of society as a whole, and influence government policies more effectively" (Besomi 2001, 18), avoiding "illusions de l'enthousiasme et de la superstition" (Smith 1790, IV, 78). The reference to religion as a source of fanaticism and superstition pushes Martínez de Irujo to delete a long paragraph. For the sake of brevity, we quote only the sentence that represents the heart of the matter:

> Dans les sociétés civilisées l'attention publique doit peut-être se porter plutôt vers l'éducation du peuple que vers celle des gens que le rang et la fortune placent au-dessus de lui; car il est très-avantageux pour l'état que le peuple soit instruit. [...] D'ailleurs un peuple intelligent et éclairé est toujours plus décent et plus réglé qu'un peuple ignorant et stupide.
>
> (Smith 1790, IV, 78–79)[9]

As is well known, Smith also criticises the system of fixed remuneration of university professors. Referring to the inadequate levels of commitment and quality of teaching "in the University of Oxford," Smith writes: "the greater part of the public professors have, for these many years, given up altogether even the pretence of teaching" (WN V, I, 761).

According to Smith, the attitude of the professors is comparable to that of the representatives of the clergy, against whom he launches similar recrimination. The latter, translated in the French version, is deleted by Martínez de Irujo:

> Les institutions, relatives à l'instruction des gens de tout âge, sont principalement celles qui ont pour but l'instruction religieuse; ceux qui la donnent tirent leur subsistance comme les maîtres dans tout autre genre,

ou des contributions volontaires de leurs auditeurs, ou des fonds dont ils jouissent par les lois du pays: ils doivent naturellement déployer beaucoup plus de zèle et d'industrie quand ils ne vivent que des libéralités ou des secours de leurs auditeurs. Voilà pourquoi les prédicateurs des religions nouvelles ont presque toujours attaqué les anciennes avec beaucoup d'avantage. Le clergé de celles-ci se reposant sur ses bénéfices, avait négligé d'entretenir la ferveur de la foi; livré lui-même à l'indolence, il était devenu incapable de défendre sa propre cause; et la seule ressource qu'il ait eu en pareille circonstance, a été communément d'appeler le bras séculier pour persécuter, détruire et chasser ses adversaires comme des perturbateurs du repos public.

(Smith 1790, IV, 79–80)

Smith describes a further malpractice of the Roman Church: the clergy obtains "la pluspart une grande partie de leur subsistance des dons ou oblations volontaires du peuple" and enriches itself through the money that pious penitents pay for absolution: "la confession leur fournit bien des occasions d'améliorer cette source de revenu" (Smith 1790, IV, 80). Obviously, Martínez de Irujo censors this last statement. The same happens in the following pages in which Smith:

(1)  dwells on the risks linked to the natural tendency "dans toutes les religions [...] à corrompre la véritable, en y mêlant une forte dose de superstition, de folie et d'illusion" (Smith 1790, IV, 82), and to the attempts of each religious sect to assert its own exclusive right to exist (Smith 1790, IV, 83);
(2)  describes the contrast between "deux différents systèmes de morale [...] dont l'un peut être appelé austère, et l'autre doux ou relâché" typical of every "société où la distinction des rangs est une fois bien établie" (Smith 1790, IV, 83–84).

This leads to

(3)  the different degree "d'improbation ou de blâme, que nous devons donner aux vices de légèreté, aux vices qui naissent assez naturellement d'une grande prospérité ou d'un excès de gaieté et de bonne humeur" (Smith 1790, IV, 84).

According to Smith—and to the French translators—tolerance towards "vices de la légèreté" can have very different consequences for different social classes:

Un homme riche, et les gens de cette classe sont assez portés à regarder le pouvoir de se livrer à certains excès comme un avantage de leur fortune, et la liberté de le faire impunément, sans être exposés à des reproches, comme un des privilèges attachés à leur rang.

(Smith 1790, IV, 85)

On the contrary, for "le peuple sont toujours ruineux" (Smith 1790, IV, 84). Against these negative consequences, Smith detects "remèdes faciles et efficaces, dont l'opération réunie pourrait corriger sans violence la misanthropie des petites sectes qui diviseraient un pays" (Smith 1790, IV, 88).

At this point, Martinez de Irujo's *Compendio* is—partially—in line with the text of the *Bibliothèque*, which announces the "modo de remediar los inconvenientes, que lleva consigo la ignorancia del pueblo"[10] (Smith 1792, 262–63). Only the reference to "small sects" disappears.

It is quite easy to detect other cuts on the issue of religion in the Spanish version as opposed to the French (book V). We prefer to focus on an analogy that Smith proposes in book IV in order to implicitly criticise the promise of happiness in otherworldly life in return for some privations in worldly life. Such an analogy could have gone unnoticed, but the attentive eye of Martínez de Irujo detected it and decided to limit the damage, making changes that, while negligible in form, are not so in substance, as one can see by comparing the French version, absolutely identical to Smith's original, with that of Martínez de Irujo:

> Les lois relatives aux grains, peuvent partout être comparées à celles du culte. Les peuples prennent un si grand intérêt à tout ce qui a rapport à leur subsistance dans ce monde, ou à leur bonheur dans la vie future, que pour le maintien de la tranquillité publique, les gouvernements sont obligés de se conformer à leurs préjugés, et d'établir les systèmes qu'ils approuvent; voilà peut-être ce qui fait qu'on en trouve si peu de raisonnables sur l'un ou l'autre de ces deux objets.
>
> (Smith 1790, IV, 22-23)

> La causa de que haya tan pocas leyes bien fundadas acerca de los granos consiste tal vez en que como la subsistencia es el primer interés de los pueblos, se ven precisados los gobiernos a conformarse con sus preocupaciones, y a establecer los sistemas que se apoyan en la opinion publica.
>
> (Smith 1792, 196)

## The case of the French linkage

The comparison between the *Compendio* and the French translation of the WN published in the *Bibliothèque de l'homme* shows that the spread of Smith's work in Spain does not imply full support for his ideas. In many cases, the literature has pointed out,

> the weakness of the influence of the essential aspects of the Smithian system, despite Smith being a well-known author translated in the last age of the Enlightenment. It is also suggested that: his influence was taken up with modifications and restrictions within a previous structure of mercantilist thought, maintained with slight adjustments; other less well-known

authors were more influential; the enlightened intellectuals learnt their main ideas on economic freedom from other previous sources; the Spanish economists' thought was characterised by a strong eclecticism not really consistent with the teachings of Smith.

(Llombart 2000a, 64)

However, on this occasion, we prefer to highlight again the role that the French channel of dissemination played in this story. On the one hand, committed to hindering any kind of information and ideas coming from France, where the Revolution had almost completely destroyed the Ancien Régime (Schwartz 2000, 178), the Holy Office is said to have blacklisted the WN because it suspected that the Scottish name hid a French Jacobin (Lasarte 1976, 22).

On the other hand, the French was "the *lingua franca* of the party of the Enlightenment in eighteenth century Europe" (Reeder and Cardoso 2002, 187). More specifically, although Condorcet was a key figure in the French revolutionary process, his name was used to introduce the WN into the Spanish institutional milieu. In his *Discurso preliminar*, Martínez de Irujo defined him as a guarantee "del aprecio que debe merecer esta obra" (Smith 1792,V).The same may have occurred in France, since using the name of prominent intellectuals in order to disseminate foreign works was a rather common strategy in the editorial circles of the age.

Our impression is that this also happened on the occasion of the publication of the abridged version of WN in the *Bibliothèque*, when the name of Condorcet, *philosophe* and much-appreciated public official, replaced that of Antoine Roucher, the real translator of the WN into French (Pisanelli 2018, 39–41). Given his perfect "knowledge of the English language" (Ross 2010, 386),Antoine Roucher decided to fully translate the WN and informed Sophie de Grouchy, Condorcet's wife and his longtime friend (Boissel 1988, 68). In 1790, Roucher published the first three volumes of the WN in French and, in 1791, the fourth and final one (Faccarello and Steiner 2002, 81–84).

Volumes I and III of this translation represent an important clue to the hypothesis we wish to advance here.The title page of these volumes announces a fifth additional volume of "Notes, par M. le Marquis de Condorcet, de l'Académie Françoise, et Secrétaire perpétuel de l'Académie des Sciences." On 26 May 1791, *Le Moniteur* wrote:"on ne peut qu'attendre avec impatience le cinquième volume, ou l'on annonce des notes d'un écrivain homme d'etat, digne commentateur d'un texte qu'il aurait pu composer lui-même."[11] We consider it unlikely that these notes were written or published and then lost, for at least two reasons. Firstly, the reference to this phantom fifth volume had already disappeared in the second edition of the translation edited by Roucher (1791–1792). Secondly, there is no trace of it even in the collection of Condorcet's works edited by Arago and O'Connor (the latter Condorcet's son-in-law).

Scurr put forward two different hypotheses about Condorcet's missing notes on WN. It is possible that Condorcet could not devote his time to a long and demanding task such as the critical commentary on Smith's powerful, complex work because of his direct involvement in French revolutionary politics. The second hypothesis is that "Condorcet may have abandoned his commentary on the WN after 1790 because he realised that *The Theory of Moral Sentiments* (TMS) was more pertinent to the process of social renewal that was fast becoming central to the Revolution" (Scurr 2009, 444). The latter supposition seems unlikely because it supports the existence of an *Adam Smith Problem*,[12] which an Enlightenment thinker like Condorcet could not have envisaged. He recognised the essential role of political economy in order to know the contemporary economic and social reality. Finally, one should not forget that Enlightenment thinkers attributed an essentially ethical dimension to political economy. By reducing social inequalities, the latter could improve human conditions on an individual and collective level. Condorcet, as a great admirer of Smith, defined WN as "un ouvrage malheureusement encore trop peu connu en Europe pour le bonheur des peuple" (Condorcet 1847 [1786], V, 54).

On the other hand, the hypothesis that "Condorcet not only paid little attention to these notes on Smith, but that he somehow allowed his name to be used for advertising purposes" is credible (Faccarello 1989, 125). Even the literature of the time confirms it: "on pensa que son nom pouvait donner plus de crédit à l'entreprise" (Lalande 1796, 155).

One final remark may be useful. Apart from some short sentences connecting the selected parts, the text of the WN summary published in the *Bibliothèque de l'homme* is perfectly in line with the complete translation by Roucher, of which it is obviously an excerpt. As a result, the considerations on the (nonexistent) volume of notes by Condorcet can be extended to his role in the summary published in the *Bibliothèque*. It is true that "M. le Marquis de Condorcet, Secrétaire perpétuel de l'Académie des Sciences, l'un des Quarante de l'Académie Françoise, de la Société Royale de Londres" is one of the editors of the periodical that aims to disseminate "les principaux ouvrages français et étrangers" in France, but also "M. de Peysonnel, ancien Consul-général de France à Smirne, & c.; M. Le Chapelier, Député de l'Assemblée Nationale, *et autres Gens de Lettres*" (*my italics*) are named. In this intellectual network, anyone could have prepared a summary of the WN suited to the journal's circulation needs. Not by chance, *Journal des révolutions* wrote:

> *Bibliothèque de l'homme public*, par MM. de Condorcet, Chapelier et de Peyssonnel; le premier n'y travaillera point, le second n'y travaillera guère; le dernier est vieux et cacochyme, il est froid et lent, deux qualités que n'avaient point Bayle, le Clerc et l'abbé Prévost. Nous n'aurons le premier numéro qu'au mois de janvier, et alors tout le temps de le louer.[13]

## Conclusions

This chapter is focused on the analysis of the case of the *Compendio* by Martínez de Irujo on two levels:

(1) the systematic comparison between the Spanish text and the French summary in the *Bibliothèque de l'homme*;
(2) the actual role of Condorcet in the diffusion of WN in Spain.

As for the first level, eminent Spanish scholars have already devoted their attention to the diffusion of Smith's WN in Spain through its main Spanish translations. In this framework, Lluch and Almenar have already highlighted the importance of the *Compendio* by Martínez de Irujo, whose reading was recommended "for educational purposes" to a minority of statesmen, to literary circles and ordinary people (Lluch and Almenar 2000, 95–96, 100). Nevertheless, there is generally less interest in Martínez de Irujo's *Compendio* than in Alonso Ortiz's complete translation. The literature has mainly reported additions and cuts visible at a glance: the long digression on the Amsterdam Bank, the only footnote added by Martínez de Irujo or the long cut of Smith's pages on religious sects. However, the systematic comparison between the *Compendio* and version of the *Bibliothèque* shows other significant modifications, eliminations and additions.

Sometimes, the judgments expressed about Martínez de Irujo's work have been too harsh. In my opinion, it is an error to say he oversimplified the Smithian analysis on the issue of price and value. On this aspect, Martínez de Irujo faithfully follows the summary of the *Bibliothèque*.

On other points, interesting interventions on the Spanish text may have been overlooked. This is the case of a not insignificant issue in the debate on the new configuration of the social order. The modernisation of European nations required the division of powers in order to avoid threats to their free exercise and to individual freedom. A particularly significant passage of the French version, regarding Smith's emphasis on the separation of legal and executive power, disappears from the text of the *Compendio*:

> Lorsque la puissance judiciaire est unie à la puissance exécutrice, il est difficile que la justice ne soit pas souvent sacrifiée à ce qu'on appelle la politique. Les personnes chargées des grands intérêts de l'état, sans avoir même de mauvaises vues, peuvent imaginer souvent qu'il est nécessaire de leur sacrifier les droits d'un particulier. Mais la liberté de chaque individu, le sentiment qu'il a de sa propre sûreté, dépendent de l'administration impartiale de la justice. Pour qu'il sente parfaitement qu'il ne sera pas troublé dans la possession de ses droits, il n'est pas seulement nécessaire que la puissance judiciaire soit séparée de la puissance exécutrice; il faut encore qu'elle en soit indépendante le plus qu'il est possible, que le juge ne soit point amovible au gré de cette dernière puissance, et que le paiement de ses gages en soit également indépendant.
>
> (Smith 1790, IV, 64–65)

As for the role of Condorcet in the diffusion of the WN in Spain, since scientific editorial news reached the Iberian Peninsula mainly through the French channel (Lasarte 1976, 37), it was taken for granted that Martínez de Irujo's *Compendio* was really "hecho por Condorcet." This seems highly acceptable if one only looks at the events that characterised the spread of Enlightenment ideas in Spain. However, if one includes in the framework of the analysis also what happened simultaneously in the French intellectual environment in which Condorcet acted, an alternative hypothesis can be put forward. The mere name of an important personality like Condorcet evoked authority and was therefore able to ensure the diffusion of a noteworthy work such as Smith's WN, even if he did not directly edit its full translation—Roucher's work—nor the volume of notes—announced and never published—nor, probably, the summary in the *Bibliothèque de l'homme* more readable for a wide audience.

As for the success that the *Compendio* had in Spain, two reasons may have contributed to it: (1) "the flavour of the forbidden that derived from the condemnation of the French translation" (Lasarte 1976, 37), but in this case, the merit would be attributed to Roucher—the too often forgotten translator; (2) the perception of Condorcet as a "moderate agrarian reform supporter", a pupil of Turgot, whose ideas were considered less dangerous for Spain than those of Smith himself (Lluch and Almenar 2000, 100).[14]

## Notes

1  Nevertheless, "this abridgement [is] full of inaccuracies and fails to convey with a minimum degree of precision and clarity Smith's economic theories" (Tribe and Mizuta 2002, 189).

2  This does not mean that French thinkers completely agreed with Smith. For instance, see the disagreement between Condorcet and Smith about the *impôt unique* (Pisanelli 2018, 91–92, 103–08).

3  For example, Martínez de Irujo removes the explicit reference to the attempt to smuggle better-made craft products, which the guilds prevent from producing in town. The original text—"you must then smuggle it into the town as well as you can" (WN I, X, 146)—in French becomes: "il vous reste encore l'embarras de le faire entrer en fraude dans la ville" (Smith 1790, III, 140) and in Spanish text completely disappears. In the discourse on *Variations in the Proportion between the respective Values of Gold and Silver*, the reference to the fact that "les diamants et toutes les pierres précieuses approchent peut-être davantage de ce bas prix de l'or" (Smith 1790, III, 155) disappears too.

4  Here, one should notice that Martínez de Irujo adds: (1) a footnote by Smith about "the prices at which the bank of Amsterdam at present (September 1775) receives bullion and coin of different kinds" (WN IV, III, 482); (2) a whole paragraph: "The sum of bank money for which the receipts are expired must be very considerable. It must comprehend the whole original capital of the bank, which, it is generally supposed, has been allowed to remain there from the time it was first deposited, nobody caring either to renew his receipt or to take out his deposit, as, for the reasons already assigned, neither the one nor the other could be done without loss. But whatever may be the amount of this sum, the proportion which it bears to the whole mass of bank money is supposed to be very small. The bank of Amsterdam has for these many years past been the great warehouse of Europe for bullion, for

which the receipts are very seldom allowed to expire, or, as they express it, to fall to the bank. The far greater part of the bank money, or of the credits upon the books of the bank, is supposed to have been created, for these many years past, by such deposits which the dealers in bullion are continually both making and withdrawing" (WN IV, III, 484–85).

5   This approach is typical of the mercantilists, who pointed out that a different level of development may imply a different kind of behaviour by individuals or the state.

6   While in the *Compendio*, Smith's name never appears, in the *Observations* he is explicitly mentioned. Nevertheless, it should be pointed out that Martínez de Irujo did not sign the *Observations*, which were attributed to him later. Also in this case, therefore, the diplomat acts with the prudence his role requires.

7   However, Martínez de Irujo does not condemn the use of slaves: "The American colonist, who by the advantageous price at which he sells his valuable produce, and by the convenience with which he purchases the articles he wants, gains yearly a considerable quantity of money, with this sum buys more negroes; these negroes clear and cultivate more ground; this cultivation offers more produce; this increases the revenue of the King by its exportation; this greater mass of produce employs more ships, more sailors, gives you more commissions on its arrival, and on its sales. The new duties in Spain still increase the produce of the King's revenue, and offer to the nation a precious way of paying to foreign ones the balance of trade, that may result against us, and which we now pay in effective money" (Smith 1792, 80–81). The reference to the necessary balance of trade recovers typically mercantilist themes.

8   Morellet used the Italian expression *traduttore traditore* with reference to the very bad French translation of Smith's TMS edited by Blavet (Morellet 1821, 237).

9   Many French Enlightenment authors shared Smith's concern. See, for instance, what Condorcet wrote: "L'action des gouvernements y est trop compliquée; ils agissent trop, et sur trop d'objets. De cette complication et de cette action inutile, résulte nécessairement une influence obscure, indirecte, qui doit exciter des inquiétudes. La marche des chefs du gouvernement, celle même de leurs agents, reste, malgré la publicité, un secret pour la généralité des citoyens qui ne peuvent la suivre." (Condorcet 1847 [1792], X, 606–07)

10   The reference is to "the study of science and philosophy" and to "the frequency and gaiety of public diversions" (WN V, I, 796).

11   *Gazette Nationale, ou Le Moniteur Universel* (1847 [1789–1799], 8, 490).

12   Since we cannot dwell on the subject here, at least see Oncken (1897), Winch (1978), Raphael (1985), Nieli (1986), Montes (2003) and Tribe (2008).

13   *Journal des révolutions* (1790, VII, 9–10).

14   See R.S. Smith (1957a, 1968b) and Lasarte (1976).

# 5 The first complete Spanish translation of Adam Smith's *The Wealth of Nations*

## José Alonso Ortiz's *Riqueza de las naciones* (1794)

*José Carlos de Hoyos*

## Introduction

José Alonso Ortiz (1755–1815) published the first complete translation of *The Wealth of Nations* (WN) (1776) at the Viuda e Hijos de Santander printing house in Valladolid in 1794, 18 years after the first edition of Smith's text was appeared. Alonso´s *Investigación de la naturaleza y causas de la riqueza de las naciones* had the support of Manuel Godoy, future Prince of the Peace; running to four volumes and 1,683 pages, the publication would remain the only almost complete Spanish version of the WN for exactly 162 years, until the arrival of a new translation by Amado Lázaro Ros in 1956.

The literature on José Domingo Alonso Ortiz Rojo states that he was born in Granada in 1755 and was awarded degrees in theology (1774) and civil law (1778) by the University of Granada.[1] He worked there for several years as a teacher of civil law and trainee lawyer, moving to Valladolid exactly a year before receiving his lawyer's licence in 1782. In Valladolid his career as a public servant began (Valladolid *Corregimiento e Intendencia*—Courts and Town Hall— the Council of Castile and the Treasury) and in 1797 he embarked on a diplomatic career on the initiative of minister Diego de Gardoqui, which would take him to Turin, Paris, Algiers and, finally, London, as consul general, where he died in 1815.

It was the years between Alonso's teaching and work as a trainee lawyer in Granada and his diplomatic career that provided the chronological framework for his work as a translator. His interest in literature and economics developed during his time in Valladolid, where he translated Macpherson's poetry (1788)[2] and Butler's *Lives of the Fathers, Martyrs and Other Principal Saints* (1789–1792; 1791) from English, also attempting to publish a translation of d'Orléans' *Histoire des revolutions d'Angleterre*, which fell foul of the censors and remained in manuscript form. The translation in question here must be added to these titles, as well as the original work *Ensayo económico sobre el sistema de la moneda-papel y*

DOI: 10.4324/9781003152804-6

*sobre el crédito público* (Alonso, 1796), considered by some critics to be "one of the pinnacles of Spanish economic literature" (Schwartz 2000, 204).

Reactions to Alonso's work as an economic translator have been extremely mixed. Some authors deem his Spanish text "well-crafted" and a "faithful translation" (Schwartz 2000), and that the *Riqueza de las naciones* is a high quality version (Lasarte 1975). However, other researchers including R.S. Smith feel that he bowdlerised too much, producing a flawed translation and disorienting readers: "Readers had no way of knowing where the cuts had been made; in fact, there were numerous omissions, distortions and inaccuracies" (Smith 2000, 307). Reeder's opinion falls halfway between these views; he felt that although Alonso had supplied a complete translation, it should be noted that it was "conveniently reworked" (Reeder 1978, 48).

These opinions only partially address the problems involved in fully assessing Alonso's translation praxis in the late eighteenth century. Without attempting to provide a solution to an unsolvable problem—how to assess a translation objectively—this chapter aims to take a close look at three aspects of the first complete translation of the WN into Spanish. The state of Spanish at the end of the eighteenth century, and the extent to which it was capable of tackling economic terminology opens the discussion, followed by a detailed analysis of the stylistic effects as real translating strategies, as well as how much, and to what ends, they change the source text. Finally, the deliberate alterations to the text of the WN are addressed, with attention focused on the footnotes and the modifications to the main body of the translation.

## Spanish at the end of the eighteenth century

Translating requires the translator to have knowledge of the source language, on one hand, and expertise in the target language, on the other, two skills that facilitate the transfer from one language to another, with a greater or lesser degree of success. In the face of this basic and mechanical model, the resources that each language actually possesses to achieve this exchange are rarely taken into account.

Although from a purely abstract point of view it is easy to imagine that two sets do not possess the same number of items, transferring this analysis to languages is more difficult, and even more so when the languages are observed from a historical perspective. While it is it is easy to deduce that the Spanish spoken today is not the same as that in the eighteenth century, it is more difficult to discern which elements are not constant, which have changed, been modified or simply disappeared. At the same time, presenting each language as a set of idiosyncratic linguistic items assumes that it is different from the others, but there can be no absolute certainty as to exactly which aspects are unique and which are common to all.

The outcome of this lack of knowledge is that a model that explains the act of translation as a simple shift from one language to another is applied, and these aspects of the context of the language are not taken into account. Thus, when a translation is described as good or bad, the question of whether the balance of linguistic resources between the language pair is equal or is favourable or unfavourable to one of them—source or target—and how all this may influence the selecting of translation equivalents, is rarely taken into account.

This issue needs to be addressed before any assessment of Alonso's translation of Smith's text is undertaken, since should there have been an imbalance of language resources that was mainly unfavourable to the target language, in this case Spanish, the translation praxis would often be subject to major linguistic modifications, which would be unjustified from a modern point of view.

Despite the long philological tradition of studying the language used in texts written in the past, diachronic research into Spanish still lacks major comparative studies of cross-language resources, which is why no indicators or techniques are available to assess these resources. There are, however, many studies whose aim is to ascertain Spanish's capacity to adapt over time to technical-scientific innovations—particularly the work by Garriga and his team—which provide valuable impressions of the development of scientific language in Spanish.[3]

Therefore, the question that needs to be asked in this opening section is whether Spanish was equipped to embrace the ideas in Smith's text when Alonso sharpened his quill to translate the WN in the late eighteenth century. Did eighteenth-century Spanish have the linguistic resources to translate the English in the WN into a text that was comprehensible to a Spanish-speaking readership?

The relevant literature for this section relates to the situation of economic vocabulary in Spanish during the eighteenth century and its establishment at the beginning of the nineteenth. Various researchers have addressed this issue (Álvarez de Miranda 1992; Gómez de Enterría 1992; 1996; Garriga 1996; Hoyos 2016; 2018), and have frequently put forward convincing arguments as to the existence of economic language in Spanish. Proof of this line of research is Gómez de Enterría's 1996 contribution *Voces de la economía y el comercio en el español del siglo XVIII*, which shows that many neologisms in this field existed in the eighteenth century in Spain, which were recorded not only in economic texts written by Spanish-speaking writers but also in the wide range of Spanish translations of eighteenth-century works on economics (Genovesi, Mirabeau, Quesnay, Rozier, Condorcet and Turgot, among others).

Although dating words is important, in itself it is not enough for forming an idea of the lexis available in this field. A term's use and visibility is not automatically proved by the first time is appears in a text; therefore, in addition to simply recording when and where the terms used appeared, it seems more appropriate to observe their historical trajectories: appearance, spread throughout the language, standardisation process. One pointer is their inclusion in dictionaries, an indicative parameter showing that both a concept and its name were widely known. However, it is clear that a wide range of terms were involved, and that everything points to the conclusion that Spanish had not entirely assimilated some of the concepts of the new economics.

An analysis of terms corresponding to concepts that Smith discussed at some length in the WN and are reflected in Alonso's translation appears below. It is based on Garriga's work (1996), and the three lexical fields in his study, which relate to finance, trade and manufacturing, have been cross-checked with dictionaries published by the Real Academia Española (RAE)—Spanish Royal Academy—(ranging from the *Diccionario de Autoridades* (1723) to the latest twenty-first-century compilations) with the aim of dating the introduction of economic terms.

Each term and the date that it first appeared with an economic meaning in one of the RAE dictionaries over the last three centuries is cited below:

- finance: *déficit* deficit (1832), *defraudar* defraud (1936), *en efectivo* in cash (1837), *gestión* management (1852), *fluctuación* fluctuation (1970), *depresión* depression (1932), *neto* net (1803), *bancarrota* bankrupt/bankruptcy (1726), *acción* share (1726), *accionista* shareholder (1780), *dividendo* dividend (1817);
- trade: *balanza de comercio* balance of trade (1852), *exportación* export (1817), *importación* import (1822), *oferta* supply (1869), *demanda* demand (1869), *mercado* market (1914);
- manufacturing: *empresario* entrepreneur/businessman (1837), *fábrica* factory (1726), *manufactura* (manufacture 1852), *factoría* factory (1970).

If the average occurrence of each lexical unit is ascertained, it can be seen that the terms related to finance appear in the RAE dictionaries for the first time around 1837, those related to trade in around 1857 and those related to manufacturing in around 1846. The year 1844 is thus the midpoint at which this set of words was first included in the RAE Spanish Dictionary, a means of language standardisation *par excellence* and recognised throughout the Spanish-speaking world as the benchmark for the language and the authority on its use.

1844 is a simple median that does not provide much information as to the dictionary compilers' perception of the use of economic terms. However, if the focus is shifted to qualitative elements regarding the use of these words, the ways the terms are defined and the lexicographers' comments show that this terminology did not become fully standard until later. The definition of *acción* (share) en el *Diccionario de Autoridades* (1726) can thus be interpreted:

> SHARES (ACCIONES). A certain type of trade introduced in Holland, England and elsewhere, the term has been communicated, and is commonly used in the press, from which some have taken it without understanding its exact meaning, and needlessly, *as this type of trade is not used in Spain.*
>
> [My italics]

The *Autoridades* definition explains that although the term *acción* exists and its appearance in periodicals can be dated, its use in the Spanish-speaking world seems fairly limited, and it is considered a "foreign" word. In any event, if the word did exist, its use would be purely anecdotal. Lexicographers working outside the RAE milieu reached similar conclusions about the use of *comercial* (trade, which is repeated so often in the WN), of which Father Terreros y Pando commented that it is "of little use, what touches on trade" (Terreros 1786–1788 [1767]). Alonso discusses the terminology used in his translation of the WN in the translator's foreword,[4] and his statement comes as no surprise:

> There are sometimes terms in the translation which, when viewed with the scrupulousness of the dictionary, might seem somewhat incorrect; but which, in view of the subject matter, should be considered optional and specific: reflecting above all that if the terms succeed in explaining the concepts well, for this reason only they fulfil the function of meaningful terms.
>
> (Smith 1794, I, "El traductor")[5]

Alonso admits that in view of the approach taken by dictionaries, some of the words used to translate Smith's text will be considered *bárbaras*, or incorrect and uneducated speech, although he considers them necessary to deal with subject matter of this type and uses them as fully meaningful political economy terms.

Given this state of affairs, there was a clear lack of balance between the set of lexical resources available to Alonso and the expressive capacities of Smith's English text. While it may be overstating the case to talk of a decisive imbalance, it is true that more than half a century went by—the long stretch from 1794 to 1844—between the inclusion of a good many of these terms in the RAE dictionary and the appearance of Alonso's translation. It should also be taken into account that not only did Alonso himself deem many of these economic terms incorrect, but that various lexicographers expressed the view that the words were rarely used when including them in the dictionary (*Diccionario de Autoridades* or Terreros' *Diccionario*), all of which suggests that economic terminology was not yet fully integrated into Spanish when the translation was undertaken. The fact that they were Alonso's only weapons in his struggle with the English text should not be forgotten in the final assessment of the *Riqueza*.

## Alonso's translating style

However, evaluating Alonso's translation praxis requires more than simply appraising the state of Spanish in the eighteenth century and the extent to which economic terminology had been integrated into the language; it is also necessary to consider what specific strategies he followed when faced with the challenge of conveying ideas expressed in English into Spanish. To this end, Alonso introduced certain modifications into the English text so that it flowed better in Spanish. The analysis (Table 5.1) is based on the definition of political economy at the beginning of book IV, *Of Systems of Political Æconomy*.[6]

The first thing that Alonso does is to reorder the discourse by placing "two objects" at the beginning of the paragraph, moving it forward in the sentence and making it the subject of the clause, when in the original English, "two

*Table 5.1* Comparison between the WN´s original version and Alonso´s translation

| WN IV, 1–2 | Smith 1794 IV, 247–248 |
|---|---|
| POLITICAL œconomy, considered as a branch of the science of a statesman or legislator, proposes two distinct objects: first, to provide a plentiful revenue or subsistence for the people, or more properly to enable them to provide such a revenue or subsistence for themselves; and secondly, to supply the state or commonwealth with a revenue sufficient for the public services. It proposes to enrich both the people and the sovereign. | *Dos objetos* son los que presenta la economía política considerada como uno de los ramos de la ciencia de un legislador, *y que debe cultivar* un estadista: el primero suministrar al pueblo *o nación respectivamente* abundante *subsistencia,* o hablando con más propiedad, habilitar a sus *individuos,* y ponerles en estado de poder surtirse por sí mismos de *todo lo necesario:* y el segundo proveer al Estado o Republica de rentas suficientes para los servicios públicos, *y las expensas, o gastos comunes:* dirigiéndose en ambos objetos a enriquecer al Soberano y al pueblo *como tales.* |
| The different progress of opulence in different ages and nations, has given occasion to two different systems of political œconomy, with regard to enriching the people. The one may be called the system of commerce, the other that of agriculture. I shall endeavour to explain both as fully and distinctly as I can, and shall begin with the system of commerce. It is the modern system, and is best understood in our own country and in our own times. | De los diferentes progresos *que se han hecho* en la opulencia en diferentes siglos y naciones nacieron dos sistemas distintos de economía política, dirigidos a enriquecer a los pueblos: el uno puede llamarse sistema de comercio, el otro de agricultura. Procuraré explicar ambos con la claridad y distinción que me sea posible, *principiando por el del comercio.* Este es el sistema moderno, el que más se entiende en nuestros días, y el que mejor ha llegado a penetrar la *nación inglesa entre otras.* |

Table elaborated by the author.

distinct objects" is the direct object of the verb "propose," which is translated as *presentar.* The syntactic focus thus shifts from "political economy" in Smith's original to "two objects" in the Spanish version. Alonso then changes the English conjunction "or" between two nouns (*statesman or legislator*) for a compound clause with a new verb with a moralising bent (*que debe cultivar*) creating the following structure: *uno de los ramos de la ciencia de un legislador y que debe cultivar un estadista* (literally, one of the branches of the science of a legislator and which a statesman must cultivate). Alonso employs the same strategy when using a gerund to avoid a new compound clause with a conjunction plus future, as in *principiando* to translate "and shall begin," and when he adds a subordinate relative clause instead of using Smith's prepositional phrase: "the different progress of opulence" becomes *De los diferentes progresos que se han hecho en la opulencia* (of the various advances made in opulence). It could be concluded at this juncture that the reordering and the use of compound clauses, gerunds and relative clauses all enhance the discourse's fluidity, despite the structural gap between the source and target texts.

Alonso also adds text that is not in the original, such as explanatory synonyms. He proposes *pueblo* or *nación* for the English version's stark "people," also adding *respectivamente*, which is not in the original but is appropriate if the chain of creating synonymic pairings is taken into account. However, not only he does add synonyms, doubtless for clarification, but he also omits them. Thus, "plentiful revenue or subsistence" becomes *abundante subsistencia* (without the binomial) in the Spanish text, and a little further on a synonym is used, once again for simplification: *todo lo necesario,* without the original "revenue or subsistence" binomial. In this way he corrects Smith's repetition of the first item on the list, probably feeling it unnecessary or poor style.

On other occasions the text may be enriched by additions that make it easier to understand or improve the style. Instead of using Smith's succinct wording "to enable them," in which the pronoun refers back to "people," Alonso extends it with a noun that is not in the original text: *habilitar a sus individuos.* As he can neither respect the English text's coherence ("them"–"people") as his first translation used two words for "people" (*pueblo* and *nación*), nor does he wish to be too abstract and use a vague co-referencing device for the pronoun and the noun *nación,* for example, he opts for using the lexical unit *individuo.* At the end of the first paragraph, he adds text again (*como tales:* "as such"), thus creating a stronger version of the WN's statement that wealth reverts both to the sovereign and the people: *dirigiéndose en ambos objetos a enriquecer al soberano y al pueblo como tales.*

There are other means of enriching the target text than by simply adding words. Alonso chose to embellish the English "has given occasion to two different systems" by using a metaphor referring to birth: *nacieron dos sistemas distintos* ("two different systems were born"). Avoiding repetition is a further aspect of text enhancement and in his translation of "shall begin with the system of commerce," "system" disappears, to be replaced by a pronoun: *principiando por el del comercio.*

Other translator additions may not be fully justified on the basis of a narrow reading of the WN. In the definition of political economy Alonso clarifies Smith's thinking in the second item on the list (starting with "secondly"), with the addition of *y las expensas, o gastos comunes,* ("and expenses, or common costs") to public services, while the original text only mentions *revenue sufficient for the public services.* The translator has added *gastos* and *expensas* to complete the idea with regard to public service. Alonso also acts along similar lines when he intervenes in the Spanish text to clarify that "own country" in the WN refers to the *nación inglesa,* English nation, since it would be futile to translate it as *nuestro país,* "our country", and readers would automatically assume that the reference were to Spain, had they not taken into account the fact that the book was foreign. Naturalising the text in order to avoid possible problems of intercultural understanding is a common strategy in Alonso's translation.

In short, three main types of translation praxis have been used: structural, semantic and stylistic changes. The first type entails manipulating the source to produce different syntactic structures in the target text, such as rearranging phrases, creating compound or subordinate clauses, and using gerunds and simplifications to avoid repetition. The second type includes creating or omitting synonyms and altering the semantic load in Smith's text. The third type is mainly related to enhancing the style of the original, or at least improving Smith's style from a Spanish-speaking perspective; this does not mean at all that Smith's style was unsuitable for his object of study in the language in which the book was originally written, but that perhaps certain adjustments were needed to adapt it to a Spanish-speaking readership.

In all but a few cases, modifications of this type had the effect of making the 1794 version of *Riqueza de las naciones* longer. Although it cannot be taken as a definitive pointer, comparing the number of words used in the English and Spanish versions at least indicates a certain tendency: the WN defines political economy in two paragraphs, with 149 words in total, while Alonso's version contains 177 words.

In the *Riqueza de las naciones* Alonso created a text that contained a great many structural, semantic and stylistic changes with respect to Smith's original text. All the modifications discussed here, which recur throughout the translation and not only in the excerpt analysed above, inevitably mean that the Spanish version is longer than the original, which, according to the interpretation above, aimed to improve the final product in order to make it easier for Spanish readers to understand, as well as to meet the requirements of good taste in the use of language at the end of the eighteenth century. In short, Alonso seems to have been guided by the principles of fluidity and clarity, and he cannot be criticised for this, as he acted within the same common framework of intervention as other translators of the time, as Gómez de Enterría points out in his work on economic lexis:

> In the translations of economic works undertaken in Spain during the eighteenth century, constant care was taken to ensure clarity of expression, so that the translated texts could be perfectly understood by the wide range of readers to whom they were addressed.
>
> (Gómez de Enterría 1996, 21)

The textual modifications detailed and analysed above are fully consistent with the effective transmission of the message, and although from a twenty-first-century perspective it may sometimes be felt that the translator has taken his interventionist attitude too far, refusing to subscribe to the criteria common to all publishing companies nowadays vis-à-vis translations—essentially, faithfulness to the original text in terms of structure, semantics and style—the translation respects the conceptual framework in vogue at the time.

## Alonso's intervention in the WN's original text: notes and alterations

The oft-repeated Italian adage *traduttori, traditori* is particularly relevant with regard to deliberate additions or deletions from the original text. Without going so far as to claim that Alonso's actions betray the original of the WN, commentators have wasted no time in pointing out differences from the original in the Spanish version. They are unanimous (Lasarte 1976; Schwartz 1990; 2000; Fuentes and Perdices 1996) in pointing out that the Alonso clearly intervenes in his translation of the original text, making basic changes of two types: modifying the original text—bowdlerising or altering, as the case may be—or adding new text that he wrote himself. In the first, the translator deliberately mutilates the chapter on religious education for people of all ages— V.i.g., G 788–814—and introduces clear qualifications in his treatment of usury rates, the Catholic religion, education, tithes and the Spanish crown and its monarchs. In the second, appendices were added that did not exist in the original version, such as the table of prices (book I), historical information on wheat and barley taxes (book I), a long section on the Bank of San Carlos (book IV), the translator's foreword, a brief index of the book at the end of Book IV, and many notes aimed at "clarifying some of Smith's ideas, disagreeing with his thought and softening some dubious ideas" (Fuentes and Perdices 1996: xlvii).

Commentators have so far dealt with the changes to the original text in a macro-structural fashion, comparing the two texts, referencing the alterations to Smith's text in precise detail—particularly Schwartz's works—and positioning the changes within an interpretative approach relating to the circulation of economic thought and its implications. While not wishing to neglect previous analyses, the aim here is to focus on a strictly translation perspective, more in terms of the text's materiality than the ideas themselves and their dissemination. As the WN is a very long text and this is the first time an analysis of this type has been undertaken, there is no precedent in the literature; therefore the part of Smith's book that contains the translator's interventions referred to above has been chosen: chapter 7, book IV, which is devoted to the colonies, a subject that will be useful for analysing both the notes added by the translator and his interventions in Smith's own text.

The notes Alonso added provide a good starting point and it is useful to give an overall account of their inclusion in the translation. On the basis of Schwartz's analysis, which this author has checked, it can be confirmed that the 1794 Spanish translation contains 169 notes,[7] which are distributed as follows: volume I, which contains book I of the WN (*De las causas del adelantamiento y perfección en las facultades productivas*), has 53 notes; vol. II, with book II (*De la naturaleza, acumulación y empleo de los fondos o capitales*), book III (*De los diferentes progresos de la opulencia en naciones diferentes*) and part of book IV (*De los sistemas de economía política*, to part of chapter 3), has 23 notes; vol. III, from the second part of chapter 3 to the end of book IV, 30 notes; vol. IV, which contains the whole of book V, the last in the work, *De las rentas del soberano o de la república*, has 63 notes.

The ratio between the length of the *Riqueza* and the notes varies somewhat from one volume to another: vol. I has one note approximately every nine pages,[8] vol. II every 17 pages, vol. III every 11 pages and vol. IV every eight pages.

A different result is obtained by performing the same calculation but dividing the work into books, instead of volumes, which is especially useful for vols. II and III, in which different sections are merged: book I contains 53 notes, with an average of one every nine pages; book II, seven notes, with one every 25 pages; book III, seven notes, with an average of one every 21 pages; book IV, 39 notes, with a ratio of one note to each 14 pages, and book V, 63 notes, with an average of one for every eight pages.

In short, there are 169 notes over 1,683 pages, which means that Alonso adds a note approximately every ten pages. The books that least aroused the translator's interest from the point of view of adding notes are books II and III, which include a note on average every 20 plus pages, while he pays most attention to books I and V, including a note at least every nine pages on average. Book IV falls somewhere in between, with a note every 14 pages.

A more detailed analysis of book IV has been carried out on the basis of its position in the middle of the scale, in the hope that its figures may be representative of the translation praxis without containing significant biases in function of the subject matter. Of the 39 notes in the book, the 17 that appear in Chapter 7,[9] *De las colonias*, have been chosen.

Alonso's additions when dealing with the colonies can be classified in three different ways. Firstly, he adds short technical notes—fewer than three lines of text—in which he clarifies terms and which he generally marks with an asterisk, such as those in the explanations of the meanings of "caiman" (Smith 1794 III, 124) and "llama" (Smith 1794 III, 141). The following is a brief illustration of the procedure.

> WN text translated into Spanish: "y pieles de aligadores grandes o serpientes feroces (*)" (Smith 1794 III, 124). Translator's footnote: "(*) The difference between the alligator and the crocodile, animals which are often interchangeably called caimans, can be seen in Mr. la Harpe, in his *Compendium of Travels*, on Mexico".[10]

These technical notes may also contain minor historical or chronological details relating to specific events in Spain, such as Columbus's departure from the port of Palos, giving the exact day (Smith 1794 III, 121), or the Catholic monarchs' place of residence on a specific date (Smith 1794 III, 124).[11] They are marked with an asterisk or a cross.

Secondly, the notes enrich the information in the text by means of comments and asides, which are somewhat less succinct than the technical notes and take up between three and 13 lines of text. The vast majority of notes of this type are marked with asterisks and crosses, although there are also examples of Arabic numerals.

The content of the notes in the second category is expressed in a variety of tones, ranging from the clearly subjective, such as those praising Smith's work,

to the equally clearly neutral, which adds elements that are either simply con-
textual or can be extrapolated to situations that are not analysed in the WN.
This is what Alonso does in the following excerpts from the notes:

> Contextual or extrapolated note, text from the WN translated into Spanish:"la
> misma fue por lo general la de Francia, y lo ha sido uniformemente desde la
> extinción de la Compañia de Mississipy (★)."Translator's footnote:"(★) This
> is similar to Spanish policy nowadays."[12]
>
> (Smith 1794 III, 157)

> Contextual and commendatory note, text from the WN translated into
> Spanish "es imposible, que en las actuales circunstancias se sometan al
> Parlamento de la Gran-Bretaña (★)."Translator's footnote:"(★) The author
> was writing this around the year 1775, when the great debates of the
> English Parliament with the Assemblies of their Colonies began: nothing
> else was at issue in Great Britain but this famous controversy; each
> proposed the means which he thought most expedient for the consolida-
> tion of peace: and Smith was one of those who reproved the conduct of the
> government towards those colonies: indeed, by the consequences which
> followed from the measures taken by Great Britain, the wisdom of our
> author's reasoning and his deep political understanding, are patent. All the
> paragraphs on the subject in this chapter are therefore to be understood as
> referring to that period."[13]
>
> (Smith 1794 III, 236)

Thirdly, and finally, there are ideological notes in which the translator justifies
and legitimises Spanish actions, frequently contradicting statements in Smith's
text. Some of these are extremely long—at times stretching over four pages of
the translation—and are numbered with Arabic numerals, from one to four in
those connecting a single topic, such as the four notes between pages 125 and
156, which Alonso justifies as follows:"The expressions used by the author in
this part could well have been omitted in the translation; but they lend themselves rather to challenge than to omission" (Smith 1794 III: 125).

The notes in this case are *impugnaciones*—*challenges*—to Smith's opinions,
but instead of cutting the views out completely, as he does on other occasions,
the translator prefers the dialectical game of refuting and contradicting Smith's
statements whenever he can. If Smith states that greed for precious metals is
what drove the Spaniards to colonisation (WN IV, VII, a21), the translator's
note qualifies this with the comment:"but it is not absolutely certain that this
was generally the case, as the author supposes, and as all foreign writers who
miss no opportunity to denigrate our nation with the taint of greed suppose"
(Smith 1794 III, 128). When Smith explains Spanish settlement in America,
Alonso rebels by saying:"this paragraph gives a very sinister idea of the facts
about Spanish settlements in the Indies, and clearly manifests the spirit of par-
tiality in which our imitators generally speak of these things" (Smith 1794 III,
131–132). Alonso intended this note to be an "impartial observation" (Smith

1794 III, 131), and also to explain that colonisation was a "legitimate project of occupation" (Smith 1794 III, 132).

When Smith praises free trade among the English colonies and their governmental structure (WN I, VII, b51), Alonso includes a note in a different register but still with an ideological bias, in which he settles the score by saying: "Experience taught the English that the principles they adhered to in governing their colonies were wrong" (Smith 1794 III, 172). Later on Alonso openly criticises Smith's opinion that Spanish internal trade and manufacturing declined as a result of the discovery of America:

> Spain lost all these advantages for various reasons which were hinted at in another note, and although the monopoly of colonial trade may not have been the cause of this decline, it is evident, as our author says, that it has not been enough to restore it.
>
> (Smith 1794 III, 214)

Alonso adds a further justificatory note in the paragraph in which Smith discusses the possibility of moving the seat of Parliament from Europe to America (WN IV, VII, c79). He translates the whole paragraph except for the last part:

> The distance of America from the seat of government, besides, the natives of that country might flatter themselves, with some appearance of reason too, would not be of very long continuance. Such has hitherto been the rapid progress of that country in wealth, population, and improvement, that in the course of little more than a century, perhaps, the produce of American might exceed that of British taxation. The seat of the empire would then naturally remove itself to that part of the empire which contributed most to the general defence and support of the whole.
>
> (WN IV, VII, c79)

Alonso's translation of paragraph 79 runs from "The people [...] in those remote parts of the empire." (WN IV, VII, c79), adding a note at the end: "Member of the English Parliament, and of a Legislative body, of any injury by a military officer, or politician in those remote parts of the Empire. (+)" (Smith 1794 III, 241):

> Translator's footnote: "(+) It is very plausible that if Great Britain had embraced the means of reunion proposed here by the author at the beginning of the revolution of her colonies, there would not have been so much bloodshed, and their complete independence may not have been achieved"[14]
>
> Smith 1794 III, 241

Faced with the impossibility of translating Smith's conclusion and proposal, Alonso feels obliged to add a compensatory note, in which he adheres to Smith's proposals without giving a clear explanation of them. It has to be assumed in this case, as in others in the chapter, that while Alonso does not accept Smith's specific analysis of Spain's situation, he does accept some of Smith's conclusions, such as the tendency to take more account of the colonies governing their own destinies, thus avoiding greater evils such as possible independence (and the military conflict that this political development would entail).

To sum up, there are four technical notes, six that enrich the text and seven with ideological content. If these statistics are extrapolated to the translation as a whole, it can be assumed that the translator intervenes via the notes as follows: 23% of the notes are technical, 35% add basic contextualising information and 42% contribute an ideological viewpoint, either criticising Smith's opinions or justifying Spain's actions. If the data are divided into two large groups according to whether they are neutral or interventionist, the technical and contextualising notes are related to a neutral attitude and the ideological to an interventionist attitude, Alonso's praxis can be characterised as neutral in just over half the notes, because these simply provide essential clarifications for potential Spanish readers. However, Alonso exceeds his remit, to the point of betraying his supposed neutrality, in almost half the notes, thus producing a biased or critical view of the original, and despite the fact that he himself states in the foreword that the notes in the margins seek not to intervene but to clarify:

> I thought it very useful to add a few remarks in the margins as to what I found peculiar to Spain in those cases, in order that readers might have more opportunity to apply the general rules to the circumstances of the country in which they live; or else they might serve as curious items to illustrate the subject somewhat. My intention is not to enter into a formal discussion of the rightness or wrongness of the author's maxims.[15]
>
> (Smith 1794 I, "El traductor")

It should be noted, as Reeder points out (1978), that it was somewhat unusual for translators to add text at the time; only those who were also experts in economics could afford to do so. This is how the translators of Herbert's *Essai sur la pólice générale des grains* and the WN proceeded: "Anzano and Alonso are the only translators who insert extensive comments in the original texts, that is, who try to relate the translated works to the context of the specific problems of the Spanish economy" (Reeder 1978, 67).

Having analysed Alonso's most obvious interventions in the original of the WN, which are his notes, the changes involving deletions and alterations in the chapter on the colonies need to be discussed. According to the translator's foreword, Alonso's initial aim was to modify the original only minimally:

> although removing some details, but very few, either because they are absolutely irrelevant to our nation, or because they do not conform to the holy religion we practise, naively protesting that if they are removed, the substance of the work is not altered in any way, and if they are not removed, they add nothing to its perfection and complement, as anyone who impartially consults the original can easily be disabused.[16]
>
> (Smith 1794 I, "El traductor")

Alonso justifies such alterations on the grounds that some of Smith's statements would make uncomfortable reading for the Spanish nation and the Catholic Church. The result, in the translator's opinion, is that the translation contains minimal changes and is faithful to *the work's essence*. Therefore, he does intervene, and acknowledges this from the beginning; but does his intervention really only involve religious matters or criticisms of Spain's actions?

An analysis of the 100 pages in chapter 7 of book IV, which is devoted to the colonies, reveals that Alonso's interventions in the original fall into one of three categories: editing, minor and overt.

Merging several paragraphs in the original into one (WN III, 181, IV, VII, c1-3), or doing the opposite and splitting one paragraph into two (WN 210, IV, VII, c47), and organising Smith's discourse into sections as in parts II *De las causas de la prosperidad de las nuevas colonias* and III *De las ventajas que ha ganado Europa con el descubrimiento…*, a division which does not exist in the WN, are examples of acting on the text for purely editing purposes. From the point of view of content, the degree of translator intervention is close to zero, but there is intervention nonetheless.

A more significant example of intervention at editing level goes beyond these stylistic changes and involves adding or deleting almost negligible amounts of text from the original—a couple of words, sometimes a sentence. These are minor interventions, which do have an impact on the content, and range from some that distort Smith's thought very little to others that clearly alter his purpose: translations of meaning, historical updates, explanatory additions and the neutralising of pejorative adjectives.

The translations of meaning retain the source content but modify its linear organisation in several respects. They are very common in Alonso's translation, and Table 5.2 is a sample highlighting one of the clearest aspects of discourse reorganisation.

*Table 5.2* Comparison between the WN's original version and Alonso's translation

| WN IV, VII, b.56 (588) | Smith 1794 III, 177 |
| --- | --- |
| But the prosperity of the sugar colonies of France has been entirely owing to the good conduct of the colonists, which must therefore have had some superiority over that of the English; and this superiority has been remarked in nothing so much as in the good management of their slaves. Such have been the general outlines of the policy of the different *European nations with regard to their colonies.* | Pero la prosperidad de las Francesas, *y de las demás Naciones Europeas en aquel Continente* se ha debido a la buena conducta de los mismos colonos, y del gobierno que las ha protegido: artículos en que los Ingleses mismos conocen haber sido inferiores a las demás naciones: y esta diversidad de conducta en nada se muestra más patente que en la versación de unos y otros con sus respectivos esclavos. |

Table elaborated by the author.

*Table 5.3* Comparison between the WN's original version and Alonso's translation

| WN IV, VII, b.62 | Smith 1794 III, 179 |
|---|---|
| The conquest of Mexico was the project, not of the council of Spain, but of a governor of Cuba; | La conquista de México no fue proyecto de la corte de Castilla, *aunque ésta lo confirmase, y prestase su autoridad para ello,* sino del gobernador de Cuba |

Table elaborated by the author.

Historical updates or explanatory asides: for example, the original "late war" (b17) becomes *penúltima guerra* (penultimate war) (Smith 1794 III, 147) and again in the translation of paragraph c64, in which the same term becomes "*las guerras anteriores al año de 1775*" (wars before 1775) (Smith 1794 III, 224). There are also additions with more straightforward explanatory ends, such as the one illustrated in Table 5.3.

Alonso thus specifies that the conquest of Mexico was authorised by the court of Castile, although, as the original says, it was the governor of Cuba's initiative. The concept of authorisation does not appear in the WN, but is added by the translator. There are further examples of the addition of brief details to the original in the translations of paragraphs b62, c43, c63 and c99. Again with the aim of increasing the information in the original, the translator adds an item to a list, for example c6 "such as Spain, Portugal, France, and England", while the Spanish text also includes Holland (Smith 1794 III, 182), *España, Portugal, Inglaterra, Francia, y Holanda* and, in c13, in which Smith only cites England, Alonso writes *Inglaterra y Francia* (Smith 1794 III, 186)—specifying England's actions (b64) and including a summarising sentence at the beginning of the chapter's closing paragraph: *El gobierno civil, y la soberanía deben estar siempre en distinta mano que el manejo de los intereses mercantiles* (Civil government and sovereignty must always be different hands from the management of mercantile interests) (WN IV, VII, c108; Smith 1794 III, 268).

Minor clarifications of broader and vaguer terms in the WN fall into this category of additions: in b7, Smith simply mentions "all sorts of European cattle" but Alonso permits himself to specify that he is referring to Spain: *por medio del establecimiento de las colonias españolas*—by means of the establishing of Spanish colonies (Smith 1794 III, 141). Spain is not mentioned in the original, and the reference there is to a larger area such as Europe.

The last type of minor intervention has the effect of sterilising or neutralising certain pejorative adjectives used by Smith: "Violent and arbitrary government of Spain" (b6) becomes simply *el gobierno español*—the Spanish government—in Alonso's version; the translation of "cruel destruction of the nations" (b9) loses the notion of cruelty, and "the absolute governments of Spain, Portugal and France" (b52) is translated as *en las colonias de España, Francia y Portugal*—in the colonies of Spain, France and Portugal. Changes of this type generally involve Spanish political acts, at least in the chapter on the colonies.

As well as these minor and editing interventions, there are also genuine manipulations of the original text that actually misrepresent Smith's thought. These have been termed overt interventions and there are at least nine in the 153 pages of chapter 7 that make up the corpus of analysis.

There is a clear illustration of this overt intervention procedure in the WN´s paragraph (IV, VII, c53) in part III—On the Advantages which Europe has derived from the Discovery of America, and from that of a Passage to the East Indies by the Cape of Good Hope—in which Smith seeks to explain the advantages and disadvantages of colonial trade and its monopoly, applied to Spain and Portugal. The excerpt is reproduced in both languages (Table 5.4).

In the original text Smith attributes the lack of balance to four causes: the depreciation of gold and silver, the exclusion of foreign markets, the restrictions of the domestic market and an erratic and biased administration of justice. Alonso, however, reworks the paragraph and begins by attributing the lack of due compensation to the constant state of war during the fifteenth and

*Table 5.4* Comparison between the WN´s original version and Alonso´s translation

| WN IV,VII, c.53 | Smith 1794 III, 214–15 |
| --- | --- |
| In Spain and Portugal the bad effects of the monopoly, aggravated by other causes, have perhaps nearly overbalanced the natural good effects of the colony trade. These causes seem to be other monopolies of different kinds; the degradation of the value of gold and silver below what it is in most other countries; the exclusion from foreign markets by improper taxes upon exportation, and the narrowing of the home market, by still more improper taxes upon the transportation of goods from one part of the country to another; but above all, that irregular and partial administration of justice, which often protects the rich and powerful debtor from the pursuit of his injured creditor, and which makes the industrious part of the nation afraid to prepare goods for the consumption of those haughty and great men to whom they dare not refuse to sell upon credit, and from they are altogether uncertain of repayment. | Las continuadas guerras, y la serie de los sucesos de los siglos quince y diez y seis no permitieron a España ni a Portugal tomar las mejores medidas para el comercio colonial, como confiesan tanto sus naturales, como los extranjeros, y así en estas naciones los malos efectos del monopolio no han podido compensarse tanto como en otros países por los buenos del comercio de las colonias: además de haber concurrido otras causas para sus desventajas, cuales son la degradación del valor del oro, y de la plata siendo este más bajo en ellas que en las demás naciones de Europa: la privación de los mercados extranjeros por razón del modo con que se impusieron en aquel tiempo los tributos sobre la extracción de géneros para el comercio ultramarino, por derechos de toneladas, San Telmo &c. extinguidos ya en el día; y otras disposiciones a que obligaron las fatales circunstancias de aquellos tiempos tan contrarias a los intereses de todos sus naturales, como ruinosas para el comercio y para la industria. |

Table elaborated by the author.

sixteenth centuries, acknowledged by both Spanish and international observers, as well as to other concurrent causes: those Smith mentions, the depreciation of gold and silver and being deprived of a foreign market—high taxation— and other unspecified but ruinous provisions which were adopted in fatal circumstances—armed conflict, it can be assumed.

While Alonso mitigates and justifies Spain's circumstances by attributing them to the delicate war situation and unfavourable economic facts—precious materials, the international trade situation—he never clearly points out, as Smith does, that the problem stems from Spain: firstly, from its excessive taxation of domestic trade and, secondly, the established institutional—justice— system, which in Smith's eyes is unlikely to create a productive society. Alonso says nothing about either domestic trade or justice, but notes that the obstacles to colonial trade, tonnage duties, San Telmo and others, are "defunct nowadays". He justifies Spain's role whenever he can, if necessary by updating Smith's data.

If the analysis of the text of the paragraph copied above is divided into three categories according to what has been added, deleted or reworked, these excepts emerge:

> Alonso's additions: at the beginning and in the middle of the paragraph, "The continuous wars, and the series of events in the fifteenth and sixteenth centuries did not allow [...] as both its natives and foreigners admit, [...] by tonnage rights, San Telmo &c. already extinct nowadays;"[17]
>
> Rewritten by Alonso and vaguely based on the original text: included at the end of the translated paragraph "and other provisions made necessary by the fatal circumstances of those times, so contrary to the interests of all its inhabitants, and ruinous for trade and industry."[18]
>
> The WN text bowdlerised from the translation: at the end of Smith's paragraph, "and the narrowing of the home market, by still more improper taxes upon the transportation of goods from one part of the country to another; but above all, that irregular and partial administration of justice, which often protects the rich and powerful debtor from the pursuit of his injured creditor, and which makes the industrious part of the nation afraid to prepare goods for the consumption of those haughty and great men to whom they dare not refuse to sell upon credit, and from they are altogether uncertain of repayment."

Using different content but similar degrees of intervention to those observed above, Alonso also acts to remove Smith's moralising device when dealing with Spanish colonisation (b7), suppresses negative mentions of the Catholic Church (b20), protects absolutist governments by attributing the possible faults of monarchs to governors or subalterns (b52 and c80), downplays English colonial superiority (b53 and b63) and distorts the original with regard to justice (c54, in a very similar way to c53).

The only real bowdlerising in these pages occurs when Smith proposes extending the British Parliament to include American representation and the possible relocation of its seat to America at some future point (c79). This polit-ical proposal runs to almost 100 words —"The distance of America ... support of the whole" (WN IV, VII, c79)—and Alonso omits them entirely, adding a justificatory note by means of compensation, as mentioned previously.

To summarise the results of the analysis of this section's interventions relating to the translation of chapter 7, "Of Colonies", Alonso makes 11 alterations that can be deemed editing—paragraph merging and division, the addition of sections—14 minor interventions—from translations of meaning to the neutralising of pejorative qualifiers—and nine overt interventions that cause considerable changes in the original meaning.

In order to assess the frequency of translator intervention in the first com-plete translation of the WN, the Glasgow edition paragraph division and the 1794 translation page count have been used. On the basis of the Glasgow edition and its numbered paragraph structure, it can be seen that book 4 is divided into three sections (a, b, c), with 22 paragraphs in the first, 64 in the second and 108 in the third. If this figure is used as a general framework for creating intervention ratios, there is one overt intervention every 22 paragraphs, one editing alteration every 18 paragraphs and minor interventions every 14 paragraphs. These figures can be interpreted by taking Alonso's translation as a reference and exchanging the paragraphs for pages. The reference value in this case is the 153 pages from 115 to 268 in volume III: there would be an overt intervention every 17 pages on average, a minor one every 11 pages and an editing one every 14 pages.

On the basis of this analysis it is possible to state that two very different types of intervention can be found in each aspect examined. On the one hand, there are notes that can be deemed technical or contextualising, which provide important information for future readers but do not distort Smith's original thought. Likewise, Alonso permits himself to alter the WN for editing purposes, but without repercussions for the content. This type of intervention would seem to remain within the bounds of what was considered good translation praxis at the time.

On the other hand, Alonso also introduces ideological elements in the notes he adds, as well as minor or overt interventions that predispose or change the content of the WN. If the proposed calculations of these interventions are merged, taking the final count per page of Alonso's translation as a bench-mark, there would be 23 minor and overt interventions and six ideological notes, that is, 29 points at which the translator voluntarily manipulates the original text without any attempt to transmit Smith's thought neutrally; a very abstract calculation would yield one visible intervention by Alonso every five pages.[19]

## Conclusion

If the 1794 translation of the WN is compared with Smith's original text, it emerges that Alonso had two basic aims in the *Riqueza*: to preserve most of the original text, adding critical, qualifying or contextualising notes if necessary, but suppressing anything that was inappropriate enough—from the point of view of the Spanish nation and religion—to prevent it being published; it is important to understand the risk of civil or religious censorship here. As he stated in the opening pages, this balance had of course to be achieved without *adulterar el fondo de la obra*—adulterating the work's essence (Smith 1794 I, "El traductor")—while at the same time bringing Smith's work closer to a Spanish audience by means of *varias notas e ilustraciones relativas a España*—various notes and examples relating to Spain (Smith 1794 I, Frontispiece)—most of which enriched the original text—notes, appendices and additions.

Therefore, did Alonso behave as a good translator should? Is the result of his work a well-crafted translation, as some commentators believe (Schwartz, Lasarte, Perdices), or is it flawed (R.S. Smith)? The answer can be expressed on three levels, following the outline of this contribution.

From the point of view of the materiality of the language, all that can be said is that Spanish was not very well-equipped to deal with all the concepts that Smith covered in the WN. Much of Smith's economic lexis was not in common use in Spain in the second half of the eighteenth century, as the dating of economic terminology in dictionaries of the time confirms. Details from lexicographers normally conform that part of the economic vocabulary was little used, and useful information is also provided by the inclusion of economic terms in dictionaries; these terms do not usually appear until 50 years after they were used by Smith or in the translation. All this seems to indicate that neither the Spanish language nor the average Spanish reader was used to economic terminology; thus the translator's basic tool, which is language, was a flawed instrument for transferring Smith's ideas to the Spanish version of the WN.

From a style perspective, Alonso does not seem to have pursued the criterion of faithfulness to the source text that currently prevails in publishing companies; instead, his praxis is based on the criteria of clarity and fluency for a supposedly Spanish-speaking readership. This clarity and fluidity imposed a series of mismatches between the source text and the resulting translation; examples of his actions are the manipulating of sentence organisation, the creating of compound clauses, the use of gerunds, the avoiding of repetition and unnecessary embellishments, among other strategies, resulting in a text that is longer than the WN but more suitable for a Spanish audience. This is a somewhat more flexible criterion of faithfulness than that currently used in modern publishing, but it in no way detracts from Smith's original and is in keeping with translation practice in the late eighteenth century.

Finally, from a purely interventionist perspective, there are two ways of interpreting the mismatches between the original text and Alonso's translation. On one hand, the technical and contextualising notes as well as the purely editorial changes would be part of the translating tradition of the time, and could not be considered true alterations but rather enrichments that pursued the same effect of clarity and fluidity as the interventions for style purposes. On the other hand, however, the ideological notes and minor and overt interventions would seem to depart from the translation praxis of the eighteenth century, instead coming close to the work of an author–editor and leaving aside any semblance of transparency in the transfer of the source text to the translated target text. According to the calculations outlined above, the latter appear in the translation on the basis of an average of one distorting intervention in the text of the WN every five pages of translation.

It has often been said that the WN is not only the product of Smith's genius, but the result of an era—the Scottish Enlightenment—condensed in its author's pen. In the same way, it could be said that Alonso's translation is not only the work of a skilful translator with good knowledge of the English language and the technical aspects of political economy, but was also the fruit of the translation context at the end of the eighteenth century. Contemporary Spanish, in which economics terminology was lacking or was at least poorly established, needs to be integrated into this context. Similarly, it is important to remember that the authorities kept a close watch on the orthodoxy of everything that was published, forcing translators to strike a difficult balance between faithfulness to the original text and respect for the censors' criteria. The reading public in Spain, meanwhile, liked a classical written style, which needed to be maintained when dealing with the world outside the kingdom of the Bourbons, and as a result of readers' demands translators were forced to adopt a different style from that of the originals they translated and to add multiple paratexts to their translations—such as forewords, appendices, notes and summaries.

The translation analysed here can be described as fluid and intellectually "Spanishised", a child of its time yet with a certain degree of timelessness, as the fact that it was reprinted until well into the twentieth century shows (Perdices 2000a, 275–77). In 1805–1806 Alonso himself published a second extended and revised edition, and the *Riqueza* was published once more in 1933–1934, again revised and in modern Spanish, which guaranteed it a certain success throughout the century. It was reissued at least four times: 1947–1949, 1954, 1955–1956 and 1983, even though there were other modern translations such as Gabriel Franco's—first published in 1958—on the market.

The number of times a book is reissued is not necessarily a good criterion for assessing a translation, but might perhaps indicate that the segment of the secondary literature that has been highly critical of Alonso's work does not concur with the text's reception. This version was the only one in the publishing market for over a century and a half. From 1956 onwards it coexisted with other publishing projects that updated the translation yet, despite this, it continued to be reprinted and read for much of the second half of the twentieth century.

Ultimately, is this a good translation or a bad one? There is no easy answer to this question, but it is certainly true that Alonso's translation of the WN is one of the rare cases of the vitality and endurance of a text on the Spanish publishing scene of translations from English. While not entirely faithful to the original, the fluidity of the Spanish, the paratextual information and its adaptation to a Spanish-speaking readership must have been ingredients that contributed to its longevity.

# Notes

1 This is a brief summary of the biographical information to be found in the following works: Schwartz (1990; 2000), Perdices and Reeder (2003), Fuentes and Perdices (1996) and Menudo (2013).

2 Described by one commentator as "the only serious one we have in Spanish of Carthon and Lothmon" (Alonso 1920, 15).

3 There are various illustrations of this dynamism in Garriga et al. (2019) and Pinilla and Lépinette (2016).

4 Since only Alonso's first translation (1794) is analysed here, citations refer to the first edition published in 1794, specifying the volume (I, II, III and IV) followed by the page numbers in the original.

5 "se hallarán a veces en la traducción algunos términos que mirados por la escrupulosidad del diccionario podrían parecer algo bárbaros; pero que atendida la materia se deberán tener por facultativos y propios: reflexionando sobre todo que si los términos logran explicar bien los conceptos solo por esto cumplen con el oficio de voces significativas" (Smith 1794, I, "El traductor").

6 The expressions from Alonso's translation to be analysed are in italics.

7 Although the aim here is not to compare the two editions of Alonso's translation (the first in 1794 and the second in 1805–1806, "much corrected and improved" as the title page indicates), it is interesting to note that the system notes has been modified from one edition to the other. The second edition contains fewer notes and seems to retain only those that are deemed in this section to be contextualising and ideological, while the purely technical ones are omitted.

8 Whole numbers have been obtained by rounding down from 0.1–0.5 and up from 0.6–0.9.

9 The change in the system of notes between the first edition of the *Riqueza* (1794) and the second edition in 1805–1806 is exemplified by the fact that chapter 7 contains fewer notes: in the second edition there are only nine.

10 "(★) La diferencia del aligador y el cocodrilo, animales que suelen llamarse indiferentemente caimanes, puede verse en Mr. la Harpe, en su *Compendio de los viajes*, tratando de México."

11 The following is an example of this procedure: "When, on his return from his first voyage, Columbus entered this court as if in triumph (+)", footnote: "(+) At that time the king and queen were in Barcelona" (Smith 1794, III, 124).

12 "(★) Esta es en el día con poca diferencia la política de España."

13 "(★) El autor escribía todo esto por los años de 1775, en que principiaron los grandes debates del Parlamento inglés con las Asambleas de sus Colonias: no se trataba en la Gran-Bretaña de otra cosa que de esta famosa contestación; cada uno proponía los medios que creía más oportunos para la consolidación de la paz: y Adam Smith fue uno de los que reprobaban la conducta que observaba el gobierno con aquellos establecimientos: en efecto por las consecuencias que se siguieron de las medidas que tomó la Gran-Bretaña, se ve patentemente el acierto con que discurría nuestro autor, y su profunda penetración política. De aquella época pues deben entenderse todos los párrafos que hablan de la materia en este capítulo."

14 "(+) Es muy verosímil, que si la Gran-Bretaña hubiera abrazado los medios de reunión que aquí propone el autor, al principio de la revolución de sus colonias, ni se hubiera derramado tanta sangre, ni acaso se hubiera verificado su total independencia."

15 "me pareció muy conducente añadir en algunas advertencias marginales lo que en aquellos casos encontré de particular en España, para que el lector pudiese con más oportunidad aplicar sus reglas generales a las circunstancias del país en que vive: o bien sirviesen de noticias curiosas que ilustrasen algún tanto la materia. No he pretendido con ellas entrar en una formal discusión de lo acertado, o errado de las máximas del autor."

16 "bien que suprimiendo algunas particularidades, pero muy pocas, o por absolutamente impertinentes a nuestra nación, o por ser poco conformes a la santa religión que profesamos, protestando con ingenuidad que quitadas, en nada se adultera el fondo de la obra, y no expurgadas nada añaden a su perfección y complemento, como puede con facilidad desengañarse cualquiera que consulte con imparcialidad el original."

17 "Las continuadas guerras, y la serie de los sucesos de los siglos quince y diez y seis no permitieron [...] como confiesan tanto sus naturales, como los extranjeros, [...] por derechos de toneladas, San Telmo &c. extinguidos ya en el día."

18 "y otras disposiciones a que obligaron las fatales circunstancias de aquellos tiempos tan contrarias a los intereses de todos sus naturales, como ruinosas para el comercio y para la industria."

19 One could also try to estimate this calculation as a percentage, by saying that 19% is altered, taking each intervention as an abstract reference and assuming that each deliberate intervention changes the meaning of one page. However, this means of calculating seems difficult to justify because the value 1 intervention = 1 modified page can not immediately be assumed. In many cases the translator's intervention only affects one sentence, and in others, a mere adjective.

# 6 José Alonso Ortiz, Adam Smith's translator

## A new interpretation

*Jesús Astigarraga*

## Alonso's Valladolid

When José Alonso Ortiz, author of the first practically complete Spanish translation of *The Wealth of Nations* (WN), arrived in the Castilian city of Valladolid in 1781, he was a young lawyer aged twenty-five with few professional achievements.[1] Originally from Granada, where he had been born in 1755, he was leaving behind his formative years at the university in his hometown, having been awarded degrees in theology in 1774 and in civil and canon law four years later. These had enabled him to become an articled clerk and to work intermittently as a teacher of civil law at the university. Once settled in Valladolid, he completed his legal training and qualified as a lawyer in 1782. In the years that followed Alonso practised law and was briefly an advisor to the Valladolid *Corregimiento* and *Intendencia*—Chancery and Municipality. He began working as a translator in 1786, and one of his works was a translation of the WN, which was published in 1794 and reissued in 1805–1806 by Casa Santander, one of the most prestigious publishers in the city.

Although Alonso's main steps through life are well known, little research has been done on his time in Valladolid. However, it is essential to reconstruct this period if his versions of the WN are to properly understood, as it was during the fifteen or so years that Alonso lived there before settling in Madrid in 1795 that he became a renowned translator. Valladolid was then a town of about 20,000 inhabitants.[2] It was a major economic hub in the interior of Castile, with activity typical of a region that focused on grains, vines and livestock, while also being an important regional centre for services (Almuiña 1974, 18; Enciso 1980, 65). Valladolid was also the seat of the bishop, the Inquisition and the Chancery, as well as housing one of the three major universities in Spain together with Salamanca and Alcalá de Henares; the Colegio of Santa Cruz (1484–1793), one of the seven main colleges in the Spanish university structure, was attached to it. Valladolid had once been home to the Court of Castile, and these institutions were now the mainstay of the city's cultural activity. Alonso was the witness in the emergence of a network of new institutions that channelled the Enlightenment culture's arrival in the city and endowed it with a thriving cultural activity for a provincial capital (Almuiña 1974, 33–54). This

DOI: 10.4324/9781003152804-7

network was forged around the Academia geográfico-histórica (1764)—the Academy of Geography and History—which aimed to educate local nobility in these two disciplines and in physics and geometry; the Real Academia de Matemáticas y Nobles Artes (1779)—the Royal Academy of Mathematics and Noble Arts—which specialised in mathematics, drawing and architecture; the Real Academia de San Carlos de Jurisprudencia Nacional (1784)—the Royal Academy of San Carlos of National Jurisprudence—oriented to spreading legal culture and linked to the powerful Chancery; and, finally, the Real Sociedad Económica de Valladolid (1783)—the Valladolid Economic Society—where the Real Academia de Medicina y Cirugía (1785)—the Royal Academy of Medicine and Surgery—was created.

These institutions were born by local initiative, although they generally followed Court directives. Such was the case of the Sociedad Económica, the only body that explored economic issues. Although little is known about the society's history due to the scarcity of sources (Demerson 1969; Enciso 1975; 2010, 319–48), it is another example of the importance of these patriotic institutions in local elites' involvement in Enlightenment ideas and social practices. It was founded in September 1783 by distinguished members of the Valladolid municipal authorities and nobility and was approved by the Council of Castile within a year because the statutes drawn up in Valladolid followed the pattern established by the Madrid Society, which it resembled in terms of internal organisation and activities. The Sociedad Económica was not particularly active in spreading economic ideas, but it did create a drive for socioeconomic reform in the city, using subsidies and prizes to promote activities for agricultural and industrial development, modernising the charity network and encouraging educational efforts through the creation of "patriotic schools" for teaching literacy and crafts. Like the Matritense, it set up a Ladies' Board and undertook advisory work for the Council of Castile with Floridablanca's guidance. Despite experiencing the usual problems facing such institutions, including a hostile environment (Enciso 1975, 155–78), it had eight dozen members drawn from four social groups: the nobility, the clergy, legal experts linked to the Chancery and university teachers (Demerson 1969, 34–38).

At the heart of this society and the other institutions named were the movers and shakers in Valladolid's Enlightenment culture, such as jurist and historian Floranes; Hernández de Larrea, bishop of Valladolid, who had previously been extremely active in Zaragoza as founder of the Aragon Society and its Chair of Civil Economy (1784); Santiváñez, who settled in the city in 1787 after teaching at the University of Valencia and the Seminary of Vergara, and various writers and magistrates such as Silvela and Del Plano. Valladolid was also the temporary residence of magistrate Mon y Velarde, during his time at the Chancery (1786–1781), and poet Meléndez Valdés (1791–1798). Some of them reinforced the reformist tendencies of these institutions and they also created other informal cultural activities and bodies, such as the meetings on Spanish law set up by Floranes, the gatherings organised by Meléndez Valdés, Santiváñez's teaching academy and the Casa Santander publishing house, a genuine *machine de guerre* in the Enlightenment cause. There must have been an intensely enlightened atmosphere in Valladolid in the 1780s when Foronda chose the Academia geográfico-histórica as the setting to read his "*Disertación sobre la libertad de escribir,*" the starting point of the struggle for freedom of expression in Enlightenment Spain, and Miguel de Lardizábal read his distinguished "*Apología de agotes de Navarra y chuetas de Mallorca.*" In short, this was the milieu in which Alonso must have matured as a translator, although there is only indirect evidence to corroborate this assumption.

## Beristain and the *Diario Pinciano*

The first piece of evidence concerns Beristain, the true architect of Valladolid's cultural effervescence in the 1780s.[3] Born in Mexico, he obtained a degree in philosophy and travelled to Valencia at a very young age, where he studied theology and Holy Scriptures at the university and worked as a substitute lecturer. He arrived in Valladolid in October 1782, having acquired extraordinary credentials: during his period in Valencia he had been given "lessons in literature and good taste" by Mayans (Millares 1972, 4–5), had republished Montegón's *Odas de Filopatro* (1782) and joined the Sociedad Bascongada. It is hardly surprising that in March 1783 he was professor of theology at the University of Valladolid, and that during his six-year stay in the city he became the epicentre of its cultural activity. A member of the Academia Geográfico-Histórica and the Academia de Matemáticas, this scholar and bibliographer was also the founder and Censor of the Economic Society and created its Academia de Medicina. His leading role was underpinned by the network of contacts he wove during his frequent visits to court seats, especially with Floridablanca in whose service he worked cataloguing the manuscripts in the library at El Escorial (Almuiña 1978, 25–30).

The clearest proof of Beristain's key role in the Valladolid of the Enlightenment was his *Diario Pinciano* (DP; Alonso 1933; Guinard 1973, 357–64; Almuiña 1978). The city's first newspaper, once Floridablanca's permission to publish was obtained at the end of 1786, it appeared every week for a year and a half, was circulated by subscription and was open to outside contributors.[4] Its aim was to put the fledgling provincial press, of which the DP was a true emblem,[5] at the service of the official policy against the anti-Spanish currents of the European Enlightenment. Indeed, according to Beristain, "newspapers" should also bloom in the provinces and stimulate the creation of "opinion" so that Europe would have a true idea of "our Enlightenment."[6] The DP plan pointed the finger at Masson de Morvilliers and several paragraphs from his controversial article *Espagne* were copied for the *Encyclopédie Méthodique*.[7] The five sections—"historical, literary, legal, political and economic"—were designed to outline the history of Valladolid and its municipal politics, on the one hand, and the activity of different local institutions including the university and the Sociedad Económica, on the other. The fact that the newspaper appeared weekly and was densely packed with news suggests that Beristain had outside contributors, at least from time to time, among which Alonso has been cited (Almuiña 1974, 85; Enciso 1980, 121ff.). The DP carried accounts of academic discussions on luxury and entailed estates; it repeatedly criticised university teaching methods; it rang with echoes of Mirabeau, Rousseau, Marmotel, Vattel, Heinetius and other Enlightenment writers, and reported Santiváñez's founding of an academy to revitalise university teaching,[8] as well as lectures by Floranes, and others given by Antonio de Ulloa and Carlos Le Maur, who were in the city temporarily. The DP also carried reviews of locally published works, among which the two longest were those devoted to the Santiváñez's translations of Marmotel and Alonso's of Macpherson. In short, the paper was a kind of unofficial mouthpiece for the enlightened sectors at the head of cultural activity in Valladolid.

Not unsurprisingly, the DP was a controversial newspaper, which came of age in a climate of "aggressive pettiness" that was expressed in the form of pamphlets, anonymous letters and public mockery originating with the city council and the university (Almuiña 1978, 63–68). More serious was the fact that in 1786 Beristain was punished by the Inquisition and forced to reapply for his professorship, and that two years later several proposals in the DP were censored (Almuiña 1978, 57–61; Prado 1996, 216). Far from hiding this persecution from his readers, Beristain enlisted the help of people like Santiváñez to use the DP to attack the "buzzing drones" who branded him "impertinent" and "unfit to be a clergyman,"[9] and who he exposed for hiding behind anonymity, claiming the "freedom to print anything" that respected religion and decency.[10] However, the intense hostility towards the DP was one of the reasons for its premature closure in May 1787, which was also linked to financial trouble difficulties and its editor's problems with the Inquisition; having obtained a canonry in Vitoria in 1788, he put an end to his Valladolid sojourn.

## Casa Santander

The second piece of evidence confirming Alonso's involvement in Valladolid's enlightened circles is his relationship with Casa Santander, which published his translations between 1786 and 1794. This was one of the city's most famous family bookshops and printing houses in the eighteenth century.[11] It owed its success to its founder, Tomás Santander, who worked as a bookseller, book dealer and paper manufacturer until his death in 1782. His widow and two sons—Raimundo and Mariano—with whom Alonso must have established a close relationship, kept the business open under various names until it closed in 1837. Thanks to Tomás's immense shrewdness, Casa Santander became an integral part of Valladolid cultural life. In 1777 he bought the printing press and much of the library of the suppressed Society of Jesus. At that time, Tomás shared his work in his printing house with various posts at the university— bursar and treasurer—for which he was also the printer. His company also worked for the city council, the hospice and the economic society, and was the DP's first publisher, also offering its premises as a meeting place for its readers.

Casa Santander was not only a printing house, but was also a prominent book dealer. Its market covered peninsular Spain and the colonies and included newspapers and banned books with dangerous regularity. The owners were in constant contact with France and supplied these publications to elites in an area that extended far beyond the city of Valladolid: according to Floranes, Casa Santander bookshop was one of the "best-served in Castile," while according to an anonymous contemporary it was responsible for "a good part of the Enlightenment that we enjoy today in Castile" (Palomares 1974, 51). Casa Santander also enjoyed close relations with other bookshops that were also known for selling banned books in Cádiz, Madrid, Valencia and Salamanca. It is therefore not surprising that his centrally-located establishment was a hub in the social network of Enlightenment life in Valladolid.

The Santander family's boldness is well illustrated by its three generations' permanent conflicts with the Inquisition. In a setting in which circulating banned books was commonplace, their persecution was one of the "most important of all those carried out by the Valladolid court during the eighteenth century" (Prado 1996, 202). Tomás was tried in 1777 but the chief victims were his two sons, against whom twenty-four cases were brought between 1792 and 1799, mainly related to the distribution of banned publications: in fact, according to witnesses at the time, "more than three parts" of the works in their bookshop had been banned (Prado 1996, 216–17).[12] They were also accused of slandering the Inquisition and of desiring its abolition. The inquisitors' statements singled out their shop as the epicentre of the forbidden books trade and of the "most revolutionary spirits" (Larriba 2013, 149). They also highlighted the two booksellers' insolence when it came to obeying the Inquisition: they served harsh sentences until 1799, which left their bookshop in a delicate financial situation.

During Alonso's years in Valladolid Casa Santander established itself as a thriving printing house. It was one of the main private printers in the country and the most successful in Valladolid (Cruz 2014, 320–21). Like all printers (Escolar 1993, 392–629), its output focused on religious themes in a range of formats and satisfied local demand,[13] which mainly centred on such subject matter (Matos 2012, 294–95); however, they are also an example of how the publishing world was gradually opening up to other topics. In 1797, the Casa Santander published Meléndez Valdés's complete poems, following these with Mably's translation in the nineteenth century. It was around this time that Valladolid libraries began to stock books that were committed to the Bourbon reform (Matos 2012, 746–50) and also to the changes that these advocated at university level. As was generally the case, these reforms reaped only meagre rewards in Valladolid.[14] The main effect of the 1771 decree had been to increase enrolment: in 1779 Valladolid was the second university in Spain in terms of student numbers, after Salamanca (Torremocha 1991, 57–61). This growth was particularly significant in the Faculty of Law, the university's largest most prestigious; together with Salamanca, it was the training ground for the Bourbon bureaucracy (Torremocha 1986, 49–50). With its services for printing handbooks and university textbooks, Casa Santander aimed to respond to this growing university clientele, which was more open to new Enlightenment publications than the rigid academic structure allowed.

It is against this backdrop that Casa Santander's gradual opening up to economic culture prior to publishing the translation of the WN in 1794 needs to be viewed. In addition to several merchants' handbooks, it published two texts: the first was Ruiz de Zelada's *Estado de la bolsa de Valladolid* (1777), a short-run production funded by the city council and covering municipal policy and supplies, while the second, *Memoria político-económica sobre el pan cocido* (1789), was more important and requires closer attention. Published anonymously in May 1789, it advocated improvements in grain milling and bread-making, a particularly pressing issue when it was written, at the height of the 1789–1790 agricultural crisis (Anonymous 1789). The delicate issue of the grain trade was addressed from the perspective of defending the liberalising line taken by the 1764 *Pragmática*, a veritable "masterful *coup d'état*" against the obstacles then hindering agricultural progress. The *Memoria*, however, contained a number of Physiocratic overtones and may have been inspired by Condillac's *Le commerce et le gouvernement* (1776), which had been translated into Spanish in 1781. The *Memoria* stressed the beneficial effects of private enterprise, which had restored farmers' "natural freedom." The freedom to store was the best antidote to monopolies and their excess profits. The text also evoked the advantages of "large-scale cultivation" and "well-off" landowners, who were spurred on by their "own interests" and ability to raise capital. In the background stood the example of successful British reforms, which Spain had accepted via the official free grain trade scheme. However, two caveats remained. The first was the land tax, which offered British landowners a system of guarantees and incentives that the Spanish tax structure lacked (Anonymous 1789, 32). The second was the price of grain. The author advocated setting an "average price" to reconcile "the just returns due to farmers with the reward and interest of merchants" (Anonymous 1789, 44). This meant going against "popular opinion," which was fuelled by the agricultural crisis, and defending a "just and moderate" increase in the price of bread (Anonymous 1789, 85–87). While wages rose in geometric proportion, prices rose in arithmetical proportion, and the proposed solution would thus benefit both sides of the market: the surplus in the hands of producers and consumers would increase at the same time, once the price had been paid. Moreover, this unusual *bon prix* would attract capital and new manufacturers, so "the largest population will always be found where bread is expensive." The *Memoria* thus laid bare Casa Santander's desire to intervene in support of Bourbon reformism, and there is no doubt that the writer was close to Beristain's DP. The *Memoria* censured Masson for his criticism of "proud" Spaniards, and dismissed his calculations of the population growth that would potentially be driven by improving Spanish agriculture, as there was no "less suspect witness" to the possibility of this improvement (Anonymous 1789, 20–30). In short, the "Valladolid son," anonymous author of the *Memoria*, came from the Beristain and Casa Santander circle in which Alonso moved.

## Alonso, translator: before the WN

Alonso produced five translations for Casa Santander between 1786 and 1794 while still practising as a lawyer and must have used Valladolid's splendid network of libraries, as well as that at the university (Matos 2012). The translations were no doubt requested by Casa Santander itself, and it should be stressed that they were produced in a provincial city, although the list of translated authors shows that the enlightened milieu in which Alonso moved was in harmony with European Enlightenment culture. The authors were Joseph d'Orléans (1786), James Macpherson (1788), Alban Butler (1789–1792; 1791) and Adam Smith (1794).

The only translation never to be published was the first, Joseph d'Orléans's *Histoire des révolutions d'Angleterre* (1693–1694).[15] Casa Santander may have requested it due to the anticipated commercial success of the enterprise: bypassing the Inquisition's checks, it was already selling the French version (Larriba 2013, 149), which was circulating "freely" in Spain, along with other works by the prolific Jesuit historian. Despite this, Alonso's work failed to get through the censorship filter; he tried to have the first volume of his translation approved three times between March 1786 and May 1789, but was prevented from doing so by the negative report from the *Academia de la Historia*—the History Academy—censors, who used numerous highly expressive examples to show that his version needed a "more diligent revision." This verdict carried sufficient weight for the Council of Castile to uphold its refusal, despite the fact that Alonso personally lobbied Campomanes, albeit unsuccessfully, in July 1788, either for the licence to be granted or for the president of the Valladolid chancery, who would undoubtedly be more inclined to cede to his wishes, to be the censor.[16]

While this issue was still ongoing Alonso embarked on a translation of Macpherson's *Obras de Ossian* (1788).[17] He began the work in the midst of a widespread controversy, which originated in Britain and was then magnified to Continental scale, over the apocryphal poems written in Gaelic by the Scottish bard Ossian, which were later "restored"—invented in fact—by Scottish poet and historian Macpherson. As he wrote in the *Prólogo*, Alonso intended his translation to involve Spanish scholars in the controversy, because "their literature, taste and application must in no way yield to that of foreigners" (Macpherson 1788, iii). In this he was closely in tune with Beristain, joining the wave of panegyrics in defence of Spanish culture, which was presented as "a part, and not the least valuable, of cultured Europe" (Macpherson 1788, iii). To this end, and very significantly, he mentioned Jesuit Andrés's work with great respect, even though he himself defended the authenticity of Ossian's poems while Andrés did not. While in exile in Italy, Andrés had been chosen by Floridablanca to lead the expelled Jesuits' subsidised literary campaign, which aimed to counteract the negative image of Spanish colonialism and culture projected by French, Italian and Scottish scholars (Guasti 2017). However, as Alonso mentioned, the interest in Macpherson's work went beyond this and was due to the fact that it encouraged the study of "barbarian" customs from earlier ages; more precisely, it nourished a conjectural history through oral transmission that sought to capture the state of nature in the soulful atmosphere of the Scottish Highlands before the advent of civil society: "the pure aspect of nature" was the work's sole aim (Macpherson 1788, xv). It was therefore a matter of exploring a seam, more romantic than rational, of introducing the ideas of the Scottish Enlightenment on the origin and basis of civil society in its contrasts with the previous stage of barbarism: Macpherson had claimed that Ossian's poems were important for analysing the effects of religion, forms of government and property on the development of social customs and the introduction of "delight" (Macpherson 1788, xxiiiff.).

After completing his translation of Macpherson, Alonso began translating works by the Reverend Alban Butler, an English literature and theology professor. This was a titanic undertaking since Butler's work contained 1,600 hagiographies of Catholic saints, arranged according to the calendar. It took Alonso four years to finish two complementary translations: *Vidas de los padres* and *Fiestas movibles*.[18] Both fitted in perfectly with Casa Santander's business activities, which prioritised books with religious themes, as pointed out above. Butler's works, however, were not hagiographies of saints as such, but were built on Enlightenment principles: Butler pointed his finger at "false authors," who he accused of making "mystique out of history."[19] Alonso only confirmed this idea: because of the "fictions, adulterations, falsehoods" with which the holy biography had been written he claimed, appealing to the Protestant Grotius, among others, that "every lie with certain knowledge is essentially a sin," for it destroyed the "sacred bond of society and of all commerce among men." The virtue of Butler's work lay in his documented examination of history, in distinguishing what was true from what was apocryphal and applying to ecclesiastical history the methods of analysis and criticism that had transformed history into a rigorous academic discipline: he "never states anything without proper substantiation." Alonso could thus present Butler's book as "a prodigious monument to critical history and moral erudition," which came to the aid both of Catholicism, which was repeatedly accused of appropriating a "raw indigestible mass of unexamined and uncritical miracles," and sacred history; far from being an unhelpful genre that was alien to good "taste in literature," this was transformed into a powerful Enlightenment channel, that was not necessarily identified with "irreligious radical" currents, as Israel did (2002), but with the idea that the Enlightenment had its own religious origins deriving from Protestant heterodoxy and Catholic reformist currents. Thus, despite the oblivion to which those studying Alonso have condemned his pre-WN translations, it is clear that these works not only have close links with the WN, but also shed light on the profile of Smith's future translator. Alonso appeared to mesh perfectly with the Casa Santander publishing machinery and also the enlightened aims that the members of Beristain's circle so longed for.

## The translation of the WN (1794)

The translation of the WN was the last of Alonso's works for Casa Santander.[20] According to available information, he translated the four volumes between 1792 and the summer of 1793. The work was not only a prosperous commercial venture for the publishing house, but also represented a prestigious project for the translator. By then the WN's circulation in Spain was well underway; this was perhaps an echo of post-revolutionary France, where the WN moved from "periphery to centre" between 1790 and 1795 (Carpenter 1995, 6–7; 2002, xxiii). Martínez de Irujo and Alcalá-Galiano's versions had been published in 1792 and 1793 and enlightened Spaniards had been citing Smith as a prestigious author for a decade. The stage was thus set for a complete translation of the work to be undertaken.

The publication of the Valladolid version was delayed until 1794 due to censorship. Obtaining the licence sparked an illuminating battle between the Council of Castile and the Inquisition, the subject of an excellent study by Lasarte (1975). After three harsh rulings by the inquisitorial censors in the first half of 1791, the Inquisition banned the 1788 edition of Blavet's French translation *in totum* by edict on 3 March 1792 (Smith 1781), "because, under a whimsical and obscure style, it favours religious tolerance and induces naturalism."[21] Martínez de Irujo and Alcalá-Galiano's versions were published shortly afterwards and represented a counter-offensive in the WN's defence, with the support of prestigious authorities such as Lerena and Godoy. In this context Alonso submitted three requests to the Council for the publication of his translation in the first seven months of 1793. He also went to Madrid in person to conduct the procedure, probably aiming to avoid a repetition of events surrounding his version of d'Orléans's work. He not approached only the Council, but also the Holy Office: anticipating the inevitable negative decision from the latter, he argued that he had already practised strict self-censorship and asked them to bow to the Council's criteria. For its part, the Council acted without hesitation, placing civil censorship in the hands of one of the most tolerant institutions possible, the Academia de la Historia, which in turn left it to Banqueri, an academic who was very close to Godoy and whose censorship would be endorsed due to his clerical status; in fact, his critical remarks regarding Alonso's translation were very succinct and readily accepted by the author (Lasarte 1975, 89–104, 233–36). All these factors contributed to the Council's swift decision to grant the licence in September 1793, and it is also not inconceivable that, in the turn of the century context, banning the work would encourage people to read it rather than hamper them. In any event, the speed at which events moved seems to reveal some official protection of Smith's work, as well as a desire to reinforce the Council's *regalista*—royalist—policy, over-reaching the Holy Office's room for manoeuvre. By this time, book censorship had become a malleable area that the Council adjusted according to each precise context (Velasco 2000).

It is not surprising that the translation of the WN should open with a dedication to Godoy, who Alonso had approached in November 1793 for permission to do so.[22] Alonso's foreword (Smith 1794, "*El traductor*") was also highly
relevant. Ground-breaking for the times, it gave biographical details for Smith
and his work, mentioning both the *The Theory of Moral Sentiments* (TMS) and
the WN—giving the wrong publication year for the latter, 1775 instead of
1776—and underlining its enormous international reputation. At the same
time, the foreword was a good reflection of the balancing act Alonso had been
obliged to perform to bring his version to fruition. He emphasised that the
WN dealt with political—or civil—economy, and therefore with matters outside the slippery terrain of "religious and moral interests" and "purely political aspects" affecting the "supreme powers." By positioning political economy
in this supposedly innocuous arena, Alonso appealed to the status it already
enjoyed among Spain's enlightened elites. With veiled echoes of Campomanes
and Jovellanos, he presented political economy as a science of the "gift" of government, useful for the "magistrate, head of the people or leader of society," and
indispensable so that "abundance, decorum and convenience rule in society."
However, the WN had its own added value, since it provided the basis for a
true "science"; it was therefore a "masterly" and "highly exceptional work of
its kind." In this context it was not incidental that Alonso expressly quoted
numerous seventeenth- and eighteenth-century Spanish economists, from Mata
and Moncada to Campomanes and Ward, going on to underline their failure to
"reduce the subject to a scientific method, a general system."[23] In contrast, the
WN transcended the "economic [political] policy" by establishing, "elementary
principles" and "universal causes" without stumbling into academic labyrinths."
Anticipating criteria that he would later transfer to his translation, Alonso ratified the soundness of these principles, acknowledging that the difficulty lay in
their being correctly applied to "the circumstances of the country, the terrain
or the society." Martínez de Irujo had put forward similar ideas a couple of
years earlier in his *Compendio*—the WN was "facultative, abstract and profound" (Smith 1792, V); however, the distinction Alonso drew between Smith
and Spanish "various classical texts" transformed his translation into the basis of
the myth-building surrounding Smith, which would go hand in hand with the
WN's circulation in Spain, and to which reviews in the Spanish press, inspired
by Alonso's introductory text, also contributed.[24]

Alonso deliberately mentioned that his version was a translation from English
on the title page.[25] This may have been Casa Santander's device to attract
readers, as translations of English originals were rare in the publishing market at
the time; however, the aim is more likely to have been to sidestep the fact that
the French translation of the WN had been in the Inquisition's catalogue since
1792. Alonso not only mentioned Martínez de Irujo's *Compendio* in his requests
to the Council, but he also argued that the banning decree applied only to the
French translation and that his version had been done "from the English original" and—falsely—before the decree. He also claimed that he had removed
the chapter that led to the ban and insisted that the work dealt with "purely

economic points" (Lasarte 1975, 236–37). In reality, however, in translating the WN Alonso operated in the same way as in previous translations, which also referred to English sources.[26] Not only did he consult the translations of the WN published in other languages (WN 1794, "*El traductor*"), but, quite certainly, he used Blavet and Roucher's French versions (Smith 1781; 1791 [1790]), which were well known in Spain.[27]

Alonso's machinations to get his translation through the censorship filter left their mark on the final version. According to his claims, while not adulterating "the substance of the work," he did remove various "particularities," mainly in defence of the Catholic religion and his own country (WN 1794, "*El traductor*"). As requested by the censors, he cut the WN's long section on "tolerance in matters of religion," which was essentially about religious teaching (WN V, I, III). Passages that were highly critical of Catholicism and the Church of Rome were deleted, which in fact left Smith's analysis of public expenditure incomplete. R.S. Smith (1957) commented that he also made notable excisions regarding tithes, usury, public education, taxation figures and other religious matters, as well as various pieces of information about British circumstances. Schwartz (1990, 15) argued that his ideas on tax shifting were inaccurate.

Meanwhile, aiming to apply Smith's "general rules" to Spain, Alonso incorporated various paratexts into the work in the form of appendices and notes. He added three appendices, two of which illustrated the workings of the Castilian grain market through a laudable reconstruction of traditional price series (Smith 1805–1806, I, 456–62) and, copying Zavala, of the historical value of the wheat rate (Smith 1805–1806, I, 462–64). The third was a brief history of the Bank of San Carlos, from its founding by Cabarrús, who was expressly cited (Smith 1805–1806, II, 352–92); this was incorporated after the translation had been finished, presumably by someone close to the bank since it provided very up-to-date information (up to July 1794) with the aim of reinforcing the "security" of the bank's funds in "public opinion". Alonso's notes also included information on other Spanish economic institutions, such as the Cinco Gremios Mayores—the Five Major Guilds—or the Compañía de Filipinas—the Philippine Company.

The notes' length and content were such that they actually made up a short treatise that laid bare the translator's economic ideology.[28] Some were common in this type of translation and explained intentional omissions, clarified terms, expressions or the equivalences of weights, measures and coins; the latter used the best merchants' handbooks in Spain, such as those produced by Cantos Benítez and Marien Arróspide. Other notes helped to contextualise the WN; Alonso recalled that it had been written at the height of the revolt in the British colonies, and deliberately emphasised that Smith had not only disapproved of London's policy of taxing its colonies yet failing to afford them political representation, but that he had also anticipated the events that culminated in their independence (Smith 1805–1806, III, 12, 15, 17; IV, 41).[29]

On the other hand, Alonso's notes were respectful towards Catholic orthodoxy. They could not have been otherwise, given that the Inquisition had banned the WN and that Alonso knew via Beristain and Casa Santander that it acted mercilessly. He was especially cautious in his handling of usury (Smith 1805–1806, I, 17; II, 10; III, 10), which is not surprising. His version was written at the height of the eighteenth-century dispute between the Inquisition and the enlightened Spaniards over usury, an issue that had caused the former to initiate various proceedings between 1787 and 1796 to request the partial or *in totum* censorship of Uría Nafarrondo's book and Condillac, Genovesi, Accarias de Serionne and Turgot's translations.[30] Alonso was at pains to present Smith as an author that respected Catholic dogmas, in no way a supporter of lucrative and morally reprehensible usury but rather of a more balanced version that justified charging interest on certain loans; as, moreover, the Bourbon laws had done, particularly since 1764 with the trine or company contract. He also embraced official reformism by supporting a reduction in the number of clergy and being sceptical of pious foundations. However, his criticisms of the Catholic Church were generally moderate and hardly touched on its privileged economic status (tithes, mortmain and tax exemptions under the 1737 Concordat).

Alonso's notes contained little mention of the WN's analytical content, and his comments dealt with its normative aspect. His chief concern was the impact of Smith's ideas on Spanish circumstances, and he approached the WN more as someone with legal training than someone who was familiar with the intense circulation of economic ideas that characterised the second half of the eighteenth century in Spain. In fact, the bibliographical sources in his notes were few and dominated by references to seventeenth- and eighteenth-century Spanish authors, with Zavala cited most. Through them Alonso tried to establish the Spanish reforms' affinities with those proposed in the WN, and to assess their usefulness for a country like his own, with a longstanding problem of socio-economic backwardness. His lawyer's gaze was particularly evident throughout. His notes contained long digressions on Spanish legislation, in which he was able to reflect the discussions that took place at the university and academies in Valladolid, which he had witnessed first-hand. He took a long view of events, exploring the historical background and giving a long and critical account of Hapsburg Spain: its "spirit of conquest" had exacerbated Spain's decline (Smith 1805–1806, I, 40). However, his notes were mainly devoted to Bourbon reforms, and those referring to laws with economic content were astonishing. Alonso did not hesitate to gloss, summarise and even copy long extracts from these laws in order to present an up-to-date perspective, and his work was imbued with an intensely apologetic sense, whose maximum expression was treatment of the colonial question (Smith 1805–1806, III, 9, 10, 11, 12, 13, 14). A fair number of Alonso's notes were also devoted to refuting Smith and other authors who "covered" Spanish colonisation "with shadows," a tacit reference to Raynal and De Paw, whose impact on the WN was noticeable. He countered their "slanders" that this colonisation had been based on the "spirit of conquest" and greed for precious metals with an account of a process of colonisation inspired by Catholic and humanist principles, as well as respect for the law of nations and the "spirit of trade," to the extent that they should be called colonial "plantations or settlements" instead of colonies (Smith 1805–1806, III, 11). Moreover, the unfortunate colonial monopoly operating under the Habsburgs did not justify the "predatory piracy" that foreign powers carried out on the Spanish high seas in breach of international treaties. In short, Alonso's acerbic criticism of Smith echoed the official programme that aimed to counter attacks on Spain from the Valladolid milieus in which he moved.

This apologetic sense ran through all Alonso's notes and was especially significant in relation to the Bourbon reforms: Alonso's oft-repeated arguments against Smith's proposals were based on the merits of these reforms, although he took a more moderate tone. The issues of the guilds and tied land provide two good examples. Where the former were concerned (Smith 1805–1806, I, 20, 21, 22, 28), Alonso reviewed the critical arguments that had surfaced in Spain since the 1760s, which partly matched Smith's ideas, to conclude that the guilds were anachronistic institutions and functioned in a way that was the opposite of their original purposes. Now, in the face of Smith and the experience in Scotland, the alternative was not to abolish them or issue across-the-board regulations, but to implement Campomanes's gradual liberalising programme, which had in fact culminated in a system in which the guilds coexisted with freedom of labour (Astigarraga 2017). Alonso also echoed the critical views on tied land that were circulating in Spain because of its "ruinous effects on agriculture and trade" (Smith 1805–1806, II, 11, 12, 13). Behind this lay the rejection of a feudal system in Castile that had conferred absolute power on the nobility, to the point at which vassalage had become confused with slavery. However, these criticisms did not lead to abolition; "fine civilisation" meant that certain families' honour had to be preserved as far as possible, without detriment to their merit; a good example of this was the 1793 Council of Castile law restricting the creation of new entailed estates.

The same affinity with official reforms was evident in the notes Alonso devoted to the question of agriculture, among which his defence of the *Expediente de Ley Agraria* was particularly significant (Smith 1805–1806, II, 3). One of the longest notes showed the importance of converting pasture into grain-producing land in order to encourage population growth. The thorny issue of the grain trade was a different matter, however. Alonso opposed establishing Smith's system of "absolute" freedom,[31] preferring the reforms enacted in Spain over the last fifty years, which used maximum prices to limit grain exports and which it felt facilitated free domestic trade in a manner that was exemplary with respect to other countries. Alonso went so far as to defend the expediency of the laws enacted in 1789–1790, which in reality had put an end to the liberalising process initiated by the 1765 *Pragmatica*. The same was true of another of Carlos III's most emblematic reforms, which concerned trade with the colonies. While the British policy of granting its colonies "absolute freedom in civil trade" had ultimately led to their independence, the 1765, 1778 and 1788 measures to open up Spanish ports to direct trade, reform tariffs and lower taxes had not only abolished the monopoly and other antiquated regulations that hindered economic growth in Spain, but had united the country's territories around a common programme.

Alonso's longest notes were prompted by volume IV of the WN. In connection to public expenditure, his views on education policy diverged significantly from Smith's. Having witnessed the poor quality of Spanish schools and universities at first hand, Alonso opposed Smith's proposal that teachers' salaries should be funded by their students (Smith 1805–1806, IV, 1, 2, 3, 4, 11, 12); this "idealistic and impracticable system" would condemn teachers to destitution and lead to the expulsion of badly-off pupils, who were the majority in Spain, thus reducing the size of both groups and exacerbating the Spanish education system's woes. According to Alonso, it was better to continue with current reforms in the sector, which were *regalista*—royalist—and secular in orientation and promoted schooling for women as well as a state education system, the only type capable of guaranteeing stable institutions and disciplined and standardised teaching methods.

On the financial side, Alonso's lengthy digressions were highly informative on the structure of the Spanish Treasury. This was a particularly pressing issue because of Spain's financial deterioration since 1780 and the country's involvement in the War of the Convention (1793–1796). Alonso approved of laws aimed at stabilising Spanish coins, preventing changes in their value and centralising minting. At the same time, he also at least partially approved of Smith's taxation principles and, with the help of Uztáriz, Zavala, Loynaz, Campomanes and Alcalá-Galiano, entered the broad fiscal debate raging in eighteenth-century Spain (Guasti 2000; Astigarraga et al. 2015), albeit in a rather ambiguous way. Establishing a single contribution in line with Zavala required respecting Smith's advice to introduce moderate tax rates (Smith 1794, IV, 24). Nevertheless, the caution that should guide any change in this sensitive area, especially after the experience of the *Catastro*—Cadastre—of Ensenada (1749), brought Alonso closer to the principles of Lerena's 1785–1787 reform and his mixed system of *rentas provinciales*—provincial revenues—and *frutos civiles*—civil fruits. By following these principles, Alonso aligned himself with a wider current in Spain that criticised the *rentas provinciales*, but he did not advocate abolishing them; nor did he share Uztáriz and Smith's belief that the *alcabalas* had caused Spain's industrial decline; rather, he praised the government's policy of establishing franchises and moderate tax rates, which should be matched by a fall in the number of civil servants.

As for other public revenues, reconstructing the series of the arrival of precious metals from America reaffirmed Alonso's belief in their strategic value for the Spanish Treasury, despite silver's continued depreciation against gold (Smith 1805–1806, I, 43, 44). Spain was fortunate enough to have some leeway to increase government revenue through public debt, and Alonso accused Smith of being misinformed about the value amassed through bonds and censuses. However, the main point of his notes was to show that the *vales reales*—royal vouchers—policy initiated in 1780 and supported by the Bank of San Carlos afforded both transparency and confidence, given Spain's relatively low debt level: "in its capital [Spain] does not import half as much as other states in Europe pay annually as the yield on their debts alone" (Smith 1805– 1806, IV, 39).[32] Finally, with regard to tariffs, far from being a mere source of tax revenue, they were a powerful weapon for stimulating economic growth. Alonso accepted Smith's theory that free trade was advantageous when it did not hinder the progress of national industry and tariff restrictions did not distort capital's tendency for natural allocation; but for an economy like Spain's, tariffs were the "only" or "main" means of compensating for the poor competitiveness of its manufacturing and overcoming its relative backwardness (Smith 1805–1806, I, 24; II, 18, 19; III, 1, 3). Alonso thus aligned himself with the protectionist approach that prevailed during the Spanish Enlightenment and led to the 1778–1782 reforms of tariffs.

In as much as it was inspired by an intense sense of patriotism, Alonso's translation of the WN was directly linked with his previous works, and the content of its paratexts ensured that it was perfectly aligned with the Spanish Enlightenment's official economic programme, which was gradualist, protectionist and moderately liberal. Alonso proposed a kind of Hispanicisation of the WN, to the point of turning his version into a type of firewall to defend the official reform programme in the arena of "public opinion" against both its domestic critics and Smith's innovative vision. Alonso also had many affinities with Smith's early readers in Spain, especially with members of the Treasury where he was later employed, among them Covarrubias and Alcalá-Galiano. It would therefore be within the bounds of possibility if his notes and appendices, some of which were included after his arrival at Court, had been written with some kind of guidance or supervision.

Together with Martínez de Irujo and Alcalá-Galiano's translations, Alonso's version of the WN shows that in the mid-1790s the work transcended its marginal status to become a major Spanish Enlightenment text. Alonso's work reaffirmed the significance of translations in the eighteenth century as crucially instrumental in counteracting competition from the leading commercial powers in international trade (Hont 2005; Reinert 2011). Thus, his work was a landmark in the far-reaching debate that had begun in the 1740s on the superiority of the commercial society over the "ancient" societies (Robertson 1983, 477– 78), of which the WN was a highly refined interpretation (Berry 2013, 204ff.). At the same time, despite Alonso's criticisms and disagreements with Smith, which were especially sharp in the area of religion, his work did not distort the WN's core message: the deregulating and liberalising of markets that went hand in hand with building trading societies would generate greater social wealth, benefiting more people and favouring moral development (Paganelli 2013). However, this did not mean that Smith immediately became recognised as the iconic author he is today; rather than bringing about a break with current economic ideology in Spain, the WN actually served—*ex-post*—to consolidate the economic reforms that had been initiated against the "mercantile system" since the 1760s and 1770s, and did not inspire any new ones. In this sense, Alonso's translation kept faith with Smith's early Spanish readers, who took their cue from their counterparts in Italy and Germany (Gioli 1972; Tribe 1988; 2002) in feeling that the "system of natural liberty" was only useful for their country up to a point. However, Alonso's "departures" should not be interpreted as intellectual incoherence, surrender to censorship or the inability to understand Smith's book (*cf.* Schwartz 1990; 2000). Alonso paid less attention to Smith's analytical ideas than to those on economic policy, respecting his conviction that the WN's main difficulty lay in understanding how its "system" should be applied to specific national settings. Like Smith, Alonso accepted that political economy was a science of the "art" of government and, like many of his contemporaries, he viewed Smith above all as a "politician." Alonso set up his "natural freedom system" against Bourbon reformism and, despite the overlaps between the two in terms of the suppression of "mercantile system" regulations, the set of government interventions proposed in the Spanish translation was notably superior to Smith's proposals, beyond the strict regulation of markets, in the provision of public goods, public health care and support to the poor.[33] In reality, however, this did not radically contravene the spirit of the work, which was conceived with a strong pragmatic and realist sense, to the point of accepting that the government "interference" agenda would vary on the basis of historical and country circumstances (Viner 1927). The rationale for the dialogue Alonso held with Smith via his copious notes was to circulate an intellectual product that could be useful in addressing his country's specific socio-economic problems.

On the other hand, from the point of view of social demand for the book, his endeavour to adapt the WN to Spain increased its appeal to the authorities and educated elites who were meant to be the translation's first readers. It is important to stress the fact that the work was above all a commercial venture and went on sale as early as September 1794, first by subscription, for a one-off payment (17 *reales* per volume), for which readers received the first two volumes and the right to the rest once printed. Individual volumes were not sold until all four had been published, and the price of the full work then increased (80 *reales* for the paperback version and 104 for the hardback). Casa Santander mobilised its entire network of contacts to make the publication a profitable enterprise; subscriptions could be taken out in numerous Spanish cities in bookshops that were similar to Casa Santander and specialised in selling French works.

## After translating the WN: the second edition of the translation of the WN (1805–1806)

The first consequence of the publication of Alonso's translation of the WN was that he joined the Bourbon administration for the first time. In November 1795 Minister of Finance Gardoqui appointed him to produce a version of Beawes's *Lex Mercatoria Rediviva* (1751).[34] This paid commission was part of a wider project promoted by Lerena, Gardoqui's predecessor as head of the Treasury, to compile a list of the tariff laws of Spain's trading partners, a project that had already begun with translations produced by several officials in the Balance of Trade Secretaría, where Alonso was employed (Astigarraga and Zabalza 2007).

Beawes was not a random choice; his book was a well-known commercial classic in Britain and he was also familiar to members of the Spanish Enlightenment, including the powerful Campomanes—who had recommended translating *Lex Mercatoria* as early as 1774 (Campomanes 1774, clxxxii)—as he had served as Consul in Cádiz and had published a work on Spain and Portugal in 1793 (Beawes 1793). Alonso, however, accepted the commission only to set it aside to produce his one original work a few months later, the *Ensayo económico sobre el sistema de la moneda-papel papel y sobre el crédito público* (1796) which had a strong Smithian flavour and was perhaps initiated by Gardoqui himself (Schwartz and Fernández 1998). As a result of its publication Alonso gained Gardoqui's confidence and in 1797 he embarked on a diplomatic career. In the same year he undertook a diplomatic journey, under Gardoqui's orders and with Godoy's tacit protection, which took him to Turin and Paris. It was not until after his return to Spain that financial hardship led him to resume in 1800 the task of translating Beawes, following the version—updated and expanded— by Thomas Mortimer; but, as Schwartz (2000) has explained, the translation was never finished.

It is highly likely that one of the unintended effects of the publication of Alonso's WN translation was the incentive to produce a Spanish version of the TMS. Sánchez (2003, 68) notes that enlightened thinkers in Aragon, at the turn of the century, knew of a manuscript translation of the work and that it is more likely to have been produced at Court during Alonso's years there. José María Magallón, Marquis of Santiago, who moved in literary circles there, explicitly referred in 1797 to the existence of a manuscript version of the TMS in Spanish, "made from the English original" and "ready to be given to the press":

> Among all those who have written on morality in ancient and present times, in my opinion (and in that of his learned nation, and even of the literary world) the best is the highly celebrated Englishman Adam Smith, author of the work *The Wealth of Nations*, which we have well translated into Spanish. I do not speak of this work here, which, like them all, is masterly on political economy, but of another entitled *The Theory of Moral Sentiments*, the translation of which, made from the English original, I have seen in manuscript ready to be given to the press. The purest moral philosophy and the surest and most proportionate principles for the happiness of man are expounded in this work, with all the energy of truth and grace and a boldness of style.
>
> (Borrelly 1797, 120–22)

Martín (2008) argues that this translation may have been done by José Deza y Goyri, a lawyer and priest. Although he obtained a printing licence for his translation with no major obstacles from the censors in August 1801,[35] the book was never published, for reasons that are not known. The version he used was not the original English edition, but Blavet's 1774–1775 French translation (Smith 1774–1775), taking the third edition of the TMS (1767) as a reference.

Thus, the Spanish Enlightenment failed to produce a translation of the TMS, which sets it apart from countries such as France or Germany, where the WN and the TMS were published in parallel. In principle, although no in-depth study has yet been undertaken, the much discussed dilemma between "sympathy" and "self-love"—"*Das Adam Smith Problem*" (Montes 2003, 15–56)—was alien to the Spanish Enlightenment.[36]

In the meantime, Alonso's translation of WN was reissued in Valladolid in 1805–1806 on Casa Santander's initiative. However, it was in fact a different edition,[37] most unusual for Spanish Enlightenment political economy translations, whose reissues were usually simple reprints. This was not so with the new version of Alonso's work: the changes included in the 1805–1806 version affected questions of both form and content, and were clear from the title page; the book was no longer presented as a translation "from English," but as a work "written in English." The reason is that Garnier's French translation of the WN was in circulation in Spain by then (Smith 1802). The title page also omitted the brief account of who Smith was, which was no doubt superfluous in 1805–1806, and although the reference to the translator Alonso was retained, the work was described as a "second, much corrected and improved edition."

The new version retained Alonso's introduction but omitted the dedication to Godoy, which was unnecessary and also damaging after his political career had been cut short. This was simply the introduction to a new text that contained a great many interventions in the form of rectifications, deletions and additions, to the extent of creating a different edition. The new translator certainly rewrote the first version, but he also introduced numerous disparate changes, restructuring paragraphs, changing punctuation (adding interjections and question marks that had been wrongly omitted in the previous version, for example); he corrected innumerable typographical and spelling mistakes, although not all of them; he used italics to highlight numerous key words ("division of labour" and "real price", for example) and for the titles of cited works; he rewrote numerous passages, correcting errors, changing the meaning and, in short, improving the syntax; he corrected author and place names, as well as those of authorities and authors from the classical world; he amended and updated various monetary equivalences, and, finally, he introduced improved translations for numerous lexical items. His work was particularly intensive with respect to the names of trades and professions, social classes, techniques used in the arts and the language of political economy; the latter was due not improvements in the vocabulary of political economy during the decade that separated the two versions, but to errors that had been carried over from the first edition.

At the same time, there were minor alterations that changed the meaning on especially sensitive subjects. The 1805–1806 edition was less politically cautious (omitting justifications for "political reasons", "public calm" and "fear of the mob", for example, and accusing the ruling class of negligence instead); it was bolder in the way the Church was treated (including the clergy among the "unproductive" classes, introducing tacit anti-Inquisition references or expressing opposition to tithes and the clergy's immunity from taxation); omitting references to "Providence", the "first Maker" and similar Catholic affiliations; defending enthusiastically the "spirit of trade" against that of "conquest;" it was more careful about merchants' social standing and, finally, it was more faithful to Smith's generally uncomplimentary allusions to Spain. Moreover, the quality of the translation was not only enhanced by the introduction of new sentences and deleting of existing ones, but new ideas that were not present in the previous version were included. These changes were particularly significant in that they added paragraphs and even whole pages, which corrected omissions—or self-censorship—that Alonso himself had in all likelihood deliberately excluded from the first edition. Despite this, the translation was not complete, as the deleted chapter was not reinstated and some censorship was thus retained (WN V, I, III).

The interventions also extended to the footnotes. Many of Smith's original footnotes were deleted, especially those containing bibliographical references and allusions to authors, texts or facts relating to Britain. Moreover, no new notes were produced, so the version ignored the innumerable comments added by Garnier in the fifth volume of his translation. On the other hand, Alonso's notes were preserved intact, except for the appendix devoted to the Bank of San Carlos, which was cut out; however, they were grouped together at the end of each volume and a clear distinction was drawn between them and the few of Smith's that had survived, which was absent in the first edition. This all affected the new edition's quality, as the fact that Alonso's notes had not been edited led to anachronisms and, more seriously, to contradictions with the new pages that were included.

In short, the changes included in this "much corrected and improved" edition were on the whole neither superficial nor cosmetic. Beyond self-censorship issues, they revealed that the quality of the 1794 translation could be improved. The 1805–1806 translation was longer, more faithful to the original and less censored, all of which showed that its nature and purpose differed from the first. The most logical hypothesis is that it was designed to create an intellectual product that would be capable of competing in the emerging political economy textbook market. When it was published, not only was Campos's *La económica* (1797) in circulation, but new editions of three of the first texts used to teach political economy in Spain had appeared: in 1800 Danvila´s *Lecciones* (1779), in 1803 Martínez de Irujo´s *Compendio* (1792) and in 1804 Genovesi´s *Lecciones* (1785-1786). Nor should it be forgotten that the second edition was published only a year before the July 1807 Caballero Law introduced political economy into the law teaching; using the WN was recommended, pending the translation of Say's *Traité* (Martín 1989).

With the new version modelled to facilitate its use in teaching, the commercial objective that inspired the original translation re-emerges, as does Casa Santander's role in the enterprise. There is no evidence to suggest that Alonso was the actual author of the second edition as he had been Spanish Consul in Algiers for some years (1802–1809) when it was produced. In all likelihood, it was written by an unknown author under the auspices of Casa Santander, still driven by the desire for commercial success. Despite the economic hardships suffered by the company and its never-ending conflicts with the Inquisition, to which were added other problems with the printers' judge, Casa Santander continued to be run by brothers Mariano and Raimundo and retained its perennial combative attitude until closing in 1837. Given that contact with the American colonies was intermittent in those years, the natural market for their books was peninsular Spain, starting with Valladolid of course. It is important to remember the interests linking Casa Santander with the university, and that the student body that would be potentially interested in a work such as Smith's was far from small: enrolment peaked in 1793–1794 and remained at high levels, particularly driven by law students from all over Castile (Torremocha 1986, 47, 51, 56, 64). The new edition was distributed via similar channels to the first, but at lower prices, and now reached another leading university: Salamanca.

A further reason favouring this interpretation is that in 1807 Casa Santander published in Valladolid the *Breve exposición de la doctrina de Adam Smith comparada con la de los economistas franceses*. This booklet was taken from Garnier's translation of the WN and presented as an appendix to the 1805–1806 edition.[38] Its starting point was that the "true" doctrine was Smith's, although the "lack of method" typical of English works made it difficult to understand (Garnier 1807, 23). For this reason, the pamphlet offered a "reading plan" for the work, which was "to suit the abilities and intelligence of those who are making the acquaintance of economic science for the first time," in order to better understand "the translation that comes from the original" (Garnier 1807, "*Advertencia*"). The author was anonymous—he signed himself N.N.—and may have been responsible for the extensive reworking of the 1805–1806 edition. In any event, Alonso was left out of this new Casa Santander initiative; by this time, the once astute translator had become a skilled diplomat. He joined the diplomatic legation in Algiers in early 1803 and then went to London in 1809; this was his last posting and the city in which he was awarded the distinguished title of Intendente Honorario del Ejército before his death in 1815.

## Notes

1  The biographical data on Alonso in this work come from Schwartz, to whom we owe the reconstruction of his biogphy: Schwartz (2006) and Schwartz-Fernández (1999, xi–xxvi); likewise, see Alonso Cortés (c.1920, 10ff.) and various statements of merit presented by Alonso in 1800 seeking honours and career advancement (AHN, *Consejos*, bundle 11.283-48) and 1815 (AMAE, bundle 22-933).

2  On eighteenth-century Valladolid and its cultural activity, see Almuiña (1974), Enciso (1984) and Vallejo (1984).

3  There is an intellectual biography written in the light of his major work, the *Biblioteca Hispanoamericana septentrional* (1816–1821), in Millares (1972). For his sojourn in Valladolid, see Alonso (1933) and Almuiña (1978).

4  The name of the DP evoked "Pincio", the Roman name for Valladolid. Forty-six issues were published between February 1787 and April 1788. Almuiña's re-edition (1978) has been consulted.

5  According to Guinard (1973, 364), the DP was the only "original and truly worth-while newspaper to appear in the Spanish provinces under Carlos III."

6  DP, "Plan del Diario Pinciano," 5.

7  DP, "Plan del Diario Pinciano," 4–5.

8  DP, no. 11, 18-IV-1788, 134.

9  DP, no. 26, 1-VIII-1787, 290.

10  DP, no. 34, 24-X-1787, 355.

11  Palomares (1974, 44–53). On his never-ending problems with the Inquisition, see Prado (1996, 204–05, 216–17) and Larriba (2013, 147–52).

12  Numerous persecuted authors were featured in his bookshop: Rousseau, Voltaire, Condorcet, Burlamaqui, Filangieri, etc. The situation recalls the effervescent atmos-phere of nearby Salamanca and the figure of Salas; see Astigarraga (2011).

13  The production of novenas, catechisms and sermons contrasted with the few books on official history, law, philosophy, medicine and university dissertations. All printing presses used a similar thematic structure: Palomares (1974, 22, 29, 32, 43–44, 50, 53–54).

14  The essential guide is Torremocha (1991, 42–49); see also Almuiña (1980, 46–54).

15  The dossier is in AHN, *Consejos*, bundle 5.552-59.

16  Alonso felt that he had Campomanes's support from then onwards (AMAE, bundle 22-933).

17  Alonso planned to publish Ossian's complete works, but only the first volume saw the light of day. The EMD published a review of his version (no. 138, 21-VII-1788, 69–79). Alonso was in the line of such brilliant Spanish Enlightenment authors as Montegón and Marchena, also partial translators of Ossian (in 1800 and 1804 respectively).

18  Butler (1789–1792; 1790). The first was reviewed in the ML (1790, XIX, 282–86; XXI, 203–04).

19  Butler (1789–1792, I, "*El traductor*"). The remainder of the quotations in this para-graph are from this text.

20  Apart from the specific case of France, Spain's experience is not very different from Italy's, where the first translation of Smith was published in 1790 (Parisi 1972, 920–21). In Germany there was an "unsuccessful" translation in 1776–1779 and a second far more successful one in 1794 (Tribe 1988, 133).

21  The censor's files, which are transcribed in Lasarte's work, are in the AHN, *Inquisición*, bundle 4.522-25, 4.484-13; and RAH, bundle 11-48, 11-58, 11-62. As usual, the censors' rulings were full of inaccuracies: they confused Hume and "Volter", and the elder Mirabeau (Marquis) with his son (Count). They called the WN "impious," "blasphemous" and "heretical;" they showed their distrust of societies based on trade and civilisation and far removed from the Stoic ideal (Bee and Paganelli 2019), and described Smith as faithful to "toleration in point of religion," "materialistic," "Protestant" and "a man without religion, either good or bad." The truth is that Smith was not only a supporter of religious freedom but that when he wrote the WN he was sufficiently independent of theology and very critical of the established Christian church (Viner 1958, 222–24; Rothschild 2001, 19ff.).

22  *Inquisición, Estado*, bundle 3.244. In his memoirs Godoy (1836, II, 281) claimed to have supported Smith's arrival in Spain.

23  This stance was put forward in the prospectus that Alonso sent to Godoy: unlike the "ingenious and erudite Smith," none of the Spanish economists "formed a scientific system from this vulgarised idea of economics" (AMAE, bundle 22-933).

24  See Chapter 9 in this book.

25  According to Alonso he had followed the 1789 eighth edition, but Smith (1957, 1228) argued that it was probably the fifth and Schwartz (1990, 41–51) the eighth. In any event, the original edition of the WN was later than the second edition of 1778, which was printed with amendments, and especially the third edition of 1784, which was extended and corrected by Smith himself (Sher 2002).

26  His familiarity with French had been seen in his translation of d'Orléans. From among the numerous French versions of Ossian (1762, 1774, 1777, etc.), Alonso translated the version that was written in poetry. As for Butler, he repeatedly mentioned the French version of his work (1763–1782) with great admiration. Alonso was able to learn English in his dealings with the Royal English and especially the Royal Scots Colleges, run between 1770 and 1779 by John Geddes, a pioneer in the introduction of the WN in Spain. There are no signs that Alonso used the fragmentary translations of the WN made by Geddes at the end of the 1770s; see Chapter 2 in this book.

27  It is important to recall the dissemination of the WN through the numerous extracts from Blavet's translation included in volumes 2–4 of a work that was well-known in Spain: *Économie politique et diplomatique* (1784–1787, 4 vols.) of the *Encyclopédie Méthodique* (Carpenter 2002, 40–53).

28  Alternative analyses of Alonso's notes can be found in Smith (1957), Elorza (1970), Fuentes and Perdices (1997) and Schwartz (2000, 223–37), who presented the complete list. On the strategies used by Alonso as translator, see Chapter 5 in this book.

29  The volume and quotation are cited following the WN edition of 1805–1806.

30  Astigarraga (2017); AHN, *Inquisition*, bundle 4.463-10, 4.482-11.

31  Smith (1805–1806, I, 34; III, 5, 6, 7, 8). His calculations on the price of grain and its correlation with the value of silver are one of the most novel added values in his notes. Alonso rejected the use of the grain rate and used the grain price series in Burgos and other Castilian markets.

32  Alonso expanded on these ideas in his *Ensayo* (Alonso 1796); see Chapter 7 in this book.

33  See recent interpretations from Rothschild (2001) and Sen (2013), among others.

34  See AHN, *Consejos*, bundle 11.283-48.

35  AHN, *Consejos*, bundle 5.564-52.

36  On the use of ideas from the TMS in Smith's translator Campos's work *De la desigualdad personal en la sociedad civil* (1799), see Cervera (2003, 131–33).

37  The print record is in the AHN, *Consejos*, leg. 5.559.

38  Accoding to Sánchez (2005), it was a faithful translation of Garnier's "Préface", which, however, omitted the third part, unrelated to Smith, devoted to a comparison of the wealth of France and Great Britain, which Garnier deemed to be favourable to the former.

# Section II

# Influences

# 7 Adam Smith's *The Wealth of Nations*

## The first Spanish readings, 1777–1800

*Jesús Astigarraga*

### The first spheres of influence: poverty and the guilds

Pedro Rodríguez de Campomanes, Count of Campomanes, Fiscal of the Council of Castile, was the first enlightened Spaniard to come into contact with *The Wealth of Nations* (WN). In 1777, a year after the book was published, he ordered a translation of the work from John Geddes, the head of the Royal Scots College in Valladolid (Smith c.1777).[1] While the translation never actually materialised, with Geddes's collaboration Campomanes may have received a copy of the book from Smith himself, perhaps also with the aid of Scottish historian William Robertson (Schwartz 2000, 172–75; Llombart 1992, 296–305). It is therefore not surprising that Campomanes should be the first Spaniard to make use of Smithian ideas. The context was poor relief, one of the themes discussed in the six dense volumes of his *Discursos* (1774–1776) and whose recommendations inspired the charitable projects of the recently created Sociedad Matritense (1775) and the other economics societies formed in its wake. To complement the *Discursos*, Campomanes drafted a *Plan para desterrar la ociosidad*, which he sent to Secretary of State, Count of Floridablanca, in early 1778, and which in the end was neither completed nor published. In keeping with Campomanes's usual *modus operandi*, the work included a compilation of current legislation in different European countries, including Britain, and he incorporated the chapter covering this from the WN (WN I, 10), which Geddes had given him in translation, into his *Plan*. At the same time, he commented favourably on Smith's ideas about the problems of the free circulation of labour and the wage inequalities created by the laws preventing labourers from seeking work outside their local area, endorsing Smith by commenting that he considered them "a clear violation of natural liberty and justice" (Llombart 1992, 297–99).[2]

New Smithian ideas emerged soon after, when Alcalá-Galiano (1788), Martínez de Irujo (1792) and Alonso Ortiz (1794) produced the first Spanish versions of the WN. The spotlight now fell on the issue of the guilds. Smith's ideas arrived at the height of the debate over these institutions' socio-economic usefulness. Campomanes was deeply critical of the way they functioned, deeming them inefficient, bureaucratic and creators of monopolies. In 1775

DOI: 10.4324/9781003152804-9

and 1776 he had published two lengthy *Discursos* on the issue, which provided intellectual support for a reform programme that would be gradual, royalist and mildly liberalising and whose execution was to be in the hands of the economics societies. The programme's three main aims were to carry out a systematic and uniform revision of guild by-laws, to promulgate technical advances and to create centres to teach the crafts of draughtsmanship, mathematics and seamanship (Campomanes 1775; 1776). Campomanes's reasoning echoed the criticism of the guilds that had originated with the Castilian *arbritristas* and were revived in the 1760s (Ramos, Arriquíbar, etc.), while also invoking Gournay circle authors (especially Cliquot de Blervache and Plumard de Dangeul) and Physiocracy. The common thread with Physiocracy was Bigot de Sainte-Croix's *Essai* (1775), one of the intellectual buttresses of Turgot's famous February 1776 *Édit* abolishing the guilds in France. The *Édit* was immediately and widely disseminated throughout Spain—there were, at least, four translations in circulation, one handwritten by Campomanes himself. Thus, this Turgot and Physiocracy-inspired abolitionist current was already well-known before the WN reached Spain and, in reality, it was through these ideas that the notion of freedom of labour as a natural right was introduced there. This is clear from the fact that Turgot's *Réflexions sur la formation et la distribution des richesses* (1769–1770), his abolitionist *Édit* and Sainte-Croix's *Essai* were all translated in 1791 under the aegis of the Sociedad Matritense, while another of Turgot's *Edit* sources of inspiration was also translated five years later: Coyer's *Chinki. Histoire Cochinchinoise* (1768) (Astigarraga 2017). Where the guild question was concerned, therefore, the WN irrupted in Spain at the height of the debate between supporters of the status quo, especially Romà, Capmany and other Catalan economists with links to the Barcelona Board of Trade (Lluch 1973), the minority first abolitionist authors (Foronda) and the mainstream affiliated with the reformist programme backed by Campomanes and the Council of Castile (Arteta, Normante, Sánchez, Danvila, etc.). At exactly the same time, the official reform programme was culminating in 1784 with the creation of an "intermediate" or "mixed" system, which was similar to that promoted by Necker in France following the failure of Turgot's policy, and made it possible for industries that were organised into guilds to coexist with those that respected the principle of freedom of labour.

It is not surprising that Smithian anti-guild ideas filtered into Spain through the Matritense Society;[3] the society was in charge of the official scheme to examine guild by-laws in order to design a "general legislation system" for trades. These ideas probably first surfaced in 1784 and came from Juan Pechenet, a Parisian craftsman who had settled in Madrid a couple of decades previously and was seeking the Matritense's support to set up a jewellery workshop. He cited Smith in connection with long apprenticeships' negative impact on salaries and the advantages of the specialisation of different tasks in improving the quality of goods and reducing their prices (WN, 1, II; Larruga 1789a, 96–97). Nine years later, in 1973, Agustín de la Cana and Sixto de Espinosa, both members of the Matritense, copied these arguments, word for word, adding

Smith's ideas about the poor productivity of forced apprentices (WN, 1, II) in a handwritten opinion that was circulated in the˙Matritense (Schwartz 2000, 176–77).

Jovellanos's 1784 *Informe sobre el libre ejercicio de las artes*, written for the Board of Trade, appeared between these two documents (Jovellanos 2008b [c.1784]).[4] This text has long been viewed by some historians as the first sign that the WN had taken root in Spain, although there is not really enough evidence to support this claim. Jovellanos's doctrinal account in defence of freedom of labour as a natural right had a Physiocratic root, since it came from the writings of Sainte-Croix and Turgot, as Smith's ideas may have done.[5] In fact, Turgot's *Édit* may have been the basis for the format of Jovellanos's *Informe*, in which a lengthy doctrinal explanation was followed by a precise and well-organised legislative regulation. Nevertheless, the WN could have helped Jovellanos to complete his historical references on the guilds and inform his long list of complaints about their harmfulness to welfare and economic development, which were grounded in the writings of these two French economists. Moreover, as Llombart has showed, Jovellanos's proposal was essentially an update of Campomanes's arguments from 12 years earlier; its ultimate aim was to support the "intermediate" or "mixed" system mentioned above. A major role was also played by the wide circulation in Spain of the volumes of the *Enciclopédie Méthodique* covering *Économie Politique et Diplomatique* (1784–1788), with their strong criticism of the guilds, inspired by Smith, the core of the Gournay circle and the Physiocrats. Grivel, a Physiocrat who was ubiquitous in these volumes, appears to have inspired the doctrinal framework for a report produced in 1786 for the Matritense by Sixto de Espinosa, Secretary of the Arts Committee. However, once again, in its translation into specific reforms, Espinosa´s report was fully in tune with Campomanes, which did not prevent it from quoting the WN with regard to the fact that the guild laws in Scotland were the least oppressive in Europe, among other reasons because they made it possible for the years of apprenticeship to be redeemed fairly cheaply (WN, 1, X, II; Sixto de Espinosa 1787, 233).

## Smithian ideas in the public finance milieu

The second focus for filtering in Smithian ideas was the Treasury. There was a pressing need to deal with the financial crisis that had begun in the 1780s, as a result of which the Treasury Department, led by Múzquiz (1766–1785), issued new public debt bonds, known as *vales-reales*—royal bounds—in 1780, and his successor Lerena (1785–1791) decreed the 1785–1787 fiscal reform following guidelines from Secretary of State Floridablanca.[6] This was the most important fiscal reform of the entire eighteenth century in Spain. It consisted of introducing direct taxation for the first time via a tax on *frutos civiles* (civil fruits), which was levied on income from leasing land, dwellings and other property; Lerena also ordered a review of tax registers and the reduction of theoretical rates of indirect taxes levied on consumption and trade (*alcabalas*, *cientos* and other *rentas provincials*—provincial revenues). The reform gave support to the legacy from the seventeenth and eighteenth centuries of criticising the *rentas provinciales*, while at the same time curbing the widespread aspirations to establish a *única contribución*—single contribution—based on direct taxation. In 1783, in one of the most radical tax reports in eighteenth century Spain, although its viability is open to question, the prestigious financier Cabarrús had demanded the abolition of the *rentas provinciales* and their replacement by a property tax, the only means of dealing with the problem of uninterruptedly issuing *vales reales*—royal vouchers (Cabarrús c.1783, 320).[7]

Once enacted, Lerena's reform became the focus of an intense taxation debate involving many and varied points of view. Radical critics (Cabarrús and Arroyal) took against it, as did tacit critics (Foronda and Jovellanos), supporters of the Physiocrat *impôt unique* (Salas and Álvarez Guerra) and the *única contribución* (Caamaño). Lerena naturally solicited the support of a range of writers, civil servants and advisers to voice their support for his reform; this was a propaganda operation that highlights the fact that, when the publication of Necker's writings was at its height, public opinion was a basic ingredient in Spanish Enlightenment politics (Astigarraga 2000; 2010). Along with Gallard, De la Torre and Mantecón, the most noteworthy of all these writers was Vicente Alcalá-Galiano.[8] Secretary of the Sociedad Económica Segoviana, he was a soldier with an excellent scientific background—he taught mathematics at the Segovia College of Artillery—and transformed the Sociedad Segoviana into an echo chamber in defence of Lerena's fiscal reform. In 1787, while a member of the Treasury, he wrote a lengthy report with Mantecón that appealed to the seventeenth- and eighteenth-century tradition in Spain criticising the *rentas provinciales* (Mata, Osorio, Moncada, Zavala, Ulloa, Campomanes and Arriquíbar) and evoked Necker's ideas on the advisability of gradually reforming the Treasury and maintaining a mixed taxation system in defence of Lerena's 1785–1787 reform (Alcalá-Galiano and Mantecón de Arce 1787.

Alcalá-Galiano first came into contact with the WN in or around 1788 and the work provided him with new arguments in favour of the reform. As Valles (2008) has outlined, in the same year he drafted the first summary to be produced in Spain of the WN's ideas, especially those on finances, which are explained in book V (Alcalá-Galiano 1793 [1788]). Although Alcalá-Galiano omitted Smith´s ideas on the public debt (WN V, III), in general he accepted those relating to public income and expenditure, except—as with all his work—the free trade principles. However, not only did he present Smith's ideas, he also read them selectively, without questioning his previous considerations, to defend Lerena's new mixed system. Naturally, Lerena himself took a similar line. In 1789 he appealed to Necker and Smith's ideas to argue that the number of Treasury civil servants and the overall cost of their salaries was lower in Spain than in France and Britain, and also copied Alcalá-Galiano word for word to evoke Smith's authority to justify the suitability of the tax on *frutos civiles*:[9]

Ordinary income from land and assets is a type of income that the owner enjoys most of the time without any work or attention; no kind of industry will be discouraged because part of this income is taken to meet state expenses. The annual produce from the land and the work of society, the real wealth and the people's income will be the same before and after such taxation; so the income from assets and the ordinary income from the land are those that can best bear any kind of individual tax.

(Lerena 1789)

Alcalá-Galiano's services to Lerena did not end there. In 1786, in order to draw up the balance of payments for the Spanish economy, Lerena ordered an annual compilation of Spanish trade data and committed Alcalá-Galiano and Gallard to writing a text on French tariff legislation (Valles 2008, 431–37), as part of a wider investigation into the customs structures of the country's trading partners (Astigarraga-Zabalza 2007). The work appeared in 1789 as the *Colección alfabética de los aranceles de Francia* (Alcalá-Galiano and Gallard 1789). In their instructive "Prólogo," the authors appealed to Smithian ideas—labour as the basis of wealth, capital as "accumulated wealth" and workers' skills as the well-spring of productive labour—to combat the Physiocrats and their ideas on the exclusive productivity of agriculture, the *impôt unique* and the free trade system (Alcalá-Galiano and Gallard 1789, I, "Prólogo"). Paradoxically, they took Smith's ideas to such extremes that they rejected the free trade system because it could only benefit the "most advanced" countries and made it impossible for "poor" and "less developed" nations to use tariffs to tackle their economic backwardness. However, this idea did not involve accepting solutions based on classical prohibitionism or high tariffs backed by a rigid "mercantile system," but required striking a "good balance." Although they did not mention this, Alcalá-Galiano and Gallard aimed to ascertain the operability of Múzquiz's 1778–1782 protectionist tariff, and also undoubtedly to defend Spain from the swing towards free trade sanctioned by the recent Eden-Rayneval trade treaty between France and Britain (1786). Thus, Alcalá-Galiano and Gallard's reading of the WN was not dogmatic.

## Smith's forgotten translator: José de Covarrubias

In defence of his reform Lerena sought the support of another distinguished writer: José de Covarrubias. He was the author of an important work on the Spanish Treasury—forgotten today—entitled the *Código, o Recopilación de Leyes de Real Hacienda*, which was written around 1790 but never actually published (Covarrubias c.1790). Lerena's aim in commissioning the work was to silence the complaints stirred up by the circulation in Spain of Necker's *De l'Administration des Finances* (1784) on the basis that Spain lacked a work with the same characteristics. In December 1789 Lerena issued a decree for the drafting of the *Código*, which would have to "gather the laws, certificates and instructions [...] that constitute the Crown Estate in one legal text"

(Covarrubias c.1790, I, 1–1v). Covarrubias was appointed to write the text and, as it was an official document, Alcalá-Galiano was assigned to assist him. The choice of Covarrubias was no accident: lawyer, public prosecutor and member of the Spanish Law Society, he was soon recruited by the Bourbon government as a civil servant, working for Floridablanca as a *plumista* to translate a range of works that were *regalistas*—royalists—or in support of Bourbon reforms. His work showed signs that he was familiar with the concept of "public opinion", which he understood as the "general fixed rule" that all good governments should respect (Covarrubias 1783, xliiff.).

Covarrubias's *Código* was divided into two main sections. The first reconstructed the history of royal revenue, in four parts, from the creation of the Crown Estate to Lerena's reform. The second concerned positive law and consisted of a systematic description of all government revenue in eight books. It was, therefore, a tremendously ambitious work, but was interrupted during the third part of the historical account and never finished. However, over and above questions of structure, the fact that it began with a "Discurso Preliminar" whose source, though this was not expressly stated, was the WN, is highly significant (Covarrubias c.1790, 21–28). Having remarked on the contractual basis of public finance, Covarrubias translated lengthy extracts from Smith's work on "the expenses of the sovereign" and the four canons to guide governments on taxation (WN V, I–II). In fact, he said relatively little about the canons, and so the main argument of the "Discurso Preliminar" revolved around the issue of public expenditure. Covarrubias essentially respected Smith's reasoning: the sovereign's first obligation was to establish a "public or military force" that was needed "to protect society against violence and invasion by other societies." Like Smith, Covarrubias suggested that the expenditure required for this differed according to each society's socio-economic structure and their "periods of progress" until the recent appearance of state-funded professional armies. Secondly, the sovereign should fund the administration of justice: again following Smith, Covarrubias related this function to the necessary protection and security required by private property in societies based on "civil government" (Covarrubias c.1790, I, 24). Thirdly, the state should finance "works and public facilities" that benefitted society as a whole and were beyond the means of private enterprise. As in the WN, this duty covered four areas: the infrastructure needed to organise trade; primary education; moral and religious instruction, and funds earmarked for the sovereign's "dignity." Throughout the work Covarrubias only disagreed with Smith on two questions: he believed that teachers should be paid by the state and not by the pupils themselves and he defended the funding and channelling of religious training through tithes, first fruits and the "multitude of benefit foundations and chaplaincies," while criticising the fact that these exceeded the limit of what was desirable (Covarrubias c.1790, 26). Finally, having described the optimum structure for public expenditure, he undertook a detailed account of the types of taxation that should fund each item, either general, local or provincial. Once again, he simply transferred Smith's conclusions to his work (WN, V, XIX).

Covarrubias's dense "Discurso Preliminar" thus consisted of a selective, condensed and bare translation of specific historical and spatial references in Smithian thought on the structure of public expenditure and his funding criteria. The political intent of these pages was unquestionable: when the reform of public revenue had been tackled from 1785 to 1787, public expenditure should be dealt with. In this respect Smith's work provided a model for the reorganising of Spain's administrative and financial structure, which Covarrubias went on to describe in detail using his dual historical and legislative criteria. His proposal sought a radical transformation in the structure of public expenditure in Spain: more than creating a "minimal state," it aimed to surmount the current fiscal-military system, which gave priority almost exclusively to two items of expenditure—the military and the monarch—in favour of an economic development programme.[10]

The *Código*'s mark is visible in a number of future compilations on public finance in Spain. The first was produced by Gallard (1795), one of the Alcalá-Galiano circle and secretary of the Balance of Trade Office; it updated Ulloa's (1768) reissue of the work by Ripia (1675) and had no Smithian features. This was not true of the text put together by Gallardo, a Treasury official, in the early nineteenth century: he cited Smith's idea that the true source of wealth was labour, arguing that if Spain had converted the *moriscos*—moorish—to Catholicism "by gentle means" instead of expelling them, it would have had a powerful fountain of wealth at its disposal (Gallardo 1805–1808, III, 272).[11] However, the real heir to the genealogical line begun by Covarrubias was Canga Argëlles and his prestigious Diccionarios of public finance in Spain during the second and third decades of the nineteenth century.

## Alonso Ortiz's *Ensayo* (1796)

In 1796, whilst Covarrubias's *Code* was being drafted, Alonso, the author of the first almost complete translation into Spanish of the WN, published his single original work: *Ensayo económico sobre el sistema de la moneda-papel papel y sobre el crédito público*. The book was published in a context characterised by the critical situation of the Treasury, headed by then by Gardoqui, but also by the uninterrupted cycle of war: Alonso wrote his work amid the Convention War against France (1793–1795) and shortly before the outbreak of a new Anglo-Spanish war (1796–1802). Although very moderate compared to Britain and France (Torres 2013), the policy of public indebtedness had begun to undermine confidence in the financial system as the issuance of *vales reales*, which started in 1780, continued and the Spanish currency depreciated. This happened indeed in 1794 and 1795, under Gardoqui's ministry, when Alonso wrote his book. As the cover page stated, it is not surprising that its purpose was to "combat vulgar concerns." That not only means that paper money had powerful enemies at the top of the monarchy (Torres 2013, 379–84), but that it was imperative to operate in the field of "public opinion," which, thanks in particular to the dissemination of Necker's ideas, had become a key force in Spanish politics

(Astigarraga 2011a). In particular, it was a matter of redirecting Charles III's traditionally cautious and fearful policy of public indebtedness by looking for new instruments for balancing public deficit apart from public savings (Torres 2013, 281–85). By then, Spain was much closer to Hume's deep misgivings about the use of paper money and public debt—his *Political Discourses* (1753) had been translated into Spanish in 1789 (Hume 1789)—than to Smith's more relaxed stance on both issues. However, as Sonenscher (2007) has explained, by then the European literature had shown that public credit was a mighty spoiler of political stability, something that Alonso noticed: his ideas, though intended to forge "opinion," shaped the "rules of a well-managed constitutional politics" (Alonso Ortiz 1796, xviii). As was usual in that kind of literature, *Ensayo*'s two sections intertwined the championing of paper money and public credit. Accordingly, it involved a theoretical endorsement of these two critical policies of late eighteenth-century Spain. In fact, *Ensayo* deepened the financial ideas set out in the notes that he drafted in his translation of the WN. Therefore, although written on his initiative, his instigator may have been Gardoqui. Consequently, it is not surprising that he immediately obtained a licence to publish it in January 1795, financed by the Royal Account.

Although *Ensayo*'s intellectual sources were broader than Smith, the latter was particularly influential as far as monetary matters were concerned, as Fernandez and Schwartz have rightly shown.[12] Following Smith (WN II, II), Alonso outlined the different types of paper money to focus on *vales reales*. Far from Hume's fears of banks and paper money (Paganelli 2014), Alonso believed that the latter's deployment instead of the metallic currency represented a great advantage for the country, at least as long as it was convertible. Following Smith, he portrayed money as a factor of production, whose cost, in terms of production and preservation, could be lowered by replacing it with paper money while maintaining a framework of strict monetary restraint: Smith's theory of money played a crucial role in his development of the superiority of the "system of natural liberty" on the "mercantile system" (Harley and Paganelli 2014). Paper money saved the maintenance cost of productive capital, which fostered society's net income growth. Metallic money, whilst being circulating capital, resembled fixed capital since, as an instrument that facilitated distribution, it could not be part of the pure income of the nation. Likewise, as fixed capital, its maintenance as an instrument of circulation entailed allocating part of the income to compensate for its depreciation. Otherwise, this income would be used for other purposes. Hence, any saving would decrease accumulation expenses and foster national expenditure (Alonso 1796, 108–09). Similarly, according to Alonso, the paper money introduced into circulation led to "another quantity of metals overflowing and spilling out of the nation equal to paper" (Alonso Ortiz 1796, 114). As cautious as Smith, he believed that these metals would not divert to luxury, but to "raw materials, artefacts, tools and machinery required by the nation" (Alonso 1796, 115), that is to say, to stimulate national economic growth. Alonso recommended, in any case, a limited monetary issuance, entailing a favorable perception of the banks, and controlled metal extraction, which would bring to the surface the hoarded gold and silver, both of which were constraining growth. All this would make it possible to avoid extraordinary taxes and achieve budgetary goals within a framework of monetary stability.

Alonso's analysis had similar weaknesses to Smith's. For one thing, he did not address the consequences of an over-issuance of *vales reales* on prices as he merely made vague generalisations about "the channels of circulation overflowing" if the money supply was excessive. He also contended that the quantity of paper money could never exceed the amount of metal that would be required in its absence, but he gave hardly any reasons for this. Finally, he conceded that the number of *vales* should be limited "to what the country's circulation will allow," according to the traffic circumstances. Given the complexity of a precise calculation, he presumed that equilibrium would be reached when the price of paper money and the demand for silver were at parity. But this ambiguity when defining the issuance volume allowed him to reinforce his advocacy of the Spanish paper currency. By neglecting its effect on prices, the main problem was its depreciation. Its value was the most reliable sign that the issuance had not been excessive, although Alonso invoked a safeguard clause: except for "accidental causes causing extraordinary public discredit" (Alonso 1796, 72). These "accidental causes" referred to active warfare. The ordinary public resources, now depleted, would be replenished in peacetime, by bringing public opinion in accordance with Bourbon reforms: "public confidence is not so much in the hands of the government as in the opinion of the vassals, and once lost, there is hardly any way of restoring it" (Alonso 1796, 151). Alonso underpinned his claim by detailing that Spanish *vales* fulfilled all the mechanisms of restraint: state warranty, limiting the number of notes, use in the wholesale trade, adjustment of the interest rate, the provision of an extinction fund and the creation of a redemption fund (Alonso 1796, 173–221).

Alonso intertwined the ideas about paper money with those ideas about public debt, which served as the "arch of the vault" (Alonso 1796, 226). This was an essential constitutional requirement to equip the economic system with the required confidence to guarantee growth. Such confidence transcended positive laws, as it relied not only on the actual wealth of the nation but also on the personal credit or "opinion that the public perceives of the economic and legal behaviour of the government." And in this particular sphere, he covered a broad spectrum of literature well known in the Spanish Enlightenment, ranging from Hume's opposing positions to Melon's favourable ones, later reformulated by authors such as Dutot, Genovesi or Mortimer.[13] Alonso tried to "seek the middle ground between one system and the other" (Alonso 1796, 270). He admitted, however, that among "modern" nations, a moderate resort to public debt was appropriate. The WN was instrumental in underpinning this approach.

On the one hand, Alonso opposed hoarding, characteristic of "primitive" communities, and indebtedness to establish perpetual income funds because they were a source of idleness. Additionally, he drew on Smithian ideas about productive labour to explain the effects of indebtedness on capital accumulation.

If the debt were external, then the domestic industry would work to "enrich the stranger"; moreover, if an increasing rate of profit did not counterbalance the payment of the principal and the interest, the rate of saving and the accumulation of capital would fall. But if the debt were domestic, capital would be shifted from the private to the public sector and, thereby, from productive to unproductive labour. Consequently, the rate of profit of capital would decrease (Alonso 1796, 285ff.; cfr. WN, IV, III). In either case, resorting to moderate public credit was preferable to raising taxes. Under Gardoqui's shadow, Alonso underpinned in this way the reversal of the Bourbon budgetary policy more prone to indebtedness, which was, however, unavoidable due to the collapse of the Treasury.

## Ramón de Campos's *La económica* (1797): a new hypothesis

Meanwhile, a year after the publication of Alonso's *Ensayo* and three years after his translation of the WN, Ramón Campos (1770–1808), a native of Castellón and professor of theology and philosophy with a strong background in science, brought out *La económica reducida a principios exactos, claros y sencillos* (Smith 1797a). It was a work of just over 100 pages that presented a concise summary of the WN. However, Campos's biography suggests, and Cervera has also clearly demonstrated (2003, 128–57), that his work seemed not to be based on Alonso's translated version, but on the WN itself. Campos worked as a teacher in Murcia and at the eales Estudios de San Isidro—the San Isidro Royal Studios—in Madrid, and then lived in England between 1793 and 1796, having been appointed Council of Castile commissioner for the study of agronomy and other sciences. He returned to Madrid in mid-1796 and obtained Godoy's support for the publication of *La económica*. The application process and publication of the book were carried out with remarkable speed, achieved in just a few weeks in January 1797.[14] Everything suggests, therefore, that it was during his stay in England that Campos came into contact with the WN and was able to write his book. In fact, the only explicit references in it are to Steuart and Smith;[15] although Campos mistakenly believed that Smith had recast Steuart's work (Campos 1797, "*Prólogo*"), *La Economica* was a laudable exercise in synthesising the ideas of "some of the best economists of the day", as he described it (Campos 1797, "*Advertencia*"), although in reality all the ideas covered were Smith's. Campos neither followed the order of the WN, nor did he include all its contents, omitting much of what related to book IV in particular. In fact, there is no real proof that his work was based on Alonso's version, since, as Cervera points out (2003, 133–35), he did not refer to any of Alonso's notes, keeping more closely to the WN—he accepted free trade—and, in contrast to Alonso's work, *La económica* was not focused on adapting the WN to circumstances in Spain, but on simplifying its content through "exact, clear and simple principles" (Campos 1797, "*Prólogo*"). The fact that the work was an informative summary of Smith's principles not only helped a wide audience to understand the complex WN, but also made it more suitable for teaching purposes.[16] However, there is no evidence that it was ever used on political economy courses, perhaps because this function was already fulfilled by Martínez de Irujo's translation of Condorcet's *Compendio* (Smith 1792), and so *La Económica* had only very limited circulation.

In fact, there is good reason to doubt the originality of Campos's work. He himself stated that the materials in the book "are not mine. The way they have been reworked is …" (Campos 1797, "*Prólogo*"). However, while putting together his book in Britain, Campos had access to texts and press articles on the WN, including several summaries of the work in publications that were not only unknown in Spain, but whose international circulation was negligible.[17] A clear example of this is a work such as Jeremiah Joyce's *Abridgement*, which is in the form of a textbook (Joyce 1797, *Advertisement*) and with which *La económica* has unquestionable similarities; although a literal and rigorous interpretation of the publication dates in the two books may cast doubt on this specific intellectual debt, it is included here more as a potential example than as a bibliographical certainty.

## Beyond the Treasury

Smith's ideas on finance had other readers beyond the Treasury. In his articles for the *Correo de Madrid o de los ciegos* (CMC), published in 1788–1789, Manuel de Aguirre, a soldier and member of the Sociedad Bascongada, recommended limiting public expenditure to maintaining the sovereign, magistrates, priests, soldiers and "certain illustrious cases that supported the homeland in important ways" (Aguirre 1974, 121, 132, 183). Morales was another of the WN's contemporary readers; this distinguished soldier and mathematician's *Discurso sobre la educación* (1790) accepted Smith's idea that labour was the origin of public wealth, as well as his division between the productive and unproductive classes;[18] the latter, which consisted of the clergy, the militia, the judiciary and the civil service, was ultimately dependent on the former:

> [A] nation's productive classes form a fund of wealth, the surplus of which puts them in a state of sacrificing part of it to preserve their good order, rest and happiness […] they provide the subsistence of the other classes that live at their expense.
>
> (Morales 1790, 5–6)

For this reason, as in Smith, the education of the "most useful class", which Morales regarded as "labouring" and the basis of "the nation's true strength" (Morales 1790, 13), was the source of public prosperity since, as well as maintaining social cohesion, it resulted in the application of specialised labour to production.

The WN's travels through Spain soon took it to the Sociedad Bascongada, thanks to Foronda. His *Cartas sobre los asuntos más exquisitos de la Economía Política* (1788–1789) were written in Bergara, in the heat of the debates that brought together the society's leaders and teachers at the village's science seminary to discuss the works of thinkers such as Raynal, Linguet, Necker, Mercier de la Rivière and Mirabeau.[19] The Smithian map for this unique Spanish Enlightenment work has been traced by Barrenechea (1984): Foronda cited the WN twice, once with regard to historical levels of interest rates and then as a guide to reading Physiocracy (Foronda 1788–1789, 403, 452); nevertheless, he also used the work tacitly. The ideas that, even in such volatile sectors as the grain trade, the rates of return in competition tended to level out in the long term and the use of substantial capital resources favoured the division of labour and productivity come from the WN (Barrenechea 1984, 29, 237). However, it was in the sphere of public finance that Smith's mark was especially clear, as Foronda used his tax principles repeatedly (Barrenechea 1984, 249–50). Therefore, taxation is the only area in which a significant flow of Smith's ideas can be observed: on the whole, the WN failed to make any particular impression on Foronda, who was in fact a great reader of political economy, mainly because his *Cartas* were structured around the three principles of freedom, property and security characteristic of the Physiocrat natural order. The pages reverberated with the names of Mercier de la Rivière, Mirabeu, Baudeau, Le Trosne and other followers of Quesnay. Foronda's reading of Physiocracy on numerous doctrinal issues, although not always in line with this—especially on issues related to the theory of utility, the productivity unique to agriculture and other principles of economic analysis—reveals that Physiocrat liberalism actually functioned as a barrier to Smithian thought, which was more flexible and mindful of historical and institutional constraints than that of the *économistes*.

## Jovellanos

When Smith published the WN in 1776 Jovellanos was beginning his prolific work on what he called the science of "political," "public" or "civil" economy. Throughout his life, he deemed it the fundamental science for a statesman and, as it was devoted to investigating the sources of public prosperity, a basic branch of the science of legislation (Jovellanos 2000 [1796–1797]). His body of work essentially consisted of reports and texts written for a variety of enlightened political bodies and institutions, mainly the Board of Trade, the History Academy and the Seville, Asturias and Matritense Economics Societies, culminating in the *Informe de Ley Agraria*, which was written for the Sociedad Matritense and published in his 1795 volume of *Memorias* when he himself was president (Jovellanos 2008c [1795]). Together with Alonso, the author of the first complete translation of the WN, Jovellanos was the eighteenth-century Spanish economist closest to Smith. His *Diarios* and the information available about his personal library show him to have had access to various versions of the WN, which he had read in both English and French on three or four occasions by 1798, and also that he wrote a summary for his own personal use, whose whereabouts is unknown. Jovellanos's supposed affiliation for Smith has naturally produced a long and controversial list of works, and there is a broad historiographical tradition that assumes that he gradually gravitated towards the WN. According to Varela (1988, 113–17), the "Smithian conversion" of Jovellanos was achieved from 1784 onwards and reached its peak in the *Informe*, a work in which, according to Polt (1971, 92ff.; 1978, 26–28), its allegiance to Smith is made very clear from the simultaneous defence of free will, private property and individual economic rights.[20] However, Llombart, the main expert on Jovellanos's economic thought, feels that accepting this affiliation amounts to a mistaken and restrictive assessment of his work: Smith's influence on Jovellanos was neither so clear nor all-embracing as has been supposed; furthermore, in no case did it lead to his breaking with Spanish economic tradition, in which he was shaped.[21]

As mentioned above, Jovellanos may have discovered Smith around 1784. Three of his texts seem to carry Smith's stamp; however, none of the apparent signs is fully convincing. The first work is the *Informe sobre la marina mercante* (1784), written for the Board of Trade. Varela noted Smith's influence in citations defending the English Navigation Acts as the cornerstone of the development of the merchant navy (Jovellanos 1859, 20–28); however, this idea had been commonplace since the 1750s among Spanish economists, who remained divided over the Acts' virtues and the possibility of enacting similar laws in Spain. The second is the *Informe sobre el libre ejercicio de las artes* (1784; Jovellanos 2008c [c.1784], 509–39) mentioned above. Schwartz held that Smith's influence, or the concurrence with his ideas, was "direct and profound." Nonetheless, as has been shown, if this influence did in fact exist, it was very limited: the principles favouring the freedom of labour originated with Turgot and the Physiocrats; moreover, Jovellanos did not accept abolitionist ideas but favoured the moderate gradual reforms designed by Campomanes to support the creation of an "intermediate" system. The third work, *Apuntes para una memoria sobre la libertad del comercio de granos* (c.1785; Jovellanos 2008d [1785], 621–28) has been represented as a precedent for the *Informe de Ley Agraria*. In this text Jovellanos tackled the delicate issue of the grain trade; his approach went well beyond the framework of the 1765 *Pragmática*—Law—which, justified doctrinally and politically by Campomanes, established the principles of "free trade" in grain in Spain, in force until 1790 (Llombart 1992, 155ff.). The reason is that Jovellanos's doctrinal premises differed from the Gournay circle's pragmatic liberalism, which had reached Campomanes via Herbert, a member of that circle, and underpinned this *Pragmática*. For the first time in Spain, Jovellanos acknowledged that "opinion" conditioned the grain market's functioning and price formation. At the same time, he underlined the fact that restrictive laws, including those on grain exporting, were inefficient because they failed to curb individual interest: "the incentive of interest is always urgent and men sacrifice future needs for the sake of present ones" (Jovellanos 2008d [1785], 626). The grain market should be based on free competition, which encouraged rivalry among growers, broke up monopolies, avoided shortages and fixed a suitable price level for both consumers and producers. This was the only regulatory framework to respect private interest that was not detached from the common interest in any way: "public interest is nothing more than the aggregate of private interests," which, when they match public interest, "secure common happiness" (Jovellanos 2008d [1785], 262). In contrast to Campomanes's beliefs, therefore, economic freedom should be extended to both the domestic and the foreign markets. However, although these liberal principles have been assumed to come from Smith, they did not. Instead, Jovellanos appears to have been inspired by Condillac, whose *Le commerce et le gouvernement* (1776) had been translated into Spanish in 1781 and which, in his opinion, contained the "conclusively established principles of sound economic science" (Jovellanos 2008d [1785], 626).

In short, interpreting the young Jovellanos as an early Smithian economist gives rise to a number of confusions, which have been accurately described by Llombart (2017). Firstly, these interpretations have not grasped the true depth of enlightened liberalism: the discovery of the principle of agents' free will and the assertion of individual economic rights predate Smith and reached Jovellanos when his influence was insufficiently documented. Secondly, his familiarity with many economics thinkers means that theoretical diversity was not only limited to British writers, whose influence on Jovellanos has generally been overestimated, perhaps because of Polt's magnificent study of the impact of Smith, Ferguson, Hutcheson and other Scottish authors on him (Polt 1978). Jovellanos's intellectual library included not only the most distinguished *arbitristas* and political economists of seventeenth- and eighteenth-century Spain, but also the major foreign writers on political economy during the European Enlightenment, who were mainly French and Italian (Clément 1980; Aguilar Piñal 1984). Jovellanos was an excellent reader and also benefitted from the fact that so many works on economics were translated and circulated during that period: the list includes Cantillon, Verri, Mirabeau, Galiani, Genovesi and Necker, as well as Condillac, Condorcet and Turgot, whose liberalism was more advanced than Smith's in many issues. He translated several entire works by these authors (Cantillon) as well as extracts (Verri, Condorcet and Smith) for his own personal use. Finally, the channels connecting Jovellanos with the WN have been analysed only narrowly: not only did he have access to several versions of the work, including those by the Spanish and French translators— on the one hand, Martínez de Irujo (1792) and Alonso (1794) and, on the other, Blavet (1778–1779) and Rouger (1790–1791)—but his writings also document other sources of Smithian inspiration such as Condorcet—with whom he shared the view that Turgot's work contained the seeds of the WN (Condorcet 1787, I, 54)—and the three volumes on *Economie Politique et Diplomatique* of Panckoucke's *Encyclopédie Méthodique*, which are known to have followed the dual theoretical line of Physiocracy and Smith (Perrot 1992; Larrère 2006).[22]

In contrast to other writings prior to the *Informe de Ley Agraria Law* (1795), Smith's influence here is absolutely unquestionable. Rooted in the *Expediente de Ley Agraria* promoted in 1767 by the Council of Castile in order to discover the causes of the decline of Spanish agriculture, the *Informe* was an applied economics text and was quasi-official in that it was commissioned by the Sociedad

Matritense. According to Jovellanos, political economy, as the main science of government, illuminated the work's two central principles: agriculture was the main source of nations' wealth and its progress required respect for the free exercise of private self-interest within the framework of justice (Jovellanos 1795, 703–05). The government should protect this interest by removing the three obstacles that hindered it, specifically, the political, moral and physical "stumbling blocks" stemming respectively from legislation, opinion and natural conditions (Jovellanos 2008c [1795], 706). The respective solution to each of these was "freedom", "enlightenment" and "aids", so that this free will became effective and stimulated agricultural development.

Jovellanos's *Informe* laid out a government programme based on these principles. Smith was mentioned twice, to justify the precariousness of using slaves for agricultural labour (WN III, II; Jovellanos 2008c [1795], 699) and the benefits to agriculture of long-term leases (WN III, II; Jovellanos 2008c [1795], 761). At the same time, as Llombart states (2017), rather than influence, there were many points of convergence with his ideas: support for enclosures, intensive agriculture and the popularising of agricultural knowledge; criticism of mortmain and entailment; rejection of privileges for livestock farming; the distribution of common land, and free for grain pricing and circulation in the domestic market. Likewise, Jovellanos's reading of Smith and Condorcet provided another of the *Informe*'s central ideas: given that labour was the origin of private and public wealth, instruction that encouraged the applied arts and labour specialisation was a strategic factor in economic development.[23] However, Jovellanos did not always concur with Smith on all these matters: his reforms were generally more cautious and moderate than Smith's, when not actually opposed to them. They disagreed on such basic issues as the defence of protectionism, refusal to accept free foreign trade in grain and rejection of guilds and entailed estates. The repeated classification of the *Informe* as Smithian is thus more confusing than illuminating. The *Informe*'s sources were many and varied (Llombart 1996) and, while explicitly indebted to a range of Spanish and foreign economists, its implicit debts were no less important. Some of these, such as Herbert, were shared with Smith, while others, like Galiani, Condillac and Necker, were core influences that left a deeper mark on the *Informe* than did the WN. The most noteworthy case is Necker, who inspired every detail of Jovellanos's refusal to accept free foreign trade in grain, as well as the law regulating this trade, which he copied literally from Necker's proposal for France (Jovellanos 2008c [1795], 776–81; Astigarraga 1998).

All these diverse and sometimes even contradictory sources underpinned the moderate pragmatic liberalism characterising Jovellanos's *Informe*. Thus, its interpretation of the exercise of free will within the framework of justice as a source of both agricultural development and wealth did not come solely from Smith and the Scottish tradition, let alone lead to a doctrinaire *laissez-faire* approach that was opposed to sovereign intervention. As Fuentes has shown (2000a), Jovellanos reserved a wider range of positive functions for the sovereign than the considerable body established in the "system of natural freedom" described in the WN; but, as is well known, Smith did not advocate *laissez-faire* if this expression is taken to mean a negative conception of the economic and social role of government or a simple and strict defence of the *ordnungspolitik* or Bentham´s *Sponte acta* (Coats 1971, 5ff.; O´Brien 1989, 375ff.). In short, according to Llombart, Jovellanos's work would function as one more step in the updating of Spanish economic thought that originated with Campomanes, Olavide, Sisternes, Pereira and the other authors who inspired the *Expediente* of the Agrarian Law. Jovellanos's contribution to this tradition was his unique construct of "political, moral and physical" stumbling blocks to agricultural growth and the trio of "freedom," "enlightenment" and "aids" to overcome them, as well as the decisive weight of the principle of free will in all this, which, strictly speaking, stemmed more from the enlightened culture than exclusively from Smith.

Much the same can be said of Cabarrús's *Cartas sobre los obstáculos que la naturaleza, la opinión y las leyes oponen a la felicidad pública* (c.1795), written as a commentary to his friend Jovellanos's *Informe*. They had a Physiocracy background that was lacking in the *Informe*, in spite of the fact that the ubiquitous Cabarrús, a financier, merchant and president of the Bank of San Carlos, remained loyal to protectionism, restrictions on grain exports and the qualified preservation of entailed estates; in sum, to a moderate liberalism that attributed wide areas of intervention to the sovereign. This did not prevent the *Cartas* from reflecting a number of ideas from the WN, again from book V. Cabarrús maintained that public expenditure should be limited to defence, justice and infrastructures, given that a fourth item, the "arts and sciences" required "no more encouragement than freedom, individual interest, public opinion and Enlightenment" (Cabarrús c.1795, 208). At the same time, he rectified the three principles of taxation set out in his 1783 *Memoria* and accepted the four proposed by Smith, which he deemed the "standards in this matter." However, Cabarrús remained faithful to his radical property tax-based fiscal project and used Smith's principles to level harsh criticism at Lerena, Alcalá and the "incomprehensible monument to ignorance and ferocity" that the fiscal reform of 1785 represented (Cabarrús c.1795, 179–81).

## Final remarks

When the eighteenth century drew to a close, enlightened thinkers in Spain had fully incorporated Smith's name onto their select list of noteworthy authors in the development of the fledgling science of political economy. The circulation of the first Spanish translations of the WN during the 1790s had undoubtedly been influential in the process, but so had the use that enlightened Spaniards had been making of the work since 1777. Yet, the first readers were a minority and they did not see in the WN the canonical book that it would become. As politicians, publicists or senior officials, they were "policy makers" and used the WN to both modulate public opinion and to inspire or to support legislative reforms. They essentially came from two focal points: the

Treasury and the economics societies, specifically those in Madrid, Segovia, Seville and the Basque Country. Their reading of the WN was highly accurate and was closer to applied economics than analytical economics. The work was interpreted in the light of the serious concerns raised by the Spanish economy at that time. Enlightened Spaniards sought ideas and proposals in the WN that would help to underpin the socio-economic reforms being developed in areas such as education, poverty, guilds and the hindrances to international trade and agricultural and economic growth. Therefore, its reading of the WN was not based only in the *ordnungspolitik* approach, but also included that of *prozesspolitik* (Coats 1971, 6). They understood that the WN was structured around a *laissez-faire* policy, but conferring numerous positive functions to the state,[24] and, as Rothschild (2001, 136–38) remarks, without appreciating that the "invisible hand" was an authentic *idée-clé* that would have epitomised all the book's content. Its activity was essential to abandon the fiscal-military system in favour of a development policy, which, in turn, required reforming the institutional framework of the Ancien Régime. In addition to all this, public finance emerged as the most privileged reading area of the WN. It was the ideas in WN's book V on the sovereign's obligations, including those referring to public debt and paper money, that spun the *filo rosso* of the first phase in the WN's reception in Spain. This confirms what the passage of time would only ratify with tremendous harshness: the critical budgetary situation that the Spanish monarchy began to experience from the 1780s became the real touchstone for its survival. In fact, the supposed virtues of the "invisible hand" as a channel for "the maximization of individual freedom within a framework of law and order" were obscured by the four Smithian principles of taxation, the idea in the WN that was most often repeated by enlightened Spaniards during the last two decades of the century.

## Notes

1  On the recent research about the outstanding role played by Geddes in the early translation and dissemination of the WN in Spain, see Chapter 2 in this book.
2  On the first Spanish readings of the WN, see Smith (1957b), Schwartz (2000) and Perdices (2000a).
3  On other uses of Smith's anti-guilds positions within the Segovia Society during the 1790s, see Chapter 3 in this book.
4  In spite of being handwritten, this *Informe* was widely circulated during the late Spanish Enlightenment (Ceán 1814, 128).
5  On the human relationship between Turgot and Smith, see Rae (1895, 118–20) and, on his intellectual influence, Groenewegen (2002, ch. 20). For a wider view of Smith's French sources, see Skinner (1997).
6  On this reform, see Hernández (1972, 3–90); on its insertion into Treasury history and the fiscal debates in the eighteenth century in Spain, see Guasti (2000) and Astigarraga et al. (2015).
7  On his dizzying rise in the Bourbon government, see Tedde de Lorca (2000).
8  On Alcalá, see Valles's excellent political and intellectual biography (2008).

9   Lerena's citations of Smith are in his *Compte-rendus,* written between 1787 and 1789 (Lerena c.1787; c.1790).

10  The most up-to-date analyses are by Torres (2012, 76–84) and Dubet and Solbes (2019, 404ff.).

11  Only a few years previously Sempere (1801, I, 19) had characterised *arbitrista* Valle de la Cerda's work as a precursor of the Smithian idea that labour was the source of wealth.

12  We follow the analysis by Fernández-Schwartz (1978) and Schwartz-Fernández (1999); also, vid. De Haro (2013) and Elorza (1970, 196–202). Alonso's case was not isolated. In the Italian Piedmont, Vasco also adopted Smithian ideas on paper money around 1790 (Parisi 1972, 926–27). For a synthesis of Smith's banking and monetary views, see Rockoff (2013). See Paganelli (2015) about Smith's significance to developed a "system of natural liberty" that would promote both efficiency and justice.

13  Melon (1736, ch. XXIII); Dutot (1738, I, 225ff.); Hume (1752, discourse VIII); Genovesi (1765–1767, III, chs. VI–VII); Mortimer (1772, 355–58, 359–91).

14  AHN, *Estado,* bundle 3014-8.

15  The mention of Steuart is quite significant as he was received in Spain with far less interest than Smith; in Germany, on the other hand, he was the most frequently cited author during the 1780s, as his work was readily assimilated into the Cameralist tradition (Tribe 1988, 133–34).

16  The fact that it was published at the same time as Garnier's *Compendio elemental* began to be circulated in Spain (c.1796) does not seem to be a coincidence.

17  Something very similar happened in Germany, where a summary of the WN was published two years after Garve and Dörrien's translation (Tribe 1988, 164–68).

18  The *Discurso* was read in the Seville Patriotic Society on 3 September 1789 and published in the EMD (18-1-1790, no. 26, pp. 49–58). Morales knew Cantillon's *Essai.* On the other hand, the Smithian affiliation usually attributed to Fernández de Navarrete's *Discurso* (1791) is less than clear. His structuring of the productive classes and the presumed nature of political economy as a suitable science for mathematical applications were unrelated to the WN. Its content is rooted in *fin de siècle* French political arithmetic.

19  The *Cartas* were reissued in book form in 1789–1794 and 1821.

20  Similar position, although with more nuances, in Schwartz (2000, 205–16).

21  See especially Llombart (1995; 1996; 2000; 2017) and, also, the cautious observations of R.S. Smith (1957, 1220–23).

22  In 1784 Jovellanos was appointed by the History Academy to carry out the censorship of the Spanish version of volume I of the Dictionary. Although it was considered more than adequate, the translation was never completed.

23  See, especially, Jovellanos (2000 [1796–1797]), in which there are echoes of Morales's *Discurso* (1789). Jovellanos praised English production methods but failed to mention the division of labour or relate this with the extension of the market. Fuentes (2000a, 387ff.) has seen precursors of human capital theory in these ideas.

24  For Smith's views respecting the legitimate functions of government, see Viner (1927) and Robbins (1961, ch. 2), and relating that question to the civic tradition, see Robertson (1983).

# 8 Nuancing Adam Smith

## The Wealth of Nations' reception and influences in Spain, 1800–1820

*Jesús Astigarraga, José M. Menudo and Javier Usoz*

### The long shadow of tradition

During the first decades of the nineteenth century, the reception of *The Wealth of Nations* (WN) in Spain was conditioned by an especially turbulent cycle of political events. Besides incessant military conflicts, the country witnessed the War of Independence (1808–1812); the simultaneous holding of the Cortes—Parliament—of Cádiz (1810–1813), which produced the first constitution in Spanish history (1812); the return of absolutism with Fernando VII (1813) and, finally, the beginning of a new constitutional phase under the Liberal Triennium (1820–1823). This continuous changing of direction did not prevent political economy from slowly becoming established in academic terms: the relationships between absolutism, censorship and the circulation of ideas did not result in a particularly restrictive framework, nor did the translation and production of economic works slow down during the reign of Fernando VII (Almenar 2000a; 2003). The process by which authors and translators became increasingly specialised was not interrupted either during his reign; as civil servants, writers, advisers, parliamentarians and university teachers, these individuals helped to equip political economy with institutional support (university chairs, boards of trade and economics and patriotic societies), promoted stable circulation networks (the press) and introduced it into parliamentary debates, all of which led to the growing acceptance of the new science in specialised literature. In turn, the War of Independence represented the beginning of a set of reforms that acted in continuity with the late Enlightenment to bring about the Ancien Régime's gradual replacement by a liberal system (Comín 2000a).

The WN did not leave its mark on all the period's economics literature. A significant number of works were based on pre-Smithian concepts, originating in economics currents in Spain from previous centuries (Perdices 2000a). Among the authors that were sympathetic to Colbertism, Smith was just one more noteworthy writer in the cultivation of political economy (Colbert 1801, "Discurso Preliminar"). For its part, Banqueri's unpublished work aimed to persuade readers of the priority of domestic over foreign trade (Banqueri 1801). Banqueri was a priest and had a close relationship with Godoy; in spite of having

DOI: 10.4324/9781003152804-10

been one of the censors of Alonso's translation of the WN, he mentioned Smith on just one occasion to endorse this idea, and to show England's diligence in putting it into effect (WN I, 11). His real sources were seventeenth- and eighteenth-century Spanish economists, especially Ward (1779).

The tendency to look back to earlier Spanish economists was rekindled during the Cortes of Cádiz. In De las Heras's work (1813), both his conception of the object of political economy and its main theme—the metalist principles in trade policies (De las Heras 1813, 51)—as well as the only reference mentioned in the text—Ward (1779)—reflect the dominance of the economic analysis that predated Smith, who in fact had no explicit or tacit influence on the work. Another contemporary work with strong agrarian tendencies by Franco Salazar (1812) was presented as a genuine compendium of eighteenth-century political economy in Spain; to this was added the name of Filangieri, whose *Scienza della legislazione* (1780–1791) was widely circulated throughout Spain at the time (Astigarraga 2005a), and argued for the establishing of a constitutional monarchy that was capable of organising a "national" economic "system"; Smith's shadow, however, was only discernible in the general principles of taxation (Franco Salazar 1812, 99ff.). Finally, it has been claimed that moderate liberal Antonio Alcalá-Galiano's book (1813) contains a summarised interpretation of Swiss Physiocrat Schmid d'Avenstein's *Principes de la législation universelle* (1776). However, in the set of economic maxims outlined there, refutating Physiocracy prevails over accepting Schmid d'Avenstein's principles, which can only be detected in a small core of economic policies—defence of large-scale farming, mechanisation and agricultural land owners (Astigarraga 2005b). Lacking any connection with Smith and containing only one generic citation of his work, Antonio Alcalá-Galiano's book had its roots in pre-Smithian economics (Genovesi, Necker), including his brother Vicente Alcalá-Galiano's ideas, and defended a moderate monarchical regime that owed a great deal to Montesquieu. In short, all these books contained a defence of reforms that was something of an anachronism, since the agenda triggered by the Cortes of Cádiz had made them obsolete. The fact that they were rooted in pre-Smith literature acted as an effective barrier to the acceptance of Smith's theoretical and applied liberalism.

Other authors such as Veranio (1807) openly opposed Smith head-on. His book was written for use by the new political economy chairs and intended to show that the works by Smith and British economists in general were mere "artifices [...] to win over opinion" (Veranio 1807, 24). He showed that the Navigation Acts, the 1786 free trade deal between France and Britain and other economic laws enacted in Britain, of which he gave a detailed account, all aimed to strengthen the British trading system vis-à-vis its competitors. His anti-British position had its roots in the late Enlightenment tradition that was opposed to accepting universal laws for fear that Spain would renounce the prohibitive trading laws discredited by "Smith and his followers," and which in reality remained in full force in Britain three decades after the publication of the WN (Veranio 1807, 34, 182).

## Versions of the WN

The main dissemination channel for Smithian thought during this period was provided by the reissues of Martínez de Irujo's eighteenth-century translation of Condorcet's *Compendio*, in 1803 and 1814 (Smith 1792), and Alonso's translation of the WN in 1805–1806 (Smith 1805–1806). To these were added the reprints in 1803 and 1814 of the latter's Smithian text on monetary theory (Alonso Ortiz 1796) and a brief piece in which Smith was compared with the Physiocrats that was taken from Garnier's translation of the WN (1807; Smith 1802).[1] After the War of Independence two works were published that were evidence of Smith's enduring popularity and whose titles showed that they had been strongly influenced by the WN, whether the authors were inspired to spread this influence or to question it.

The first was written by Ramón Lázaro de Dou y de Bassols, whose magnum opus *Instituciones de Derecho público general de España* (1800–1804), one of the best summaries of public and administrative law in eighteenth-century Spain, contained an early reference to Smith. A Catalan lawyer and professor at the University of Cervera, Dou proposed levying tariffs on foreign manufactured goods, citing Uztáriz and Ulloa as references for these policies. At the same time, he criticised free market policies and the authors that supported the elimination of tariffs for "hiding behind Smith's authority, who they present as an Achilles of opinion" (Dou 1800–1804, V, 247). Dou cited three arguments in support of his preference for protectionism over prohibitionism: the latter created hatred in excluded nations; it put an end to domestic competition and, as domestic industry could not provide for the colonies by itself, it caused shortages (Lluch 1973, 195). Without further citations or references to the WN, due to his work's pre-Smithian content and perhaps also to the fact that it had been finished in 1793, almost a decade before publication,[2] Dou disagreed with "Smith's system" where backward nations were concerned, although he admired Smith for the depth of his work on other matters:

> What cannot be overlooked is that the further a nation is from drawing equal to or surpassing others in industry, the further it must be from adopting Smith's system. Some of them are so far ahead in physics, mathematics, machines and all the aids that can be provided by study and application that have been encouraged and rewarded for two centuries, they would not allow factories to be set up in the backward nations, because the others would sell everything finer, more perfect and cheaper.
>
> (Dou 1800–1804, V, 247–48)

Years later Dou published a work whose explicit aim was to disseminate the WN. This is reflected by the title, *La riqueza de las naciones nuevamente explicada* (1817). He used the second edition of Alonso's translation of the WN to write it (Smith 1957a). Having introduced Smith as the "Newton of political economy," Dou explained that his work aimed to "raise the profile of the inquiry into the wealth of nations published by Dr. Adam Smith" (Smith 1817, VII). This was another aspect of Dou's project; as well as explaining the causes of Spain's economic backwardness, which included ignorance of economics, he proposed appropriate institutional reforms (Lluch 1973, 200). If the *Instituciones* introduced economic science to public law jurists, this new work made it accessible to a wider public.

Dou's work was a compendium of the WN, which was cited multiple times, and covered almost all the chapters; however, it also included a critique of Smith based on the "mercantile system" and mainly using references to the *Instituciones*. The work has been patchily interpreted in the literature: while R.S. Smith (1957a) believed that Dou accepted Smith's overall framework, Lluch (1973), more correctly, maintained that he supported both the "mercantile system," which was the focus for criticism in the WN, and an agrarianism that was an exception in the Catalan industrialist tradition, which united the Barcelona Board of Trade from Romà to Jaumeandreu: Dou accepted Smith's sequence of investment priorities favouring agriculture (Lluch 1973, 198).

In the first two sections of his work, Dou set out to show an inconsistency between Smith's critique of the "mercantile system" and his labour theory of value:

> According to this system gold and silver cannot be exchanged, except for wares, or goods, that contain an equal, or almost equal amount of work: then the nation, which adopts the mercantile system, acquires precious metals solely with the annual product of its labour; and the more it wishes to acquire, the more it must work, and the greater the annual product of its labour must be: so that the legislator, adopting this system, says to the citizens: *work without stopping in the fields and workshops, for you shall all have a just reward and wages for your labour:* and this is what Smith intends.
>
> (Smith 1817, 116–17)

Dou considered Smith's labour theory of value a brilliant theoretical principle, and accordingly defended labour as the only source of wealth. Land and capital also created it but only in function of the labour they contained. The three remaining sections of the work were devoted to capital, land and taxation, and here Dou presented Smith's ideas more critically. Smith's condemnation of usury in the chapter on capital was in fact due to changes Alonso had made in his translation of the WN; specifically, Dou mistakenly believed that Smith was unaware of the existence of "legal usury" as interest on loans permitted by the *lucrits cessans* and *damnun emergens* doctrine (Smith 1957a, 199). On the issue of agricultural income, Dou disagreed with Smith over the problem that mortmain, or entailed estates, represented for agriculture, and defended the use of emphyteusis. The work's last long section covered taxation and contained a summary of Smithian thought, with which Dou was in full agreement.[3] The WN's taxation principles enabled him to explain that the final tax burden fell on agricultural landowners and he therefore advocated a single tax; this led to a heated disagreement with Alcalá-Galiano, which inspired Dou to write several texts during the 1830s.[4]

Valladolid liberal Gonzalo de Luna criticised Smith from a different point of view. His *Ensayo sobre la investigación de la naturaleza y causa de la riqueza de las naciones relativamente a España* (Smith, 1819–1820) did not aim to either explain or disseminate the WN; rather, it was a critical interpretation that accepted the work's importance (Menudo 2005; 2007). In the introduction to the *Ensayo*, Luna presented his main sources: on one side, were those that were essentially applied, rooted in Spanish authors—Ortiz, Saavedra, Mariana and Ward—and, on the other, were the theoretical, which stemmed from Smith's work, although Luna distanced himself from Smith on basic issues such as wealth, value and productive labour. Filangieri and Alonso Ortiz were other clear influences, the latter concerning monetary theory put forward—the theory of monetary circulation (Lluch and Almenar 2000, 103)—and Quesnay was another source. Like Dou, Luna used the second edition of Alonso's translation for his many quotations and references to Smith.

Luna's first reference concerned the definition of wealth. He followed the categories established in book IV of the WN regarding the differences between the mercantile and *économistes* systems (Smith 1819–1820, 131), and it is here that his first criticism of Smith appears (1819, ch. IV), which was based on Ward (1779): a plea for the contribution that what were called the "sterile" sectors made to production. Thus, services were granted a productive category and the impossibility of developing an analysis of production without considering demand was emphasised. Smith's ideas were presented in a later chapter on the division of labour, in order to discuss their relevance and, more specifically, their limitations. Just as the market for goods restricted the division of labour, effective demand, defined as the "arrangement of arms and labour", limited the labour market and thus production (Smith 1819–1820, 152). Luna's third reference to the WN concerned monetary issues. He described Smith's monetary thinking together with that of Say and Spanish author Marien Arróspide to show that Smith's monetary policy did not contradict theirs. He proposed a monetary policy that altered the value of the currency on the basis of the same principles or benchmarks: the real value of the goods–currency. To be specific, Spain should increase the face value of its currency when its real value was higher (Smith 1819–1820, 305). This economic policy recommendation was underpinned by Luna's own model of economic growth, and to illustrate this he even evoked Smith's analogy between the liberalisation of the international flow of capital and opening the floodgates of a dam:

> Open the flood-gates, and there will presently be less water above, and more below, the dam-head, and it will soon come to a level in both places. Remove the tax and the prohibition, and as the quantity of gold and silver will diminish considerably in Spain and Portugal, so it will increase

somewhat in other countries, and the value of those metals, their proportion to the annual produce of land and labour, will soon come to a level, or very near to a level, in all.

(WN IV,V)

The final reference to the WN appeared in Luna's critique of the foundations of the quantity theory of money used by Smith and Filangieri in their classical formulas for the Spanish economy (Smith 1819–1820, 355ff.). Luna believed that the classical solution for inflation in Spain was based on the quantity theory, just as Smith described it in book IV of the WN: if the velocity of circulation and production are constant, reducing the amount of cash—via the importing of foreign goods—would reduce prices. Luna suggested that if the money supply remained unchanged—given the balance between the money market and goods, the supply of goods also remained constant—in Classical thought absolute prices were fixed according to the velocity of circulation (Smith 1819–1820, 382–83). The modification of this velocity meant that there was a point to holding monetary balances; thus, the demand for goods did not only depend on relative prices. This was the analytical structure that enabled Luna to state that money could not be neutral. Neither the velocity of circulation nor production remained constant, and thus an expansionary monetary policy was not necessarily passed on to prices. In short, both Dou and Luna's works represented a reasoned rejection of the WN's core ideas, and, in so far as both were based on Alonso's translation, they proposed interpretations that sought to curtail the influence of Smithian thought.

## Reading Smith in the context of development strategies

The problems of interpreting the WN in one way only are rooted in attempts to reconcile the work with other economic doctrines (Steiner 1995). From 1800 to 1820 the usual agrarian or neo-Physiocrat interpretation of the WN was backed up by the Spanish translations, not only those by Condorcet and Garnier, but also others by cutting-edge economists who favoured agriculture, such as Young—published in the SAP (1796–1808) and the VCLA (1803–1805)—Herreweschand (1800) and Canard (1804). The most influential of these was Garnier. Before his agriculture-oriented translation of Smith appeared (Smith 1802), his *Abregé élémentaire* had already been in circulation since 1796, the year it was produced, in a handwritten translation attributed to the future Finance Minister Martín de Garay (Garnier c.1796). However, Garnier's free-market agrarianism, which was close to Peuchet, who was also well known in Spain, showed profound differences with both the Physiocrats and Smith (Breton 1990) due to the mark of authors such as Condillac, Hume, Turgot and especially Cantillon (industrial productivity, the income circuit, the population–subsistence ratio, a positive view of luxury and the hegemony of the agricultural landowner). Cantillon's influence is also visible in the work of another author, who in fact was less close to Physiocracy than it is normally deemed to be: the Swiss writer Herreweschand (Gislain 1995).

Smith left only a marginal imprint on economists who were followers of the schemes of Physiocracy or Turgot, such as Álvarez Guerra (1813) and Orense (1813).[5] Agrarians who were not associated with the *économistes* normally intermingled Smith's ideas with those from the late Enlightenment. In 1820, in the midst of drafting a new law on entailed estates (mortmain), Cambronero (1820, 42–45) appealed to Smith's authority, as well as that of Bentham, Say and Sismondi, to expose the socio-economic harm done by this institution, but in the end his acceptance of mortmain with strict conditions in a monarchical system was more faithful to the tradition of Jovellanos—and Montesquieu. Cañedo (1814), an author who specialised in fiscal issues, accepted various Smithian ideas (the priority of agriculture in investments, the notion of unproductive labour, the criticism of entailed estates and the principles of security, freedom and property), but the late eighteenth-century Spanish agenda (defending British agrarian laws, instructive pamphlets for agriculturalists, using the army for public works and limitations on entailed estates) resurfaced in the appendix to his work, which was devoted to arguing for the priority of agriculture.[6]

Smith's reception in Aragon was aided by teaching activity at the pioneering Chair of Civil Economics and Commerce. Founded in 1784 by the Aragon Economic Society, the WN was first taught there at the end of the eighteenth century, following on from Condorcet's *Compendio*. Chair-holder Cistué may have been reflecting the state of opinion in the society in 1804 when he singled out Smith as the "greatest economist" because, unlike the "mercantile" and Physiocrat systems, he had identified the real laws of a nation's wealth. Behind the veil of a debatable patriotism, political authority's traditional incursions into economic life not only created monopolies, but were particularly harmful to agriculture. They also hampered the shaping of a Smith-inspired institutional framework in which the stimulating of individual interest—"under justice's watchful eye"—and the free use of property and capital favoured wealth creation and generated public funds to support the non-productive classes; at the same time, the division of labour and mechanisation were key factors for improving their country's international competitiveness (Cistué 1804, 36–39, 44). Around the same time, Calomarde, another supporter of agriculture from Aragon, was using the quantitativist tradition in Spain (Zavala, Arriquíbar, Ward and Campomanes) and abroad (Genovesi and Mirabeau) to illustrate the possibilities of exporting grain from the region. Against Physiocracy, he mentioned the WN to validate his opposition to rewarding grain exporting, as according to Smith (WN V, V) this had not been the real reason for the development of British agriculture (Calomarde 1800, 70–71).

In nearby Navarre Smithian ideas filtered into the 1817–1818 Cortes, which were studying the integration of the kingdom's *foral*—chartered—system into Spain's common system of laws.[7] Their main economic debates took place against the backdrop of pressure from a combination of low agricultural prices and the urgent need to dispose of the surplus wheat and wine produced in the south of the region, which were seen as its main source of wealth. The debates evoked the authority of Say, Jaumeandreu, Foronda—who was consulted by the Cortes themselves—and, above all, Jovellanos, culminating in Law LXII repealing existing obstacles to the internal trading of Navarre's grain and raising its maximum export prices. In order to overcome resistance from ecclesiastical deputies, the Cortes asked the University of Salamanca for an opinion in favour of the economic advantages of free internal trade, as well as its moral probity. The resulting *Dictamen* (1817) mentioned not only Campomanes and Jovellanos, but also Smith, evoking two of his ideas: competition was the only system that levelled market prices with natural prices, and thus "covered all production costs and left a moderate profit for farmers"; and the evolution of British grain prices showed that free internal trade was the best price leveller (Anonymous 1817, 18, 31). In response, Zuaznabar, an official with close ties to the viceroy or royal representative in Navarre, drafted one of the Cortes's best-argued texts, with the aim of moderating the excessively liberalising content of the *Dictamen* and Law LXII (Zuaznabar 1818). His theoretical framework did not involve breaking with the Enlightenment heritage, either in Spain (from Zavala to Jovellanos) or abroad (from Melon to the Physiocrats) (San Julián 2000, 157ff.). In fact, his relativist methodology (Necker, Galiani, Filangieri) derived from just this, as did his pragmatic solution, which was akin to Jovellanos, opposed to the Physiocrat or Smithian free grain trade "apologists" and in favour of a pricing system to regulate grain exports. He was unique in using the Smith-Say theory of prices to calculate the natural price of Navarre grain in normal years, when production was assumed to be proportionate to consumption and wages, incomes and profits were all covered. A further aim was to establish the maximum price above which exporting would be allowed, although in practice the system simply estimated a value that was adjusted to regular market peaks and troughs (Zuaznabar 1817, 100–12).

Smithian ideas also filtered into early works by two pro-agriculture economists that were destined to set the course of Spanish economic thought from the 1820s onwards. Treasury Secretary and future minister Canga Argüelles specifically cited the WN to establish the four conditions for agricultural prosperity: property ownership, freedom of crop cultivation, free management of production and the "freedom to dispose of [its products] without hindrances or regulations that encumber it" (Canga Argüelles 1813, 24).[8] For his part, Flórez Estrada represented the culmination of a growth model based on agrarianism and free trade. According to Almenar (1976, 58–81; 1997, 145–49), in the *Examen imparcial de las disensiones de la América con España* (1811), criticising the "restrictive system" practised in Spain enabled him to account for its "economic decay" and to propose "absolute freedom for trade and industry", albeit unilaterally (Flórez Estrada 1811, 293), to promote the development of the peninsula and the American provinces. Flórez accepted Condillac's theory of value, Hume's theory of specie-flow mechanism—the main argument against the "restrictive system" in Spain—and a range of ideas put forward by seventeenth- and eighteenth-century Spanish political economists, including Campomanes and Ward, in order to develop a model in which prosperity was identified not with the accumulation of precious metals, but with feeding the population and producing goods. This in turn depended on an active employed population, and demographic growth relied on plentiful staple foodstuffs; hence the agricultural sector became key to boosting population growth and invig-orating the Spanish external sector on the basis of this comparative advantage. Almenar has found conceptual hints of Smith in issues such as the priority of investment, the absolute advantages of trade and the theory of surplus for export; but there is no reference to the WN in the text, except perhaps via its citing of a "well-documented Englishman" in pursuit of prioritising taxation over public debt (Smith 1957a).

The field of pro-industry economists encompassed not only the Classical mainstream, but also the Spanish industrialist tradition of seventeenth- and eighteenth-century political economists, traces of German Cameralism and, most importantly, links with the "economists of the nation" (Chaptal, Ganilh, Ferrier or Arnould); the latter had grown up with the negative effects on France of the 1786 trade treaty with Britain and, as a result, had turned manufacturing into a *raison d'état* (Démier 1990; Almenar 1997, 165; Lluch et al. 1999, 1436). All this encouraged a desire to modify or even oppose the mainstream, espe-cially in the defence of certain policies inherent in the "mercantile system" and the rejection of free trade; however, French "industrialist liberals" moved away from prohibitionism towards a "dynamic and measured" protectionism (Démier 1990, 294).

López de Peñalver, the first head of the Conservatorio de Artes y Oficios—the Conservatory of Arts and Crafts—and promoter of early exhibitions of Spanish industry, as Lluch detailed (1992, ciii), epitomised these positions.[9] His business, academic and political career were all marked by the Chaptal's maxims: "industrialism, protectionism, technological innovation and technical education." His *Reflexiones sobre la variación del precio del trigo* (1812) are note-worthy for their pioneering mathematical economics content, which was partly the successor to political arithmetic but also had sources in Say, Smith, Steuart, Dyannière and Canard. Peñalver's work was closer to Steuart than Smith and showed no particular interest in the theoretical issues or political economy covered in the WN. His references to Smith were drawn from the second edition of Alonso's version and dealt only with his account of wage behaviour in Britain, while briefly mentioning errors of government intervention in the corn market (Peñalver 1812, 7–8, 60).

The narrow agrarian interpretation of Smith was in fact corrected by the ideological pluralism of the period.[10] Aragon native Polo y Catalina's 1804 *Informe* lambasted Spanish Enlightenment Physiocracy and agrarianism (Campomanes), as well as the attempt to reconcile them with the WN (Polo c.1804). Although Mirabeau, Serionne and Herrenschwand also came in for criticism, the main focus was Garnier, whose *Abregé elementaire* (c.1796) and pro-fusely annotated translation of the WN (1802) had already begun to influence

Spanish economists. Polo was opposed to all this, proposing instead an industry-led development strategy that drew on the Spanish tradition (Mata, Arriquíbar) and an interpretation of the WN that invoked a greater harmony between industry and agriculture and anticipated Say's forthcoming success. However, he also restored various measures that typified the "mercantile system" and defended protectionism. Although his *Informe* was never published, its import-ance should not be underestimated. Polo had been educated in the pioneering Zaragoza Chair of Civil Economics and Commerce, and his text was in fact an important official statistics report to be created under the auspices of the Department of Public Works and Balance of Payments.

In Catalonia, meanwhile, Jaumeandreu and Gassó's works contributed to the consolidation of the Barcelona Board of Trade's industrialist and anti-free market programme (Lluch 1973). If Jaumeandreu was essentially inspired by Say, although he moved away from Say on matters relating to free trade,[11] Gassó was proof of the growing importance of Chaptal's political economy. The title of his work left no room for doubt as to its content: *España con industria, fuerte y rica* (1816). The text was mainly descriptive, with arguments rooted in the recent his-tory of Spain and Catalonia, and not lacking in praise for the Bourbon reforms and the economists that inspired them (Uztáriz, Campomanes and Jovellanos). Gassó defended the priority of industry (Lluch 1973, 217), and to foster its growth he advocated protecting domestic manufacturing with prohibitions and tariffs, promoting the structuring of the internal market, "nationalising con-sumption" by encouraging demand for Spanish goods and creating a "constant and secure" system (Gassó 1816, 60). In principle unrelated to Smith, his work contained several tacit references to the WN on the desirability of adopting a good economic system, the functions of the Treasury, fiscal data on Britain and the possibility of creating a federative system with the American colonies (Buenaventura 1816, 81, 109, 110, 133).

In 1821 Smith's work found a warm reception in the writings of Basque industrialist Foronda. The third reprint of his *Cartas* (Foronda 1994 [1788–1789]) appeared that year with numerous notes referring to the Classical Franco-British tradition, from Smith, Condillac and Turgot to Say and Ricardo. As Barrenechea (1984) pointed out, Foronda's aim was not to refute his *Cartas's* principles, which were based in Physiocracy, but to find authoritative arguments in these authors' writings to endorse his own liberal strands. When Say's popu-larity was at its height, Foronda identified with Condillac, due to his theory of value, but most of all with Smith, who he read through Garnier's transla-tion—reprinted a year later—and the comments of other economists (Ganilh, Canard et al.). The "oracle" and "profound" Smith was cited again and again in his defence of consumer interests and the expansion of labour and property rights, as well as his opposition to guilds, prohibitions, low wages, monopolies, the spurious interests of merchants and hindrances to domestic trade. Above and beyond these issues, however, he was championed as an early advocate of free trade, which, according to Bentham, emerged as a benevolent unifying prin-ciple of the whole economic system, generating benefits for all kinds of citizens and nations (Foronda 1994 [1788–1789], 112). Foronda criticised advocates of the prohibitive system for not having read Condillac and Smith, as well as the latter for establishing exceptions to free importing and defending the Navigation Acts, and he favoured multilateral tariff dismantling, whose result would be similar "to that of the provinces in an internal trade system" (Foronda 1994 [1788–1789], 426).

## Readings of Smith on taxation

The beginning of the nineteenth century saw the continuation of the Enlightenment tax debate inspired by Lerena's 1785–1787 revenue reform.[12] After the milestone represented by the 7 August 1809 decree abolishing provincial revenues, the reform's influence was first visible in the liberalism of the 1812 Constitution and the 13 September 1813 decree introducing direct tax on productive activities. As was the case in the late eighteenth century, the economic writings that informed these achievements were inspired by Smith in a broad and sometimes particularly radical sense.[13] This was especially true where the liberalising approach to property ownership and economic activity were concerned, as well as to the long overdue reform of taxation, which was marked by the Smithian ideas that tax should be levied on subjects that were able to pay and that it should be exacted in the time period and by the means that were least harmful for economic activity and collected as cheaply as possible (WN V, II).

These decrees were followed by reflections from prominent personalities such as Vicente Alcalá-Galiano, Canga Argüelles, Martínez de Montaos, Ranz, Porcel, Uriortua, Luyando, Gómez Rombaud, Polo de Alcocer, Conde de Toreno, Antillón, Antonio Alcalá-Galiano (Cádiz deputy and Vicente's brother), López Ballesteros, Santillán, Gallardo, López Juana Pinilla and Aribau. On the whole, these authors show no explicit influence from Smith, beyond their liberal inspiration, with the exceptions of Vicente Alcalá-Galiano, Canga Argüelles and Martínez de Montaos.

In 1810, at the request of Finance Minister Francisco Saavedra, Treasurer General Alcalá-Galiano produced an *Informe* on the decree, which was a defence of the revenue system established by Lerena in 1785 (Valles 2008). While the defence accepted that taxes on consumption "are not the most suitable for a free people" (Alcalá-Galiano 1810, 81), it also embraced the conviction that Spanish society lacked the necessary conditions for abandoning such taxes, incorporating Smith's ideology (López 1999, xxxiv).[14] In this respect, Alcalá-Galiano stated that the 1785 *rentas provinciales*—provincial revenues—respected the economic principle according to which the accumulated capital that determined future investment should not be taxed. Such a system did not increase wages, since these depended to a large extent on causes that were unrelated to consumption. Smith's influence on this Spanish author and politician was actually related to his general approach, and not to specific tax solutions, which Smith himself is known not to have favoured. According to Alcalá-Galiano's *Informe*, Smith's doctrines on the division of labour and the use of capital were "the thread that led me joyfully through this political economy maze," which included a correct and critical understanding of Physiocracy (López 1999, xxxvi–xxxvii).

The next reference to Smith in relation to tax relates to the activity of the Cortes of Cádiz, which were first convened on 24 September 1810 and on 4 October created the Finance Commission to follow the trail of the *única contribución*—single tax—for which the Cortes cited both eighteenth-century financial policy-makers in Spain and foreign authors—such as Necker, Turgot and Say—and Smith. Among the Commission's most noteworthy achievements was Finance Minister Canga Argüelles's *Memoria sobre las rentas provinciales* (1811), which proposed a Treasury linked to the objective of economic development, and thus inspired by the new science of economics.[15] When it came to deciding on a tax system, Canga Argüelles argued that, following the examples of Aragon, Catalonia and Valencia, while the *única contribución* was oriented towards agrarian property, it respected the Smithian principles of taxation with which he himself identified by preventing the division of labour and circulation of money from slowing down.

A third contemporary reference to Smith and taxation appears in a text by Martínez de Montaos in response to one by Luyando. Both were published in 1813 and were given serious consideration by the Cortes of Cádiz Finance Commission.[16] The two texts disagreed on how the ability to pay should be measured: according to Martínez de Montaos it should be based on territorial, industrial and commercial wealth, while Luyando preferred expenditure or consumption, following the line set by Zavala in the previous century. Following the constitutional mandate, Martínez de Montaos's approach strove to reconcile the new law's liberal principles with a vision of economic development and public affluence that was a long way from a more typically Smithian spending programme. However, the spirit of Smith, who Martínez de Montaos considered the best author on economic matters, manifested itself in his forceful defence of free trade. This was based on the principle of absolute advantage and on the Constitution's implementation of direct tax, which should be levied on products not capital, and not only on income from land in accordance with a refutable Physiocratic doctrine, but also on the income from labour and industry (López 1999, lxxxvi–xcviii).

These contributions were linked to an important Cortes tax document that was intended to inform a future law: the *Informe sobre nuevo plan de contribuciones* drafted by the Finance Commission (Anonymous 1813). It was presented to the Cortes on 6 July 1813 and led to the 13 September 1813 decree introducing direct taxation—only to be abolished by the decree on 23 June 1814 which re-established *rentas provincials*. Attributed to Porcel (López 1999, cviiff.), although the text contained references that could be credited to Smith or even Physiocracy in a generic sense, such as its liberal background and the notions of unproductive labour and sterile occupations, the strongly protectionist customs policy proposed there distanced the text from such influences. However, parliamentary responses to the *Informe* did refer explicitly to Smith, and Antonio

Alcalá-Galiano therefore complained that the Commission had not followed Smith and Giraudet's taxation principles and thus breached certain basic tenets such as not directly taxing productive, commercial and industrial capital. His comments were answered by Toreno, who referred to Smith as the "patron saint of political economy" and concluded, like Argüelles, that Smith had not opted for a specific tax and that the Commission had tried to apply his maxims, while at the same time raising his criticism of customs duties. Toreno also criticised Antillón's positions from a Smithian point of view, deeming them Physiocratic due to the central importance Antillón gave to land as the sole source of wealth.[17]

The enacting of the decree of 13 September gave rise to a number of reactions in published form. Noteworthy among these were texts by Duaso (1814), Plana (1820), who followed in the former's footsteps, and López-Juana Pinilla (1814a; 1814b). None of their writings show any particular acceptance of Smith's ideas;[18] however, they contain clear echoes of Say's doctrine of taxation, especially on questions of limiting state intervention and the desirability of neutrality and voluntary taxation, which was best achieved by taxing consumption or expenditure. This did not prevent some writers, especially Duaso, from reviving Necker and Steuart's conceptions of finance, as well as the line proposed by Vicente Alcalá-Galiano.[19]

Beyond the reflections prompted by the Cortes of Cádiz, it is useful to refer to some publications on taxation that were directly influenced by Smith, if more for use as a general framework for interpretation than to follow his specific guidelines. This is certainly the case with agrarian economist Ramón Cañedo (1814). His work's overall approach, which was typical of the late Enlightenment and opposed the *única contribución* of 1813, showed clear signs of Smith's influence, albeit more tacitly than explicitly (Cañedo 1814, 37–38, 92–93), in its references to individual interest, the principles of security, freedom and property ownership and tariff policy, defending the latter only in very exceptional cases and for national security reasons. Where taxation was concerned, Cañedo took up Smith's distinction between productive and unproductive work, warning that capital should not be taxed excessively so as not to diminish the former. He also proposed a mixed system, taxing the consumption of certain luxury goods and levying moderate taxes that would be paid and could be collected quickly and cheaply; again, very much in Smith's style.

Morant's *Discurso sobre contribuciones* (1820) showed various affinities with Cañedo. A member of the Ministry of Finance, Morant argued against direct taxes, adhering instead to the mixed tradition represented by Alcalá-Galiano; he advocated the reform of the current mixed system, indirect taxes and *rentas provincials* and levying light direct taxes on property, trade and industry. To defend this approach Morant cited various examples from Spain, such as Jovellanos, Arriquíbar, Ward, Cabarrús and Alcalá-Galiano, as well as foreign thinkers like Montesquieu, Mirabeau, Necker, Say, Canard, Steuart and, particularly, Smith. Described as "the prince of economists", Morant referred to a range of sometimes lengthy quotations from the WN on issues such as the defence of indirect taxation, capitation, the impossibility of ascertaining individual wealth as the basis for direct taxation, and data on the taxing of bread in Holland and coal in Great Britain (Morant 1820, 8, 10ff., 20, 54, 70, 74).

## Reading Smith through Say

The rise of industrialism from 1800 to 1820 was inseparable from the growing acceptance of Say's work. It was translated with great enthusiasm from 1804–1806, when the first Spanish version of the *Traité d'économie politique* (1803) appeared, followed by versions of *Epitome* and *Cathecisme*.[20] This did not only contribute to the indirect dissemination of Smith's work, but also helped to reinforce a view of industrialisation that was more positive and optimistic than Smith's. Moreover, like Garnier, Peuchet and other free market agrarians, and in contrast to the "economists of the nation", Say did not abandon free trade principles. However, Say's first Spanish followers (Jaumeandreau, Gutiérrez, Orense) realised that he had not simply made a compilation of Smith's ideas, and identified notable differences between the two authors with regard to methodology, the theory of value, productive labour and the formation of capital. In addition, as had previously been the case with Garnier (c.1796, 4–11), not only did they criticise the method and explanatory criteria used in the WN, but they accused Smith of having made mistakes. which, as the Spanish press of the day highlighted,[21] had largely been corrected by Say.

This partially critical view of Smith flourished among the promoters of the first university chairs in political economy to emerge at the end of the 1810s. Jaumeandreu, who held the Barcelona Chair, was the author of the only teaching handbook published between 1807 and 1823; based on a summary of Say's work (Martín 1989, 43), it contained a wide range of criticisms of Smith. These went beyond the rejection of the free market and covered issues linked to both form—poor organisation—and content, relating to its theories of value and capital, support for colonial trade and policies on education and the administration of justice (Jaumeandreu 1816, VII, 45, 102, 105, 216, 274, 277–78). In his 1818 *Discurso* to inaugurate the Economics Chair promoted by the Consulate of Malaga, its holder Gutiérrez, who was also Say's translator, stressed that Smith's work contained errors and a number of "obscure truths," which had been resolved by Say, the true architect of political economy's conversion into an exact science (Gutiérrez 1819, 20). Not only did Gutiérrez overwhelmingly prioritise Say over Smith, but he also intertwined Say's ideas with those of authors who both predated him (Verri, Genovesi, Steuart et al.) and came after him, such as Destutt and Ganilh, who were used instead of Smith to present the different systems of political economics. Lastly, in Orense's written application for the Madrid Chair, the brief quotations from Smith relating to class division, mechanisation and the critique of Physiocracy were contrasted with quotations from Say, around whom the text was structured (Orense 1820, 10, 12, 14, 15). All these works stressed that Say's work's concise and methodical nature made it more suitable for teaching—a replacement for the WN had been sought to promote the study of political economy since 1796, when the translation of

Garnier's *Abrégé* was written (c.1796, 17)—as well as being an essential milestone, together with Ganilh, in establishing political economy's independence as a discipline from political arithmetic and statistics (Luna 1819). In short, Jaumeandreu, Gutiérrez and Orense's works all showed that the shift towards Say and his defence of the new industrial order had strong supporters at the opening of the Liberal Triennium Courts in 1820.

## Final remarks

Readership of the WN increased notably during the first two decades of the nineteenth century. In conjunction with other contemporary sources, especially the works by Say, Garnier and Ganilh, the book contributed to political economy's emergence as a science with its own academic status (Steiner 1995). During 1800–1820 six editions or reissues of different kinds of the WN saw the light, so that it is not entirely true, as Palyi (1966 [1928], 191) emphasises, that Smith became popular in Spain through Say. Moreover, the two first decades of the nineteenth century proved to be different regarding the previous period on two issues: on the one hand, a greater focus given to theoretical principles of the WN; on the other, a wider application of the WN's ideas beyond public finances including, among other issues, its use in the debates about the most appropriate strategy of economic development for Spain. Unlike all this, reading of the WN remained fragmentary and eclectic—without any pejorative connotation. In Spain there were almost no pure Smithian economists, solely eclectic doctrinal positions that qualified the theories in the WN and intermingled them with those of late Enlightenment Spanish economists, thus dissolving some of the most innovative contents of Smith's work. Furthermore, while some translations of the WN from the time were faithful versions, some contained significant theoretical departures from the original (Luna and Jaumeandreu); but the fact that the WN failed to become firmly established facilitated the successful emergence of Say's work, which fairly quickly began to dominate Spanish intellectual circles after the War of Independence. In fact, as in France or Germany, during this period the WN became a canonical work in Spain (Carpenter 2002), althought, as was, in particular, the German case, its principles were not completely understood (Tribe 1988).

Acceptance of the WN was patchy and uneven. This can be explained firstly by the problems involved in achieving a single interpretation of the book, which stemmed from attempts to reconcile it with other economic doctrines and, secondly, in the nature of Spain itself, which was economically backward and barely industrialised and in which Ancien Régime structures were still well established. The work was less influential than it could have been, given the extent to which it was circulated and known; at the same time, as generally occurred during the late eighteenth century, it was mainly read in the light of its usefulness in the debates and economic reforms promoted by the Enlightenment and early Spanish liberals (Perdices 2000a). On many occasions, and more tacitly than explicitly, the WN contributed to the deepening of liberal tendencies in Spain over the last 30 years of the eighteenth century, especially with regard to the creation of an institutional framework based on free initiative and individual economic rights. Nevertheless, many of the old obstacles to liberalisation remained and, although the WN favoured the emergence of the first free market currents, protectionist positions continued to hold sway.

The development strategies met a similar fate: the WN helped to extend the liberal agrarianism that characterised the Spanish Enlightenment mainstream in the second half of the eighteenth century, but it was less relevant in the defence of industrialism, especially in comparison with the role played by other doctrinal currents. In terms of specific economic policy on issues such as the guilds, the grain trade and entailed estates, this Enlightenment current contributed to the consolidating of liberal positions, but around pragmatic compromise formulas that were usually more moderate than those put forward in the WN. The work's relative ambiguity in key areas such as taxation meant that its principles were accepted in a broad sense, even though they were later vindicated by different ideological currents and intermingled with demands for reform originating in the previous century.

## Notes

1　See Chapters 3 and 6 in this volume.
2　Written in the context of the conservative University of Cervera, both Dou's personal library and that of the university itself were very limited. This is reflected in the scant references to writers on economics in the work: Smith, Jovellanos, Uztáriz, Ulloa, Campomanes, Ward and Galiani. According to Lluch (1973), the last two had most influence on Dou.
3　Lluch (1973, 201). The work closes with a brief sixth section with the title "On private individuals, whose interests are linked with those of the nation," in which lengthy paragraphs from the WN on the three factors of production are transcribed.
4　See Chapter 9 of this book.
5　Smith's imprint on the latter was limited to a defence of the general principles of taxation; on his work, see López (2000, 351–68).
6　Alonso López has been included in the list of authors that defended the priority of agriculture and a liberal industrialism (Dopico 2005). His *Consideraciones generales* (1820) contained a couple of tacit references to the WN but none of them referred to development strategies. Alonso criticised Smith for using abstract generalisations when market price determination is explained in WN. There is also a reference to Smith regarding the estimation of the quantity of metallic money in England (Alonso López 1820, I, 174; II, 275).
7　For a general framework, see San Julián (2000).
8　Cited by Almenar (1997, 150).
9　Following Lluch (1992; 2001).
10　Following Sánchez (2005; 2018).
11　See Chapter 9 in this book.
12　See Chapters 3 and 7 in this volume.
13　See especially Uriortua's reform project (Uriortua 1811), reviving the old scheme to establish an *única contribución* on land, that would apply to all social classes

including the clergy and the nobility. This would replace the unfair and "barbarous fiscal system" of *rentas provinciales* and monopolies, based on a rigorous defence of individual rights to property ownership and freedom and on a personal interpretation of Smithian principles of taxation and public expenditure.

14 Due to their breadth and depth, our analysis is especially indebted to the works of López (1995; 1999).

15 Canga Argüelles's writings contain references to a wide range of authors, such as Spanish writers Ensenada, Martínez de Mata, Campomanes, Gándara and Zavala, among others, and Verri, Colbert, Sully, Young and also Smith; however, the most important are Garnier, Sismondi and Necker (López 1999, lxiv).

16 Martínez de Montaos (1813) and Luyando (1813a; 1813b). The first of Luyando's two works received an answer from Gómez Rombaud (1813).

17 Cited through López (1999, cxxvii, cxxx, xxxv, cxxxix).

18 This is also true of López de Araujo's work (1813).

19 There is a specific analysis of Duaso and Plana's contributions in López (2010).

20 The most thorough analysis is in Menudo and O´Kean (2005; 2019).

21 MHP, 15-III-1804, 355–84; 31-III-1804, 426–39. The publication was then known as the *Mercurio de España*.

# 9 "Readings" of Adam Smith's *The Wealth of Nations* by Spanish economists, 1820–1840

*José M. Menudo*

## Introduction

There is a vast array of literature that tackles in depth the way in which Smith was received in Spain, but it focuses essentially on the translation and circulation of *The Wealth of Nations* (WN) in Spanish or on the dissemination of Classical thought in Spain.[1] Among the few papers on "readings" of the WN in Spain, Schwartz (1990) argued that Smith's influence in Spain concluded in 1814, specifically in the opening lesson for the Chair in Political Economy of the Provincial Council of Mallorca, where Jaumeandreu mentions the decree of 8 June 1813 to emphasise that Say's work would take precedent in the teaching of economics in Spain and that Smith was "hardy methodical." Lluch and Almenar (2000) claim his influence extended until 1820, including Luna and the early writings of Flórez Estrada and Canga Argüelles. Finally, Perdices (2000a) offers the longest timeframe of influence for the WN, encompassing specifically up to the free trade work of Pastor in the 1860s, concluding that neither teachers nor politicians preferred Smith, but that Say became the preferred author in teaching and Bastiat the key reference for politicians.

This chapter provides a systematic review of the economic works published by Spanish authors between 1820 and 1840, with a view to analysing national "readings" of the WN. We begin by examining the sources through which such works entered Spain, once summaries and partial translations had become popularised. We also intend to define which of the five books into which the WN was divided were the most influential in order to know the issues or question in which Smith had the greatest presence. Finally, we examine whether Smith's line of thinking was linked to any school, current or group of authors, and the criteria used to establish such links.

To answer these questions, we analyse the "readings" of the WN offered between 1820 and 1840, distinguishing texts linked to teaching from those published to address specific issues. We began this work with an introductory section on the complex institutionalisation of economics teaching in nineteenth-century Spain. We then analyse the major economics textbooks and manuals published by national authors. The second part of this chapter will

DOI: 10.4324/9781003152804-11

focus on studying economic publications on particular issues, such as public finances, agrarian reform, free trade or social issues.

We conclude that the WN enjoyed great prominence during the 1820s and 1830s, even though the work of Say dominated the influx of foreign works during the first half of the nineteenth century in Spain. The WN is a reference in the major handbooks used to teach economics and in public debates in which Spanish authors publish texts to defend proposals for trade policy and agrarian reform, mainly. In these writings, many mentions are made, although actual references are less frequent, and quotations are scarce. We also find that the manuals that most use and cite Smith do not use the Spanish translation of his works. This raises the question as to whether translations are an appropriate criterion for measuring a nation's intellectual underdevelopment. Finally, Smith is positioned as the forerunner who lays the foundation for turning political economy into a new science and also as a theoretical reference used both to defend free trade and advocate the use of tariffs on international trade.

## The WN in the teaching of political economy (1820–1840)

Economic science in the first half of the nineteenth century in Spain was marked by the emergence of economics as an academic subject in our country. The process of institutionalising the teaching of political economy was long and intermittent, but the dynamics were unstoppable and the obstacles were continually overcome.

The enlightened elites in the second half of the eighteenth century demanded economic teachings, and, in response, a comprehensive education programme was developed in the 1770s through two new institutions: trade consulates and economic societies. The Bascongada and Matritense economic societies took the initiative, but in both cases the creation of a chair in economics failed. In the early 1780s, the Aragon Society returned to this idea and, in 1784, the Chair in Civil Economy and Trade was founded within this society ushering in an intense period of proposals to promote economic teachings (Cádiz, Valencia, Barcelona and Madrid). But the denunciation of the professor appointed to this chair, Normante, before the Inquisition in 1786 for alleged heretical propositions contained in his teachings and the revolutionary events of France, capped expectations of generalising the Aragon experience. The last advance in economic teachings occurred around the turn of the century, through two parallel lines. On the one hand, the Royal Order of February 1796 issued by the Council of Castile incorporated mercantile studies into the traditional technical training (drawing, nautical, mathematics, etc.) provided to the trade boards and consulates. On the other hand, sporadic experiences of economic teachings continued within a diverse set of institutions: the Chair in Moral Philosophy at the Madrid College of Nobles (1779), the Academy of Law at the University of Salamanca (1788) and the Academy of Political Economy within the Mallorcan Economic Society of Friends of the Country (1793). In this initial phase of teaching institutionalisation (1776–1806), the work of

Smith played a prominent role, but it was not the sole influence. The *Lezioni di Economia Civile* by Genovesi, Cantillon through *Lecciones de Economía Civil* by Danvila, *Cartas sobre los asuntos más exquisitos de la economía política* by Foronda and *Discurso sobre Economía Política* by Ramos were also teaching texts in Spain.

Say's *Traité d'économie politique* (1803) marks the beginning of a new era. The journal *Mercurio de España* presented the *Traité* over two issues (15 and 31 March 1804), under the title *"Noticia del Tratado escrito en francés por Say."* This is an extensive commentary that begins with a brief exploration of Smith's forerunners—Steuart, Condillac, Condorcet—as this is considered the turning point after which the concept of political economy is clarified, and it distinguishes two different methods of addressing economic problems: Say's deductive method—referred to as the French method because it is also used by Condillac—and Smith's method—not named. The balance tips in favour of Say's work, which comes onto the scene in Spain with a great deal of influence, as a work of reference, in accordance with educational plan of the Marquis of Caballero of 1807. However, the teaching of economics practically ground to a halt until the restoration of Caballero's curriculum in the 1820s. In any case, the so-called Say Era in Spain was ushered in (Martín 1989, 40), during which direct influence through translations of Say's work extended from 1804 to 1846.

With the restoration of academic life and chairs in economics in the 1820s, the influence of Say's *Traité*, which was even included as part of the chair competition, intensified.[2] These times were marked by the emergence of chairs in economics and the extension of economics teachings, each of them linked to Say. At the beginning of the Liberal Triennium (1820–1823), Caballero's curriculum was taken up once more, placing political economy and statistics in the final—eighth—year of a compulsory branch of secondary education for the study of jurisprudence.[3] The subject was also extended to the new special schools for trade education, where a course in economics was also taught. Schools were created in Madrid, Málaga, Cádiz, Alicante, Barcelona, La Coruña, Bilbao and Santander (Martín 1989, 29), but the teaching of economics once again disappeared between 1823 and 1836. Subsequently, it appeared only during the sixth year of the bachelor's degree of the Faculty of Law and, from 1842 onwards, also in the fifth year of the new Faculty of Jurisprudence. Teaching of the subject gradually spread, through the appearance of administration studies, now separate from those of jurisprudence, where the subject of political economy was included during the first year (Martín 1989, 31). This expansion of teaching meant that, at the beginning of the 1840s, Spain's General Directorate of Studies decided to publish a list of works from which texts could be selected. On 9 October 1841 an initial list was drawn up, encompassing the Marquis of Valle Santoro's *Elementos de economía política con aplicación particular a España*, Flórez Estrada's *Curso de economía política*, Torrente's *Revista general de la economía política,* and Rossi's *Curso de economía política*—the following year, Droz's *Economía política, o principios de la ciencia de las riquezas* was also added.

### Orthodox academic readings of Smith

This section looks at authors who acknowledge their reference to Say, viewed as such by the secondary bibliography. Linked to teaching, they write their works while the *Traité* is being taught—sometimes by these authors themselves—in classrooms and in order to disseminate economic science. They represent alternatives to the French author by incorporating new features in the structure, adding in the form of applications to Spain's own economy, or by using references that are not inconsistent with Say. Writing in the form of a manual or handbook, the aim is to differentiate themselves from Say but not to distance themselves too much, either through fear of falling into a theoretical vacuum or of seeing doors closed to them in classrooms accustomed to the work of Say. However, all this does not imply Smith's disappearance from the textbooks.

The first author to highlight in this regard is Orense, a clear example of the need to integrate Say's work into an analysis based on previous doctrines (López 2000), namely the introduction of Say's thought into schemes anchored in Physiocracy (Orense 1820), with the resulting theoretical problems and a clear manifestation of the need for theoretical evolution that goes beyond agricultural primacy. The influence of Classical economics can be glimpsed, coming mainly from Smith, evident in his ideas about capital accumulation, the division of labour, and taxation—although Orense opts for a single contribution. However, explicit references to Smith are almost non-existent, and any that are included refer to book I only.

The works of Jaumeandreu have a theoretical grounding in the writings of Say, although in this case he offers an early response to Classical economics from an industrial perspective. Jaumeandreu treads a similar path to that of Flórez Estrada and the British Classics (Martín 1989), whilst maintaining content based on Say's work. His *Rudimentos de Economía política* (1816) becomes the only Spanish-language university textbook for economics between 1807 and 1823 (Martín 1989, 43), rooted in the work of Say, to the extent that one of its objectives is to correct the work of the French economist. His modifications focus on aspects such as industrial development, protectionism and the defence of emphyteusis (Lluch 1988). Some commentators argue that Jaumeandreu tried to adapt Smithian thought to Spain just as Say had done for France. However, we do not agree that this was his objective in *Rudimentos* (1816), as Jaumeandreu himself mentions in the prologue. Here Smith's work is presented as the first systematic effort, albeit one "without order or method […]. Smith's lack of method is corrected to a large extent in the work of Say" (Jaumeandreu 1816, vii). Smith is mentioned frequently, but references to his ideas are less common. First we find the defence of legal certainty required for capital to flourish, and in this case he supports his argument with a note at the end of the book, citing chapter 1, book 2, of the WN (Jaumeandreu 1816, 322).[4] Subsequently, when addressing the issue of trade protection, Jaumeandreu attacks "Smith's system," understanding this as the exposition of the collective benefits offered by freedom of international trade (Jaumeandreu 1816, 120).

Smith is again present in the lessons on price and value, both in relation to the tendency of market prices to align with natural prices (Jaumeandreu 1816, 339) and in the use of the value of labour as an invariable measure of value:

> Q. Is there an accurate measure of values? A. None, because none has been imagined or could be imagined to be unchanging, which is the first hallmark of measurement. Q. But does the value of man's labour not serve as such a measure? A. No sir; and the reasons on which Smith founds this proposition, although plausible, are not convincing as two quantities of labour.
>
> (Jaumeandreu 1816, 216)

A quote from Smith also appears in lesson VII of book IV, once again in the notes at the end of the book, to defend the existence of high wages and low profits against the idea of a reduction in wages to increase competitiveness (Jaumeandreu 1816, 343). Finally, lesson X of book IV uses, by way of a quotation in a note, a case set out by Smith about the rise in interest rates due to an increase in capital demand (Jaumeandreu 1816, 344).

Twenty years later, Jaumeandreu revealed that his first work was only a textbook, with no greater pretension than to spread political economy, while his *Curso Elemental de Economía política* (1836) does seek to elaborate a theory critical of orthodoxy, accusing it of starting from the false benefits of free trade (Jaumeandreu 1836, I, iv). At this point in time, new influences are added to those of Say and Smith, such as Flórez Estrada, Herrenschwand and Sismondi (Martín 1989, 50), and Cantillon (Estapé 1971, 84ff). The presentation of Smith changes substantially: references to Smith move from the footnotes up to the main body of the text, they are greater in number, and even the perception of the WN changes. Now Smith is the author of the first and excellent work of political economy, after which nothing elementary is published in the eighteenth century, and comments about the absence of method disappear:

> Half a century ago Adam Smith laid out the principles of political economy, when in 1776 he published his excellent work on the nature and cause of the wealth of nations, demonstrating in it economic truths, destroying the systems that confounded them, and setting the general principles of this science on such a solid and eternal basis as reason itself.
>
> (Jaumeandreu 1836, I, iii)

The reference to Smith used in the *Rudimentos* is expanded, encompassing more topics and an increasing number of citations. Jaumeandreu brings Smith into the question of the division of labour with the case of the pin factory and the three causes that "Smith points out for the production of such a marvellous effect" (Jaumeandreu 1836, I, 29). On the question of capital, references to Smith abound, and Jaumeandreu adds to the reference to the legal certainty of investment the need to incorporate "the talents or useful knowledge of all manufacturers and members of a society […] into the national capital" (Jaumeandreu 1836, I, 52). Smith is also brought into the issue of taxation, and Jaumeandreu inserts a long quotation from the WN on the maximums necessary for taxes to cause as little damage as possible to the taxpayer and to achieve maximum collection (Jaumeandreu 1836, I, 334–36). In this case, the quotation does not correspond to the translation of Alonso or to Roucher's French translation of 1793—it is most similar to Garnier's translation of 1802. Jaumeandreu might also have used the original English text.

A second manual that featured Smith extensively was compiled by Professor Paso y Delgado, from the University of Granada. In his *Elementos de economía política* (1841), he essentially follows the path trodden by Say although he takes the reader on a journey through this subject, firstly mentioning Quesnay and Smith, then foreign contemporary authors (Say, Ricardo, Sismondi, Malthus, Ricardo, Jones and Ricci). The text makes frequent references to Smith: the pin factory (Paso y Delgado 1841, 44), natural price (127), the objectives of public expenditure (206) and the four maxims of taxation (212–14). He quotes Smith with respect to debt rates (257) and public debt (260–62), although the quotations are not taken from the translation by Alonso.

The rest of the texts used to teach political economy closely linked to Say's work make some reference to Smith but indicate that the authors had not used the WN in any of its formats. The Marquis of Valle Santoro, in his *Elementos de Economía política con aplicación particular a España* (1829), opts for an alternative approach to Say that allows him to introduce innovation in terms of content and form, but without straying too far from the French author. The alternative was Rau (Martín 1989, 51; Perdices 2000a, 288), and it worked editorially. As far as our object of study is concerned, the literature notes that Valle Santoro displayed good knowledge of Smith (Martín 1989, 14), and his *Elementos* have even been described as a "hypersimplification of the work of Smith and Say" (Smith 1968a, 328). However, analysis of the references and quotations taken from Smith would indicate the opposite. Valle Santoro uses Smith's quotes as used by Say (Valle Santoro 1840, 92), specifically the translation of Say's *Traité* by Sánchez Rivera in 1821. Another highly significant author in the teaching of the new science is Espinosa de los Monteros who, in his *Tratado de Economía Política aplicado a España* (1831), takes Say as a reference, using a disorderly and, in some cases, inconsistent structure (Martín 1989, 61). Espinosa de los Monteros does not use Smith and merely comments that the object of his work is to depart from all that he considered erroneous and to try and correct Smith and Say's mistakes. Torrente's *Revista general de la economía política* (1835) was also intended to be a textbook to be used by "university chairs in political economy." Torrente seeks an alternative theoretical reference, in this case Gioja, although he goes much further and approaches the limits of translation (Lluch and Almenar 2000, 126). He criticises Smith and Say about the possibility of increasing production without having to increase capital but without making reference to the ideas of the Scottish author (Torrente 1835, II, 8).

### Ricardian heterodoxy

So far all the authors discussed have had a doctrinal or theoretical affiliation to Say. This next section explores the texts of writers who know of Say's work, but who steer away from it, finding their foundations in economists we know as Ricardians. In this case, in the period studied here, only Flórez Estrada's textbook would fit the bill. Flórez lays the foundations for a model of growth, with three fundamental pillars in Classical economics: the division of labour, the accumulation of capital and the defence of property.

Smith enjoys a broad presence throughout the text. Right from the preliminary speech, Flórez exhibits extensive knowledge of the WN and even how it was received in France, with references to the particular interpretation of Smith given in Garnier's *Abrégé*. Smith represents the "industrial system," the third system, or "revolutions in general opinion," after the commercial and agricultural systems, which precede the birth of political economy as a science. This system is based on the consideration that wealth comes only from labour, which allows us to move beyond the two previous systems. Flórez Estrada also attributes to Smith the "wise policy [of] leaving the complete individual freedom to embrace the branch of industry that he would like." Furthermore, he denounces the policy of

> directing capital towards special branches or determining the kind of trade that should be made between the different provinces of the state or between different nations [...] because, in addition to harming the rights and interests of the individual, it is an obstacle to the economic progress of the national industry.
>
> (Flórez Estrada 1835, I, 38)

There are also references to Smith, without quotes, regarding the need to establish a salary higher than the subsistence wage (I, 334), the causes of wage differences (I, 329), Smith's maxims on taxation (II, 450), the causes of wealth in Britain (II, 191) and the determination of wages (II, 396). Similarly, Flórez Estrada considers that Smith has masterfully demonstrated the growing productivity flowing from labour division and the extension of the market.

The main effect of this division is to significantly increase the effectiveness of labour. Smith, who masterfully addressed this point, notes that the division of labour contributes to increasing the productive virtue of industry in three ways: firstly, by increasing the knowledge and skills of the worker; secondly, by providing the worker with savings in the time that would necessarily be lost if he had to suspend one occupation to move on to another; thirdly, by enabling the worker to invent machines, instruments or means of abbreviating the work (Flórez Estrada 1835, I, 110).

In this vein, he credits Smith the merit of demonstrating that "a country's industry will never become as large as it would be with the free competition of producers and consumers" (Flórez Estrada 1835, I, 38). Something similar happens regarding taxation principles (II, 450). Summing up, regarding competition, division of labour, economic freedom and taxation Smith is still a reliable source and did, according to Flórez Estrada, make permanent theoretical advances. Along with his praise for the Scottish economist, Flórez also takes time to criticise the WN:

> Despite the great merits of Smith's work, it cannot be denied that it has flaws and errors of great transcendence. The former consist of the lack of clarity, on many occasions, the lack of method or order of matters and finally the digressions with which it is filled, which, although not ever entirely useless, are so at least in relation to the matter at hand. The second consists of considering agriculture as the most productive branch of industry, claiming that internal trade is more advantageous to society than direct external trade, and believing that this branch of industry is more productive than that of transporting or chartering goods.
>
> (Flórez Estrada 1835, I, 37)

In the *Curso*, precisely, Flórez Estrada abandoned the economic development model based on the promotion of modern export-led agriculture in a free trade context that characterised his economic thought before his exile (Almenar 1980, xlvi–xlvii). Finally, Flórez Estrada points out a third group of "capital errors" like the invariability value of wheat, the links between worker's wages and the price of consumer goods or the eventual tax burden destination. Over the course of the following chapters, Flórez goes further with these criticisms with quotes from the WN: unproductive labour (I, 149; II, 263, 307), the theory of value-labour (II, 16), the definition of individual wealth (II, 50), the value of coin (II, 56), the effect of foreign trade prohibitions (II, 257), tax-raising systems (II, 331) and the effects of land tax (II, 336). Smith's quotations are a faithful translation of extracts from McCulloch's *Principles of Political Economy* (Almenar 1980); however, these quotes do not match in the different editions, which suggests that Flórez could also use a French translation of WN.[5]

Consequently, without disdaining the substantial contribution of Smith, Flórez Estrada proceeds to a systematic refutation of a broad spectrum of topics analysed by Smith in WN in the light of the then recent contributions to economic science, which in his opinion, had been made by a large group of economists like Sismondi, Lueder, Storch, Destutt de Tracy and, more recently and profoundly, by James Mill and McCulloch (Flórez Estrada 1835, I: 48). Ricardo, who also left his footsteps in *Curso*, is not mentioned, but there is no doubt about his influence (Almenar 1980: lxvi). In doing so, he picks out a series of episodes from the WN that, for the most part, he takes from McCulloch, to demonstrate that Smith's theory was but a starting point on which other Classical economists have worked to build a more advanced and consistent doctrine.

Summing up, Flórez Estrada considers that Smith's legacy is valid and useful in labour division, competition, economic freedom, commercial policy and taxation. But Smith's view has been overtaken by the advances of political economy. More than the content of the very excerpts of WN, the selection made by Flórez Estrada himself is of greater interest. Such a choice allows us to accurately assess a late reception of WN and how the Smithian doctrine as a whole is purged in a way that some elements survive, others transformed into new ones and, finally, many others surpassed by the new economic theories of the later Classical economists, and McCulloch in particular.

## Smith in books on economic policy

The economic literature of the period is not limited to the publication of manuals and textbooks, although the activity of its authors might be linked to academic life. In general, there appear to be four issues that incite the authors of the period to publish their proposals: the question of public finances, the free trade debate, agrarian reform and the social question.

### On the treasury and public administration

The first half of the nineteenth century in Spain witnessed a series of historical processes that promoted the tax reforms of the 1840s: the liberal agrarian reform, the loss of the American colonies and the administrative construction of the liberal state launched from Cádiz (Vallejo 1999). The first attempts at fiscal reform failed—the 1804 San Millán bill and the 1842 bill put forward by Surrá and Calatrava—but the tax reform law of 23 May 1845 eventually passed. During this process, a plethora of publications came out on the question of taxation in the period, and Spanish administrative science even emerged as a discipline.[6] But the presence of the WN in texts is very minor. The *Ensayo sobre la Hacienda Pública* (1820) was the first book published by the Marquis of Valle Santoro. Although this is a work of which few copies are known, it is cited in other works that deal with the management of the public treasury. The book focuses on taxation, making no reference whatsoever to Smith. There are also no references to Smith in *Examen económico, histórico-crítico de la hacienda y deuda del Estado, proyecto de su reforma general y la del banco* (1840) by Pita Pizarro or in *Situación de la hacienda pública de España en marzo de 1822, y medios de mejorarla* (1822) by López Juana Pinilla, as well as in any of the main texts on administrative sciences.[7]

   Together with *Elementos de la Ciencia de la Hacienda con aplicación a España* (1825) by Canga Arguelles (see Chapter 13), the WN appears only in reference to lending and public borrowing (1838), a translation by Pita Pizarro of excerpts from the work *La Magia del credito* (1824) by De Welz. This publication examines the work of illustrious authors who highlighted the importance of credit: Necker, Forbonnais, Melon, Genovesi, Steuart and Smith. There are no quotations or references, only mentions of the author of the WN, most often when dealing with public debt. Pita Pizarro advocates budgetary balance but argues for budgetary deficit in extraordinary situations. To defend an intermediate position, he presents Smith's arguments about the limits of the governor's role, for example, in defending the state's policies of land confiscation:

> However, as Smith showed, it is not convenient for a state to have property: firstly, because it has to entrust its cultivation to managers who do not apply the same care as private owners, constantly excited by their personal interest: secondly, because state goods become stagnant when out of circulation; and thirdly, because they are exempt from common taxations and duties.
>
> (Pita Pizarro 1838, 8)

There are also references to Smith to reject registered public debt, in other words, perpetual-time debt issues where the government could return the principal without the consent of the holder (Pita Pizarro 1838, 15).

### Debates about freedom of trade

In the first half of the nineteenth century, Spain began to take hesitant steps towards liberalising foreign trade. The 1820 decree had set out the protectionist policy, at least until Figuerola's reform of 1869. Minister Ballesteros laid down the protectionist tariff of 1825, which increased industrial costs: discriminatory tariffs on foreign flags, levy on foreign vessels, a list of balance and port duties and another list of prohibited plant general, establishing the reserved market principle that would disappear with the 1849 tariff. From 1835 onwards, free trade interventions gained support in all Spanish provinces with influence on the Board of Tariffs. Opposing them were figures such as Jaumandreu and Madoz. Smith was a reference in publications focusing on the free trade debate.

The *Memoria sobre la balanza del comercio y examen del estado actual de la riqueza en España* (1830) by Marquis of Valle Santoro was structured in a unique way. It was divided into three parts, each of which reviewed the approaches of a different author. In the first, it deals with Smith, in the second with Say, and it concludes in the third section with the considerations of the Marquis himself. Valle Santoro's review of Smith's position comes from reading the first seven chapters of the WN book IV, entitled "Of Systems of Political Economy," taking paragraphs from the Spanish translation by Alonso (Serrano 2012a). This work questions freedom of trade, defended by Smith and Say, without making any distinction between the two authors. Valle Santoro shares the theoretical approaches of Smith and Say, called absolute freedom of trade, although he points out that different national interests make the desired free trade harmony impossible.

In this line of moderate free trade we find Vadillo, who, after his *Discurso sobre los medios de fomentar la industria española y contener o reprimir el contrabando* (1821), published when the reform of tariffs was discussed in the Cortes

(Parliament), proposes a review of the arguments employed by advocates of protectionism—Chaptal and Ganilh—and of the arguments put forward by the "great economist Smith" for eliminating or, exceptionally, maintaining tariffs.[8] Vadillo had been familiar with Smith's work since 1805 when he presented a report entitled *Discursos económico-políticos: sobre la moneda en común medida de los géneros comerciables y el examen del influjo de la legislación y de los gobiernos en el valor de la moneda y del interés del dinero* (1805) at the Seville Economic Society (Vadillo 1844, 9–10)[9]. References to the WN abound, even though there are no direct quotations of Smith. In these speeches, Smith is brought into matters of international trade, interest rate determination and the issue of colonial trade. In all these cases, Vadillo provides an interpretation of Smith's arguments:

> I understand that in order to proceed methodically on this issue, we must assume two of the bases set forth by Smith. Firstly, for there to be a stimulus to buy, there needs to be a proportion to sell, because one who does not find an outlet for his goods will neither be able nor want to buy others without exchange […] Secondly, so as not to be bewildered by vague exclamations, it must be known that the matter of adopting the prohibitive system is not concerned with admitting or rejecting certain fine articles of the kind made or produced by common or ordinary people in the country for, with regard to those which are neither made nor produced in any way, and which are necessary or useful, there can be no question.
>
> (Vadillo 1844, 73–79)

Vadillo defends the welfare generated by international trade and the barriers necessary for emerging nations to be able to share in the benefits of the trade circuit. Smith's WN will also appear in a later work on colonial trade entitled *Apuntes sobre los principales sucesos que han influido en el actual estado de la América del Sud* (1829) and published in London during Vadillo's exile. This text repeats references to cases where Smith allows for tariff barriers (Vadillo 1836, 204), and the issues of colonial monopoly present in the WN are introduced (Vadillo 1836, 179).

Offering a more radical defence of free trade, we find Mora, an author almost exclusively involved in the matter of foreign trade. His economic work *De la libertad del comercio* (1843) was once again a specific essay on the tariff debate that underpins freedom of trade in Smith's arguments, although it also tackles economic problems with a specific theoretical background, in this case moving away from Say and towards Ricardo (Martín 1989; Schwartz 1999). It contains 13 chapters that analyse the influence of free trade on productive activities and that provide a defence against objections to free trade. To this end, Mora turns to the bulwarks of economic literature, such as Smith and Storch's *Traité d'économie politique*, and cites paragraphs from *Commerce Defended* by J.S. Mill and especially McCulloch. Although he opens the introduction by presenting Smith as the founder of political economy, references to the Scottish author are very few. Mora uses, in a footnote, a single quotation from Smith to define wealth as "the annual product of land and labour" (Mora 1834, xiii), taken from the *Compendio* by Martínez de Irujo or from the translation by Alonso.

At the other extreme we find Gutiérrez, a required reference in the transmission of economic ideas in Spain. In 1837, Gutiérrez published his well-known *Impugnación a las cinco proposiciones de Preber* in which, following or refuting famous economists, he presented the means used by England to impose a free trade model on all of Europe, as well as the real causes of Spain's late industrialisation (Martín 2018).[10] The only reference to Smith points out that the love for his country prevented the famous Scottish economist from expounding his true views on the limits of free trade (Gutiérrez 1837, 168). Years later, in his *Nuevas consideraciones sobre libertad absoluta de comercio* (1839), Gutiérrez returns with the same idea, now justifying Smith's exceptions to freedom of trade as an argument for his tariff proposals (Gutiérrez 1839, 102–03). In this text, Smith is presented as the father of economic science although Gutiérrez distinguishes himself from Smith on the issue of international trade:

> I translated Say's treatise, admired it then and still admire it now, because it is written with a great deal of method, and with a great deal of philosophy, because he is the disciple of Smith, to whom science owes its language and the development of its doctrines. Less well advised than today, now that years and experience have made me aware of the dangers of a freedom that flatters and seduces a fiery youth, or men with little knowledge of the administration business, I was perhaps the most fiery of his students; but I will always weep to have inspired such a dangerous doctrine in my own.
>
> (Gutiérrez 1839, 72)

In short, Smith's work was built on that same free trade debate and continues without interruption until the 1840s. Smith is a theoretical reference for both the defence of free trade and the defence of protectionism.

### The debate on agrarian reform: emphyteusis

With the dismantling of the feudal regime initiated in 1811 by the Cortes of Cádiz, different debates appear on how to define property rights and contractual relations with regard to the lands that emerge following the abolition of their lordly and ecclesiastical privileges. One of them is the recognition of the rights of emphyteusis as private property rights.

Dou enters this debate by dealing with the issue of emphyteusis and proposing this particular system so that unused lands in Spain could be exploited after civil and ecclesiastical expropriation. To defend his thesis, Dou publishes two works: *Conciliación económica y legal de pareceres opuestos en cuanto a laudemios y derechos enfitéuticos* (1829) and *Pronta y fácil ejecución del Proyecto sobre laudemios, fundada principalmente en una autoridad del Dr. Adan Smith* (1831). In both cases,

Smith is brought in to defend Dou's theses, even though emphyteusis was not a subject dealt with by the Scottish author.

The work *Conciliación económica* aims to propose "a new agrarian law, based on that of 1795 with several exceptions" (Dou y Bassols 1829, vii). The problem posed by Dou is part of the need in Spain, and also in the rest of Europe, to exploit more land. In view of the variety of proposals in circulation, the author defends the system of emphyteusis and proposes its application to the rest of the Spanish nation. Dou also proposes a number of improvements to the system and explains his rejection of certain proposed modifications to improve the situation of the leaseholder or tenant in relation to the landowner.[11] There must be arbitrage between the two parties to ensure that there are no abuses in such a long-term contractual system. To defend this necessary balance between the parties to the emphyteusis contract, Dou uses several references to Smith on two issues. Firstly, there are references to explain the exchange: the theory of the value of labour and how the exchange occurs through agreement on price in terms of man hours, the introduction of the use of coin or the types of contract established (Dou y Bassols 1829, 20–24). Dou also quotes Smith with regard to exchange (WN I, IV). The defence of agriculture is the second issue on which the WN is introduced. In his particular reading of Smith, Dou uses the WN to explain two arguments in favour of agriculture: the exclusive productivity of agriculture and the contribution of owners to the nation's prosperity:

> How Adan Smith [sic] also speaks in favour of agriculture itself, in whose work I have read two reasons, which have always seemed to me particularly convincing and subtly reasoned. [...] One is that manufacture and trade only reproduce what has been spent [...]. The other reason, I have indicated, is that Smith divides all men in a state into three classes: firstly those who have the right to rule over different species on the lands: these, he says, and rightly so, have essentially joined their interests to those of the state: no one can increase the fruit of the farm without its improvement being also of the state: one who has a mill or irrigation, which he did not have before, is richer afterwards.
>
> (Dou y Bassols 1829, vii)

Years later, Dou responds to the comments that his "project" drew, in a short essay, the aforementioned *Pronta y fácil ejecución del Proyecto sobre Laudemios* (1831). The text begins with a quote from chapter II, book V, of the WN, in which Smith proposes the sale of uncultivated public land to farmers. This increase in farmlands would increase production, population and public revenue. Dou ponders what happens if there are no owners who want to buy the land. The emphyteusis contract overcomes this difficulty because the tenant or leaseholder can be a farmer without resources and the agreement generates the same positive consequences as a purchase–sale. This presentation would be the motivation to begin responding to the objections made to his proposal to extend the practice of emphyteusis throughout Spain.

### Debate surrounding the "social question"

Smith's work is a central theme in the controversy between Sagra and Flórez Estrada regarding property rights. Sagra publishes an article in *El Corresponsal* (19 December 1839), entitled "Propiedad", where he comments on the work *La Cuestión Social* by Flórez and states that the latter has not understood Smith's definition of wealth: "A staunch supporter of Smith's doctrine, Mr. FLÓREZ ESTADA cites him as an oracle, whose decisions may not be doubted, and bases upon this his own proposition to draw consequences, the meaning of which subsequent economists have failed to grasp." In *La cuestión social, o sea origen latitud y efectos del derecho de propiedad* (1839), Flórez Estrada argues that the consequence in the lives of peasants of concentrating land in the hands of a few landowners was that:

> the subsistence of these [peasants] was precarious, for either they could not work since they had not obtained the permission of the one who, without further entitlement than his own will, called himself the owner, or, if they were working, were unable to obtain the full reward for their exerts.
>
> (Flórez Estrada 1839, 9)

Flórez had opposed Mendizabal's confiscation of land because he considered that the purchase of land could not be considered an investment and because it would concentrate land ownership to an even greater degree. Essentially, his alternative was the nationalisation of all agricultural lands, which would then be leased via emphyteusis to settlers, something he himself defines as "almost ownership," turning these rents into public revenues. This proposal was popular among those who:

> claim that man owes any goods and amenities he enjoys to ownership and that it deserves such consideration that the object of a well-constituted society can be none other than that of protecting it […] the others, on the contrary, say that property is the germ of all the physical and moral calamities that afflict this wretched humanity […]. In order to discern them from one another, I believe it is necessary to constantly take Smith's principle as a guide; the first are in perfect harmony with this, the latter in the most complete discordance.
>
> (Flórez Estrada 1839, 6–7)

He found in Smith's theory on the value of labour a theoretical foundation to consider that land cannot be owned. Work is the origin or cause of wealth and it is a natural right for each individual to own the product of their labours. The question is to apply the right of ownership only to the product of labour, and land is not the product:

> the effects of the right to ownership, we will find that, when it is strictly limited to the objects that are the product of labour, the idea of those who

consider it as the origin of all the physical and moral progress of society is accurate in all its parts. Hence, the idea of those who consider it the primary cause of the various calamities endured by humanity is erroneous and absurd.

(Flórez Estrada 1839, 6–7)

Sagra does not share the notion that an economist, such as Smith, can obtain any solution from those who consider that "ownership is not in line with the future progress of human society" (Sagra 1839, 1). Sagra refutes Flórez Estrada's proposal because it makes no sense to hand over land to a population

without capital, without knowledge, without direction, or space to develop […] In vain the government would offer limited lots of land to those with no more than their own nails to dig it. How often have they been offered without result!

Flórez published *Contestación de Don Álvaro Florez Estrada* (1840) in response to Sagra regarding his interpretation of Smith and many other questions. He says that, in spite of his respect for the Scottish author, his "work of economics" is full of criticism for Smith, both those known to all and errors that Flórez himself has discovered, as in the case of territorial contributions (Flórez Estrada 1840, 4). He adds in his reply that Sagra himself, in *Lecciones de economía social* (1840), praises Smith for linking wealth to labour. But these are not isolated comments; Flórez devotes much of the work to discussing the relationship between his idea of ownership and the "Smithian principle," that is, that "wealth is the product of man's industrialism and which man desires" (Flórez Estrada 1840, 15).

## Conclusions

Although the work of Say dominated the influx of foreign works during the first half of the nineteenth century in Spain, the WN was very present in these decades. Through a systematic review of the economic works published by Spanish authors between 1820 and 1840, we conclude that the WN is a reference in the main manuals and textbooks used to teach economics, *Curso de economía política* by Flórez Estrada and *Curso elemental de economía política* by Jaumeandreu. The WN also appears in public debates where Spanish authors publish texts to defend political economy proposals, such as trade policy, tax reforms or agrarian reform. Especially interesting is Smith's limited presence in the texts on public finances, even though Smith was a key reference in the sections on taxation in some political economy manuals.

The issues or problems in which Smith enjoys the greatest presence are free trade, value and prices, taxation, the division of labour and wealth. On these and other issues where Smith appears less frequently, references are supplemented by Smith's "doctrines"—for example, Smith's maximums on taxation—or quotes from the WN. The sources of these quotes are diverse. Some use the translation of Alonso, French translations of Smith, original editions and indirect references, for example, the use of Smith's quotations used by Say in his own writings. In particular, the manuals that most use and cite Smith do not use the Spanish translation. This raises the question as to whether translations are an appropriate criterion for measuring a nation's intellectual underdevelopment.

Finally, we examined whether Smith's line of thinking was linked to any school, current or group of authors. In textbooks, Smith is often presented as the forerunner to economic science or as a member of the group of authors that lay the foundations for turning political economy into a new science. Also in trade policy debates, Smith is positioned as a reference among authors who advocate free trade. There is no use of a specific approach established by Smith as an argument against protectionism.

## Notes

1 Regarding research exclusively devoted to the translation of the WN into Spanish, see, for example, Lasarte (1976), Fuentes and Perdices (1996), Calderón (2000) or Schwartz (2001). On Classical thought in Spain, see Smith (1957a; 1968a), Almenar (2000a), Lluch and Almenar (2000) or Menudo (2016).

2 The Spanish translation of the *Traité d'Economie politique* was introduced as a textbook in the Chair of Civil Economy and Trade of the Aragonese Economic Society by its holder in 1807, Rivera, and would continue to be used in the teachings of Alcaide (1815–1821) and Soto y Barona (1828–1836), translator of Say´s *Catéchisme* (Martín 1989).

3 In 1814, a general restructuring of teaching was attempted, following a report of the University of Salamanca, which entailed a greater presence of political economy at three levels of teaching. A 10-year period of secondary education was established before entering the faculty, with an added year for those wishing to study jurisprudence, where the subject of political economy and statistics was inserted (Martín 1989: 28), in addition to one subject in the bachelor of jurisprudence—political economy—and another in the doctorate—trade and its laws—recommending the *Traité* by Say as the textbook. However, the reform was not ultimately implemented due to Ferdinand VII's ascension to the throne that same year, marking a return to the 1771 curriculum, which did not include the subject of economics.

4 He seems to use the translation of Alonso (II, 16), but there are differences noted when comparing the two texts.

5 "The same capital and labour employed in manufacturing, Smith says, can never provide such a large reproduction as when it is used in agriculture. In manufacturing, nature does nothing; everything is the work of man: and the result of the production of wealth must always be provided to the agents who cause it" (Flórez Estrada 1835, I, 149). "The same capital or work employed in manufacturing, Smith says, can never occasion such a large reproduction as if used in agriculture. In manufacturing, nature does nothing, rather man does everything; and reproduction must necessarily be provided to the agents who cause it" (Flórez Estrada 1831, 170).

6 Gómez de la Serna, Oliván and Posada Herrera all wrote administrative science handbooks, and the Special School of Administration was set up in Madrid.

7 *Exposición a Fernando VII* (1826) by Burgo or *De la administración pública en relación a España* (1843) by Oliván.

8 On Vadillo's ideas on free trade, see Martín (2012, 244–49).

9 The works *Discursos económico-políticos: sobre la moneda en común* and *Discurso sobre los medios de fomentar la industria española*, among others, were published jointly in 1844 under the title *Discursos económicos-políticos y sumario de la España económica de los siglos XVI y XVII.*

10 Gutiérrez devoted three articles to hemp, linen and cottons, respectively, in which he again explained his idea that national production had to be protected by an appropriate use of tariffs: "Why should we pay the wages of foreign industry and condemn our own, Ganilh rightly argued, refuting Smith's chimeric freedom, founded on specious reasons and the insignificant example of the father seeking thrift in all objects of trade?" Neither the division of labour, which increased productivity, nor the lower cost of consumption, were sufficient arguments in the face of the advantages of preserving domestic incomes (Martín 1989, 127).

11 Like other Catalan authors, Dou has a very optimistic view of this system (Lluch 1973, 207). In fact, Lluch (1973) suspects Dou's criticism of Oliver's proposals to reform the emphyteusis contract.

# Section III

# Institutions

# 10 Adam Smith in the Spanish press, 1780–1808

*Jesús Astigarraga*

## Introduction: the Spanish press in its "Golden Age"

In the early 1780s the Spanish press entered a period of brilliance described as its "Golden Age." It began in 1781, the year that *El Censor* (EC), one of eighteenth-century Spain's most emblematic journals, was published, and lasted—although not without a few ups and downs—until 1808.[1] This period saw an exponential increase in the number of titles published, both in Madrid and the provinces, and the fact that it was relatively long-lived was closely linked to an improvement in quality. All this was connected to factors that were both internal and external to the press itself: in the first place, it was a consequence of population growth and a rise in literacy levels, both of which created a larger potential readership. It was also the result of improvements in circulation due to advances in editing techniques and reduced postage costs, together with the emergence in the "Republic of Letters" of new cultural agents, the "scribblers" or "public writers" epitomised by Joaquín Ezquerra, Cristóbal Cladera, Luis García Cañuelo and other "journalists" of the *fin de siècle* generation (Álvarez Barrientos 1999, 31–32). This flourishing period was also underpinned by the shift from private funding and patronage to the subscription system, which began to become widespread during the 1780s (Larriba 2013, 22–24), while other favourable influences were the "proto-liberal" cultural climate that was gradually being established and the campaign in support of freedom of expression and the press led by emblematic Enlightenment figures such as León Ángel de Gándara, Miguel Arroyal, Manuel Aguirre, Francisco Cabarrús and, mainly, Valentín Foronda: his "*Disertación sobre la libertad de escribir*" (1780) is considered a turning point in the process leading up to the Cortes de Cádiz' recognition of the right to freedom of the press in 1812 (Larriba 2012, 19–41). In turn, the print law reform decreed on 19 May 1785 by Secretary of State Count of Floridablanca was the first government regulation aimed at promoting and protecting the press. While it abolished neither the civil and religious "double ideological filter" entailed by censorship,[2] nor political oversight of the sector, it did give the press far more room for manoeuvre and greater commitment to ideological freedom. A further contributory factor was the success of the Council of Castile's *regalista*—royalist—policy, which gradually

DOI: 10.4324/9781003152804-13

whittled away the Church's powers of censorship. In short, in the exuberance that characterised this golden age, the press became an important mouthpiece for Smith's *The Wealth of Nations* (WN).

In fact, the emerging science of political economy was so effective in carving out its own space in the "newspaper hydra" appearing during the late Spanish Enlightenment that, after a tentative beginning during the 1750s and 1760s, marked by journalistic initiatives from Juan Enrique Graef, Francisco Mariano Nifo, Mateo Antonio Barberi and Juan Pedro Saura, these years can be considered the origins of the economics press in Spain (Astigarraga 2021, 47–89). Nevertheless, most papers still carried no economic content at all or, if they did, it was almost marginal. However, there were some exceptions; multi-disciplinary journals published entire texts on political economy, while the more general, literary and cultural press carried introductions to discourses, articles, letters and essays with economic content. This was a clear sign that political economy had begun to enjoy unquestionable social recognition and to play a pioneering role in the shaping of both the public sphere and public opinion (Usoz 2015, 105–27). One outcome of this was that the discipline became not only a routine object of information among the general public, but also a benchmark of press quality and it was no accident that the golden age's best publications began to carry economic content. EC (1781–1787) was the first to do so, but it was also true of the major publications at the forefront of the regeneration of the Spanish press during the final decades of the eighteenth century: the *Miscelánea instructiva, curiosa y agradable* (ML) (1784–1808), the *Correo de Madrid o de los ciegos* (CMC) (1786–1791) and the *Espíritu de los mejores diarios literarios que se publican en Europa* (EMD) (1787–1791). Two government initiatives that represented the start of the specialist economic press in Spain surfaced in this context: the *Correo mercantil de España y sus Indias* (CM) (1792–1808) and the *Semanario de agricultura y artes dirigido a los párrocos* (SAP) (1797–1808). It was precisely this cluster of titles, which carried cultural, literary and, finally, economic content that was responsible for disseminating Smith's ideas and works in the press in the wake of the EMD's publication of the first news item about him in 1788, in a context in which the multiple ideological currents of the late Enlightenment were reaching Spain (Almenar 2000a; Lluch and Almenar 2000), and the figure of Say was beginning to emerge (Menudo and O'Kean 2019). The following lines describe the three main channels for this process: reviews and bibliographic information; adaptations, and finally, quotations and tacit and explicit mentions of Smith and the WN.

## Reviews and bibliographic information (1790–1808)

The Golden Age of the press witnessed the creation of a new cultural genre: reviews of books on political economy (Astigarraga et al. 2020). The genre was essentially created by the broadening of the seventeenth-century European tradition of journals that specialised in book reviews to include a new disciplinary field. It burst into life during the 1780s when the bibliographic information published in the two official journals of the period, the *Gaceta de Madrid* (GM) and the *Mercurio histórico y político* (MHP), was complemented by an inrush of more specialised journalistic enterprises. The ML (1784–1808), which mainly covered the book world, played a major role in this sense (Urzainqui 1990; Astigarraga 2021, 146–72). A monthly culture magazine, brilliantly edited by Joaquín Ezquerra, the ML devoted a large amount of space to books on political economy, both Spanish and translations, especially between 1784 and 1797. Furthermore, specific journals that compiled or recompiled bibliographic news had a clearer social function; they mainly followed the example of two Belgian journals that were published in French, *L'Esprit des journaux* (EDJ) (1772–1818) and the *Journal Encyclopédique* (JEN) (1756–1794), and the Spanish prime examples were Francisco and Joaquín Escartín's *Correo literario de la Europa* (CLE) (1781–1782; 1786–1787), Cristóbal Cladera's *Espíritu de los mejores diarios literarios* (1787–1791) and Blas Román, Antonio Cruzado and Antonio Ulloa's *Miscelánea instructiva, curiosa y agradable* (MI) (1796–1800). The journalists were normally the translators of reviews that had been published in foreign journals such as those mentioned above. Smith's works were thus disseminated via reviews and bibliographic news that formed part of a wider publishing operation, thanks to which these journals circulated the most important developments in political economy among the general public.

Six journals published information about Smith's works, carrying a total of 16 bibliographic news items and essays.[3] They provided information on the WN and also on other works by Smith that were less widely circulated in Spain than his economics *magnum opus*. In 1798 the ML included a lengthy review, certainly translated from French, of "Of the Affinity between Music, Dancing and Poetry," one of the chapters in *Essays on Philosophical Subjects* (1795) compiled by Dougald Stewart, clear proof that the French translation of Pierre Prevost's 1796 work had reached Spain.[4] The ML review highlighted the notion that the advance of civilisation fostered progress in the arts: in contrast to "ancient" times, in the "modern" world, dance, drama and music were no longer mere imitation arts, very close to nature. In the same year the journal published a full and very precise bibliographic reference, quite certainly the first in Spanish, of Smith's *The Theory of Moral Sentiments* (TMS) following the seventh edition of the work's French version by Sophie de Grouchy.[5]

The WN was disseminated through 13 items of reviews and book news, nine of which (reviews) were published between 1790 and 1808 and referred to the different translations and versions of Smith's work, while the other four (book news) appeared between 1800 and 1804 and were written by a variety of authors. The journals in the first group were the EMD (1), the GM (3), the CM (3) and the MI (2). The reviews, one of which appears twice, referred to translations by two French writers, Jean-Antoine Roucher (1) and Germain Garnier (3),[6] and two Spaniards, Carlos Martínez de Irujo (2) and José Alonso Ortiz (3).[7] They all appeared without by-lines, although those in the ML and EMD can be assumed to have been written by the editors, Joaquín Ezquerra and Cristóbal Cladera, respectivley.

The reviews' main social function was to attract readers to the WN, in accordance with the enlightened scheme of encouraging the reading of "useful writings" lauded by Campomanes, the powerful *Fiscal* of the Council of Castile, and other distinguished Spanish economists. It is thus no accident that the appearance of these reviews coincided with the publication of different versions of the WN. This was the case with details of Martínez de Irujo's version (Smith 1792), published in the CM and the GM in 1792, the year that the book appeared,[8] and three pieces devoted to Alonso Ortiz's translation (Smith 1794). All of them were on the first line of what Tribe (2002a, 8ff.) calls the "construction of a reputation." The first of these appeared in the GM in 1794 and unabashedly aimed to promote what was actually the first complete Spanish version of the work.[9] To this end, pieces of text from Alonso Ortiz's "*El traductor*" were copied—Smith's "deep understanding" of political economy "made him conceive of and put into practice the idea of reducing it to basic method"[10]—along with other details, all with the purpose of guaranteeing that the work would have a good reception in Spain, as it had had in other countries, including Britain, where, as the review remembered, several editions had already been issued. As a piece published recently in the GM had done,[11] the review identified the book's potential readership, which included members of the economic societies, civil servants and high-ranking government officials. Undoubtedly aiming to attract their attention, the text highlighted the fact that Alonso Ortiz's work had been adapted for Spain: his version not only included "several illustrations and appendices on points relating to Spain," but also various "notes and appendices provided by the translator, many news items and thoughts regarding our nation to facilitate the application of these principles and make it more interesting to read."[12] The two reviews published in the ML in 1794 and 1795 also carried information taken from Alonso Ortiz's "*El traductor*"; they included biographical information about Smith, praise for the work and reports of its success in the publishing world. However, Ezquerra wisely devoted a good part of these reviews to detailing the index and contents of Smith´s WN.

The three reviews of Garnier's French version followed a similar pattern. The piece published in the CM in January 1802 warned readers that it was not about an edition in use, but a "new translation with a great many notes and observations,"[13] and went on to provide a detailed list of the contents. A new review of a work by Garnier devoted to a brief booklet aiming to contrast Smith with the Physiocrats appeared in the CM in January 1808, coinciding with the booklet's publication the previous year;[14] the GM copied it in its entirety a month later.[15] Not only did the review underline the superiority of Smith's work over that of the Physiocrats, but, by remarking on "the way and method" that should be used to study the WN, also highlighted its potential for use in teaching,[16] once government minister José Antonio Caballero had introduced the teaching of political economy into Spanish universities in 1807.

Over and above the purpose of making the WN more accessible to readers and underscoring the possibilities of applying it in a variety of contexts, such as Spain, other reviews appeared to be aiming to fulfil a different function: promoting the translation of the work into Spanish. This is certainly true of the first piece, which was published in the EMD in 1790 when there was still no Spanish version of the WN.[17] As was usually the case with Cladera, the editor of the magazine, it was not an original review but the translation of one that had appeared in the JEN. The aim was to publicise Roucher's French translation and, for the first time in the Spanish press, the headline consisted of a correct translation of the book's full title. The review praised Smith handsomely: he was described as the best interpreter of a commercial society in which avarice had become "the only bond between men" and in which any restriction of personal freedom "whether in industry or commerce, can have no other effect than to hinder the multiplying of wealth."[18] However, there was a second objective: in spite of the continuing demand for a French translation of Smith, and the fact that Roucher was a renowned translator, the author was unsparing in his criticism of the quality of the French version. Not only did it contain numerous misstatements, contradictions and errors, but it was also inferior to the anonymous 1776 French version, which, moreover, it had copied "word for word": "the new translator can only be understood when he uses the same expressions as the previous one."[19] Roucher's use of Condorcet's name on the front of his translation, far from being a guarantee of quality, could only be interpreted as bait to attract readers. In short, the review was a sharp warning for forthcoming Spanish translations of the WN.

It should be recalled that the publishing venture surrounding Smith and his work was in fact part of a larger project, which was the creation of a new readership for the new science of political economy. It is thus important to understand that the review genre was also useful for presenting different opinions, some of them critical, of the WN and this can be said of four reviews in which less prominent authors appraised the work. The most favourable to Smith appeared in the MI and was devoted to *Sketch on the Causes of the Advance and Decline of Nations* (London, 1795). The review presented this anonymous British work as "a supplement to Smith's excellent treatise"; in fact, it was one of the many summaries generated by the WN, hence its usefulness for a readership such as that in Spain. The recognition that Smith deserved in the historical development of economics was no impediment to the aspiration to turn political economy into an "exact science," being "almost new" and a far cry from being reduced to "a small number of simple and irrefutable principles." The review had a fiscal orientation (the work was subtitled: *Structures on Systems of Finance, Particularly Applied to those of France and Great Britain*) and was favourable to the WN, in which, in the face of the harmful practices of the "mercantile system," its central theory stood out. However, it was particularly useful in the context of Spain as it judged the "issuing of paper currency to be the fairest and least ruinous type of extraordinary contribution that can be imagined," and presented a comparison of Britain and France's financial situations that was favourable to the former: Britain had fewer resources but almost the same level of expenditure as France.

Other visions of Smith's work with more critical connotations surfaced though three reviews devoted to analysing the works of French authors Charles-Philippe-Toussaint Guiraudet and Jean Baptiste Say. The two covering the former's work (*Doctrine sur l'impôt,* 1799) in the MI and the CM in 1800 were genuine rebuttals of Smith, especially his ideas on taxation:[20] the Scottish economist had embraced false theories; he had done nothing more than "modify the Physiocrats' doctrine,"[21] and lay down principles that were simply unrealistic, as were his famous four rules of taxation. Moreover, he was far from being a successful author: his theories on foreign trade and the national debt had few supporters in Britain itself. A lengthy review of Say's *Traité d'Économie Politique* (1803) published in 1804 is perhaps more significant.[22] As well as publicising Say's work, the content of which was described in detail, it also aimed to show-case its strengths vis-à-vis Smith's book. Although the anonymous author did qualify some of Say's criticisms of the WN, so as not to undermine Smith's work, the review stressed the discrepancies between the two texts rather than the similarities. A substantial part of the criticism was aimed at the question of method: Say's synthetic and deductive method was more appropriate than Smith's analytical and inductive approach, so much so that Smith's work did not fit in with the French tradition: some of Smith's passages were obscure and were a far cry from the method adopted for basic books in France. Say's *Traité* was reappraised: its merit consisted in the "many new things it contains and its novel and original way of expressing the truths that Smith had presented previously."[23] In short, the review was a vindication of economic science, but its aim was to invite readers to incline towards Say's *Traité*, following majority opinion in France, where it undoubtedly originated. In a way it set limits on the circulation of Smith's writings prior to the appearance of Say's work and, in a more general sense, exemplified the fact that the review genre had reached maturity in the hands of the journalists writing during the late Enlightenment in Spain: it did not only educate and inform readers, but it did so with an overtly critical eye.

## An adaptation of Smith's work: Samuel Crumpe's *Essay* (1793)

Throughout the months of November and December 1802 the SAP published a very broad synopsis of Irish scientist Samuel Crumpe's *An Essay on the Best Means of Providing Employment for the People* (1793; 2nd ed. 1795) in four consecutive instalments.[24] By then the work had been translated into both German (1796) and French (1801), and it was the latter version that facilitated its arrival in Spain. In 1801 Adrien Dusquenoy had included the French version in his lengthy *Recueil de mémoires sur l'établissemens d'humanité* of essays devoted to public health, hospitals and hospices (Dusquenoy 1798–1804; Crumpe 1801). The collection contained descriptions of numerous European experiences in all these areas of caring for the sick, including those of the Madrid Hospice, and included various reports by distinguished enlightened thinkers. Given the special attention paid to policy towards the poor, it is not surprising that the work of American-born British scientist Sir Benjamin Thompson, Count of Rumford, occupied a place of relative importance in the work—his contribution opens the collection—nor that other iconic authors such as François de La Rochefoucauld and Jeremy Bentham were also included. The *Recueil* was entirely the personal endeavour of its science editor, Dusquenoy himself. He was not only a politician and member of the Constituent Assembly, but was also a prolific translator of authors such as the German statistician Hock, Rumford and Bentham, and was among the first to introduce the two latter writers into France. However, it was not a private initiative but a commission from the Ministry of the Interior that encouraged the collecting of the most important information on charitable institutions from around Europe with the aim of designing a complete overhaul of the French hospice system (Dusquenoy 1798–1804, I, 1–4). The result was a highly diverse and lengthy work, which was used extensively by Juan Antonio Melón, the SAP's chief editor. He took numerous extracts from it that related to policy towards the poor, one of his publication's main topics. From 1800 onwards Rumford's immense work was included and he became one of the journal's star turns. The SAP in fact provided an ideal route for Rumford's entry into Spain, at the same time as his *Essais politiques, économiques et philosophiques* (1799–1806) were partially translated in 1801 on the initiative of the *Sociedad Ecónomica Matritense*—the Madrid Economic Society.

Crumpe's *Essay* was a highly significant piece of work. It had been awarded a prize by the Royal Irish Academy in 1792 for the foremost dissertation on the "best system of national education." The main theme was how to "provide a general occupation for the entire population" and how to "make them industrious" (Crumpe 1793, 7, 17). The work was divided into two parts, one dealing with theory and the other applying the theory to the specific context of Ireland. The version in the SAP carried a summarised translation of the first part and appeared to contain signs of censorship (or self-censorship): for example, a quotation from a text by Rousseau was omitted, as was the idea that establishing colonies in New Holland had not civilised the inhabitants but had instead made them "attacher plus fortement à leur état de barbarie originelle" (Dusquenoy 1798–1804, X, 35). However, the SAP version's defining feature is that it was actually a summary of the original and left out most of the references to Ireland as well as quotations from a variety of authors such as Davenant and, more especially, the many citations devoted to its main source: the WN. Crumpe's treatise was not a summarised version of Smith's work but an astute adaptation. The author repeatedly acknowledged his debt to the WN, which he deemed an "ouvrage politique inestimable" and "un fond inestimable de connaissances politiques" (Dusquenoy 1798–1804, X, 26, 101), and from which he copied numerous passages word for word. He also cited other authors, such as Davenant, Franklin, Hume, Raynal, Steuart, Morellet and Uztáriz, frequently by means of the quotations that appeared in the WN itself.

The work's structure was relatively simple. Its starting point was a study of the means by which individuals became industrious in a "state of civilisation." Where this issue was concerned, Crumpe stressed the importance of imitation as a key factor underpinning industriousness, an idea that he took from Hume. He went on to detail the obstacles to increasing employment levels, using a variety of central ideas from the liberal analysis at the heart of the WN, especially books I and II. If labour were the source of wealth, wages that were above subsistence level were the main guarantee of population growth and industriousness. The latter required the suppression of social ills and the creation of a good education system. For its part, the level of employment was determined by the rate of economic growth, which in turn depended on capital accumulation, and this was therefore the factor that ultimately boosted industriousness and occupation. However, given the fact that employment was "the most sacred" of all rights, society's institutional and legal framework had to be built on the principles of property, freedom and security so that all individuals could freely choose the occupation that most benefited them. For its part, capital accumulation required individuals to be thrifty, avoid extravagance and circumvent various erroneous public policies: "the use [...] capital is one of the best means of encouraging industry among people. This, says Smith, is its chief origin and most secure support."[25] Franchises and privileges, exclusive trading companies, guilds and restrictions to free domestic trade, the main source of wealth, seriously damaged the cornerstones of economic growth. This was also true of certain taxes, such as those levied on staple goods and industrial activity, as they hindered the accumulation of capital.[26] In short, appropriate public policies were essential to tackle the shortage of employment and transform the unemployed into industrious workers.

Crumpe's *Essay* culminated with a lengthy digression devoted to analysing which economic sector guaranteed higher employment. His line of argument followed book IV of the WN in its extensive analysis of agricultural and mercantile systems, which he called "of trade." His main theme was the priority of the agricultural sector in economic growth, a criterion that was totally alien to the hegemonic mercantile system. This system was based on the mistaken supposition that the government knew what individuals' interests were better than the individuals themselves did. It was also based on innumerable erroneous notions: the balance of payments theory was wrong; tariff protectionism and prohibition ran contrary to the principle of comparative advantage in foreign trade, and privileges and regulations totally distorted capital's natural destiny: according to Crumpe, Smith had clearly shown that the privileges typically found in the mercantile system "reduced a nation's general wealth and capital" to one extent or another, and national employment along with this, to the advantage of a limited number of manufacturers and merchants: that is, "at the expense of the majority and to the detriment of industry and employment as a whole."[27] Like Smith, Crumpe only accepted the use of tariffs in support of national industry in three specific cases: the defence industry, the Navigation Acts and compensation for tax burdens.[28]

His harsh criticism of the mercantile system contrasted with the benefits provided by the agricultural system. Crumpe repeatedly copied Smith's praise for Quesnay and the Physiocrats: "none of those that had previously written about this branch of political economy had come so close to the truth."[29] However, his analysis was not only influenced by book IV of the WN but also by a second source: Benjamin Vaughan's *New and Old Principles of Trade Compared* (1788), which had been translated into French in 1798, possibly by the author himself. The agrarian and anti-urban, anti-Colbertist tradition struck a tremendous chord with Crumpe, as did the Physiocrat argument defending the "agricultural nation," the *produit net* and the strict divide between productive and non-productive labour which aimed to show that capital's most beneficial destination was agriculture. Crumpe presented this as the priority sector on which both industry and trade depended, as well as being a natural and steady source of wealth creation without which economic power was precarious, short-lived and artificial. This all materialised in growth and employment; as it was the most productive sector: "it is agriculture that increases the general capital of a country more than any other branch of industry"[30] and, with it, national wealth and real incomes; it generated more employment than the other sectors, created stable occupations for future generations, activated work in trade and factories and, ultimately, boosted population growth. All these ideas underpinned harsh criticism of a mercantile system that had traditionally subordinated agricultural to industrial growth. This agrarian reading with Physiocratic overtones of Smith's work, originating in Ireland—which like Spain, was agrarian and with a low level of industrialisation—must certainly have facilitated its publication in the SAP, specialising as it did in agricultural matters, and strengthened the WN's reading favourable to agriculture; it was very characteristic of its first arrival in Spain.

## Citations of Smith (1788–1808)

How was Smith read in Spanish journals? How did the journals use his ideas? In the two decades that elapsed between 1788, when the WN was first cited, and 1808, when this study ends, the Spanish press carried more than 40 tacit and explicit mentions of the book and, much more marginally, its Spanish translator José Alonso Ortiz. Four journals in the vanguard of the Spanish press during its Golden Age picked up the WN: the ML, the EMD, the SAP and the CM. The increase in the number of citations resulted from the real acceptance of Smith's work when the two latter journals appeared, both of which were specialist (see Table 10.1) the CM (19/40) and the SAP (14/40) accounted for 80% of the total number of citations; given the ML's very marginal role (1/40), the remainder appeared in the EMD (8/40). The specialist press emerged at a late stage of the Enlightenment, and the same is true of its interest in Smith: around 85% of the citations were between 1799 and 1808, while the remaining 15% appeared in the previous ten years between 1788 and 1797 (see Table 10.2). It should be remembered that Alonso Ortiz's Spanish translation of the WN, the first almost complete, was published in 1794.

*Table 10.1* Number of WN´s citations in the Spanish journals

| Journals | Number of citations |
|----------|---------------------|
| ML | 1 (1804) |
| EMD | 8 (1788–1790) |
| SAP | 14 (1800–1808) |
| CM | 19 (1799–1807) |

Table elaborated by the author.

*Table 10.2* Number of WN´s citations by years

| Years | Number of citations |
|-------|---------------------|
| 1788 | 2 |
| 1789 | 5 |
| 1790 | 2 |
| 1799 | 5 |
| 1800 | 4 |
| 1801 | 9 |
| 1802 | 2 |
| 1803 | 2 |
| 1804 | 1 |
| 1806 | 2 |
| 1807 | 5 |
| 1808 | 3 |

Table elaborated by the author.

Smith was frequently cited in conjunction with other authors, which had the effect of diluting the purported novelty of his ideas. Very late on, in 1804, the ML provided a highly illuminating example of this, linking Smith's name with Bernardo Ward's to defend the priority of domestic over foreign trade.[31] Nevertheless, Smith's ideas mainly appeared in the Spanish press via intermediaries: the WN was repeatedly mentioned in reviews and bibliographical information published in the EMD, the SAP and the CM. The first was the most genuine case. The EMD was the pioneering and most important journal during the first phase of the use of Smithian ideas.[32] There were two reasons for this: firstly, its publication of Foronda's well-known *Cartas sobre los asuntos más exquisitos de la economía política* (1994 [1788–1780]), which contained two of the first mentions of Smith in the Spanish press;[33] and, secondly, its special interest in Scottish authors: beyond Smith himself (1790), the EMD published reviews of John Millar (1787), John Playfair (1788), Joseph Priestley (1789), John Sinclair (1790) and Arthur Young (with J. Banks, 1790). Through these and a further review devoted to the French author Lesperat (1788), Smithian ideas such as the criticism of exclusive privileges and France's economic and demographic debatable comparison with Britain were circulated.[34] However, the idea that appeared most frequently actually referred to a central problem in the Spanish politics of the day and a very present topic in the WN (Winch 1978, 121–45): the "monster" of the national debt.[35] While Playfair, Sinclair and Priestley's works presented this as an invention of "modern" times, Smith's ideas warned of the inappropriateness of excessive government borrowing (WN V, III). The example of Britain showed that the national debt had grown disproportionately due to frequent wars, and given that its citizens already bore an over-heavy fiscal burden there was limited leeway for future tax increases.

An anonymous contribution to the SAP, whose content was clearly Smithian, was one of the first in Spain to remark on WN´s ideas on the advantages of the division of labour (WN I, I).[36] It may have originated in Spain's pioneering scientific institution in the application of engineering to industry, the Real Gabinete de Máquinas (1788)—the Royal Cabinet of Machinery—as its founder, the engineer Agustín Bethancourt, was mentioned there. In fact, promoting mechanisation was one of the SAP's focal points; the aim was to stop Spain from paying foreign manufacturers for everything, "even wafers and toothpicks." Britain provided a good example to look towards; its successful mechanisation process was due to a happy combination of the division of labour and market size. As everything depended on increasing the "*gran despacho*"—or exports—Spain had to ensure that it was goods of the country that were consumed in the colonies, take advantage of the war with Britain (1796–1801) to appropriate its markets and boost the consumption of Spanish wares inside the country. The division of labour created more skilful workers and using machinery improved the end product, all of which made the division of labour a key factor in improving the competitiveness of domestic goods.

In the long-lived SAP, mentions of Smith normally appeared in reviews of works by other authors such as the Count of Rumford, Ambroise H. Arnould, George L. Staunton and Arthur Young. While problems for an even social balance deriving from overspecialisation and the division of labour cropped up in writing on Rumford,[37] the excerpt devoted to Arnould reflected a common asymmetry in Smith's reception in Spain.[38] His works brought out the advantages of specific institutional factors in the liberal substratum for boosting economic growth. Arnould's review aimed to persuade readers of the benefits of having an official body designed for this propose and used the notions of the division of labour, respect for individual interests and the defence of property and security as a suitable framework for the proper use of capital; but, at the same time, he championed tariff protection to promote the advance of domestic industry. The special body that he recommended should be funded by income raised from tariffs.

The SAP had an agrarian orientation and the agricultural ideas in the WN struck an especially intense chord there. The numerous extracts it published about Young's work evoked Smithian criticism of the "mercantile system": merchants' greed, trading privileges, the colonial empire, English policy towards Ireland and the national debt. These were accompanied by the conviction that monopolies proliferated under this system and that agriculture had been pushed aside; in short, "the purely mercantile government is the worst of all."[39] Even more significant were the appearance in the SAP of citations of the WN in writings related to the *Expediente de Ley Agraria—Agrarian Reform Law*—a topic that had been a matter for concern among enlightened Spaniards since the 1760s and which acquired new relevance after Melchor G. Jovellanos published his well-known *Informe de Ley Agraria* (1795). The *Expediente* provided an excellent prism through which to reread Smith: self-interest was defended in the SAP as the best driving force for agricultural development and the dividing up of large pieces of land into smaller plots to improve crop cultivation. Alonso Ortiz linked Smith's name to enlightened Spaniards' traditional demand for a reduction in the numbers of the clergy and chaplaincies.[40] Finally, Staunton's works served to remind SAP readers of the Smithian idea that moderately fertile land supported a larger population if it was devoted to agriculture rather than to livestock (WN I, XI, III).[41]

In line with its specialisation in commerce, it was the CM that carried most citations of Smith.[42] In this case, the mentions were almost entirely via third parties, which explains why they were concentrated into the years from 1799 to 1808 when the CM was in the hands of Diego María Gallard and specialised in publishing reviews and developments in the book world aimed at entrepreneurs. The WN received mixed treatment. Many general citations presented it as an essential work for the study of economic principles,[43] while others were critical of its ideas on both taxation (Guiraudet) and trade. A contribution by Veranio reminded readers that Smith not only supported the English Navigation Acts but that the WN as a whole was in the service of British trading interests: public opinion was wrong in enabling Smith's name to allow themselves to "become entangled in the niceties of numerous purely theoretical economists or those who just repeat what they have heard."[44] In any event, most citations defended the validity of specific ideas in the WN, such as the critical view of the balance of payments theory and prohibitions, as well as of Physiocracy, and the positive analysis of the functions of paper currency. It is important to highlight the fact that Smith was mentioned as an authoritative author in several reviews devoted to prominent economists: Morellet reminded CM readers that, as the example of the United States showed, economic prosperity was based on high wages, and that the use of capital should respect a natural order: agriculture, manufacturing and foreign trade;[45] Saint Aubin pondered Smith's data on the amount of money in the economy in Britain;[46] Young discussed his support for a free grain trade,[47] and Anquetil his rejection of an exclusive trading system;[48] finally, Sismondi highlighted the fact that the WN´s content had been confirmed by events occurring after it was written and boasted of having managed to "appropriate for France and its legislation the advice that Adam Smith meant especially for England."[49] However, while the CM did not reject Smithian ideas on economics, it was a long way from subscribing to them. The publication did not support doctrinaire liberalism, and even less so the radical variety, instead favouring pluralist, eclectic, moderate liberalism, informed by sources in France, from where most of the reviews published there were taken. Its roots in the late Spanish Enlightenment model of "freedom" and "protection" led it to defend tariff protectionism and numerous exceptions to the exercise of free domestic trade (guilds, subsidies and privileged companies), thus distancing itself from Smithian liberalism and, in general, from the mainstream of the first Classical political economists.

## Final remarks: a survey of the use of the WN in the Spanish press

The fact that the Spanish press was an active, diverse and persistent channel for the spreading of Smith's ideas renders recent Spanish historiography's omission of the issue even more glaring. However, the information that Spanish journals provided on the WN was in fact belated, cautious and patchy: apart from reviews, they actually carried very few texts about Smith. Moreover, not all Spanish publications presented Smith's ideas in the same depth. Leaving aside routine references devoted to praising the WN, the main division was between citations relating to the work's central theories (books I and II) and those that discussed the advantages of specific economic systems and suitable policies for good governance (books IV and V). The bulk of the citations were concentrated in the second group (Table 10.3). In general terms, readers of the Spanish press had a one-sided and incomplete view of the analytical innovations in the WN, owing to the fact that the journalists who contributed to the golden age of the Spanish press interpreted the book from the perspective of the economic problems facing Spain, upon which the "immortal" Smith could shed some

*Table 10.3* WN's topics cited in the Spanish journals

| *General citations* | *Economic systems and applied economics* |
| --- | --- |
| Generic, 2 | No theory of the balance of payments, 1 |
| WN is a source for other authors, 2 | Pro-free trade, 1 |
| WN is applicable to France, 1 | Anti-free trade, 1 |
| WN is not applicable to Spain, 2 | No exclusive privileges, 1 |
| | No privileged companies, 1 |
| Central analysis | Pro-Navigation Acts, 2 |
| Natural order/Property-security, 2 | Mercantile/monopoly system, 2 |
| Self-interest /Self-love/Harmony, 2 | Preference to domestic trade, 2 |
| Division of labour/Market size, 3 | Ideas on agriculture, 3 |
| Theory of wages, 1 | Reducing the number of clergymen, 1 |
| Theory of capital, 2 | Disseminator of Physiocracy, 2 |
| | Taxation, fiscal burden, 3 |
| | National debt, 2 |
| | Quantity of money, 1 |
| | Paper currency, 1 |
| | Data on interest rates, 1 |

Table elaborated by the author.

light. Two focal points stood out: trade policy and fiscal policy relating to government income and expenditure; the Spanish press disseminated the central ideas of Smith's work on both of these, although it did not always support his positions. The CM was undoubtedly the closest to the heterodox currents of the Classical economics mainstream, which, openly defended protectionism and, in general, the so-called "economists of the nation" (Almenar 2000a, 25–26; Lluch and Almenar 2000, 154).

## Notes

1 Guinard (1973, 219–20); see also Sempere (IV, 176–98), Urzainqui (1995, 125–216) and Larriba (2013).
2 See especially Velasco (2000, 217–75), Domergue (1982) and Defourneaux (1973).
3 Smith´s reception in the Spanish press was later with respect to France, Germany and Italy; see, Faccarello and Steiner (2002, 14–15), Carpenter (2002, xxix), Tribe (1988, 136–37) and Gioli (1972, 920–21).
4 MI (VII, 48–54). The essay was translated as "*Del baile como arte de imitación, fragmento traducido de una obra inglesa, intitulada Ensayo sobre diferentes asuntos, por Adam Smith.*" The original was: "Of the Affinity Between Music, Dancing, and Poetry;" see Smith (1795, 179–84; 1797b).
5 MI, VII (1798), 124. *Teoría de los sentimientos morales o ensayo de los juicios que forman naturalmente los hombres de sus acciones y las de los otros, acompañada de una disertación sobre los orígenes de las lenguas, por Adam Smith, traducido todo de la séptima y última edición inglesa de Sophia Grouchi (así le cita), viuda de Condorcet, la que ha añadido ocho cartas acerca de la simpatía.* The French edition was: Smith (1798). This bibliographic reference could be related to the elaboration of a translation of the TMS into Spanish, which remained manuscript; see chapter 6 in this same book. On the reception of the TMS in France from 1760 onwards, see Faccarello and Steiner (2002, 8–13).
6 Smith (1791 [1790]; 1802).
7 Smith (1792; 1794).
8 CM (no. 2, 4-X-1792, 16).
9 GM (13-IX-1794, 1099–100).
10 GM (13-IX-1794, 1099).
11 GM (4-IX-1792, 615–16).
12 GM (13-IX-1794, 1099).
13 CM (no. 31, 19-IV-1802, 242).
14 CM (no. 7, 25-I-1808, 56).
15 GM (19-II-1808, 186).
16 CM (no. 7, 25-I-1808, 56).
17 EMD (no. 260, 22-XI-1790, 282-85). *Investigaciones sobre la naturaleza y las causas de las Riquezas de las Naciones, escritas en inglés por Mr. Smith, y traducidas al francés por Mr. Roucher, con un tomo de notas, por el Marqués de Condorcet, de la Academia francesa y Secretario perpetuo de la de las Ciencias. Tomos 1° y 2°, en casa de Buisson, 1790.*
18 EMD (no. 260, 22-XI-1790, 282–83).
19 EMD (no. 260, 22-XI-1790, 285).
20 MI (IX, no. XXV, 76–92); CM (no. 5, 16-I-1800, 34-36; no. 6, 20-I-1800, 42–45; no. 7, 23-I-1800, 51–53).
21 CM (no. 5, 1-I-1800, 35).

22 MHP (15-III-1804, 355–84; 31-III-1804, 426–39). The journal was then called *Mercurio de España*.

23 MHP (15-III-1804, 374).

24 On the SAP, see Díez (1980), Larriba-Dufour (1997) and Astigarraga (2021, 252–59). Crumpe's essay appeared in the SAP (no. 309, 2-XI-1802, 359–66; no. 310, 9-XII-1802, 377–84; no. 311, 16-XII-1802, 387–95; no. 312, 23-XII-1802, 404–15).

25 SAP (no. 309, 2-XI-1802, 364).

26 SAP (no. 310, 9-XII-1802, 379ff).

27 SAP (no. 311, 16-XII-1802, 395).

28 SAP (no. 311, 16-XII-1802, 391).

29 SAP (no. 312, 23-XII-1802, 409).

30 SAP (no. 312, 23-XII-1802, 410).

31 ML (VI, no. XLVIII, 84).

32 On the EMD, see Elorza (1970, 119–38), Guinard (1973, 265–72) and Astigarraga (2021, 182–91).

33 See chapter 7 in this same book.

34 EMD (no. 245, 9-VIII-1790, 345; no. 142, 18-VIII-1788, 281).

35 See mainly EMD (no. 160, 22-XII-1788, 716–18; no. 161, 29-XII-1788, 719–21; no. 187, 29-VI-1789, 199–205; no. 248, 30-VIII-1790, 415–22; no. 249, 6-IX-1790, 1–8).

36 SAP (no. 181, 19-VI-1800, 386–93): "Diálogo sobre la perfección de las artes industriales".

37 SAP (no. 193, 11-IX-1800, 170).

38 SAP (no. 239, 30-VII-1801, 65–71): "Medios de fomentar la agricultura, la industria y el comercio".

39 SAP (no. 243, 27-VIII-1801, 130–31); see also, for example, SAP (no. 246, 17-IX-1801, 190; n. 247, 24-IX-1801, 193–94).

40 SAP (no. 592, 5-V-1808, 282, 285; no. 594, 19-V-1808, 319).

41 SAP (no. 297, 9-VIII-1802, 171).

42 On the CM, see Enciso (1958) and Astigarraga (2021, 229–37, 248–52).

43 See, for example, CM (no. 56, 15-VII-1799, 444; no. 19, 6-III-1800, 147).

44 CM (no. 93, 23-XI-1807, 740).

45 CM (no. 53, 4-VII-1799, 419; no. 59, 24-VII-1799, 466).

46 CM (no. 67, 22-VIII-1799, 532–33).

47 CM (no. 26, 30-III-1800, 204).

48 CM (no. 24, 25-III-1799, 186–87).

49 CM (no. 47, 23-VI-1803, 371).

# 11  Adam Smith in the chairs on political economy in Spain, 1780–1823[1]

*Javier San Julián Arrupe*

## Introduction

This chapter explores the presence of Smith's *The Wealth of Nations* (WN) among the sources used for economic teaching in Spain in the period roughly comprised between its publication and the Liberal Triennium (1820–1823). Spanish enlightened authors underlined the importance of economic instruction throughout the second half of the eighteenth century, in the belief that the dissemination of economic principles would lead the country to the path to prosperity. Prominent public officials of King Charles III shared this enthusiasm. Political economy was however regarded with suspicion by Ancien Régime powers as a vehicle for subversive ideas—in Spain and elsewhere—so initiatives for economic teaching were steered and monitored by the government and its contents submitted to political scrutiny. At universities, controlled by the Church, old scholasticism was still championed and innovations were hardly expected. Therefore the new science required a different outlet. This was mainly provided by economic societies, which, under the patronage of the government, bourgeoned all over the kingdom since the 1770s. The process of institutionalisation of political economy began there, slowly and hesitantly. The first Chair on Civil Economy was founded in Zaragoza in 1784, moulded after that of Naples, with Genovesi's *Lezioni* as the main teaching source. It was the time of the dissemination of civil economy of a Neapolitan background in Spain. Other initiatives ensued. However, the convulsions of the 1790s opened up a period of political retrenchment, which affected the diffusion of political economy and teaching efforts. This coincided with the diffusion of Smithian political economy. The WN was known in Spain almost immediately after publication, but, despite its dissemination, well-earned prestige and influence, it would be scarcely used in economic chairs, then struggling to survive. In 1807 university syllabi eventually included political economy, opening a new channel for economic teaching, but the new chairs gave preference to Say's *Traité*. Smith's time had passed.

In spite of difficulties and amidst the turbulences of a period of changes, economic teaching developed in Spain and, within it, the WN managed to find its place, albeit intermittently and timidly. This chapter has three sections. The

DOI: 10.4324/9781003152804-14

first sets the scene, reviewing the increasing demand for economic education and the supply of economic ideas in Spain. The second section analyses the presence of Smith in the Economic Chair of Zaragoza and other contemporaneous institutions. The third deals with economic teaching at Spanish universities. Some concluding remarks end the chapter.

## The demand for economic teaching and the supply of ideas

Political economy increasingly gained reputation among Spanish authors throughout the eighteenth century. Enlightened intellectuals believed that its principles, conveniently applied, would increase people's wellbeing and happiness. For Llombart (2000, 79), the program of economic liberalisation under Charles III, influenced by those intellectuals, rested on an "enlightened public interventionism" grounded on a conception of political economy as the science of government. Many prominent authors underlined the need for policymakers, the literate and the well-educated to acquire economic notions: Arriquíbar, Normante, Olavide, Sempere, etc.[2] Jovellanos condensed the enlightened fervour for education, linking it to material, moral and political progress: "a virtuous circle of Enlightenment" (Llombart 2013, 53–76). Holding a utilitarian conception of political economy as a basic instrument for social progress, Jovellanos stressed the need for instruction in political economy, both as a "useful" (this is, non-speculative) science aimed at the increase of production, and as a philosophical knowledge supplying its recipients with the ability to design the right policies to boost the economy (Llombart 2000b, 157).[3] His late works developed the analytical connections between political economy, education and growth: political economy taught the skills to efficiently apply capital and labour; education in turn would lead to an improvement in regulations, institutions and the people's virtuous sentiments. All opened the path to wealth. Jovellanos conclusion was that "the first source of public prosperity is to be sought in education" (2000 [1796–1797]), 541–44). So, in 1798 he addressed the king: "There is not any reform as necessary and important as that of education" (2010 [1798], 799).

This state of opinion led enlightened officials to conceive the idea of arranging some kind of regular economic instruction. The Count of Campomanes would be the architect of the establishment of economic teaching in Spain. In his six-volume work on the promotion of industry and education (Campomanes 1774; 1775; 1775–1777), he developed his program of "economic patriotism" aimed at attaining "public happiness." The lights of political economy would illuminate the path to the wealth of the nation (Campomanes 1775–1777, iii–lii). The central piece of his plan was setting up economic societies. "A particular by-product of Spanish Enlightenment" (Llombart 2000a, 52) and a personal enterprise of Campomanes, the *sociedades económicas de amigos del país*—economic societies of friends of the country—were assemblies of local enlightened elites, intended to supply information on the economy of each region, promote the diffusion of technical and economic knowledge, and aid in the implementation of economic regulations.[4] Drawing inspiration from the Basque society, founded in 1765, Campomanes sponsored the creation of the Economic Society of Madrid in 1775, the model for the rest that—always under his protection—spread all over the territory.[5]

What sources should be used in the economic courses at the societies? The supply of economic ideas in the last decades of the eighteenth century was diverse. Spain had a mercantilist tradition (Uztáriz, Ulloa, etc.), but new ideas coming from abroad were making their way into the country, conveniently reinterpreted in order to fit the needs of local readers. The dissemination of a particular trend or author at the time of the institutionalisation of economic teaching would influence the education provided. The government and the Church scrutinised the introduction of texts of political economy, as this was a "suspicious discipline" (Llombart and Astigarraga 2000, 703),[6] but the arrival of foreign ideas also depended on the political competition among parties and factions struggling to get government positions at a particular time. These parties had their own economic agendas for which they sought doctrinal support. As Cervera (2019, 99) put it, factors such as religion, philosophical traditions, the legal and educative framework, political interests and economic circumstances influenced the processes of circulation of ideas at that time, the case of Spain not being an exception.[7]

In the 1760s the government was under the control of the Count of Aranda and the so-called "Aragonese" or "military party." They were fond of a style of political economy of British and French ascendancy, which provided intellectual support to their liberalising reforms. This is why Aranda sponsored a program of translations of English liberal mercantilists (mostly from their French versions by the group of Gournay), to back his economic program: Grenville, Chamberlayne, Butel-Dumont, but also Plumard, Accarias de Serionne and others were edited in Spanish. The fall of Aranda in 1773 gave way to a policy shift led by Floridablanca and Campomanes, who sponsored the advent of civil economy, of Neapolitan origins and Catholic adscription, into Spain.[8] The 1770s and 1780s would be the time for the dissemination of Genovesi. In 1792, the accession of Manuel Godoy as plenipotentiary minister of Charles IV fostered the dissemination of political economy of Smithian ascendancy.[9] Godoy himself sponsored the translation of Condorcet's *Résumé* in 1792 and the WN in 1794, opening a period of explicit diffusion of Smith (the WN was known soon after its first publication in 1776, at the peak of the influence of civil economy). 1800–1820 was a period of analytical pluralism where a diversity of interpretations of Smith coexisted with neo-Physiocratic trends, the old mercantilist approaches and the new (and eventually hegemonic) systematisation suggested by Say.[10] The translation of foreign books continued mirroring political and intellectual struggles.[11]

These circumstances were reflected in the texts used in the newly founded chairs on political economy, and in the existence of the chairs themselves. Partisan options and political events are important to understand the preference for Genovesi—the civil economy approach—in the chairs of economic societies in the 1780s, and the late diffusion of Smith—the political economy approach—and his weak presence in economic teaching in the following decade, more difficult for economic courses. Martín (2000, 606–07) observed that political circumstances explain the open support for economic education in the 1780s and the absence of references in the first half of the 1790s, mirroring fear of revolution: economic teaching was subject to political fluctuations.[12] Cervera (2019, 111) hypothesised that the preference of Campomanes's party for the civil economy—it would be called, explicitly, the "civil party"—could supply a reasonable explanation for the long interval between the arrival in Spain of the first news of the WN and its translations. Civil economy would shape Spain's "autumn of the Lights" (Llombart's expression), to which a decade and a half of dissemination of political economy would ensue, with renewed energies concerning publication of economic works. The hypothesis that the fall of Aranda in 1773 and the ensuing advent of civil economy prevented an earlier diffusion of Smithian political economy in Spain should not be discarded.[13]

## Smith in the economic chairs of economic societies

The Chair on Civil Economy and Trade opened in Zaragoza in 1784, "a first experiment of economic teaching in Spain [...] with the aim (unsuccessful) to expand it to the rest of the nation" (Usoz 2000, 590).[14] Inspiration was taken from Intieri's Chair of Naples, run by Genovesi (1754). Aimed at youngsters with a background in law, the contents taught were basic economic principles, under a broad "science of government."[15] Two clergymen elaborated the planning of the chair, Arteta de Monteseguro and Pérez de Larrea. The latter, the true factotum of the chair, highlighted the importance of instituting a proper school able to analyse economic theoretical issues—beyond the usual practical application—and to assess the right policies to promote the development of Spain. He suggested Normante to run the chair, and Danvila's *Lecciones de Economía Civil* and Genovesi's *Lezioni* as textbooks (Sánchez et al. 2003, 127–28). Normante, a liberal mercantilist, followed Genovesi—his main influence—in his concept of civil economy, and supported agricultural supremacy over industry. He also had cameralist influences, from Bielfeld (Lluch 1996, 172). The chair started with a set of plural and updated sources, in which Genovesi and, to a lesser extent, Melon, stood out (Astigarraga and Usoz 2008–2009, 433). However, the chair immediately had to face hostility: Normante was denounced to the Inquisition and, although government intervention solved the matter, the polemic pitch of the chair was toned down.[16]

Progressing from his former agricultural mercantilism and embracing liberal positions, Larrea guided the evolution of the chair towards Smithianism, slowly abandoning the civil economy tradition and the subordination of economics to ethical and political principles, and opening to a new approach based on economics as autonomous science. Larrea approached Smith, he becoming convinced of the need to eliminate the obstacles to the progress of industry—the cause of underdevelopment—and supporting labour division and the introduction of machinery.[17] His concept of political economy concentrated on personal interest as the element capable of dynamising society (Sánchez 2003, 61–62). Polo y Catalina followed this path. A former student at the chair, where he became acquainted with Smithian work, he was the substitute of Normante (1800–1801). Polo wrote a critique of the works Normante used, approaching Smith and Say. His evolution was reflected in his *Informe sobre las fábricas e industria de España* (1804), where he resorted to Smith, Canard and particularly Say to support industrialist positions for the development of Spain, and facing the neo-Physiocratic ideas of Garnier (Sánchez 2005, lxxxvi).

The next professor, appointed in 1801, was José Benito de Cistué, a close follower of Larrea. He established the 1792 translation of Condorcet's *Résumé* as a textbook. The chair now diffused an eclectic political economy, which merged mercantilism with Smith—filtered through Condorcet—and later Garnier and Say. Smithian ideas that conflicted with Spanish economic policy, essentially concerning free trade, were ignored. This coexisted with some influence of Cantillon and Cameralism (Sanchez et al. 2003, 167–68). The analysis of Cistué's docent model allows concluding that there was a significant doctrinal evolution in the chair, from a "limited Smith" of agricultural tone—Cistué's agricultural leaning influenced Smithianism at the society—embodied in the Condorcet 1792 translation, to the "more authentic Smith"—less censored—of the WN 1794 translation (Sánchez et al. 2003, 174). In all, Polo and Cistué entailed a watershed in the chair, due to their assimilation of the influences of Smith, together with other French and English economists, who focused on applied issues and statistical work. Cistué stated that Smith's "incomplete plan" should be improved with other works, such as those by Herrenschwand, Garnier, Canard and Say, which were translated those years under the protection of the government (Sánchez 2003, 60). The chair thus evolved from the ideas of Genovesi, Melon, Bielfeld and Cantillon (in Danvila's version) to Smith and Say (Usoz 2000, 591).

There were some attempts to replicate the model of Zaragoza in economic societies and other institutions.[18] The Economic Society of Majorca, founded in 1778 by José Antonio Mon de Velarde—the brother of the head of the Aragonese Society—created the Academy of Political Economy in 1788, sponsored by the king himself. It taught "the theory and practice of commerce," addressed to officials and merchants, following the ideas of Genovesi (Astigarraga 2021, 210). According to Planas and Ramis (2011, 65), the society lobbied to create a chair on political economy at the University of Majorca, although economic teaching only started in 1814, in a chair funded by the provincial government led by Jaumeandreu. He taught there only for a few months. That same year Jaumeandreu took the chair opened by the Board of Trade of Barcelona. Although he showed esteem for Smith, Jaumeandreu used as textbook Say's *Traité*, considering that "following substantially the system of Smith, [it] explains with more order and clarity the principles of this science."[19]

In 1805 Antonio de Regás presented a project to the Economic Society of Madrid to set up an economics chair, but this was discarded for fear of facing similar opposition as the chair of Zaragoza. Regás again presented a project for a chair in 1813, this time getting approval. Manuel de la Viña, a former town counsellor under the French authority, offered himself to translate the works of Smith and Say, "the two best modern economists of present day." Antonio Osteret, an attorney at the National Court, volunteered to teach (Martín-Valdepeñas 2015, 127). The *Gaceta de Madrid* (GM) pompously announced the opening of the chair in January 1814, adding that "the sublime objective of this science is to expose how wealth is formed, distributed and consumed."[20] Osteret used Say's *Traité*, because it was "clearer in its assertions, [had] a better language and [was] more understandable to students." He was quickly substituted by Miguel García de la Madrid, another follower of Say.[21] After a small interruption, the chair reopened in May 1815, led by José Felipe de Olivé and later again by Osteret (Martín-Valdepeñas 2015, 196–98).[22] The following years seem to have been years of inactivity. In 1819 a new professor was appointed, José Antonio Ponzoa, who won the competition for the chair where a good knowledge of Say's *Traité* was required (Martín 2000, 596).[23] The society adopted the *Traité* as the textbook. All these events fit the hypothesis of Menudo (2016, 326) that the diffusion of Say in Spain in the second decade of the century was a collective project of the Madrid Economic Society—in fact Say would be appointed a member of the society in 1817.

The Consulate of Trade of Malaga in turn opened a chair on trade and political economy in 1818, taken up by Gutiérrez. According to Martín (2000, 601), "he undoubtedly used Smith and Ganilh, but very especially Say and Destutt de Tracy"—whose works he had translated: the second edition of the *Traité* and the economic part of the *Élements*.[24] In 1820, the Economic Society of Seville opened another chair on political economy led by José Díaz de Yabarrena, who most probably resorted to Say's work. He was quickly replaced by the young Peregrino de Lora (Martín 2011, 146–47). The Athenaeum of Madrid also opened a chair on political economy in 1820, active until 1824, run by Casimiro Orense, who had taught public economy at the University of Valladolid in 1815, and later Manuel Flórez Calderón, who was close to Flórez Estrada. Orense had competed with Ponzoa for the Chair of the Economic Society of Madrid. In his exercise he used as sources Say, Smith, Destutt, Mercier and Quesnay (López 2000, 363–64). All this information about economic chairs in the second decade of the nineteenth century indicate that by then Say had displaced Smith as the main source for economic teaching. Say's success was actually linked to the need of textbooks (Lluch and Almenar 2000, 110). The *Traité* was considered more didactic, and besides corrected some "mistakes" of Smith. By 1821 it had been edited seven times in Spanish.

The *Seminario de Nobles*—the Seminary for the Nobility—in Madrid supplies a case of special interest regarding economic teaching. Designed to provide education to courtesans, servants and the military, and run by the Jesuits, their expulsion in 1767 prompted a modernisation of teaching, introducing moral philosophy, natural law and civil economy. The Chair of Moral Philosophy was occupied by Danvila in 1774, who intended to use Heinetius's *Elementa*, but until 1779 he also explained Scottish moral philosophy using the *Compendium* by Francis Hutcheson, although to refute it (Hutcheson's sensualist, non-providentialist explanation of moral, at the base of modern political economy, did not fit well with Catholic tradition).[25] Eventually Danvila composed his own textbook, *Lecciones de economía civil*, in 1779. According to Cervera (2020, 20), Hutcheson's text in the Seminario was a "pioneering contribution to the progress of moral philosophy towards the domain of political economy in Spain." When Danvila passed away in 1782, economic teaching continued with Manuel Joaquín del Condado. Of Physiocratic leaning, he taught civil economy. In 1799 moral philosophy was taught with Hutcheson and Genovesi's texts. Isidoro de Antillón, a former student at the Aragonese, was appointed to the chair, but before he took possession in 1804, Josef Cía and Julián José Negrete, professors of logics and metaphysics, taught modern political economy, using the WN (especially book I) and Herrenschwand (Cervera 2020, 48–49).[26]

## Political economy in Spanish universities: the triumph of Say

The presence of political economy in Spanish universities was full of controversies, partisan struggle, frustrated decrees and political interferences. The panorama of universities in the eighteenth century was unpromising. In spite of the reformist plans of Mayans and Olavide, scholasticism was in command (Peset and Peset 1974, 223). Campomanes realised that he could not count on universities for his pragmatic plans of education. However, concerns for modernisation slowly spread. In Law studies, some voices demanded replacing traditional courses in Roman law with courses on national legislation, natural law, international law and political economy. Education should be less speculative and more useful and pragmatic (Alonso 2012, 452).

### The attempts of Salas at Salamanca

The reform of the study plans of the University of Salamanca was approved in 1771, one of the first in a wave of reform of universities.[27] It had three objectives: modernise contents, start a new pedagogy (after Mayans) and update knowledge to new circumstances (Peset and Peset 1974, 104–06). The modernising feature was the insertion of a course in moral philosophy in Law studies. Within this atmosphere, Ramón de Salas y Cortés founded the Academia de Derecho Real y Práctica Forense—the Academy of Royal Law and Forensic Practice—with the aim of teaching political economy to law students, where "everything related to policy, industry, agriculture and trade" would be studied (Robledo 2014, 401). It opened in 1787, lasting five years. Salas was the author of a collection of notes to Genovesi's *Lezioni*, the *Apuntaciones* (c.1787–1790), where he kept progressive positions influenced by Montesquieu, Locke, Filangieri, Condillac and others. Salas criticised Genovesi (and also Villava's translation of *Lezioni*), showing that Genovesi, a main source for early economic teaching in Spain, had diverse interpretations. Salas used this text for teaching and discussion at the Academia. Rodríguez (1979, 133) ventured that Smith awakened interest in Salas, but Astigarraga (2011a, 174) showed that there is no footprint of the WN in the *Apuntaciones*. Even more, taking into account the noteworthy differences between Physiocratic natural liberalism and Scottish liberalism, he hypothesised that some Physiocratic marks in the *Apuntaciones* became a barrier for the acceptance of Smithian ideas. This discards a presence of Smith in this early attempt to disseminate political economy at Salamanca, even if in later works Salas would reveal influences from Smith (Astigarraga 2011a, 187).[28] Salas would be another victim of the reaction, condemned by the Inquisition. Reforms of study plans yielded some modernising outcomes in the universities of Granada and Valencia, where chairs on natural law were created in 1776 and 1786. The textbook was Almici, who had adapted Heinetius (López-Cordón 2020, 257). All chairs on natural law were suppressed in 1794 after the events in France, as their activities were considered breeding grounds for ideas against the constitution of the kingdom. The opportunity to study authors as Grotius or Pufendorf was short-lived.

### The Caballero plan

In 1807 a decree of Minister José Antonio Caballero established a new plan of studies for the University of Salamanca, which was to be applied to all universities in the kingdom. It included for the first time a course in political economy in the Law degree.[29] The Caballero plan aimed at modernising and centralising Spanish universities, establishing single plans of studies and academic organisation. Preliminary works, in which Jovellanos intervened, included a report by Simón de Viegas, who demanded chairs on civil economy at every university. Moral philosophy replaced old Aristotelian ethics, and a course on national law was introduced. The ninth year of the Law degree was devoted to political economy,

> in which [students] will review the Inquiries on the Wealth of Nations by Adam Smith, and the professor will try to make as many mentions to ours [Spain] as possible. All this while the translation into Spanish of the work of Jean Baptiste Say [*Traité*] is finished, which will be preferred.
>
> (*Real Cédula* 1807, 12)

Was this an opportunity for the dissemination of Smith? The text urged universities to apply the plan immediately, but circumstances made this difficult. The Napoleonic invasion in 1808 plunged the country into turmoil until 1814. Say's *Traité* was about to be fully published in Spanish. All this conspired against Smith's dissemination through university chairs, and awarded Say with a prominent role in the following years, despite a new wave of Smithianism in the editing business: the second edition of the WN translation was released in 1805–1806, with Garnier's *Breve exposición de la doctrina de Adam Smith* as an appendix.[30] The GM praised it as a guide to study Smith's text: It "supplies everything one could miss in Smith's work for its teaching in all universities and public schools, in which according to government disposition, the useful and interesting study of political economy has just been established."[31] In spite of this, it seems improbable that Smith would become an actual source for teaching. Caballero was an enemy of Godoy (who had patronised the advent of Smith), and it comes as no surprise that he did away with Godoy's program.[32] It seems however that some universities created chairs and appointed professors. Sevilla created the chair in December 1807.[33] The University of Granada appointed José Vicente Alonso in 1807 (Martín Rodríguez 2000, 607). In Valencia, the syllabus of the chair followed exactly the table of contents of Say's *Traité* (Hernando 2002, 325–30). Peset (1995, 275) held that Felipe Benicio Navarro had a chair at the University of Alcalá in 1810. However in Majorca, Cervera and Salamanca there were no economic chairs.[34]

### The action of the liberals

Within the context of a liberal surge, a new sympathy for political economy resurfaced, and requirements for economic teaching re-emerged. In June 1813 the constitutional Parliament issued a decree urging the foundation of chairs of civil economy in all universities, after the works of the Commission for Education appointed in 1810, chaired by Jovellanos.[35] A new commission was formed to deliver a report to reorganise public instruction. The *Informe Quintana* (1813)[36] demanded a radical shift in the system of education, which should be universal, uniform and free, and divided into primary, secondary and university levels. It was to a great extent inspired by Condorcet (Araque 2013, 42). The plan set up a course on political economy and statistics in secondary education, within the section of moral and political sciences: the subjects enhancing national wealth, "with all its useful applications," should be an essential part of the education of the young Spaniards (Quintana 2013 [1813], 196–97). A new report issued one year later to clarify aspects of the *Informe Quintana* defined political economy as the science of "how wealth is formed and distributed," the subtitle of Say's *Traité*, which allows thinking that Say would be the source for teaching (*Dictamen* 1814, 10). It established that political economy was compulsory for admission to the Law Faculty, and proposed erecting schools of commerce in the main ports of the kingdom. Both the *Informe* and the *Dictamen* considered political economy under a pragmatic and applied perspective, less theoretical.[37] The replacement of Smith for Say's text might also be regarded with this perspective. At the request of the government, the University of Salamanca issued a report on this plan in 1814. It suggested a six-year degree in Law, with a course in political economy in the second year, where "Say's work will continue as textbook" (*Informe* 1820, 66).[38] The restoration of absolutism in 1814 stopped this evolution. Universities demanded returning to the old plans of the 1770s, on the reasoning that new plans presented too many difficulties. This entailed the extinction of economic chairs, but a decree in 1818 confirmed their survival, due to their usefulness.[39]

The liberal upheaval of 1820 led to the provisional re-enactment of the 1807 plan with some slight modifications. A new plan for the Law degree introduced natural law (with Heinetius) and placed political economy in the seventh year, with "the classical work of Mr. Say" (Martínez 1998, 158). However, the *Reglamento general de instrucción pública* of 1821 included again political economy and statistics in secondary education. The textbook would be Say's *Traité* (Martínez 1998, 160). Amidst this regulatory chaos and the catastrophic circumstances of the universities, some of them hosted economic teaching. According to Castro (2012), Manuel León Moreno and Alonso were in Granada, and Diego Antonio Saa and Francisco de Paula Yberri in Seville. Juan Sorá held a chair arranged by liberal provincial authorities in Majorca.[40] Even if data about texts used are scarce or non-existent for all this period, it seems that any direct trace of Smith's WN in university teaching had vanished after the 1807 plan, replaced by Say's *Traité*. In 1823 the liberal experiment ended. Economics entered again a dark age: only four handbooks were published in Spanish in the decade.[41]

## Conclusions

The dissemination of foreign economic ideas in Spain in the last decades of the eighteenth century and the first years of the nineteenth century is a fascinating history of political struggle, enlightened efforts, ephemeral successes and big disappointments. Competition between civil and political economy, sponsored by different factions, the tribulations of the kingdom facing the Convention and later Napoleon's armies and the shadow of old Ancien Régime powers are the background against which the institutionalisation of economic teaching in Spain struggled to blossom. The authorities feared the subversive flavour of the new science, which led to strict control of its dissemination, particularly teaching; but at the same time, policymakers trusted the new economic science as a lever for economic progress, and sought to select and promote specific economic ideas as an intellectual reinforcement of their policy programs. Diffusing economic ideas from chairs had to cope with gigantic constraints.

These circumstances combined to the detriment of the use of the WN in economic chairs: Smith became trapped between the triumph of civil economy, when Genovesi took over the chairs of Zaragoza and Salamanca, and the flattening wave of Say, which dominated economic teaching from the end of the first decade of the new century. Was there any room for the dissemination of Smith? His turn seemed to arrive in the 1790s, but was frustrated by the *cordon sanitaire* imposed to avoid revolutionary contagion. It is nevertheless possible to affirm that the WN was used in Zaragoza: Smith "was widely diffused in the chair, by Larrea and his disciples, especially Cistué" (Sánchez 2003, 24). And it is not hazardous to hypothesise that the WN was something more than just mentioned in the courses of Cía and Negrete at the Seminario de Nobles, Orense in Madrid and perhaps Gutiérrez in Malaga. The university plan of 1807, the first attempt to unify higher education, appointing textbooks, might have furnished another opportunity. But, although the WN was declared an official source, Say's era had arrived, he becoming the economist that influenced most economic teaching in Spain at that time (Lluch and Almenar 2000, 110). It is naturally possible to speak of an influence of Smith ... under Say's reworking.

It is very plausible that general economic teaching in all these chairs ended up being quite eclectic, as Spanish economists adapted their sources to the circumstances of the nation and the particular problems they wished to tackle. The Chair of Zaragoza combined Smith with mercantilism, avoiding slippery topics as free trade; the early Say supported a non-radical industrialism, which made him compatible with Smith's positions; the sources of some professors were varied and even opposed. It is plausible that the economy transmitted through these chairs included Smithian ideas merged with many other influences. Smith would nonetheless remain an everlasting symbol and source for Spanish economists in the nineteenth century, even if their main influences might be others.

## Notes

1  I thank the support of the research project PGC2018-095821 of the Ministry of Science, Innovation and Competitiveness of Spain and the Centre d´Estudis Antoni de Capmany d´Economia i Història Econòmica.
2  For instance, Arriquíbar (1987 [1779], 93) suggested setting a "political seminar" to teach the "science of the State", containing "the fundamental economic and political laws of the country." Normante wrote a *Discurso sobre la utilidad de los conocimientos económico-políticos y la necesidad de su estudio metódico* (Normante 1784). Sempere (1801, 8) stated the "absolute need to promote and spread the study of political economy with all conceivable means." This was the general tone.
3  Jovellanos encouraged the study of political economy from his early works. The *Elogio de Carlos Tercero* epitomised his views: it was actually a eulogy to political economy: Royal decrees "must emanate from its principles," which embodied the spirit of the Enlightenment (Jovellanos 1789, 38).
4  See Llombart and Astigarraga (2000). Sánchez-Blanco (2002, 159) was very pessimistic about the actual reformist action of societies.
5  The introduction to the records of the society states that it was founded as "a school of economic science;" RSEM (1780, xv–xvi).
6  For Astigarraga (2011a, 18) political economy was the gateway through which progressive political ideas expanded in Europe. Governments and the Church resorted to censorship in Spain, but its effectiveness should be assessed, as there were ways to circumvent it. The case of the translation of the WN is a clear-cut example.
7  Cervera (2019) suggested a periodification to assess the introduction of foreign economic ideas into Spain grounded on political competition.
8  For Cervera (2019, 112), civil economy was just the adaptation of enlightened political economy to an eclectic Catholic environment, the outcome of conservative resistance to modern protestant philosophy that separated revelation from strictly economic issues.

9 Differences between civil and political economy were not always clear-cut. Cervera (2019, 111) warned that, as they shared common traits, many enlightened authors did not make distinctions between them "for ignorance, usage or prudence." Jovellanos himself named them indistinctly (Llombart 2000b, 17). This is not to disregard the fact that at some precise moments, due to the suspicion that political economy (especially Smithian) engendered, authors were ambiguous, especially after the problems of Normante and Salas with the Inquisition.

10 Lluch and Almenar (2000, 106) point out that although Smith remained the most credited economist, his real influence decreased and his ideas were disseminated indirectly, through Condorcet, Garnier and eventually Say.

11 Translations of Herrenschwand, Rumford, Bielfeld, Young, Crumpe, Neufchateau, Bentham, Canard and Say, and the re-edition of Genovesi's *Lecciones* appeared between 1800 and 1804. In addition were the re-edition of the translation of Condorcet's *Résumé* (1803) and of the 1794 translation of the WN (1805–1806), and the anonymous translation in 1807 of the first two parts of Garnier's introduction to the 1802 French translation of the WN, in which he made a synthesis between Smith and the Physiocratic doctrines. These sources were used in debates between industrialist and agricultural positions, both using Smith (Sánchez 2018, 231–34).

12 Godoy (1839, II, 125) confirmed that political economy turned hazardous after 1791: among the measures that the government took to avoid revolutionary contagion, he named suspension of reforms, closure of journals, and that "all directors of patriotic societies [economic societies] received secret orders to slow down their activities and to avoid discussions on issues of political economy."

13 I thank Professor Cervera for this suggestion.

14 Previous attempts were made in the Basque Society in 1775 (to set up studies on the "science of government") and the Madrid Society in 1776 ("science of commerce") (Astigarraga 2003, 136–37; 2009, 154–55). This scholar (2021, 200) hypothesised that the chair was set in Zaragoza and not in Madrid to avoid conflict with reactionaries at Court.

15 The chair fitted into the framework of German Cameralism that expanded to Italy before reaching Spain, allowing Astigarraga to speak of a German–Italian axis in Zaragoza (Usoz 2000, 591). In 1785 the Aragonese Society created two chairs on moral philosophy and public law, thus hosting three disciplines that attempted to renew social thought. The content taught in those two chairs was "very moderate;" Astigarraga and Usoz (2008–2009, 429).

16 This lower profile was reflected in the handbooks used—Danvila, Genovesi, Bielfeld—of an eclectic tone, more descriptive than analytic. Although Smith was already known, perhaps the fear of attacks led professors to hold back liberal ideas (Sánchez et al. 2003, 167).

17 Larrea targeted guilder, whose power he aimed at limiting. Cistué (1804, 22), in his elegy to Larrea, stated that "the lights of political economy have unveiled the prejudices that farmers suffer from the excessive protection to urban artisanship." He used the expression "political economy," not civil economy. It was the time when the influence of Genovesi had waned.

18 Manuel Belgrano noted in 1798 that Spain was "full of economic societies" where the study of political economy "is not unknown" (Robledo 2014, 277).

19 In 1816 Jaumeandreu wrote *Rudimentos de economía política*, a compendium of Say's *Traité*. For Lluch and Almenar (2000, 111) the "correction" that Say had made of

Smith was a good excuse for Jaumeandreu to correct Say in turn, regarding industrial development, protectionism and some agrarian contracts.

20  This expression was precisely the sub-title of the translation of Say's *Traité* into Spanish by Toreno in 1804–1807; *Gazeta de la Regencia de las Españas* (1814, 18–19).

21  He published in 1820 *Principios o máximas sobre los impuestos deducidas de las obras del Say*, a pamphlet containing a precise summary of the 1816 translation of Say's *Traité*.

22  According to García Hurtado (2003, 136), Olivé had taught before in Murcia (1807), also with Say's *Traité*.

23  Ponzoa would translate the fifth edition of Say's *Traité* in 1835.

24  Speaking of the same chair, Lluch and Almenar (2000, 112), mentioned Say (main source), Destutt and Ganilh, but not Smith.

25  Danvila's early work *Theses Logices* and his later *Lecciones* sought to conciliate Christian philosophy with natural law, in a thread that ran from Pufendorf to Heinetius (more acceptable to Catholics); Cervera (2008, 20).

26  Herrenschwand's *De l'economie politique moderne*, translated into Spanish in 1800, was made compulsory for economic teaching at the Seminario in 1804. This book triggered a debate on agricultural exploitations, to which the ideas of English agronomists, especially Young, whose texts seemed to be well-known in economic societies, joined. In front of them, there stood industrialist positions as that of Polo (Sánchez 2018, 231–32).

27  The plan for Sevilla was passed in 1769; Valladolid, Salamanca and Alcalá in 1771; Santiago and Cervera in 1772; Oviedo in 1774; Granada in 1776 and Valencia in 1786.

28  In the Salas group there were intellectuals who might have known of the WN later. Meléndez Valdés, friend to Jovellanos, published in 1798 a report on the liberalisation of the wine trade, which Astorgano (1998, 96–97) believed could have got inspiration from the WN, which was in Meléndez's library. Arenas-Dolz (2015, 184) pointed out that Miguel Martel, a progressive liberal clergyman fond of Condillac and Destutt's sensualism, who taught at Salamanca since 1790, disseminated ideas of Helvetius, Locke and Smith.

29  Caballero had issued two orders for the unification of Law studies in 1802, which essentially entailed a reinforcement of the study of national law.

30  This booklet was the translation of two sections of the introduction to Garnier's 1802 translation of the WN, where he attempted a conciliation between Smith and the Physiocrats (Sánchez 2005, xci–xciv).

31  GM (19-II-1808, 186).

32  Godoy (1839, II, 264) said that Caballero "attacked all my projects and reforms", blamed him for the fall of Jovellanos, and accused him of obstructing the publication of a translation of Bielfeld (Godoy 1839, III, 158).

33  Yñiguez (2000, 21) stated that the instructor appointed was Antonio José Santervaz, a professor of Roman law. Castro (2012, 201) said that it was Joaquín María Uriarte, with Francisco Javier de Oviedo as his substitute. According to Martín (2011, 146), there is no evidence that the chair effectively started.

34  In Majorca, the town council, which patronised the university, demanded a chair on political economy (Planas and Ramis 2011, 60). At Cervera the plan triggered conflicts between conservative and progressive professors and was never applied (Prats 1993, 387–94). In Salamanca, a report by Thiebault (1811, 37) wondered at "the multitude of chairs on Roman Law and the total absence of chairs on political

economy, natural law and national law." He designed a plan for the Law Faculty with seven chairs, one on political economy (1811, 120–21).

35 Jovellanos delivered his *Bases para un Plan General de Instrucción Pública* in 1809, where he recommended once again the study of civil economy.

36 After Manuel José Quintana, the chairman. Quintana had some knowledge on economics. He was acquainted with the works of Filangieri, Turgot, Condillac, Smith and others; Sánchez (2006, 86)

37 The *Dictamen* (1814, 10) said that generalisation of economic knowledge would allow public opinion to scrutinise the government, especially regarding taxation. Its study should "be accompanied of statistics, indispensable to make useful applications of the principles of that science."

38 The liberal spirit of the report emerged when dealing with the course on natural law: it praised Locke, Beccaria and Bentham, whose moral calculus "are the true logical instruments required for legislation" (*Informe* 1820, 64).

39 There are scarce data on economic teaching during this turbulent period. Castro (2012) gave some information, although not on textbooks. Alonso was in Granada at least in 1813–1814; Uriarte in Sevilla until 1811–1812, when he was replaced by Oviedo until 1815–1816. Álvarez was in Oviedo in 1814–1815, with Albarez Roxo as his substitute. Orense was in Valladolid in 1815.

40 Majorca's liberal authority distrusted the university loyalty to the constitution, and created its own chairs. Authors suggested for teaching were Locke, Condillac and Filangieri; Planas and Ramis (2011, 67); Longás (2015, 236). Conflicts between conservatives and liberals were very common in the Triennium, posing difficulties for the renewal of university teaching.

41 Mora (1825) and Flórez Estrada (1828) in London, and Valle Santoro (1829) and Espinosa de los Monteros (1831) in Madrid.

# 12 Adam Smith and the Cortes of Cádiz (1810–1813)

## More than enlightened liberalism

*Javier Usoz*

### 'Constituting' a brand new liberal state

While *The Wealth of Nations* (WN) first reached Spain in the late eighteenth century, it enjoyed what could be described as the second phase of its reception in the first decades of the nineteenth.[1] During this period this work transcended the spheres of economics publications and early teaching of economic science and entered the realm of politics and legislation, in which the most significant event was the holding of the Cortes generales y extraordinarias—Parliament—from 24 September 1810 to 20 September 1813, at the height of the War of Independence with France.[2] During the period that began on 25 August 1811 and ended with its enactment on 19 March 1812, the Cortes drew up the first Spanish constitution, which was ground-breaking not only in Spain but throughout the world. The constitution was abolished in 1814 when Ferdinand VII returned to the throne, only to be reintroduced later in his reign during the Liberal Triennium, before it was finally suppressed in 1823. It never became positive law again, but was instead transformed into a legend of the Spanish liberal spirit, especially during the hundred years that followed.[3]

Addressing the Smithian ideology in this radical political and legislative transformation required examining the lengthy and detailed session journals of the Cortes, which were charged with the mission of creating the rules of a new state.[4] They were held in the face of the Ancien Régime's reaction, on one side, and, on the other, open war against the *afrancesados*—frenchified—Napoleonic power that was attempting to impose itself throughout the country by force; this included the area around the Cortes, which was initially held on the island of León before moving to the nearby city of Cádiz a few months later. It should not be forgotten that there were two warring claims in Spain during those years: one was the official regime, led by the king, Joseph Bonaparte, who was Napoleon's brother and was protected by both the Constitution of Bayonne (1808) and the most powerful army in Europe, while the other had risen in rebellion against the king and was supported by the Spanish armed forces and popular militias. The latter source of power had established *juntas*—boards—in the areas under its control, presided over by the Junta Suprema Central y Gubernativa del Reino—the Supreme Central Board of the Kingdom—which

DOI: 10.4324/9781003152804-15

on 29 January 1810 became the Consejo de Regencia de España e Indias—the Council of Regency of Spain and the Indies—the body that convened the constituent Cortes.

The text of the 1812 Constitution certainly contains Smith's ideas, if they are somewhat disguised. Behind this lies the fact that once suitable concessions had been made to conservative sectors,[5] the views of the liberal group in the Cortes held sway, not only over defenders of the Ancien Régime, but also the more moderate Enlightenment that Jovellanos represented. The outcome was that despite radical aversion to their French invaders, the Cortes nevertheless adopted the rational constitutional model from France rather than the British model of a historic constitution. In contrast, however, the 1812 Constitution had a clearly liberal background in which British economic ideology was essential; this was deeply marked by the WN, whose author was expressly mentioned on several occasions during the sessions in question, as outlined below.[6]

It is therefore true to say that although the Constitution was fundamentally devoted to the political and legal structure of the new state, it contained economic references that manifested Smithian liberalism. Article 4, for example, stated: "The nation is obliged to preserve and protect by wise and just laws the civil liberty, property and other legitimate rights of all the individuals of which it is composed." To talk of freedom, property and rights, above all in individualist terms, was a significant advance on the economic Enlightenment that had proposed incorporating the "happiness of the nation" as a whole into politics. Article 31 of the constitution thus stated that "the government's objective is the nation's happiness," but in accordance with a clearly individualist liberal approach, specifying that "the aim of all political society is none other than the welfare of the individuals who compose it," which transcended the collective approach. On the other hand, it is also telling that the article retained the concept of "welfare," since in the preamble, where this first appeared, it was altered to the term "good" on the grounds that, at that time, the text referred to the whole nation.[7] "Welfare" would therefore have a more material, concrete and individual meaning.

This individualist sense went beyond other liberalising concepts of enlightened discourse, which the constitution also incorporated. Thus, article 131 on the "powers of the Cortes" included the economic power to "promote and encourage all kinds of industry and remove hindrances to it," one of Jovellanos's characteristic expressions, and frequently used by the Cádiz deputies.[8] Similarly, article 321 concerning local council functions contained another liberalising nuance, which seemed to transcend the Enlightenment vision when it referred to the aim of "promoting agriculture, industry and trade, according to locality and circumstances"; although, and this is the nuance, this promotion of the economy was conditional on its "being useful and beneficial," which expressly implied that it could also be harmful.[9]

The following pages outline the most significant examples of Smithian individualist liberalism in the Cortes that drafted the 1812 Constitution. Although this was in conflict above all with the reactionary views of the privileged classes of the Ancien Régime, the Church and the landed aristocracy, which were represented in Cádiz, it also had to overcome more moderate Spanish Enlightenment reformism. At the end of the eighteenth century this individualist liberalism was viewed as radical by the mainstream Enlightenment; however, the most liberal Cádiz deputies clearly linked it to "good political economy," taking a step that was neither dramatic nor flamboyant but certainly decisive to transcend the models inherited from the liberalising Enlightenment so eminently represented by Campomanes and Jovellanos. On the other hand, this advance in terms of economic liberalisation was in line with the enactment of a constitutional rule that went beyond the remit entrusted to the deputies who drafted it, who were initially confined to restoring the best tradition of national historical rights.

## A brief reference to the treasury

With a view to outlining the Smithian themes in the parliamentary debates in Cádiz, this chapter briefly discusses many but not all of the political and socio-economic issues in which their influence was present. These issues fall into different categories, but it is necessary to mention tax policy, an important aspect that was as omnipresent as it was separate, a fact that was clearly recognised at the time, when the constituent deputies drew a distinction between the Ministry of the Treasury and the Ministry of the Interior, with the latter responsible for promoting different sectors of the economy.[10] Partly on the basis of this differentiation, and also because the tax issue gave rise to many wide-ranging and specific treatises, Smith's influence on taxation in the Cortes of Cádiz—especially evident in the views of Vicente Alcalá-Galiano, José Canga Argüelles and Román Martínez de Montaos—is discussed at greater length in Chapter 8 of this book.[11]

The liberalism of "good political economy" always prevailed when the Cortes addressed certain specific treasury matters. Thus, for example, in the discussion on the taxes to be levied on silversmiths, deputy Manuel Luján opposed the "extraordinary tax" on silver proposed by the Treasury Committee, on the grounds that such a measure "would suggest that we are either not governed by principles of justice and political economy, or that we are seeking solutions and means of imposing this tax contrary to what has already been decided," adding that "contractual freedom, particularly to buy and sell, must be this business's true point of view."[12]

It was never disputed in the Cortes of Cádiz that the main source of this "good economics" in general, and not only where taxation was concerned, was Adam Smith. When addressing the tobacco tax, deputy Pedro Silves stated:

> [M]y opinion is irrelevant in this regard, but that of the best economist we know is not, I mean the great Smith, who explains this matter in a few words in chapter V, volume 4, saying: "tobacco is a commodity which is not considered a necessity of life anywhere; which has been made a very

general and almost universal object of consumption, and is therefore also a suitable object for taxation.[13]

In fact, the discussion regarding fiscal issues in which Adam Smith was most frequently quoted during the Cortes of Cádiz sessions was the debate on suppressing the complex system of indirect taxes on consumption and trade called *rentas provinciales*—provincial revenues—the responsibility of the Extraordinary Finance Committee appointed for the purpose. Among the most prominent figures to participate in the debate, which took place in July 1813, were the Count of Toreno and Antonio Alcalá-Galiano. Objecting to the committee's proposal to abolish the *rentas provinciales*, the latter defended the cautious policies applied thus far in view of the practical difficulties involved and the country's specific circumstances. To do this he relied on the authority of Geneva economist Necker, who was enormously influential in the Spanish Enlightenment, and "his book on the administration of France's revenues" (Necker 1784). Alcalá-Galiano said that the work contained the arguments that the author had used in the French Constituent Assembly to defend the established system, however flawed it might be, against the dangers of the new. As well as citing Necker he adopted an anti-Physiocrat and industrialist position, using the "principles laid down by economists" and expressly mentioning Smith, Guiraudet and his brother Vicente, who he considered to be the precursor of the most advanced ideas on this matter in Spain.[14]

The Count of Toreno made a lengthy speech in answer to Alcalá-Galiano in the Cortes session the following day, in which he presented a summary of Smith's thinking on taxation, at least part of which is worth reproducing here:

> The Committee has not forgotten, as Mr. Galiano believes, the principles of good economists, in particular Smith; and how could it have departed from the doctrine of this sainted father of political economy? It is Mr. Galiano who has forgotten. Smith advocated neither direct nor indirect taxation; he laid down four rules or maxims, namely: first, that the subjects of a state should pay in proportion to their incomes; secondly, that the levy should specify the time, manner, and amount to be paid; thirdly, that it should be exacted in the way that is most convenient to the payer, and fourthly, that no more should be taken than enters the Treasury, that is, as little as possible of what ought to enter should be spent, as occurs either when many clerks are employed or when industry is hampered.

Toreno then went on to expound Smith's ideas on direct and indirect taxation in different contexts, and concluded that

> the Committee has not departed from the doctrine set out by Smith, who neither approves nor disapproves of direct or indirect contributions, but discusses the evils of them all, offers suitable improvements, and lays down certain canons or rules to which they must conform.[15]

## Liberalising trade and production

On the whole it is true to say that the tendency during every session and intervention in the debates of the legislature that produced Spain's first liberal constitution was to opt for broad economic liberalisation in the aspects of trade and production, both agrarian and industrial; however, given that the country was at war, reality frequently imposed less liberal outcomes. The contributions from Lázaro Dou and Francisco Gutiérrez de la Huerta, who spoke out against the "exclusive privileges" of weapons manufacturers and based their arguments on "the maxims of good political economy" and "knowledge of political economy", are examples of this.[16] When opposing a tax on jewellery purchases, Luján also appealed to the "principles of political economy," which expressly include "contractual freedom."[17] Similarly, José Miguel Gordoa, deputy for Zacatecas, Mexico, advocated liberalising the mining sector, in line with what "political economy" demanded.[18]

The appeal to "good political economy" certainly encompassed liberalising principles such as contractual freedom, free initiative and frequently "individual" or "private" interest. One of the most forceful and explicit examples of this is to be found in the Agriculture Committee's opinion on liberalising horse breeding. The initiative came from deputy Francisco Garcés and consisted of repealing the legislation regulating the sector, which dated from 1789 and was viewed as an extremely harmful web of privileges and obstacles that "restricts private owners' freedom," because "this is and always will be the effect of inappropriate government intervention in the operations of individual interest."[19] Garcés also noted "how detrimental the urge to make regulations has been to us," and that "the government's hand in the operating of private interests only serves to hinder or prevent them," while "farmers and stockbreeders know more about their business than the most skilful ministers and the most experienced councils." For all these reasons he requested the "restoring of property rights," while at the same time, in return, owners should "not enjoy exemptions and privileges to the detriment of other citizens." An entirely Smithian ideology.

Another fundamental issue that could not be omitted from the liberalising policy was the question of the grain trade, which the Treasury Committee put before the Cortes at the height of a shortage that was aggravated by the war.[20] The proposal involved "renewing" the free import of grain and its distribution throughout the country in accordance with the provisions of the repealed "*Real Pragmática* of 11 July 1765," while also liberalising the export of "prohibited goods," meaning the raw materials used to pay for wheat imports. In the end the committee proposed granting "premiums" to grain importers, with the aim of promoting "individual interest," the "key player in trade negotiations." Several deputies including Dou, who asked for a transitional period, Juan Polo, Felipe Aner and Agustín Argüelles, defended these measures by appealing to the principle of "individual interest" that "economists" talked about. Although some deputies raised protectionist objections, as far as the export of raw materials in defence of domestic industry was concerned, all points of the proposal were approved.[21]

The debates in the Cortes also featured granary policy, which was linked to the grain trade.[22] They also included references to "individual interest" and "freedom" as principles that could be reconciled with the granaries' two aims, which were investing in seeds and guaranteeing subsistence. The granaries were officially legitimised in the hope that "the principles of free trade laid down by political economists" would be applied to prevent farmers from being "victims of the same freedom that arouses their interest" and which raised grain prices excessively due to "the physical and legal obstacles to domestic trade," just as Jovellanos had suggested in the *Informe de Ley Agraria* (1795). In line with this, the Cortes approved measures based on local initiatives and the management of the *diputaciones*—provincial councils. It is worth recalling at this point that the Spanish Enlightenment had already proposed a leasing system as a way of managing the granaries privately, not for the sake of individual interest or freedom, but rather to oppose the aristocracy's prerogatives and tackle commercial speculation, thereby furthering the interests of farmers and consumers. However, liberalising views of this type, pre-dating the arrival of Smithian economics and exemplified by the approach to guild policy, did not presuppose a conception of the right to property ownership such as that upheld by Felipe Aner when he requested

> that it be decreed by law that the owners of estates and inherited land have absolute freedom to hedge or enclose them, and have the exclusive right to all the fruits and pastureland there in the exercise of the sacrosanct right of property ownership.[23]

A further economic liberalisation-related issue that was dealt with in the Cortes of Cádiz and displayed clear Smithian features was the abolition of the seafarers' registers, which limited access to fishing activity, and the forest ordinances, which restricted the freedom to cultivate private land. These regulations both constrained economic activity in order to guarantee the supply of sailors to man battleships and to protect timber production for the construction of these same vessels.[24] The liberalising arguments put forward by deputies Aner, Francisco Javier Borrull, José María Queipo de Llano, who was Count of Toreno, Manuel García Herreros and José Zorraquín made ample use of the principles of "individual interest," which was considered "a powerful agent that motivates and energises states," the "sacrosanct right to property ownership" and the "harmony between state and individual interests," along with statements such as "the nation is happy as long as its individuals are happy."[25] It was eventually decided to abolish the registers in America but not in peninsular Spain, due to the fact that the country was at war.

With respect to the forest ordinances, the arguments for privatisation included an Agriculture Committee report that used highly Smithian expressions to stress that "society's general interest needs to be united with citizen's private interest, so that when they work to further state interests, they are also working for their own private and individual interest," which is nothing less than a version of the Smithian invisible hand.[26] The Cortes repealed the forest ordinances and approved the freedom to cultivate on private land, while proposing the privatisation of "municipal land, wasteland and Crown land," although the second issue was contingent on a subsequent reform that in fact came to nothing.[27] It is worth noting that the decision opposing the reform also made an appeal to "the principles of political economy," with deputy Antonio Oliveros recalling that its implementation required taking each case's circumstances into account, so that "the experience and political economy axioms that came from it" showed that privatisation caused more harm than good for village dwellers, who were deprived of common pastures, woodlands and wasteland.[28]

Despite the pressing need to swell state coffers, the Cortes of Cádiz's liberalising policy was also applied to the mining sector, at least partially. In his proposal to substantially reduce the "duties" levied on the sector, Gordoa described mining as based on "true economics," stating that

> there is no branch of the Treasury in which the object of economic legislation is so identical with personal interest as mining, whose operators, taken as a whole, can propose nothing more than to increase their own wealth as much as possible.[29]

It was probably inevitable that the economic liberalisation sought by the Cortes of Cádiz would also be aimed at the industrial sector, and in this respect mention should be made of the project presented by the Agriculture Committee during the session on 31 May 1813, following the Count of Toreno's "opinion" "that factories or machinery of any kind could be set up without the need for any type of permit or licence whatsoever." José Rech expressed his reservations in the subsequent debate on 3 June, pointing out that the freedom requested had already been partially granted by the Board of Trade and Currency in 1800 and then extended by decree on 6 August 1811, albeit with regulations and safeguards to avoid fraud and harm to the Treasury. Toreno replied that the Board of Trade regulations effectively prevented factories from being set up at will and that the provincial authorities still put up obstacles, and appealed to the principle that consumers themselves would be responsible for identifying fraud and poor quality.

The main issue here, as Toreno explained during the same session, was the guilds. He expressly followed Smith—saying "one cannot quote [Smith] in these matters without veneration and respect"—on the question, stating that "in England one notices the benefits produced" by the absence of guilds "in certain cities," specifically "Birmingham, Westminster and others" which have made more headway "in certain matters" than London. The Smithian arguments Toreno then put forward leave no doubt as to his position, namely that "these things should be left to the interests of private individuals, who will use their funds where it best suits them," and that "this government itch to interfere in the actions of private individuals is the surest means of hampering national prosperity." Toreno was seconded by Dou, although he did call for specific regulations to replace the guild ordinances, and even more forcefully by Argüelles, García Herreros, Isidoro Antillón and José María Calatrava.[30]

## Against the vestiges of the Ancien Régime

There are also explicit references to Smithian thought in the question of the reform of property ownership and feudal power over land. The Cortes proposed abolishing seigniories and entailed estates, while also aiming to privatise common and uncultivated land. Once again, as with trade and production policy, there was an attempt to complete the work of Enlightenment *regalismo*—royalism—but with the new liberal principles of British economics to reinforce it.

The debate on the abolition of seigniories began on 1 June 1811. The basis for the discussion was a report presented by Alonso López, which spoke of "the rights of Spanish citizens" and of "banishing without delay from Spanish soil and from public view the visible feudalism of gallows, shackles and other signs of tyranny and insults to humanity erected by the system of feudal rule." This would be achieved in terms of property through reversion to the Crown, and in terms of jurisdictional power by suppressing the authority exercised by the seigniorial nobility.[31] It was clear from the outset that resistance would need to be overcome, including from the liberal sector, which supported the proposal, and Dou therefore warned during the first session that the measure should not undermine "citizens' right to property ownership" and called for a thorough examination of the matter, including the question of compensation for current owners. In the session held four days later Dou backed up his position by explicitly relying on "the liberal principles of the English economy," linking these principles to the notion that "citizens must be free and their persons and property protected" and to the "sacrosanct right to property ownership." He said that "30,000 citizens" could not be "stripped" of rights they had enjoyed for eight or nine centuries, and concluded by asking "Is this in the English spirit?"[32]

Using arguments with the same bases but positioning themselves decidedly in favour of the reversion of the seigniories to the Crown, Polo, José Luis Morales Gallego, Francisco López Pelegrín, Francisco de la Serna and José María de Beladiez made speeches containing repeated references to "property ownership," "individual," "economy," "individual security," "civil liberty" and "individual property," deeming the latter "one of mankind's most sacrosanct and primitive rights." Especially noteworthy among these was a political, legal and historical report containing specific details on the situation of the seigniories in Spain, and particularly Aragon. This was presented in the session on 11 June 1811 by Polo, a deputy from the region, and advocated the reversion of the seigniories, saying that "the state of the seigniories has been and would be one of the biggest obstacles to re-establishing the due proportional equality that the interests of public prosperity both demand and claim."[33]

However, not only did the latest wave of essentially British and Smithian liberalism survive in the Cortes of Cádiz, but so did the more specifically economic liberalism of the Enlightenment, which associated the abolition of the seigniories with the development of agriculture. Such was the case with the Physiocratic agrarianism expounded by José Joaquín Castelló when he alluded to Jovellanos's idea of "removing all the obstacles that hinder it," among which were "entailed lands," having previously stated that agriculture was the "nation's main or only source of wealth."[34] Also represented in the Cortes were positions such as that adopted by Jaime Creus, who declared himself a "lover of citizens' true freedom" and favoured "voting and accepting means that curtail abuses and free the people from oppression." Creus nevertheless opposed the decree to abolish the seigniories because it breached national law and endangered the nation's unity, holding that the institution was also well-loved in Catalonia and other regions, including American territories such as Peru. Creus used the authority of the "celebrated Montesquieu" to support his views, arguing that "he considers these intermediate powers necessary in a well-constituted monarchy" and putting forward the thesis that the less influence the nobility had, the greater "the arbitrariness of kings."[35] Another deputy who was reluctant to abolish the seigniories and called for a committee to examine the issue in more depth was Antonio Capmany.[36]

Parallel to the abolitionist trend with regard to the seigniories there was an attempt to privatise common and uncultivated land, although, as with entailed estates, the Cortes of Cádiz did not reach a firm decision over specific regulation.[37] The ideas of some of the major Spanish Enlightenment figures were used to argue the case, including Campomanes, Floridablanca and Jovellanos and his *Informe de Ley Agraria* Law, all expressly cited by Dou.[38] A Wasteland Committee was set up to examine the matter, which submitted an opinion on regulating the sale of "municipal land and wasteland."[39] However, the Cortes decided to call off the proposed privatisation of common lands and wasteland, mainly on the basis of Dou's argument that under current circumstances the land would fetch excessively low prices.[40]

A few months later the Agriculture Committee's final opinion on the privatisation of wasteland, municipally-owned, bonded and Crown lands was presented to the Cortes, although this never came to fruition in any legal sense. The report stated that while part of the proceeds from the sale of the land would be used to pay off the public debt, part was earmarked for compensation to soldiers who had retired or been declared unfit because of their war wounds.[41] In any event, it is worth noting that the first explicit reference to Adam Smith in the constituent legislature session journals appears here, in the Count of Toreno's defence of privatisation during the session on 18 April 1812. Toreno specifically defended the purchase of common land, even by "great capitalists," as long as its "amortising or entailment" was then forbidden, since via inheritance the "dual advantage of the improvement in the property and its division among many" owners would be achieved, with the consequent increase in the "national wealth." Toreno then referred to the fact that "Smith, a father in these matters," had said that

> when in England, about fifty years ago, it was a question of extending the roads to the counties furthest from London, the counties adjacent to the capital appealed to Parliament, complaining that the action would be detrimental to them and that the value of their produce would diminish.

However, Toreno continued, paraphrasing Smith: "Parliament wisely disregarded these petitions and after a time it was seen that the remoter counties became richer and multiplied their produce and those near London became considerably more prosperous" due to the rise in consumption produced by the growth in general prosperity, which he himself trusted would result from the privatisation of these lands.

With regard to the gradual suppression of vestiges of the Ancien Régime, another example appears in January 1811 in Dou's appeal to the "maxims of good political economy," which for him were largely Adam Smith's, when a regulation on the "promotion of armament factories" proposed by the War Committee was debated and approved.[42] Dou objected to the fact that the villages with under 300 inhabitants in which weapons were manufactured should be "free from all taxes," a measure in article 3 of the regulation, warning that "it is the granting of exclusive privileges that is most at odds with the maxims of good political economy, and what has lost us most in our legislation." Dou was back up by Aner, Creus, Argüelles, Polo, Mariano Blas Garoz, García Herreros and Gutiérrez de la Huerta, with the latter stating that "the issue is among the most important and requires knowledge of political economy," going on to add that protection "in accordance with common rights" is good, but that "what is proposed, being very general, is extremely harmful" and referring to the large losses of income that the measure would generate if applied to many places. Even though Pelegrín stated time and again "I am not asking for a privilege, but an incentive," the Cortes rejected the exemption proposed by the War Committee in the end. The liberal sector had prevailed.

A liberal Smithian argument was also put forward when the *mita*—mandatory public service—to which Native Americans were subjected was abolished during the session on 21 October 1812. The proposal was passed unanimously and ratified as a decree in the session on 9 November. The committee was chaired by Florencio del Castillo and had been appointed for the purpose in April; during the discussion on 21 October not only were economic criteria used to show the harm that the *mitas* had done to industry and agriculture, but also the argument—put forward by Castillo himself—that the institution attacked "the essential principles of society, destroys the most precious rights of free men, is incompatible with civil liberty, the right to property ownership and the individual safety of citizens," on the grounds that "civil liberty cannot be violated without also impairing the right to property ownership, and this cannot be impaired without violating that." Castillo added that "the *mita* destroys the choice that every free man should have to practice the profession, art or any other kind of industry that best suits him," together with the principle that "economists want a nation's land to be divided among its individuals to give them stronger roots, to inspire them to love their property and motivate them to work," a "sorrow" that only "individual interest can ameliorate."

## More Smithian ideas about economics

In addition to the issues referred to previously, a glance through the Cortes of Cádiz session journals shows that ideas and expressions that clearly revealed the liberal camp's familiarity with some of the WN's most characteristic concepts cropped up from time to time in the course of the debates. Joaquín Lorenzo Villanueva, for example, argued for the need to guarantee the security and inviolability of enemy investments in Spain, in the face of the confiscations to which they were subject because of the war. He stressed that respect for private property encouraged trade, prevented smuggling and stopped capital from leaving the country. Surprisingly, Argüelles and Díaz Caneja, representing the Cortes's liberal front, replied that "exquisite theories" were not always applicable, and that the differences between agrarian and trading nations had to be taken into account, as well as the need for any measures taken to be reciprocal.[43]

Another strong Smithian touch, which referred to labour as the source and measure of economic value, can be seen in the proposal laid before the Cortes by the Minister of Finance, José Canga Argüelles. His idea was to draw up a liberalising reform of tariffs and "customs laws, which hinder the rapid distribution of goods," stating that "Spanish economists had found the wellspring of wealth in labour, and centuries before the English proclaimed this truth, which we have deemed new because we were unaware of our forefathers' teachings." The minister also read out a memorandum "on the remedies to be applied to promote trade and true national wealth," a clearly Smithian concept, and it was decided that the report should be printed.[44]

There was an apt application of the notion of the division of labour to the legislative and institutional sphere, anticipating the approach taken by future developments in the economic analysis of law and demonstrating Florencio del Castillo's excellent grasp of Smith's concept. In the debate on article 222 of the constitution, Castillo argued for separating "overseas" from peninsular government, arguing that "the more an individual's attention and application is confined to a small number of objects, the more he progresses and improves in that kind of work because he acquires more skill and ability in those tasks every day," adding that

> among ignorant peoples, where a single person prepares the raw material, spins, weaves and sews a garment, the product of this labour is incomparably smaller and the work of lower quality than in developed countries, where it passes through an incredible number of hands.

Thus "from these advantages which society derives from the division of labour it may be inferred how much benefit will accrue to America from dividing the Ministries."[45] These were probably the statements that were literally closest to the WN to be uttered during the Cortes of Cádiz sessions.

Of course, the same cannot be said of the literalness of references to Smith's work in discussions of other economic issues, but it is clear that when the term "political economy" was used, it was an appeal to the science in which the WN was a fundamental milestone. It was a liberalising yet pragmatic approach to economics with a very Smithian spirit, which had no place for dogmatic solutions but preferred remedies that were tailored to each set of circumstances.[46] That is to say, its proposals were far less universal and abstract than those put forward by the Physiocrats, and also those that would later be framed by Classical economics, via a more formalised discourse, in the work of David Ricardo.[47]

Smithian thought on applied economics was to be found, for example, in the understanding of price theory and its tax implications that emerged in the debate on whether to tax imported Havana cigars, as Felipe Aner proposed, stating that "according to the principles of political economy," when "demand for an item exceeds supply, tax can and should be levied on that item" because as it is a "luxury item" the tax is paid by the "well-to-do."[48] The Cortes did not approve the proposal, however, and the arguments as to why not also included an appeal to "political economy," specifically to the liberal principles of free cultivation and free circulation of goods and the risk of smuggling, together with the protectionist idea that the price increase would make Havana cigars, a "national product," less competitive than other foreign luxury goods.

There is a similar example in the Cortes debate on March 1811 over whether the worth of public debt securities, the famous *vales reales*—royal bouchers—should have their nominal value or the real value attributed to them by "public opinion." Lázaro Dou, a follower of Adam Smith, albeit at his most pragmatic and moderate, favoured the second option, "following the opinion of one whom I recognise as being of superior merit in public economics," who could only be Smith. Dou differentiated between the "voucher" (literally, *vale*) and the "currency" for this purpose: in the latter, the "intrinsic value" must be the same as the "extrinsic value."[49]

## Conclusion: Smithian "self-interest" versus "the times of ignorance"

As shown in the preceding pages, the Cortes of Cádiz was receptive to Adam Smith's thinking on issues relating to the liberalisation of economic activity, both in terms of production and trade, including the grain trade, as well as the principles of private interest and the free exercise of property rights unencumbered by arbitrary interference from political power. More specifically, this also extended to issues such as abolishing seigniories, entailed estates, the seafarers' registers and forest ordinances, as well as privatising common and uncultivated land and land enclosure. The all-pervasive taxation issue also carried the mark of Smith, and the Cortes can thus be viewed as reflecting a second wave in the acceptance of his ideas in Spain. While the first wave was related to the late or mature Enlightenment and was dominated by the adapting of the more strictly economic contents, which undoubtedly contained a latent moderate and veiled political reform, in the second the most radical political elements of Adam Smith's thought are visible, essentially structured around the principle of unambiguous individual freedom, although its implementation in specific reforms did not always match his proposals. Accordingly, this acceptance of Smith's thought, which took place in the context of the parliamentary activity that gave rise to Spain's first liberal constitution, did not focus on the technical aspects of economic theory but rather on the institutional ones that eventually had to serve as a framework of economic policy, according to Coats's terminology (Coats 1971, 14), i.e. the setting up of an appropriate institutional framework for the development of the market.

With a view to drawing some conclusions, there are two anecdotes in particular from the Cortes that reflect both the type of liberal spirit that inspired them and the underlying economic factor. The first illustrates their politically innovative spirit and consists of the president's words during the session on 27 September 1811, spoken as the result of spontaneous demonstrations of jubilation in the public gallery during the previous day's session to applaud the fact that someone had said: "I am a deputy, I wish to speak, I am accountable to the nation." Faced with this "disorder," the president of the chamber stated, "it was my duty to adjourn the session immediately," which he did not do "in view of the fact that the commotion arose from hearing the sort of language that Spain had hitherto been deprived of." He went on to ask, "What Spaniard would not be moved to hear these expressions, when we have seen that we were not even allowed to speak or complain about our ills?," adding that "now that we are a free people, why is it strange that we should be glad to hear such new and glorious language?" The president's next comment leaves no doubt as to his conviction that a change of regime was underway: "in the last reign, if anyone had said 'I am accountable to the nation,' he would have paid for it with nothing less than his head." For all these reasons, he continued, the people's joy "after groaning on the bed of ignorance and slavery until last year," was not surprising. The profound change implied by this understanding is even clearer if it is borne in mind that the president of the Cortes, Bernardo Nadal Crespí, was bishop of Majorca at the time.

There was thus a deliberate attempt in Cádiz to turn around the current political system, which was of course the very system that had convened the sessions, represented by the Junta Central and later by the Consejo de Regencia. It is true that in this parliamentary assembly it was argued that the Cádiz undertaking would attempt to revive the Spaniards' ancient freedoms, which were essentially the historic rights of the Cortes in the old kingdoms and those that governed town councils. These medieval rights had been in decline for centuries and were dissolved all over Spain by the Bourbon governments, with the exception of the Basque Country and Navarre, as stated in the *Discurso preliminar*—Preliminary Speech—at the Constitution (Argüelles (1981 [1812], 76–77). In reality, however, from the outset the Cortes of Cádiz were inspired by a subversive and "revolutionary" idea, to use the language of the time, which essentially consisted of implanting a political liberalism in the country that even the Spanish Enlightenment figures that favoured economic liberalisation and social reforms had previously deemed radical. The principle was successfully defended in the Cortes by a small group of deputies, the most prominent being the Count of Toreno, Argüelles, García Herreros, Pedro Antonio Aguirre, Creus, Dou, Aner, Pelegrín and Polo, who eventually won the support of the majority of the chamber. Nevertheless, as previously pointed out, there were compromises on religious matters due to the constitutional regime's official Catholicism, and the reform of institutions such as entailed estates, Church taxes, the privatisation of common resources and the forest ordinances was put off until later, just as it was a very long time before the seigniories were actually abolished.

Where this liberal principle is concerned, a second anecdote reveals a strong doctrinal component with an eminently economic nature. During the debate on the functions to be attributed to the *diputaciones* by the Constitution, Miguel Ramos Arizpe read out some passages from the preliminary speech drafted by the Constitutional Committee, in which economic affairs attained an undeniable political status.[50] Ramos read part of the speech that included the idea according to which "no doctrine has ever been introduced that was more fatal to public prosperity than that requiring the stimulus of the law or the government's hand in simple person-to-person transactions." He criticised the fact that "the political leader and the head of the Treasury would meddle constantly in economic matters," and added:

> [I]n other paragraphs in the speech, government influence in economic affairs is condemned as extremely harmful to the provinces, attributing this tendency to the notion that prosperity and development in the provinces depended on government influence, which wrongly subrogated itself in place of individual interest.

This reference to individual interest is telling, and so is the fact that the liberal Count of Toreno responded to Ramos by indicating that the *Diputación* provided for in the fledging constitution could "take care of common prosperity" while at the same time "leaving individuals to use their private property and industry," in accordance with a kind of harmony between the general and the particular that had strong Smithian overtones.

In one way or another the use of such terms as individual interest and its reconciling with the common interest without the need for government intervention, and the many expressions and ideas of this nature uttered by the liberal sector of the Cortes of Cádiz, drawn directly from "good political economy" or "English political economy" and including the "sacrosanct right of property ownership," "private interest," "individual security," "civil liberty" and "division

of labour," revealed a liberalism that was steeped in British and Smithian economic thought, confirmed by specific quotations from Smith.[51] In any event, it
was a liberalism that on the whole went further than the version proposed by
the sector of the Spanish Enlightenment represented by Jovellanos. However,
this moderate Spanish Enlightenment ideology, which advocated an economic
liberalisation that was promoted and protected by the authorities and less open
to purely individual acts, also asserted itself in Cádiz. This is clear from the fact
that there was no break with the tradition of sumptuary laws or trade protection, particularly in view of the war and the socio-economic circumstances of
the period.[52]

In short, it is possible to state that historiography has not addressed the
economics component until now, instead focusing on philosophical and more
directly political aspects. This omission is clear from Sánchez Agesta's thorough and insightful analysis of the *Preliminary Speech* at the 1812 Constitution,
in which he concludes that the Cortes of Cádiz proposed the key ideas of
Spanish constitutionalism, which were to be "the foundation of modern
Spain." According to this analysis the ideas were the following: the Spanish
tradition of institutions of freedom; the sovereignty of a nation fighting for its
independence in a "national" war; freedom of expression, which identified the
nation with its representatives; that in the exercise of its sovereignty the nation
established the Cortes as the representative of the same, together with the king,
the pinnacle of executive power; the defence of the freedom and equality of all
Spaniards and, finally, "the importance of a local democracy that left freedom
for individual interests to be the agents of well-being and progress" (Sánchez
Agesta 1981, 62).

On the basis of the evidence set out in this chapter, the last of Sánchez
Agesta's ideas does not include or sufficiently emphasise the scope of "personal
interest" for the triumphant liberal sector of the Cortes; this was linked less to
local politics than to a certain concept of economics without which the doctrine that inspired constitutional liberalism cannot be understood. This was a
conception with Smithian resonances, for which, in the words of Argüelles,

> no doctrine has ever been introduced that was more fatal to public pros-
> perity than the one requiring the stimulus of the law or the hand of the
> government in simple person-to-person transactions, in the investment of
> their resources for the common benefit of those who care for, produce and
> own them and in the application of their labour and industry.
>
> (Argüelles (1981 [1812], 115)

It is also important to note that the reference in Argüelles's speech to town
councils as spaces for civil liberty, as opposed to the impositions of "foreign
dynasties," should not conceal the importance attributed to the *diputaciones*,
which were also understood as "purely economic bodies" (Argüelles (1981
[1812], 119).

When addressing the question of the *diputaciones* the *Preliminary Speech* referred to some strongly liberal economic principles with regard to the government agenda, which was limited to guaranteeing order and freedom, the army and state education. This was so when it spoke of the "fair balance that must exist between the authority of the government, as responsible for public order and the state security, and the liberty that the subjects of a nation must not be deprived of to promote for themselves the increase and improvement of their goods and property," adding that "true encouragement consists in protecting individual liberty in each person's exercise of his physical and moral faculties according to his needs or inclinations," while "the disastrous endeavour to subject all the operations of civil life to the regulations and mandates of authorities has brought about the same or even greater evils than those it was intended to avoid" (Argüelles (1981 [1812], 118). Further on, when the *Preliminary Speech* dealt with the budgetary power of the legislature, in which "the sovereign power of the nation" resides, it pointed out in a similar vein that the government held the initiative in so far as "it can gather sufficient data, news and knowledge to form an exact idea of the state of the nation in general and of the particular state of each province with regard to agriculture, industry and commerce" (Argüelles (1981 [1812], 121). These are no longer times, continued the *Speech*, in which "the false principles adopted by economists to furnish governments with the means of satisfying their greed in the times of ignorance can prevail" (Argüelles (1981 [1812], 122). Rather, they could be said to be Adam Smith's times.

## Notes

1  With regard to the presence of the WN in works by Spanish economists during 1800–1820, see Chapter 8 in this book.
2  The usefulness of analysing the parliamentary activity was first suggested by Coats (1971, 20), and, later on, regarding the Spanish case, by Smith (2000, 314–45). Such an approach has been widely pursued in Italy through a series of works edited by Augello and Guidi from 2005 onwards. In this respect, it is noteworthy that Alonso Ortiz remarked, in the "Prologue" to the first Spanish translation of WN ("El traductor"), that Smith had been widely mentioned in the sessions of the British Parliament (Smith 1794, I, np.).
3  On the origin and establishment of the Cortes Generales y Extraordinarias in Cádiz. For the political significance of the 1812 Constitution and its place in Spanish constitutional history, due to the depth, breadth and current relevance of its interpretation, see also Varela (2020).
4  Sessions were held every day of the year, including on public holidays. The *Diarios de sesiones*, or Cadiz Sessions Journals, are open access and the digital versions are available on the of the Congress of Deputies official website (www.congreso.es/).
5  For example, the fact that, as a means of benefitting the Catholic Church, religious tolerance was not recognised, see Varela (2020, 91ff.).
6  The first time was during the session on 18 April 1812. Three decades earlier, in 1783, Smith had been mentioned in the British Parliament (Rae 1895, 169–72).
7  Session 25-VIII-1811.

8  The Cortes's other economic powers were as follows: "to set public administration expenditure;" "to establish annual contributions and taxes;" "to borrow money when necessary on the nation's credit;" "to approve the distribution of taxes among the provinces;" "to examine and approve the accounts for the investment of public funds;" "to establish customs duties and tariffs;" "to provide for the administration, conservation and disposal of national assets;" "to set the value, weight, law, type and denomination of coins," and to adopt the most convenient and just system of weights and measures deemed." For its part, article 335 established that the *diputaciones*—provincial councils—were to "oversee the good investment of towns' public funds and examine their accounts, so that with their approval, they can also be approved by higher authorities, to ensure that the laws and regulations are observed in everything."

9  The Constitution also contained more specifically economic provisions: article 8, which established the "obligation of all Spaniards, without any distinction whatsoever, to contribute to state expenses in proportion to their assets," which, when it was approved (session 2-IX-1811), left the regulating of ecclesiastical immunity for another time; article 172 established the "restrictions on the authority of the King," who, without the consent of the Cortes, cannot "sign trade treaties, cede or dispose of national assets, impose taxes, grant exclusive privileges to any person or corporation, or take the property of persons or body"; and finally, the all-important Title VII "On Taxes," which encompassed articles 338–355.

10  The Cortes had already made such a distinction by creating a Finance Committee and a Trade, Agriculture, Arts and Mines Committee on 3 and 7 October 1810 respectively. This split would later be converted into a Ministry of Finance and a Ministry of the Interior of the Kingdom, the latter being responsible for health, public instruction, municipal policy and public works, as well as for "factories and other branches of national industry in the part that the Government must play in their promotion and prosperity, as well as everything related to the advancement of agriculture ... mines, quarries, livestock breeding of all kinds, navigation and domestic trade ... and, in a word, statistics and political economy in general" (session 11-XI-1811).

11  There were three major milestones during this period: the decree of 7 August 1809, which abolished provincial revenues; the 1812 Constitution, and the decree of 13 September 1813 on direct taxation. The last two were the fruit of the Cortes of Cádiz. In turn, the August 1809 Junta Central regulation was preceded and prepared for by two other texts: the document of 13 October 1808, which acknowledged the public debt and proposed an administrative reform of the revenue system, and the decree of 22 May 1809, by which the country was consulted on the convening of the Cortes, resulting in a vast range of responses that formed the basis of Spanish public opinion on the question of taxation and proposed the future adoption of the single contribution that the Cortes of Cádiz finally enshrined in the decree of 13 September 1813. However, clashes over the distribution of tax burdens among the regions, technical difficulties and the social, political and economic circumstances made the implementation of these measures and those approved in Cádiz unfeasible. With regard to the thinking on taxation in the Cortes of Cádiz, see López (1999).

12  Session 3-III-1811.

13  Session 30-VIII-1813.

14  Session 18-VII-1813.

15  Session 19-VII-1813.

16  Session 27-I-1811.

17  Session 3-III-1811.
18  Session 26-IV-1811.
19  Session 10-III-1812.
20  Sessions 21,22-III-1811.
21  Session 20-X-1811.
22  Session 19-VIII-1811.
23  Session 16-XI-1811.
24  The debates took place during the sessions from 17–23-XII-1811.
25  Session 21-XII-1811.
26  Session 17-XII-1811.
27  The Cortes finally approved the measure during the session on 10 January 1812 and the corresponding decree dates from 14 January. Further liberal ideas, this time with respect to the question of forests and plantations, can be found in the session on 9 October 1812, when two deputies from Cuba, Jáuregui and O'Gavan, lamented the fact that the decree, legislation suppressing the "ordinances contrary to property and to the free action of individual interest," which "the healthiest principles of political economy urgently demand" was not to be implemented there.
28  Session 22-XII-1811.
29  Session 26-IV-1811.
30  Lastly, due to the Smithian influence, the Spanish Parliament approved the decree of 8 June 1813 concerning the establishment of factories and the practice of any productive industry. In this way, the Parliament settled the freedom of labour and brought to an end the debate about the guilds that dates back to the late eighteenth century (Astigarraga 2017, 371–72).
31  The debates on this issue lasted until the decree abolishing the seigniories was finally passed on 6 August 1811. The vote was held on 1 July 1811, a month after the debates opened, and the result was 128 votes in favour and 16 against, although some amendments were still approved during the sessions on 4 and 5 July. In contrast, the Cortes did not reach a final decision on the related question of the abolition of entailed estates, which García Herreros, Calatrava, Castelló and other deputies had advocated during several sessions at the end of February 1812, a year after Joaquín Díaz Caneja had proposed it on 12 January 1812. In the end none of these proposals, in which principles such as "individual interest" were also invoked, was accepted.
32  Session 5-VI-1811.
33  Session 11-VI-1811.
34  Session 14-VI-1811.
35  Session 12-VI-1811.
36  Session 14-VI-1811.
37  In the session on 12 January 1812 the Cortes decided not to proceed with the proposal from Díaz Caneja, seconded by Castillo, to repeal "entailments and entailment trusts of any kind whatsoever," making the "current holders" the owners, as well as to "absolutely prohibit the power to bind or entail."
38  Session 2-II-1811.
39  Session 23-VIII-1811.
40  Session 27-VIII-1811.
41  Session 22-II-1812.
42  Session 27-I-1811.
43  Session 15-II-1812.

44  Session 14-XII-1811.

45  Session 23-X-1811. As regards the application of the ideas of the WN to the institutions and activity of politics, they could also have come via the works of Emmanuel-Joseph Sieyès, author of *Qu'est-ce que le Tiers-État?* (1789), which was well known to early Spanish constitutionalists; see Larrère (1992).

46  In this respect, see Viner (1927).

47  In any case, and following the aforementioned approach by Viner, the analysis carried out from the perspective of liberal orthodoxy (Robbins 1961, Coats 1971, O'Brien 2017) show how the most academic and representative examples of Classical economics were steered away from dogmatism. Furthermore, they were close to the real socio-economic problems that may demand public policies.

48  Session 27-VII-1811.

49  Session 5-III-1811.

50  Session 12-I-1812. The *Discurso preliminar* was essentially the work of the deputy Agustín de Argüelles with help from José de Espiga; on the text's drafting and contents, see Sánchez Agesta (1981).

51  This liberalism could also have been informed by versions by other authors such as Say, who was very widely read in Spain during the period, although his name was not mentioned during the Cádiz sessions.

52  For example, Alonso López made a proposal with regard to the sumptuary laws based on the defence of nationally-produced goods (session 10-XI-1811). In the same vein, Villanueva proposed a regulation against the ostentation of military apparel, forcing a committee on the issue of luxury to be created (session 13-XI-1811). However, there is no record of any of these proposals materialising into specific regulations during the period of the Cortes Generales y Extraordinarias.

# 13 Adam Smith in the economic debates during the Liberal Triennium (1820–1823), the Second Liberal Exile and Hispanic America

*Juan Zabalza*

## The political and institutional environment

The first constitutional period in Spain came to an end in 1814 when absolutism was restored. The old regime's major institutions, such as the Council of Castile, were re-established, and liberals repressed. However, the constitutional flame was not extinguished entirely and, throughout the decade, several of the so-called military pronouncements aimed at overthrowing the absolutist regime. Most of them failed, but finally, in the early 1820s, General Riego proclaimed the Constitution of Cádiz (1812), giving rise to a series of uprisings that resulted in the encirclement of the royal palace of Madrid and the acceptance of the Constitution of Cádiz by the king.

The revolution's triumph paved the way to a new constitutional period known as the Liberal Triennium. The Constitution of Cádiz and the liberal Parliament, which was to meet in Madrid, were restored in July 1820. This three-year period saw a frenetic parliamentary activity that carried out many legislative reforms, many of which referred to economic issues that resulted in bitter debates amongst the liberals, split into moderates and radicals, who demanded the abolition of the monarchy and deeper reforms. The economic environment was also quite unstable as a result of the removal of most of the employees in the public administration, the so-called Independence War, the economic consequences of the independence of the Hispanic American territories, the calamitous economic performance of the economy in the early nineteenth century and the financial burden of the growing public debt (Lucas 2017).

At the same time, the king of Spain joined the so-called Holy Alliance that emerged from the Congress of Vienna that eventually decided to invade Spain in April 1823 through the army known as the 100.000 sons of Saint Louis. The absolutist troops encountered hardly any military resistance and, finally, the absolutist monarchy was restored at the hands of Fernando VII. The result was abolishing the Constitution of Cádiz, dismantling the Parliament and the forced exile of thousands of liberals who emigrated to France, South America and, mainly, to London, where they settled in the Somers Town district (Llorens

DOI: 10.4324/9781003152804-16

1979). All this took place in the context of profound changes in the political setting of the Spanish monarchy. Some of the Hispanic American possessions, coinciding with Spain's Napoleonic invasion, had started to politically separate from the Spanish monarchy, giving way to new republics. Moreover, liberal thought in economic matters also flourished in these republics.

This chapter aims at searching for the footprints of Smith's *The Wealth of Nations* (WN) in the parliamentary debates during the Liberal Triennium, on the one hand, and the exile in London and Hispanic America, on the other. The primary sources used in this work are the parliamentary records during the three legislative periods between 1820 and 1823 and the exiles' publications in London and Hispanic America, whether monographs or articles in periodicals.

The exile of Spanish liberals exemplifies the transoceanic nature of the spread of the WN in Spain and Hispanic America. Before the independence of the Hispanic American republics, both sides of the Atlantic Ocean belonged to the same intellectual realm, and economic ideas flowed following similar paths in the entire territories of the Spanish monarchy. After independence, these intellectual links continued to some extent for an extended period. Therefore, a brief epigraph analysing the coming of the WN to Hispanic America is appropriate.

## The shadow of Smith's WN in the parliamentary debates of the Liberal Triennium

Historians have pointed out how the Liberal Triennium continued the parliamentarian debates in Cádiz that came suddenly to an end in 1814 after the return of absolutism. Therefore, the central economic discussions focused on the reform of Spanish public finance, domestic free trade, custom duties, the property of the land, the abolition of the entailed dominions, the laws of progeniture—the so-called *mayorazgos*—and the economic relationships with the territories of the Spanish monarchy in Hispanic America and Asia. The analysis of the parliamentary records demonstrates many generic and specific mentions of "economists" and "political economy" in the debates on these topics, which undoubtedly refer to Classical economists and Classical political economy, respectively. Furthermore, there are indications of the use of ideas, frames of reference, suggestions and policies of Classical economists in general and Smith in particular when some members of the Parliament refer to the "public happiness," "individual interest," "the wealth of the nation" or to the establishment of liberal economic institutions like the guarantee of property rights, individual security and economic and political freedoms. The principles of political economy are the point of reference to debate the different economic and financial issues—not only by well-known economists like Flórez Estrada and Canga Argüelles, but also by the members of Parliament who were not connected to the circles of economists but used these principles for backing liberal economic reforms and policies. Furthermore, even those who opposed the liberal reforms also referred to Smith and Classical political economy to support their respective points of view, in some cases by refuting Smith's ideas and in others by reinterpreting them in terms of the Spanish economic and political context.

However, Smith's specific influence was quite visible in the Memorandum presented in 1820 to the Parliament by Canga Argüelles, by then Secretary of State and Minister of Treasury, in charge of public finances. The Memorandum included a detailed plan for rearranging Spanish public finances that combined the principles of Classical political economy on this topic and the particular circumstances of the Spanish public finances, characterised by a growing public deficit, an astronomic public debt and an inefficient tax system.[1] Indeed, the starting point was setting out the principles that the reform of public finances must abide by, inspired by the reform planned in 1813 in the Cádiz Parliament and Smith's maxims of taxation. Many of the elements composing the four "maxims" of taxation in book V of the WN are apparent: the ability to pay principle as the basis of the equality of taxation, which, on the other hand, article VIII of the constitution embodied; the certainty and not arbitrariness of taxes; the principle that taxation ought to take out from the "pockets of the people" as little as possible; and, finally, the critical idea that taxation should not discourage the most productive branches of industry.[2]

Along with the Memorandum, Canga Argüelles analyses the administrative structure of the tax collection. He explicitly refers to Smith's maxim of tax efficiency that aimed at reducing costs by developing officers' skills and simplifying as much as possible the method of collecting taxes.[3] Generally speaking, the plan relied on direct taxation and rejected indirect taxes as the latter endangered the sources of wealth. On this criterion, he discarded, as Smith did, consumption excises as they were "destroyers of industry."[4] Also, like Smith, Canga Argüelles rejected any state monopoly, like the so-called *estanco* of tobacco, which, according to him, does not fit with the "principles of political economy." However, the overriding need for revenues led him to adopt a middle way, inspired by Necker: the government should maintain the tobacco monopoly but, at the same time, should bring prices and taxes on tobacco down.[5] A parliamentary committee examined Canga Argüelles's plan and released its opinion, which made many nuances to Canga Argüelles's proposal by reducing direct contributions and increasing the indirect collection of taxes (Lucas 2017).

By January 1822, the government's lack of popularity and other problems like worsening economic figures led to the appointment of a new administration. Sierra-Pambley replaced Canga Argüelles as State Secretary of Public Finances in the third parliamentary period. Sierra-Pambley presented a report in the Parliament analysing the causes of the failure of the reform of public finances and suggesting some modifications to Canga Argüelles's plan.[6] During the debate, some members of the Parliament opposed the rearrangement of the public finances. They indicated that the logic of the domestic economy should apply to public finances. That is, expenses should adapt to the capacity of collecting taxes. Sierra-Pambley answered them by arguing that the principles of political economy had nothing to do with the principles of the domestic economy. Thus, the government must finance some essential public expenses, like national defence, justice, public works, and the institutions favouring commerce like "the education of people of all ages." He faithfully followed Smith on these issues.[7] Furthermore, the government should determine public expenses and plan contributions to finance them.[8] This point of view was not unique, and some members of the Parliament pointed out some of the functions that Smith attributed to the government. Nevertheless, as Canga Argüelles mentioned in the same debate, most Parliament members generally accepted the budget equilibrium.[9]

Both memorandums by Canga-Argüelles and Sierra-Pambley gave way to a series of lively debates during which Classical political economy and Smith backed different views. For example, the member of the Parliament, the Count of Toreno, when supporting general direct contribution and rejecting the so-called *alcabalas* that taxed every kind of commerce, affirmed that the committee had consulted the works of the leading economists, among which he mentions Smith.[10] Even those members of Parliament opposing the reforms and their "principles," like Sebastián de Ochoa, also draw on the "economists" for arguing that they did not establish who was going to pay taxes.[11] Canga Argüelles's plan faced many difficulties and, by 1822, the growing deficit made unfeasible the reform proposed in his Memorandum. Still, its principles would inspire the first liberal reform of public finances enacted finally in 1845.

The inherited public debt and the continuous deficit that the Spanish public finances experienced due to the inefficient taxation system led to a debate about public credit (Toboso 1996, 402). As Minister of Finance, Canga Argüelles took charge of drafting a new Memorandum to determine the causes behind the failure in the trust in Spanish "credit" and the high level of the public debt. The Memorandum remarked on the need to pay the principal and the debt's service to preserve the "credit" and promote economic development (Canga Argüelles 1820, 2). To demonstrate this, Canga Argüelles relies on chapter III in book V of the WN that inspired his historical account about the Spanish public debt and the financial policies of the successive Spanish governments that impoverished families and discredited the treasury as a consequence of the reiterative delinquencies of the service of the debt. On the other hand, to show that the growing magnitude of the public debt threatened the "credit" of the Spanish treasury and, therefore, the possibility of future borrowings, Canga Argüelles quotes an excerpt in the WN (Canga Argüelles 1820, 42):

> When national debts have once been accumulated to a certain degree, there is a scarce, I believe, a single instance of their having been fairly and completely paid. The liberation of the publick revenue, if it has ever been brought about at all, has always been brought about by a bankruptcy: sometimes by an avowed one, but always by a real one, though frequently by a pretended payment.
>
> (WN V, III, 929)

Canga Argüelles quoted from Garnier's French version of the WN. He uses Garnier's comments to demand a correct administration for guaranteeing the service of the debt and, therefore, the "credit" of the Spanish treasury (Canga Argüelles 1820, 42).

The debates that followed the presentation of the Memorandum to the Parliament showed two points of view. Those like Canga Argüelles and Count of Toreno supported Smith's opinion about the need to meet the service of debt, the entire public debt, and others who fiercely rejected the Smithian perspective. Furthermore, the supporters of the Smithian approach connected the public credit to confiscate the land in the hands of the Church. For them, guaranteeing the service of the debt by winning back the trust of foreign and national lenders prevailed over any other issue, which explains the fierce opposition of those who opposed Canga-Smith's view (Toboso 1996, 411).

The third parliamentarian discussion in which Smith's shadow is quite visible focused on the rearrangement of custom duties. Canga Argüelles introduced the debate in an epigraph in the above-mentioned Memorandum on the Spanish public finances. In addition, he quoted excerpts in the WN for supporting his view on custom duties that favoured moderate duties for foreign goods and rejected prohibitions:

> By removing all prohibitions, and by subjecting all foreign manufactures to such moderate taxes, as it was found from experience afforded upon each article the greatest revenue to the public, our own workmen might still have a considerable advantage in the home market, and many articles, some of which at present afford no revenue to government, and others a very inconsiderable one, might afford a very great one.[12]

On this principle, Canga Argüelles planned the rearrangement of Spanish custom duties by combining the interest of the Spanish public finances and the demands of individuals limiting custom duties and guaranteeing the free circulation of commodities, which eventually would result in a higher collection of taxes. The relationship between commercial policy and collection of taxes, as posed by Smith-Canga, was the reference point for the debate that followed the reading of the Memorandum in the Parliament and the report that prepared the Committee of Finance and Trade in the light of the tariffs proposal made by the Junta Especial de Aranceles—the Special Tariff Board.[13] The proponent of custom duties prohibition, Guillermo Oliver, who read the committee's report, opposed Smith-Canga's view by arguing that the primary goal of tariffs is to "support the permanent wealth of the nation" and not the collection of taxes itself.[14] Therefore, the government must protect domestic productions and promote the domestic market, including the colonial possessions.[15] Behind Oliver and other Catalan members of the Parliament, like Valle, underlies "an infant industry" theory that opposes free trade and backs prohibitionism for promoting industrialisation and a "genuine economic freedom". This view was standard in the circles that promoted custom duties prohibition in Catalonia, and they argued so by relying on the "principles of political economy."[16]

Nevertheless, as Lluch (1971–1972) pointed out, the knowledge of Smith's WN by the proponents of prohibitionism was not as in–depth as they said in their addresses to the Parliament. However, proponents of moderate protectionism, like the Count of Toreno, who explicitly quoted Smith on agricultural protectionism, argued that the most advanced countries, and, in particular, England, did not reduce tariffs. Therefore, all of them rejected applying the theory supported by Classical economists to the Spanish economy.[17] However, all this happened before enacting the Reciprocity of Duties Act in 1823, designed by William Huskisson, opening the road to free trade in Great Britain. On the other hand, the proponents of free trade, like Romero-Alpuente or Freire, insisted on Smith's link of free trade and tax collection in the way that Canga Argüelles had done in the Memorandum or by connecting free trade to prosperity.[18] Flórez Estrada, who opposed any protectionist policies, did not abandon the strategy of economic development based on the priority of the agriculture sector within a context of free trade and the international division of labour, mentioned above.[19]

Proponents of free trade like Vadillo, Moreno-Guerra and Flórez Estrada also linked high tariffs, growing goods smuggling and falling incomes for the Spanish treasury in a way that recalls what Smith argued in book V in the WN.[20] Summing up, the Classical political economy, the principles of political economy and the economists were a continuous intellectual source during the debate on Spanish customs duties. Given Canga's quotation of Smith, there is no doubt that they also refer to the Scottish economist.

Another area in which Classical economists' presence is self-evident is the suppression of the entailed domains of clergy and the so-called *mayorazgos* or law of primogeniture. This issue was of particular interest in Spain and, therefore, was widely debated in the Parliament. Liberal economists employed arguments and ideas easily identifiable in Classical economists to underpin their view that abolishing these domains could make Spanish agriculture thrive. Something similar applies to *mayorazgos* and the relationships with the colonial territories in Hispanic America in their various dimensions. However, although we may notice similar views to Smith in the WN, the deputies who supported this perspective relied mainly on the Spanish members of the Enlightenment like Campomanes or Jovellanos, whom Classical economists had softly influenced. Regarding monetary matters, however, the debates were anachronistic, as the problems of Spain were quite different from those of the rest of Europe (Prieto and De Haro 2012, 142, 144–46).

## Smith in the works of Spanish exiles in Britain and Hispanic America

### The shadow of Smith in the writings of Spanish exiles in London

Many of the Spanish exiles settled in London were able to earn a living in using their intellectual activity. They worked for publishers based in London and channelled their commitment to liberal ideas through a series of periodicals that dealt with a wide range of issues, like arts, technical advances, literature, politics, poetry, history, and sometimes political economy. *Ocios de los españoles emigrados* (1824–1825) published some articles about the history of political economy in Spain and the state of Spanish public finances. Still, the mentions of Classical political economy are too generic. *El emigrado observador* (1828–1829) follows this pattern. In practice, it was a platform for preparing the return to absolutist Spain of Canga Argüelles, the former Secretary of the Treasury Department in the Liberal Triennium (Simal 2012). Canga Argüelles, indeed, included some articles on economics throughout the pages of this journal. However, most refer to specific aspects of English public finances or generic mentions of contract enforcement. Still, no particular mention of Smith is found, although his shadow is visible in some of Canga Argüelles's comments.[21] However, *Museo de Ciencias y Artes* (1824–1826), edited by the German publisher Ackermann and run by Mora, paid more attention to political economy. In general, the journal conveys the agenda of Classical economists: strong support for private business, uncompromising advocacy of free trade and a limitation of state intervention. On countless occasions, Mora refers generically to "the economists," and it is apparent that he is referring to Classical economists when he does so. The periodical shows some of Smith's ideas about trade and public finances.[22] Still, they are primarily conveyed through Say, who was quite influential in Spain during these years and whose works were repeatedly translated into Spanish from 1804 onwards (Menudo and O'Kean 2019). Smith's shadow, however, was much evident in a series of monographs published by Spanish exiles in Britain by Flórez Estrada and Canga Argüelles. They, as mentioned, had played a significant role in the parliamentary debates of the Liberal Triennium.

During his exile in London, Canga Argüelles published two works on public finances: *Elementos de Hacienda Pública* (1825) and *Diccionario de Hacienda* (1826–1827) in five volumes. His contribution to public finances has been largely ignored or considered as merely descriptive. However, in recent times, historiography has retrieved Canga's stature and has noted how his works positively contributed to spreading the science of public finances in Spain and Hispanic America (Comín 2000b, 413-16; López 2005). At the very beginning of the *Elements*, Canga Argüelles advanced that:

> it is not enough to study Smith abstractly, Say, Ricardo and Storch, but rather to apply the principles of this modern science to the political business, to the liberal arrangement of trade, to the distribution of contributions, and o the usefulness of loans.
>
> (Canga Argüelles 1825, 1)

The use made by Canga Argüelles of the WN, indeed, fits with these principles. In his *Diccionario,* Smith is a theoretical authority in three entries. In "Comercio Balanza" (Trade Balance), chapter I in book IV of Smith's WN helps to dismantle the mercantilist argument of gold accumulation. However, it is true that Canga Argüelles also resorts to Spanish economic history to demonstrate that the mercantilist doctrine of the trade balance is false (Canga Argüelles 1826–1827, I, 263; WN, IV, I, 429–51). An excerpt from book II, chapter 5, *Of the different employments of capital*, in the WN backs the need to promote domestic trade. In this chapter, Smith tries to demonstrate how the capital employed in the domestic market "make twelve operations, or be sent out and returned twelve times, before a capital employed in the foreign trade of consumption has made one," and therefore "twenty times more encouragement and support to the industry of the country" (Canga Argüelles 1826–1827, II, 146; WN, II, V, 368–69). Finally, the famous excerpt from the WN in which Smith describes the operation of a pin factory is introduced under the heading "División del trabajo"(Division of Labour) to illustrate the increasing productivity of dividing the labour within a unit of production (Canga Argüelles 1826–1827, II, 375; WN, I, I, 14–15). However, although Canga Argüelles lived in London, he consulted and quoted from the French edition of the WN by Garnier, which was the edition that he probably managed to acquire many years before migrating to England (Canga Argüelles 1826–1827, II, 211).

However, in his *Elementos*, Canga Argüelles resorts to Smith's authority for a rather practical purpose. This aimed at supporting the economic reforms and policies of the liberal agenda that he had attempted in 1812 and 1820 in the Spanish Parliament. Canga Argüelles quotes excerpts in chapter II of book II of the WN (*Of the Discouragement of Agriculture in the antient State of Europe after the fall of the Roman Empire*) for analysing the so-called *mayorazgos*, its origins and its negative consequences—"obstacles"—over the industry (Canga Argüelles 1825, 59; WN, III, II, 384). Canga Argüelles also uses the WN to argue in favour of the "free circulation of grains" since it is "not only a remedy against famine but a preservative against hunger." According to him, providing agricultural products to the people required promoting individual interest and eliminating any burden to agriculture (Canga Argüelles 1825, 62; WN, IV, V, b, 526–28). In general, the WN is used to demand falling custom duties. The observations that he included in the entry "Inglaterra. Relaciones comerciales de esta potencia con España"—England. Commercial Relationships with Spain—in *Diccionario*, for example, consists of a series of remarks that he had planned to submit to the Spanish government before the signature of the Treaty of Amiens. Among other considerations, Canga Argüelles sought to influence the government to reduce customs duties by using some episodes in book IV of the WN in which Smith explains the benefits derived from the reduction of customs duties (Canga Argüelles 1826–1827, III, 413; WN, IV, VI, 545). Furthermore, Canga Argüelles, relying on the same book in the WN, advocates creating a global market. Accordingly, trade treaties that privilege a single nation are, in his view, detrimental to all countries, including the country most favoured by such privilege (Canga Argüelles 1825, 66; 1826–1827, V, 187–88; WN, IV, VI, 545–46).

Canga Argüelles also used Smith as an intellectual source in *Elementos* regarding minor aspects of public finance; for example, when he tackles financing the burdens of the magistrate. Canga Argüelles finds in book V of the WN the remedy when he suggests that "litigants pay fees to the administration of justice, the amount of which distributes among the judges after sentencing based on the days and hours they have worked" (Canga Argüelles 1825: 99). However, he is cautious in applying the suggestions he finds in the WN and considers that Spanish magistrates, unfamiliar with receiving their salaries based on productivity, would reject such an idea as do the "roughest classes of the people." Such an opinion is understandable within a broader context of a general critique of the judicial system of the Ancien Régime (Canga Argüelles 1825, 99; WN, V, I, b, 719). Finally, Canga, as Smith did, warns about the problems associated with a high level of public debt, which may lead to the suspending of debt servicing (Canga Argüelles 1825, 182; WN, V, III, 929).

Flórez Estrada was, as seen, one of the most active liberals of the radical wing in the Parliament of the Liberal Triennium. Consequently, when the liberal troops finally surrendered, he moved to London, where he remained until 1830. Unfortunately, there is no complete account of his London activities and his contacts with British economists. However, his involvement must have been intense. He published *Reflections on the present mercantile distress* (1826), the *Curso de Economía Política* (1828) and numerous contributions, although not strictly on political economy, to the journals edited by the Spanish exiles.

*Curso de Economía Política* (1828), which Flórez Estrada entirely prepared during his British exile between 1826 and 1828, had seven editions up to 1852 and was the most significant theoretical contribution in Spain during all the nineteenth century (Almenar 1980, l). Flórez Estrada himself declares his purpose of disseminating the political economy's progress in recent years in the Hispanic sphere. From our perspective, *Curso* is mottled with countless quotations and excerpts taken from the WN directly or indirectly through other works like McCulloch's *Principles of Political Economy* (1825), which demonstrates how Flórez Estrada was familiar with British economic literature at the time. Flórez Estrada attributed to Smith theoretical advances in labour division, competition, economic freedom, commercial policy and taxation, which, according to him, belong to a timeless and everlasting doctrinal heritage. However, he also points out how some of Smith's contributions to political economy are wrong and overtaken by the breakthrough findings of many economists like Sismondi, Lueder, Storch, Destutt de Tracy, James Mill, McCulloch and Ricardo (Flórez Estrada 1828, 48; Almenar 1980, lxvi). As a result, Flórez Estrada proceeds to a systematic rebuttal of a wide range of topics in the WN by contrasting Smith's ideas to the most up-to-date contributions to the science of political economy at the time. Therefore, Flórez reinterpreted the Smithian doctrine as a starting point for a more advanced and consistent theory developed by the second generation of Classical economists.[23]

### Mora and the spread of Smithian ideas in Hispanic America

Spanish liberals, and in particular those exiled in London, became firmly committed to establishing liberal institutions in the old colonial territories of Hispanic America. Mora, who had published *Catecismo de Economía Política* (1825) in London to be distributed in the Hispanic America market, fits with this pattern. Although some Smithian rhetoric flavours are visible in *Catecismo*, there are no mentions of the WN. However, Smith's influence on Mora would be more apparent in successive works that he would produce in Hispanic America, specifically in the journal *El Mercurio Chileno* (1828–1829) published in Santiago de Chile (Astigarraga and Zabalza 2017). After a brief stay in Buenos Aires, Mora moved to Chile as a prestigious intellectual and promoter of educational institutions. Besides contributing to drawing up the republic's first constitution and being a direct counsellor of president Pinto, he published a series of articles in *El Mercurio Chileno*, a periodical financed by the government. In these articles, Mora drew up a plan of economic development for the Republic of Chile backed by a theory of economic growth complemented by a conceptual architecture that embraced three areas: monetary theory, the theory of international trade and public finance. The plan embraced an institutional reform and an economic agenda that aimed at securing liberal society in Chile and powering economic growth. In doing so, Mora used central concepts of Classical political economy and Smith's approach to economic growth.

The central role of productivity, savings and capital accumulation in Mora's model show how indebted he was to Smith's theory of economic growth. Nevertheless, the introduction of the interest rate as a critical variable suggests that he follows Smith's canonical interpretation by McCulloch (1825). McCulloch treatise indeed contributed to extending Smith's sway during the 1820s, and 1830s. According to Mora—who follows the Smith-McCulloch's model—the second determining factor of economic growth is the international division of labour. Chile, according to Mora, has an absolute advantage in agriculture thanks to the Chilean climate. However, relying on Smith-McCulloch, Mora thought economic development is bound to a series of institutional requirements. In particular, he remarks on the need of developing a bank system for guaranteeing money and capital supplies, a legal environment that favours economic growth, a tax system for financing the public administration of the liberal state and, finally, a policy of free trade. The size of the market limits the latter. By analysing all these requirements in *El Mercurio*, Mora shows an apparent Smithian influence.

The shortage of coins and the financial system's weakness during the 1820s resulted from the subordination of monetary policy to the Spanish monarchy's commercial and economic interests (De Haro 2013, 203–27). Mora finds an answer to such a problem in Smith, who suggested the creation of commercial banks "that do not lend metallic money, but a 'sign' that represents it and whose real value comes from the trust and confidence enjoyed by the banks that issue money" (Mora 1828b, 155). In this way, these institutions—by issuing convertible note banks—can feed "the industry, agriculture and trade with capital and credit" (Giacomin 2007, 181–89). Accordingly, following a tradition starting by Cantillon and followed up by Smith and some other Classical economists, Mora attributes to money supply and the financial institutions a central role in economic growth. The detailed analysis of the monetary articles in *El Mercurio* demonstrates how Mora attributes to money the function of deposit of value as "mercantilists" did; but also the role of serving as a means of payment so that money plays a central role in the theory of economic growth, as Classical economists such as Smith had pointed out. Thus, in Mora's view, both money and goods relied on the operation of the supply and the demand in such a way that "the rate of interest moves up when the consumers, namely the speculators that want liquidity, demand money beyond the money holdings of capitalists" (Mora 1828b, 155). Thus, Mora regards the interest rate as a central component of the production cost that directly impacts the profit rate. Behind these causal relationships is, without doubt, McCulloch's view on economic growth in which the money supply has an impact on the level of economic activity (O'Brien 1989, 153–59).

The institutional development of the Republic of Chile also demanded, according to Mora, who follows Smith faithfully, a profound reform of the system of public finances. On the one hand, regarding public spending, Mora shows an apparent Smithian influence when he attributes to government the tasks of financing the administration of justice, guaranteeing law and order and the national defence, promoting public infrastructures and education, and the legal guardianship of contracts and property rights. Furthermore, all this demands regular incomes for the Treasury through a well-designed tax system (Mora 1828a, 62; WN, V, I, a, 689–816). The core issue when drawing up the tax system is the distribution of the tax burden that Mora introduced by synthesising Smith's famous canons (equality, certainty, the convenience of payment and economy of the collection) and Sismondi's tax prescription from which he derived three principles that the tax system should adhere to: minimising the contact between tax collectors and taxpayers by eliminating the coercion practised by intermediate tax collectors—it owes much to Smith's view on public finance (O'Brien 1989, 337); supervising "thoughtfully the natural development of productive labour" in such a way that the industries that required stimulus would be under-taxed and the rest over-taxed (Mora 1828a, 56); finally, the tax structure should subordinate to the general principle of *laissez-faire* by minimising taxes on trade and more specifically import duties, which Mora shared with Classical economists (Mora 1828a, 60). On these principles Mora advocates for direct taxation on "production and capital."

Mora's rhetoric on free trade relies on a simple but effective international trade theory that connects economic growth to free trade based on Smith-McCulloch's absolute advantage theory. In this vein, Mora attributes the origins of international trade to the diverse structure of "absolute" costs in various countries that results in differential productivity of some goods that have lower prices (Mora 1828d, 249). As mentioned above, Chile's natural environment and property structure were well suited for agricultural development, as Mora enthusiastically pointed out. On the other hand, according to him, the nascent industry could not lead the republic's economic growth. Relying on Smith's theory of the four stages,[24] he points out that Chile should be developed based on agriculture and free trade. On these theoretical grounds, he planned an economic agenda that primarily pleads for removing import duties, particularly on industrial goods. The latter merely "enrich" the treasury, results in lower levels of international trade (exports and imports), and eventually erodes "domestic consumption [...] and public welfare" (Mora 1829, 761). In this vein, he also remarks, following Smith, that high import duties encourage smuggling resulting in falling duties collection (Mora 1828b, 205-207; WN, V, II, k, 897–933). This approach sets the debate on import duties in the broader sphere of economic development theory as Mora sizes up their influence on the profit rate and, ultimately, economic growth.

## Smith in Hispanic America: a general overview

Mora was, without doubt, a significant player in the diffusion of Smith in Hispanic America. His stay in Santiago de Chile and articles in *El Mercurio Chileno* are the best known of his journey in South America. Nevertheless, he was also active by promoting liberalism in general and political economy in Argentina, Peru and possibly Bolivia. Even the pamphlet *De la libertad de comercio* (1843) that he drafted in the early 1840s, in which he proved to be a radical supporter of free trade, was also published in Mexico. But almost nothing is known about his role in spreading Classical political economy in these countries except for promoting some periodicals in Buenos Aires (Amunátegui 1888).

Therefore, it is worth saying some words about the impact of the WN in Hispanic America, beyond the contribution of Spanish liberals, which had been analysed synthetically by R.S. Smith almost seven decades ago (1957). The influence of Smith in Hispanic America preceded the independence of the new republics. It was part of a more general and comprehensive spread of the political economy of the late Spanish Enlightenment and early Liberalism in the territories of the Spanish monarchy. Prominent intellectuals and reformers like Belgrano, Villava, Arango and Parreño, among others, took part in transferring ideas from the metropolis to the colonial territories of the kingdom.

On the other hand, Smith spread all over Hispanic America through different and multiple channels. He was read in some cases directly from the English versions. Still, Smith´s ideas also jumped the Atlantic Ocean through the Spanish translation of the WN by Alonso, the Spanish translation of Condorcet *Compendium* and the influence of Jovellanos and other representatives of the late Spanish Enlightenment (Hurtado 2019). On the other hand, in the subsequent decades, liberal Spanish economists also committed to spreading Classical political economy in Hispanic America, like the above-mentioned Mora or Flórez Estrada, who declared to have drafted *Curso de Economía Política* to spread Classical political economy to Hispanic America (Flórez Estrada 1828).

There is an agreement that liberalism in general and Smithian ideas came to Hispanic America notably in the context of the political independence from the Spanish monarchy (Mendes-Cunha and Suprinyak 2017). The cultivated young generation of the former territories of the Spanish kingdom became interested in Smith as a supporter of economic and political reforms like the monetary system, the fiscal and trade policies or the promotion of economic development. But, in many cases, they believed in the motivations of "self-interest" for fueling economic growth, which they considered incompatible with the colonial dependency on Spain (Smith 1957a, 1246).[25] It is also generally accepted that, similarly to Spain, Smith's ideas spread not only directly from the WN, but also through Say and Bastiat's works. Generally speaking, these ideas adapted to the cultural, religious and economic context of the newly created republics.

In one way or another, Smith was handled by merchants, politicians, reformers and intellectuals in most of the new republics. Argentina indeed experienced one of the most intense Smithian influences. As soon as 1797, there are indications that Argentinian merchants had encountered Condorcet's *Compendium* in the Spanish version by Martínez Irujo in the context of the debates about free trade in Buenos Aires (Perpere 2020). Much better known is the impact of Smith once the independence revolution broke out. Shortly before, Vieytes, a hero of the May 1810 Revolution, founded the periodical *Semanario de Agricultura, Industria y Comercio* (1802–1807), where he supported profound economic reforms and specific projects. The articles show the influence of many Smithian ideas adapted to the particular contexts of Argentina (Rodríguez-Braun 1997, 448–54). Vieytes, who was also influenced by the Italian "Civil Economy" approach of Genovesi, became strongly attracted to Smith's idea of "self-interest" and his writings in *Semanario* continuously referred to the links between it and economic development (Perpere 2014, 2021).[26] Belgrano, one of the republic's founding fathers, was educated at the University of Salamanca in the late eighteenth century, under Professor Salas (Astigarraga 2011a). In Salamanca, Belgrano knew many intellectual sources of the late Spanish Enlightenment, possibly Condorcet's *Compendium* in Martinez-Irujo's translation. Once he returned to Argentina, he published in the periodical *Correo del Comercio* (1810–1811) a summary of chapter I in book IV of the WN. Furthermore, many Smithian concepts mixed with ideas of the "mercantile system" are apparent in its pages (Smith 1957a, 1247). The long shadow of Smith's influence extended throughout the nineteenth century among supporters of liberalism like Mariano Moreno, Antonio Nariño or Juan Bautista Alberdi, who based his plan of modernisation of Hispanic America on "free trade with the entire civilised world" (Subercaseaux 2016, 12–14).

Beyond Mora's articles, there are indications that Smith was well known in liberal circles in Chile. For example, Manuel de Salas, Juan Egaña and Camilo Henríquez, the group of liberals who founded in 1813 the Instituto Nacional— the National Institute—in Santiago of Chile, recommended the works by Genovesi, Say and Smith to follow the course on political economy organised by the Instituto (Smith 1957a, 1248). On the other hand, the economic debates in Chile, particularly those that referred to the foundation of a central bank and free trade that extended during a long period (1790–1870), paved the way for introducing foreign ideas that adapted to the economic and institutional environment of Chile. Although the "neo-Mercantilism" approach coming from Spain prevailed in many ways, liberal ideas gradually gained ground. For example, Camilo Henríquez, a convinced "neo-mercantilist" in the early nineteenth century, became increasingly open to liberal ideas. He contributed, indeed, to spreading the ideas of French and British liberal thinkers like Smith (Edwards 2018, 374). During the first half of the nineteenth century, there was a specific knowledge of Smith in Chile. Still, a pragmatic and practical approach prevailed when applying his reform proposals and his economic policies. José Antonio Rodríguez Aldea, Diego José Benavente and Pedro Félix Vicuña are canonical examples of such a view. Although they managed Smithian ideas, they supported economic policies that contrasted with Smith. Things changed dramatically when the French liberal economist Courcelle-Seneuil came to Chile (Edwards 2018, 372–78).

The institutional development that followed the independence of the Republic of Peru from the Spanish monarchy is the realm in which we find one of the most significant influences of Smithian thought. As in Chile, the monetary disturbances and the crisis of liquidity inherited from the colonial period that had been worsened by the Independence War paved the way for reforming the monetary and financial systems. From our perspective, the monetary system finally adopted the Banco Auxiliar de papel moneda—the Auxiliary bank of fiduciary money—specifically created for issuing money, it took as a reference *Ensayo económico sobre el sistema de la moneda papel y sobre el crédito público* (1796) by Alonso, the first translator of an almost complete version of the WN into Spanish. *Ensayo* was reprinted in Lima in 1822 and was the first economic essay published in Peru after independence (Alonso Ortiz 1822). An anonymous author enlarged the Peruvian version by adding a second part entitled *Adiciones al Ensayo sobre el Papel-Moneda escrito por D. José Alonso Ortiz impreso en Madrid en 1796*. Schwartz and Fernández (1978) have demonstrated how *Ensayo* relied on Smith's monetary ideas and approach to fiduciary money, which had thoroughly influenced Alonso. Despite the Peruvian enlargement of *Ensayo,* a series of analytical nuances regarding the original edition, the Smithian influence remained as it was in the first part of *Ensayo* (De Haro 2013). Thus, many Peruvian civil servants and policy-makers, and even San Martin himself, the founding father of the Republic of Peru, used the *Ensayo* and Smith ideas.

Alonso Ortiz's translation of the WN circulated in the Viceroyalty of New Granada from 1794, and some enlightened creole like Pedro Fermín Vargas proved to be influenced by Smith (Cárdenas 2020). In the early period of the Republic of Colombia the prevalence of liberalism was pervasive and became the doctrinal support of the institutional building of the state (Jaramillo 2001). Together with Bentham, Quesnay, Ricardo, Say or James Mill, Smith was profusely read by intellectuals, politicians and businessmen to organise the postcolonial economy (Chaparro and Gallardo 2015, 232, 242). Similarly to other republics in Hispanic America, they were more interested in the practical issues of economic policy than in economic theory. Such a fact applies to the reception of the WN. For example, Salvador Camacho, who widely quoted Smith in his writings, supported the ability to pay tax principle and Smith's maxims of taxation. On the other hand, the politician Miguel Samper, committed to change the tax system inherited from the colonial period, demonstrated a deep knowledge of Smith and particularly Say's ideas (Chaparro and Gallardo 232, 238–42, 247–49). Indeed, as in Spain, Say's works indirectly spread the WN in the new republic. The first chair of political economy established in Colombia in 1820 prescribed Say's works as a handbook (Hurtado 2017).

Regarding the other territories that had composed the Viceroyalties of New Grenade, New Spain and Cuba during the colonial period, R.S. Smith (1957a, 1251–53) affirms that there are clear indications that Smith was relatively known and used in educational and political spheres. The Mexican experience exemplifies all this. The classical monograph by Silva Herzog showed that after the republic's independence, a relatively numerous group of Mexicans paid particular attention to political economy (Silva Herzog 1967). Further research confirms the considerable impact of Classical political economy and Smith. R.S. Smith points out how the member of the Mexican Parliament Manuel Ortiz de la Torre, whom he considered the first Mexican economist, opposed monopolies, prohibitions and custom duties by "interpreting correctly the doctrines of French and English economist," among which is Smith (Smith 1959, 510–13).

In some cases, however, Silva Herzog proved to be too optimistic about Smith's influence. For example, recent research casts doubts on the impact of Smith on the conservative politician Lucas Alamán (Calderón 1985). The classical works by Hale (1972) and Reyes Heroles (2002) note, respectively, the influence of Bentham, Constant, Filangeri, Say, and Smith in the early parliamentarian debates on politicians like Mora, Zavala, Antuñano or Valentín Gómez-Farías, and, on the other hand, the Spanish intellectual sources in the formative years of liberal thought in Mexico during the first half of the nineteenth century. A later generation of politicians who took on responsibilities in the successive republican governments, like Miguel Lerdo de Tejada, a supporter of free trade and promoter of the land confiscation laws in the 1850s, Ignacio Ramírez and Francisco Zarco had to a greater or lesser extent some contacts with Smith's writings (Blázquez 2002; Ibarra 2012).

The spread of Smith in Hispanic America was not limited to the old territories of the Spanish monarchy but also extended to Brazil. Bento da Silva´s 1811–1812 translation of the WN into Portuguese circulated there, although it remained virtually unknown outside Brazil (Reeder and Cardoso 2002). In this country, the spread of the WN was apparent in questions like free trade or slavery (Coutinho 2017). Similarly to the old territories of the Spanish monarchy, the recipients of the WN in Brazil adapted Smithian ideas to the backward environment of an agricultural and colonial economy (Almeida 2018). In general, Hispanic Americans used the WN in several ways: for educational purposes, for backing the proposals of the liberal economic reforms and, in some cases, rhetorically. In this respect, there is an undoubted will to adapt Smithian ideas to the backward economies and institutional environments of the newly created republics, which in many cases means to contradict the approaches of economic reforms suggested by the Scottish economist. Finally, the intellectual link to the former metropolis due to a significant circulation of economic ideas between the two sides of the Atlantic Ocean intermediated in Smith's spread in Hispanic America, even, logically, after the foundation of the new republics. Therefore, to some extent, the fate of the WN walked parallel paths in Spain and the former colonial territories. In this context, to have a complete account of the reception of the WN in peninsular Spain, the reception of the WN in the late Enlightenment and early Liberalism looks imperative.

## Final remarks

The analysis of the parliamentary records during the Liberal Triennium demonstrate that the works of Classical economists, in general, and Smith, in particular, were known by a wide range of members of the Spanish Parliament. They were well-known economists and proponents of Classical political economy in Spain like Flórez Estrada or Canga Argüelles, but also for others who had nothing to do with political economy. Even opponents of Classical economists' ideas and policies demonstrate a relative knowledge of WN's main ideas. Smith's quotations are relatively profuse but significant enough as the WN backed crucial reforms in the Spanish Parliament. Smith, indeed, is evident in public finances, public debt and the different aspects of commercial policy. Indirectly, we may find a greater influence on the suppression of clerical domains and *mayorazgos*, public debt, colonies and all the issues related to economic freedoms. However, the WN's theoretical issues are not present in the parliamentary debates. There are no references to Smith's theory of value and distribution, although there is an indirect reference to the theory of economic growth. Books IV and V in the WN are the most quoted and referenced parts of Smith's work.

Regarding the exile of Spanish liberals, Spanish economists handled Smith in different ways. First of all, he was used to criticise the "mercantile system," back competition, or promote labour division. Spanish economists also assumed public finance and taxation principles to reform public finances in Spain and Hispanic America. By far it is Canga Argüelles who most often relies on Smith for supporting specific aspects of the reform of the Spanish public finances. However, Smith is a starting point to illustrate the advances of economic science in the Classical period. In this sense, Smith's late reception by authors in exile, such as Flórez Estrada himself or Mora, is intermediated through the Scottish economist John Ramsay McCulloch and considers the advances experienced by political economy in the meantime. Finally, a correct and complete understanding of the coming of the WN to Hispanic America requires considering the previous reception of Smith's work in peninsular Spain.

## Notes

1  *Diario de sesiones*, 13-VII-1820, 79–122.
2  *Diario de sesiones*, 12-VII-1820, 100-10; WN V, II, b, 825–28.

3  *Diario de sesiones*, 13-VII-1820, 117–18; WN V, II, b, 825–28.

4  *Diario de sesiones*, 13-VII-1820, 103; WN V, II, j-k, 869–906.

5  *Diario de sesiones*, 13-VII-1820, 106–07.

6  *Diario de sesiones*, 20-III-1822, 28. Later on Sierra-Pambley was substituted by Egea, but this last period of the Triennium was by far less interesting from the point of view of Smith's influence.

7  *Diario de sesiones*, 20-III-1822, 432, WN V, I, a, 689–816.

8  *Diario de sesiones*, 20-III-1822, 440.

9  *Diario de sesiones*, 20-III-1822, 473–74.

10  *Diario de sesiones*, 23-V-1821, 1807; 31-V-2821, 1899.

11  *Diario de sesiones*, 27-V-1821, 1895.

12  *Diario de sesiones*, 13-VII-1820, 10; WN V, II, k, 884.

13  This Board was created in 1816 for rearranging and proposing the reform of custom and tariffs. Canga-Argúelles's *Memorandum* proposed tariffs coming down, but the Board reccommended high tariffs and prohibitions to foreign commodities. Finally, *Junta*'s suggestions were introduced into the custom duties legislation (Serrano 2012b, 629).

14  *Diario de sesiones*, 4-VIII-1820, 737.

15  *Diario de sesiones*, 4-VIII-1820, 739.

16  *Diario de sesiones*, 4-VIII-1820, 741–45; 5-XI-1820, 2095–97; see, also, Lluch (1973).

17  *Diario de sesiones*, 9-X-1820, 1522; 31-X-1821 (Extraordinaria), 459.

18  *Diario de sesiones,* 24-X-1820, 1873–1876.

19  *Diario de sesiones*, 24-X-1820, 1877; see, additionally, Almenar (1980).

20  *Diario de sesiones*, 6-XI-1820, 2121; 4-III-1821, 101–02; WN, V, II, k, 883.

21  *El emigrado observador*, 1829 (February), 41–51.

22  See *Museo Universal de Ciencias y Artes*, II (1828).

23  See Chapter 9 in this book.

24  On this issue, see Skinner (1975) and Berry (2013, 38–50).

25  R.S. Smith (1957) contends that the WN encouraged the independence of the colonial territories of the Spanish monarchy, but Rodríguez-Braun (1997, 47) disagrees with him on this point.

26  On the economic thought in *Semanario*, see Martínez (2009, 6–9).

# 14 Spanish translations of *The Wealth of Nations*

## Beyond the Enlightenment, 1792–2020

*Juan Zabalza*

### The "Spanish Smith" beyond the Enlightenment

During the early reception of *The Wealth of Nations* (WN) in Spain, several Spanish versions were translated or circulated among the late Enlightenment and early Liberalism members. Martínez de Irujo's translation of Condorcet's compilation in 1792, which was republished again in 1803 and 1814 (Smith 1792; 1803; 1814), was followed by a summary, mainly, of book V of the WN, published in 1793 by Alcalá-Galiano (Smith 1793; Alcalá-Galiano 1793 [1788]), and in 1794 the complete translation, but partially censored, of the book by Alonso (Smith 1794). A new revised, and expanded edition saw light in 1805–1806 (Smith 1805–1806). Between both editions, Campos published a concise summary of the WN with no reference to book IV in the form of a textbook edition (Smith 1797). Finally, the circle of Spanish early translations of the WN was closed by Dou y de Bassols and Gonzalo de Luna. The first one published in 1817 is just a series of excerpts of the WN taken from Alonso's second edition. Dou y de Bassols added critical comments from the perspective of a supporter of protectionism (Smith 1817). Gonzalo de Luna chose different excerpts of the WN to make an even more severe criticism of Smith's ideas (Smith 1819–1820; R.S. Smith 1961, 45–46). Comparing with the spread of the WN in other European countries, we may find similarities with Italy and Germany (Guidi 2002; Tribe 2002b).

Despite the continuous references found in many Spanish treaties and monographs of political economy during the nineteenth century, the WN did not see any new translations into Spanish from the third decade of the century onwards. The absence of complete or incomplete editions of the WN, whether original or not, continued during the early twentieth century. Finally, the WN was edited, although incompletely, in two volumes, vol. I (book I, chapters I–XI and Disgression of book I) and vol. II (books II, III and IV) in 1933–1934 by the members of the editorial board of *La España Bancaria*, a financial periodical based in Barcelona and published by Bosch publishing house. The publisher reproduced Alonso's first translation of the WN into Spanish, which was reviewed and adapted to modern Spanish by *La España Bancaria*'s editorial board. However, as R.S. Smith (1961, 46) remarked, they

DOI: 10.4324/9781003152804-17

only corrected orthographical and grammatical mistakes without a significant revision of Alonso's original, incomplete and censored translation. Josep
Maria Tallada, indeed, a renowned Catalan economist by then interested in
the debates about economic systems, added a "modest" preface in which he
praised the virtues and current relevance of liberalism against interventionism
and mainly Soviet collectivism (Tallada 1933–1934, 5–25). During the Spanish
Second Republic (1931–1936), the country experienced a cultural revival.
Economics experienced a great leap forward, and it seems to have been a
period of growing interest in Smith. Something similar happened regarding
economic literature. The publisher Manuel Aguilar, rooted in Madrid, had
demonstrated significant interest in publishing books on economics, as part
of the collection *Biblioteca de Ideas y Estudios Contemporáneos* (1924–1939),
such as the first complete translation of Marx's *Capital*, and other works by
Mises, Ricardo, Proudhon, Gonnard, Rosentock-Frank and Cassel. Within this
collection, the publisher had planned to publish the WN in 1936, but, finally,
the breaking out of the Spanish Civil War thwarted the publishing project.
The destruction of Aguilar's archive hinders us from knowing whether it was a
reprint of Alonso's first edition or a completely new contemporary translation
into Spanish. After the Spanish Civil War (1936–1939), *La España Bancaria–*
Bosch's incomplete edition of the WN was reprinted successively in Barcelona
in 1947, 1954 and 1955–1956. The latter included book V of the WN that had
not been part of previous Bosch's editions.

It took several years before the Aguilar publishing house embarked on
the abandoned project of publishing the WN in Spanish.[1] The company had
promoted the collection *Biblioteca de Ciencias Económicas, Políticas y Sociales*
(1946–1960). The collection targeted the market opened by the foundation
in 1943 of the Facultad de Ciencias Políticas y Económicas—the Faculty of
Political Sciences and Economics—in Madrid, the first Spanish faculty of economics, and other similar institutions in Spanish-speaking countries.[2] The
Keynesian economist Manuel de Torres, who directed the collection, also
selected the monographs to spread Keynesian ideas in academic spheres. Still, he
also tried to fill the gaps in Spanish economic literature by publishing the classic
economics texts. Aguilar's edition was made by translating into Spanish the
1904 WN edition published by Methuen & Co., Ltd. Still, the Spanish version
omitted the footnotes, the "marginal summaries," the editor's "Introduction"
and the "Preface" drawn up by Cannan.[3] Nevertheless, it included an index of
authors and topics of about 50 pages, which corresponds to the analytical index
attached at the end of Cannan's edition of the WN.[4] Amando Lázaro-Ros, an
employee of Aguilar, who had translated into Spanish a wide range of English
literary works but who had no economics background, translated the WN
into Spanish (Guzmán 2019). The work enjoyed a second edition in 1961. The
self-made economist Germán Bernácer drafted a new prologue. But Bernácer,
the first Spanish economist who originally theorised on the economic crisis,
does not demonstrate particular feelings towards Smith, whom he considered
a supporter of the Classical theory of equilibrium. His prologue, indeed, is

just a claim about the theory of economic disequilibrium and crisis to which Bernácer adhered (Bernácer 1961).

Fondo de Cultura Económica, the Mexican publisher founded by Spanish exiles, quickly captured the weaknesses of Lázaro-Ros's translation. Sánchez Sarto, who had been brought up as an economist in Germany and had edited the significant economic collection of Labor publishing house during the Spanish Second Republic, was responsible for the economics section (Perdices and Ramos 2021). There he promoted the collection of books "Master works of economics" that included Mun's *Wealth*, Cantillon's *Essay*, J.S. Mill's *Principles*, Marx's *Capital,* Ricardo's *Principles*, Smith's *The Theory of Moral Sentiments* (TMS) and many other classical works. The collection and other economic works by Fondo de Cultura Económica competed with Aguilar publishing house for the Spanish and Hispanic American markets in a period of growing interest in economic education. The WN was translated from the American edition (1937) by Random House Inc. of Cannan's original edition in 1904. The Spanish version incorporated Max Lerner's introduction for that edition and the footnotes, the "marginal" summaries and the two indexes drawn up by Cannan—analytical and bibliographical indexes. Gabriel Franco, a Spanish economist who had served as Minister of Finance during the Spanish Second Republic and was exiled in Mexico after the Civil War, translated the work into Spanish. Sánchez Sarto, who translated the footnotes and apostilles made by Cannan, suggests that Aguilar's edition had a lower analytical quality, a poor literary style and was not complete. The new Mexican edition, indeed, tried to overcome these shortcomings (Sánchez Sarto 1959). Franco added a personal contribution as he included a summary of the TMS that he had translated for Fondo de Cultura Económica in 1941, and a "Preliminary study" claiming a central position for Smith in the history of economics and supporting Smith's views on many issues (Franco 1958, vii–xxxii).[5] The footnotes in Cannan's 1904 edition included many bibliographical references, which, in the Mexican edition, are also included. However, when they have a Spanish translation, it is this one that is quoted.

The 1980s and 1990s were particularly fruitful regarding new Spanish versions of the WN.[6] In 1988, the bicenntenial edition (edited by Skinner, Campbell and Todd) was fully translated into Spanish by Collado Curiel and Mira-Perceval for Oikos-Tau publisher. Their version included the "General Introduction", the footnotes—including Adam Smith's own references, in some cases enlarged by the editors, the substantive textual variants and the editors' own commentaries—and the three indexes. Afterwards, in 1994, the successful translation by Carlos Rodríguez-Braun, a historian of economic thought, saw the light. The translation by Alianza Editorial publishing house that targeted graduate education in the Spanish and Hispanic American universities included books I, II, II, a selection of approximately half of the books IV and V and a brief index of authors and topics of ten pages. According to Rodríguez-Braun (1994, 22), the criteria driving the selection includes what is analytically significant, leaving out the details and the "incidental, historical and illustrative accounts."

On the other hand, there is no clear information about the English edition that served as the source. Rodriguez-Braun, who introduced the book by providing some of Smith's biographical details and a summary of the WN, contributed to the so-called *Das Adam Smith's problem* (Montes 2003), by remarking on the continuity between the TMS and the WN. According to him, both works should be interpreted as a whole (Rodríguez-Braun 1994, 11–12). The first Catalan and Galician translations should also be mentioned, as languages that are co-officials in Catalonia and Galicia. The former was published by Edicions 62 in 1991 and the latter by Universidade Santiago de Compostela-Fundación BBVA in 2019; both are translated from the bicentennial edition of the WN.

As far as we know, there are no new versions of the WN into Spanish after Rodríguez Braun's translation.[7] However, the available Spanish versions of the WN were extensively republished and reprinted due to growing market demand. Publishers greatly use the España Bancaria-Bosch updating of Alonso's translation in Spain, and Hispanic America (Orbis, Planeta Agostini, Orbis Hyspamérica, Folio or even the Kindle edition) for targeting the broad demand for Smith's WN.[8] Notwithstanding, two facsímile editions from Alonso's first translation in 1794 are worth mentioning. The first one, published in 1996 by the autonomous regional government of Castilla and León, the region where Alonso's edition was originally published, starts with an introductory study of two historians of economic thought, Fuentes and Perdices. The second one is a facsímile edition published in 2014 of a printed copy of the first edition owned by the Ministry of the Economy and Competitiveness. The Spanish translation of Condorcet's *Compendio* was also reprinted in 2012 (Brontes) and the bicentennial edition by Skinner Campbell and Todd in 2010 (Síntesis-Fundación ICO).

Nevertheless, it is worth remarking that Rodríguez-Braun and Franco's translation were the most successful versions of the WN in the academic and popular spheres. Rodríguez-Braun reached a third edition in 2011 and the tenth reprint in 2020 by Alianza Editorial publishing house, but many publishers in Spain and Hispanic America reprinted entirely or partially Rodríguez-Braun's translation (Tecnos, Pirámide, Folio, Liberalia Ediciones, Skla, Biblioteca Nueva, El País and Prisa Innova). On the other hand, in marked contrast with the fate of Cannan's original edition in English, Franco's translation continues being reprinted, reaching its twenty-first edition in 2018 (Tribe 2002c, 49).

## The WN's translations and reprints in Spain and Hispanic America

Taking as a starting point Tribe and Mizuta's catalogue (2002), below is included the Spanish translations of the WN published in Spanish, as well as in Catalan and in Galician, during the twentieth and twenty-first centuries. It does not include reprints by the same publishing house, and probably some partial reprints by minor publishers that are not in the catalogues of the national libraries in Spain and Hispanic America (Argentina, Chile, Colombia, Costa Rica, Cuba, México and Perú).

(1)  1792. *Compendio de la obra inglesa intitulada Riqueza de las Naciones, hecho por el Marqués de Condorcet, y traducido al castellano con varias adiciones del original, por Don Carlos Martinez de Irujo*. Madrid: Imprenta Real.

(2)  1793. "Sobre la necesidad y justicia de los tributos, fondos de donde deben sacarse, y medios de recaudarlos". In *Actas y Memorias de la Real Sociedad Económica de Amigos del País de la provincia de Segovia*, edited by Real Sociedad Económica Segoviana de Amigos del País, vol. IV, 269–358. Segovia: Antonio Espinosa.

(3)  1794. *Investigación de la naturaleza y causas de la Riqueza de las Naciones. Obra escrita en inglés por Adam Smith, Doctor en Leyes, e individuo de la Real Sociedad de Londres y de Edimburgo; Comisario de la Real Hacienda en Escocia: y Profesor de Filosofía Moral en la Universidad de Glasgow. La traduce al castellano el Lic. D. José Alonso Ortiz, con varias notas e ilustraciones relativas á España*, 4 vols. Valladolid: Viuda e Hijos de Santander.

(4)  1803. *Compendio de la obra inglesa intitulada Riqueza de las Naciones, hecho por el Marqués de Condorcet, y traducido al castellano con varias adiciones del original, por Don Carlos Martínez de Irujo, Oficial que fue de la primera Secretaría de Estado*. Madrid: Imprenta Real.

(5)  1805–1806. *Investigación de la naturaleza y causas de la Riqueza de las Naciones. Escrita en inglés por el Dr. Adam Smith, y traducida al castellano por el Lic. D. José Alonso Ortiz, con varias notas e ilustraciones relativas a España. Segunda edición muy corregida y mejorada*, 4 vols. Valladolid: Viuda e Hijos de Santander.

(6)  1814. *Compendio de la obra inglesa intitulada Riqueza de las Naciones, hecho por el Marqués de Condorcet, y traducido al castellano con varias adiciones del original, por Don Carlos Martínez de Irujo, Oficial que fue de la primera Secretaría de Estado*. Palma: Miguel Domingo.

(7)  1817. *La Riqueza de las Naciones, nuevamente explicada con la doctrina de su mismo investigador* [...]. *Su autor Ramón Lázaro de Dou y de Bassols, maestre-escuela de la Santa Iglesia de Lérida, y Cancelario de la Pontificia y Real Universidad de Cervera*, 2 vols. Cervera: Pontificia y Real Universidad.

(8)  1819–1820. *Ensayo sobre la investigación de la naturaleza y causas de la Riqueza de las Naciones relativamente a España, o sea, la economía universal teórica aplicada a la nación española* [...] *por el Lic. D. Gonzalo de Luna*, 2 vols. Vol. I (1819). Valladolid: Aparicio. Vol. 2 (1820). Madrid: Espinosa.

(9)  1933–1934. *Investigación de la naturaleza y causas de la Riqueza de las Naciones*, 3 vols. Barcelona: España Bancaria and Bosch.

(10)  1956. *Investigación de la naturaleza y causas de la Riqueza de las Naciones*. Madrid: Aguilar.

(11)  1958. *Investigación sobre la naturaleza y causas de la Riqueza de las Naciones*. México: FCE.

(12)   1961. *Indagación acerca de la naturaleza y causas de la Riqueza de las Naciones.* Madrid: Aguilar.

(13)   1971. *La Riqueza de las Naciones.* Río Piedras: Universidad de Puerto Rico.

(14)   1976. *La Riqueza de las Naciones.* Mexico DF: Publicaciones Cruz OSA.

(15)   1983. *Investigación de la naturaleza y causas de la Riqueza de las Naciones,* 3 vols. Barcelona: Orbis.

(16)   1983. *La Riqueza de las Naciones: investigación de la naturaleza y causas de la Riqueza de las Naciones.* Buenos Aires: Orbis Hyspamérica.

(17)   1986. *La Riqueza de las Naciones.* San José: Universidad Autónoma de Centroamérica.

(18)   1988. *Investigación sobre la naturaleza y causas de la Riqueza de las Naciones,* 2 vols. Vilassar de Mar: Oikos-Tau.

(19)   1991. *Indagació sobre la naturaleza i les causes de la Riquesa de les Nacions,* 2 vols. Barcelona: Edicions 62.

(20)   1994. *La Riqueza de las Naciones.* Madrid: Alianza.

(21)   1996. *Investigación de la naturaleza y causas de la Riqueza de las Naciones. Obra escrita en inglés por Adam Smith, Doctor en Leyes, e individuo de la Real Sociedad de Londres y de Edimburgo; Comisario de la Real Hacienda en Escocia: y Profesor de Filosofía Moral en la Universidad de Glasgow. La traduce al castellano el Lic. D. José Alonso Ortiz, con varias notas e ilustraciones relativas á España,* facsimile reedition by Fuentes and Perdices, 4 vols. Valladolid: Junta de Castilla y León.

(22)   1996. *La Riqueza de las Naciones.* Madrid: Pirámide.

(23)   1996. *La Riqueza de las Naciones.* Barcelona: Folio.

(24)   1997. *Investigación de la naturaleza y causas de la Riqueza de las Naciones,* 3 vols. Barcelona: Planeta Agostini.

(25)   2005. *Ensayo sobre la investigación de la naturaleza y causas de la Riqueza de las Naciones relativamente a España, o sea, la economía universal teórica aplicada a la nación española* [...] *por el Lic. D. Gonzalo de Luna,* reedited by José Manuel Menudo. Valladolid: Ayuntamiento de Valladolid.

(26)   2009. *La Riqueza de las Naciones.* Madrid: Prisa Innova.

(27)   2009. *Una investigación sobre la naturaleza y causas de la Riqueza de las Naciones.* Madrid: Tecnos.

(28)   2010. *Investigación sobre la naturaleza y causas de la Riqueza de las Naciones,* 2 vols. Madrid: Síntesis and Fundación ICO.

(29)   2010. *La Riqueza de las Naciones.* Madrid: El País.

(30)   2011. *La Riqueza de las* Naciones. Barcelona: Ciro.

(31)   2012. *Investigación sobre la naturaleza y causa de la Riqueza de las Naciones. Compendio de la riqueza de las naciones del Marqués de Condorcet.* Barcelona: Brontes.

(32)   2014. *Investigación de la naturaleza y causas de la Riqueza de las Naciones,* 4 vols. Madrid: Ministerio de Economía y Competitividad.

(33)   2018. *La Riqueza de las Naciones.* Santiago de Chile: Liberalia Ediciones.

(34)   2018. *La Riqueza de las Naciones.* Bogotá: Skla.

(35) 2018. *Indagación acerca de la naturaleza y causas de la Riqueza de las Naciones*. Lima: Ebisa Ediciones.
(36) 2019. *La Riqueza de las Naciones*. Madrid: Biblioteca Nueva.
(37) 2019. *A Riqueza das Nacions*, 2 vols. Santiago de Compostela: Universidade de Santiago de Compostela and Fundación BBVA.
(38) 2020. *La Riqueza de las Naciones*. Edición Kindle.

## Notes

1 R.S. Smith (1961) refers to some excerpts of the WN embedded in a monograph (*Los economistas*, 260 pp.) published by González Alberdi in 1947 in Buenos Aires.

2 The collection was renamed in 1952 *Biblioteca de Ciencias Sociales*, but preserved the three original sections of the collection: politics, sociology and economics (Martín 2019, 7).

3 Cannan took the fifth edition of the WN collated with the first. In the footnotes, he accounted for the modifications between both editions. He also included a set of marginal notes summarising the book's content, and appended two indexes at the end of his edition of the WN. The first index matches the index of the third edition of the WN supervised by Smith himself but enlarged with "additions by the present editor." The second one, drawn up by Cannan himself, contains the books quoted in the editor's notes (Smith 1904, 439).

4 R.S. Smith affirms that Lázaro Ros translated from the fifth edition, which is correct, but surprisingly he does not mention that Lázaro Ros translated Cannan's edition. Furthermore, he praises Aguilar's edition for including an index of authors and topics of 50 pages (Smith 1961, 46). However, Lázaro Ros merely copied from Cannan's edition of the WN.

5 The incomplete first edition of the TMS by Franco in Fondo de Cultura Económica publishing house based on a previous Mexican edition in the 1930s, reprinted in the 1940s by El Colegio de México. However, it was not until 1997 that Carlos Rodríguez-Braun made the first complete translation of the work (Trincado 2014).

6 During the 1970s, there were no new translations. The Tribe and Mizuta (2002, 305) catalogue includes a translation made in Puerto Rico. However, the monograph is a brief selection of books I and II of barely 61 pages, apparently published for students' use (Smith 1971).

7 The choice of excerpts of the WN by Ramón Tamames, translated into Spanish by Carlos González in 2011 for a commercial collection of books, may be the exception. Still, the short size of the book, 143 pages, does not deserve further comment (Smith 2011).

8 The 2018 edition by the Peruvian Publisher Ebisa Ediciones seems to be a reprint of Lázaro Ros's translation.

# Sources and bibliography

## Adam Smith's editions

All references and citations of Adam Smith are to the *Glasgow Edition of the Works and Correspondence of Adam Smith*:

WN Smith, Adam. 1976. *An Inquiry into the Nature and Causes of the Wealth of Nations*, edited by R.H. Campbell, A.S. Skinner and W.B. Todd. Oxford: OUP.

TMS Smith, Adam. 1976. *The Theory of Moral Sentiments*, edited by D.D. Raphael and A.L. Macfie. Oxford: OUP.

The rest of the editions cited in this book are the following (see, also, Chapter 14):

Smith, Adam. 1774–1775. *Théorie des sentiments moraux*, translated by Jean-Louis Blavet, 2 vols. Paris: Valade.

———. 1776. *An Inquiry into the Nature and Causes of the Wealth of Nations*, 2 vols. London.

———. 1778. *An Inquiry into the Nature and Causes of the Wealth of Nations*. The Second Edition, 2 vols. London.

———. 1781. *Recherches sur la nature et les causes de la Richesse des Nations*, translated by Jean-Louis Blavet, 3 vols. Paris.

———. 1790. "Recherches sur la nature & les causes de la Richesse des Nations." In *Bibliothèque de l'homme public, ou analyse raisonnée des principaux ouvrages français et étrangers*, edited by Marie-Jean-Antoine-Nicolas de Condorcet, Charles de Peyssonel and Isaac-René-Guy Le Chapelier, vol. III, 108–216. Paris: Buisson.

———. 1790. "Recherches sur la nature & les causes de la Richesse des Nations. Suite de la Richesse des Nations de M. Smith." In *Bibliothèque de l'homme public, ou analyse raisonnée des principaux ouvrages français et étrangers*, edited by Marie-Jean-Antoine-Nicolas de Condorcet, Charles de Peyssonel and Isaac-René-Guy Le Chapelier, vol. IV, 3–315. Paris: Buisson.

———. 1791 [1790]. *Recherches sur la nature et les causes de la Richesse des Nations*, translated by Jean-Antoine Roucher, 4 vols. Avignon: Fortis d´Urban and J.J. Niel.

———. 1792. *Compendio de la obra inglesa intitulada Riqueza de las Naciones, hecho por el Marqués de Condorcet, y traducido al castellano con varias adiciones del original, por Don Carlos Martínez de Irujo*. Madrid: Imprenta Real.

———. 1794. *Investigación de la naturaleza y causas de la Riqueza de las Naciones. Obra escrita en inglés por Adam Smith, Doctor en Leyes, e individuo de la Real Sociedad de Londres y de Edimburgo; Comisario de la Real Hacienda en Escocia: y Profesor de Filosofía Moral en la Universidad de Glasgow. La traduce al castellano el Lic. D. José Alonso Ortiz, con varias notas e ilustraciones relativas a España*, 4 vols. Valladolid: Viuda e hijos de Santander.

Reedited by Enrique Fuentes and Luis Perdices, 4 vols. Salamanca: Junta de Castilla y León (Smith 1996 [1795]).

———. 1795. *Essays on Philosophical Subjects*, edited by J. Black and J. Hutton. London: T. Cadell, jun., and W. Davies.

———. 1797a. *La económica reducida a principios exactos, claros y sencillos. Por Ramón Campos*. Madrid: Benito Cano.

———. 1797b. *Essais philosophiques précédés d'un précis de sa vie et de ses écrits par Dugald Stewart*, translated by Pierre Prévost. Paris: Agasse.

———. 1798. *Théorie des sentiments moraux*, translated by Sophie de Grouchy, 2 vols. Paris: Buison.

———. 1802. *Recherches sur la nature et les causes de la Richesse des Nations, par Adam Smith*, edited by Germain Garnier, 5 vols. Paris: M. Agasse.

———. 1803. *Compendio de la obra inglesa intitulada Riqueza de las Naciones, hecho por el Marqués de Condorcet, y traducido al castellano con varias adiciones del original, por Don Carlos Martínez de Irujo, Oficial que fue de la primera Secretaría de Estado*. Madrid: Imprenta Real.

———. 1805–1806. *Investigación de la naturaleza y causas de la Riqueza de las Naciones. Escrita en inglés por el Dr. Adam Smith, y traducida al castellano por el Lic. D. José Alonso Ortiz, con varias notas e ilustraciones relativas a España. Segunda edición muy corregida y mejorada*, 4 vols. Valladolid: Viuda e Hijos de Santander.

———. 1814. *Compendio de la obra inglesa intitulada Riqueza de las Naciones, hecho por el Marqués de Condorcet, y traducido al castellano con varias adiciones del original, por Don Carlos Martínez de Irujo, Oficial que fue de la primera Secretaría de Estado*. Palma: Miguel Domingo.

———. 1817. *La Riqueza de las Naciones, nuevamente explicada con la doctrina de su mismo investigador [...]. Su autor Ramón Lázaro de Dou y de Bassols, maestre-escuela de la Santa Iglesia de Lérida, y Cancelario de la Pontificia y Real Universidad de Cervera*, 2 vols. Cervera: Pontificia y Real Universidad.

———. 1819–1820. *Ensayo sobre la investigación de la naturaleza y causas de la Riqueza de las Naciones relativamente a España, o sea, la economía universal teórica aplicada a la nación española [...] por el Lic. D. Gonzalo de Luna*, 2 vols. Vol. I (1819). Valladolid: Aparicio. Vol. 2 (1820). Madrid: Espinosa. Reedited by José Manuel Menudo. Valladolid: Ayuntamiento de Valladolid (Smith 2005 [1819–1820]).

———. 1933–1934. *Investigación de la naturaleza y causas de la Riqueza de las Naciones*. Barcelona: España Bancaria and Bosch.

———. 1956. *Investigación de la Naturaleza y Causas de la Riqueza de las Naciones*. Madrid: Aguilar.

———. 1959 *Investigación sobre la naturaleza y causas de la Riqueza de las Naciones*. México D.F.: Fondo de Cultura Económica.

———. 1994. *La Riqueza de las Naciones*. Madrid: Alianza.

## Manuscripts

ADB, *Censura de Llibres*, Llig. 1, exp. 28.
AGI, *Estado*, 44–68.
AHN, *Consejos*, 5.552–59; 5.559; 5.564–52; 11.283–48.
AHN, *Estado*, 3.014–8; 3.244.
AHN, *Inquisición*, 4.4463–10; 4.482–11; 4.484–13; 4.522–25.

Alcalá-Galiano, Vicente. c.1788. *Juicio de la memoria intitulada "Abusos que reinan generalmente en la administración de las principales rentas del real patrimonio, y explicación de varios medios prontos y eficaces para evitarlos", presentada a la Sociedad Económica de Segovia para obtener uno de sus premios* (9 June 1788). AMS, RSESAP, 12–263.

AMAE, 22–933.

Banqueri, Juan José. c.1801. *Discurso sobre la libertad, facilidad y utilidad del comercio interior.* RAH, 9–4.729.

Covarrubias, José de. c.1790. *Código, o recopilación de leyes de Real Hacienda,* 6 vols. BIEF, 5.7223–5.7227.

FUE, AC, 14–21, 14–23, 20–2, 31–8, 32–13, 35–45, 37–35, 48–73.

Garnier, Germain. c.1796. *Compendio elemental de los principios de la economía política.* AMH, FA-1.941.

Lerena, Pedro de, Count of. c.1787. *Manifiesto presentado a su Majestad por el Ministro de Hacienda, del estado de las rentas reales con respecto a los valores que tuvieron en el año 1787.* BNE, 9.362.

MNM, 1.181.

RAH, 11–48, 11–58, 11–62.

RSC, 19/36, 20/1, 22/9/10, 22/9/10, 22/9/11, 51/2/24, 51/2/54, 51/2/68, 51/2/86, 51/7/61, 52/7/54, 57/2/64.

SCA, B/2/4/2; BL 2/292/2, 3/312/1, 3/312/4, 3/312/16, 3/322/12, 4/159/1; CA 4/52/18, 4/55, 4/56, 4/60, 4/62/5; CS/1/2.

## Primary sources

Aguirre, Manuel. 1974. *Cartas y discursos del Militar Ingenuo al Correo de los Ciegos de Madrid,* edited by Antonio Elorza. San Sebastián: Izarra.

Alcalá-Galiano, Antonio. 1813. *Máximas y principios de la legislación universal.* Madrid: Vega y Compañía.

Alcalá-Galiano, Vicente. 1793 [1788]. "Sobre la necesidad y justicia de los tributos, fondos de donde deben sacarse, y medios de recaudarlos." In *Actas y Memorias* [...], edited by RSESAP, vol. IV, 269–358. Segovia: Espinosa.

———. 1810. *Informe de D. Vicente Alcalá-Galiano sobre el Decreto de 11 de Agosto de 1809 en que se mandaron suprimir las rentas provinciales.* Valencia: Benito Monfort.

———. 1992. *Sobre la economía política y los impuestos. Segovia 1781–1788,* edited by José Manuel Valles. Segovia: BCA.

Alcalá-Galiano, Vicente, and Diego María Gallard. 1789. *Colección alfabética de los aranceles de Francia, precedida de observaciones preliminares sobre los derechos de aduanas de aquel reino,* 3 vols. Madrid: Lorenzo de San Martín.

Alcalá-Galiano, Vicente, and Vicente Mantecón de Arce. 1787. "Perjuicios del antiguo sistema de rentas provinciales." In *Actas y Memorias* [...], edited by RSESAP, vol. III, 81–363. Segovia: Espinosa.

Alonso López, José. 1820. *Consideraciones generales sobre varios puntos históricos, políticos y económicos, a favor de la libertad y fomento de los pueblos, y noticias particulares de esta clase, relativas al Ferrol y a su comarca,* 3 vols. Madrid: Repullés.

Alonso Ortiz, José. 1796. *Ensayo económico sobre el sistema de la moneda papel y sobre el crédito público.* Madrid: Imprenta real; 2nd ed. 1803. Madrid: Imprenta Real; 3rd ed. 1814. Palma de Mallorca: Miguel Domingo.

———. 1822. *Ensayo económico sobre el sistema de la moneda papel y sobre el crédito público. Se escribía contra algunas precauciones vulgares por D. José Alonso Ortiz el año de 1796, y con el mismo fin se reimprime en Lima, con adiciones sobre el Banco Auxiliar.* Lima: Imprenta de los huérfanos.

———. 1999 [1796]. *Ensayo económico sobre el sistema de la moneda papel y sobre el crédito público*, edited by Pedro Schwartz and Francisco Fernández. Madrid: IEF and Ministerio de Economía y Hacienda.

Álvarez Guerra, Juan. 1813. *Modo de extinguir la deuda pública.* Palma: Miguel Domingo.

Anonymous. 1789. *Memoria político-económica sobre el pan cocido y medios de tenerle en abundancia, de superior calidad, y a precio equitativo.* Valladolid: Viuda de Santander.

———. 1813. *Informe de la Comisión Extraordinaria de Hacienda sobre un nuevo sistema de contribución directa y extinción de rentas provinciales y estancadas.* Cádiz: Diego García Campoy.

———. 1817. *Dictamen del gremio y claustro de esta Universidad de Salamanca sobre la consulta hecha por los tres estados del Reino de Navarra, acerca del comercio de granos.* Pamplona: José Domingo.

Argüelles, Agustín. 1981 [1812]. *Discurso preliminar a la Constitución de 1812.* Madrid: CEPC.

Arriquíbar, Nicolás de. 1987 [1779]. *Recreación política*, edited by Jesús Astigarraga and José Manuel Barrenechea. Bilbao: Instituto Vasco de Estadística.

Beawes, Wyndham. 1751. *Lex Mercatoria Rediviva.* London: R. Baldwin and S. Crowder and Co.

———. 1783. *Lex Mercatoria Rediviva,* edited by Thomas Mortimer, 4th ed. London.

———. 1793. *A Civil, Commercial, Political and Literary History of Spain and Portugal,* 2 vols. London: Faulder.

Bigot de Sainte-Croix, Louis-Claude. 1775. *Essai sur la liberté du commerce et de l'industrie.* Paris: Lacombe.

Borrelly, Jean-Alexis. 1797. *Elementos del arte de pensar o la lógica*, translated by José María Magallón y Armendáriz. Madrid: Aznar.

Butler, Albano. 1789–1792. *Vidas de los Padres, Mártires y otros principales Santos escritas en inglés por Albano Butler,* translated by José Alonso Ortiz, 13 vols. Valladolid: Viuda e hijos de Santander.

———. 1791. *Fiestas movibles, ayunos y otras observancias y ritos anuales de la Iglesia Católica,* translated by José Alonso Ortiz. Valladolid: Viuda e hijos de Santander.

Cabarrús, Francisco. 1808 [c.1783]. "Memoria al Rey Nuestro Señor Carlos III para la extinción de la deuda nacional y arreglo de contribuciones en 1783." In *Cartas sobre los obstáculos que la naturaleza, la opinión y las leyes oponen a la felicidad pública* (c.1795). Madrid.

———. 1808 [c.1795]. *Cartas sobre los obstáculos que la naturaleza, la opinión y las leyes oponen a la felicidad pública.* Madrid.

Cadalso, José. 1979. *Escritos autobiográficos y epistolario*, edited by Nigel Glendinning and Nicole Harrison. London: Tamesis Books.

Calomarde, Francisco Tadeo. 1800. *Discurso económico-político leído en la Real Sociedad Aragonesa.* Madrid: Gerónimo Ortega.

Cambronero, Manuel María. 1820. *La institución de los mayorazgos, examinada histórica y filosóficamente con un proyecto de ley para su reforma.* Madrid: Imprenta de Collado.

Campomanes, Pedro Rodríguez de, Count of. 1761. *Itinerario de las Carreras de Posta de dentro y fuera del Reino, que contiene también las Leyes y Privilegios con que se gobiernan en España las Postas, desde su establecimiento. Y una noticia de las especies corrientes de Moneda extranjera, reducidas a la de España, con los precios a que se pagan las Postas en los varios Países. De orden de S. M.* Madrid: Antonio Pérez de Soto.

————. 1774. *Discurso sobre el fomento de la industria popular.* Madrid: Antonio Sancha.

————. 1775. *Discurso sobre la educación popular de los artesanos.* Madrid: Sancha.

————. 1775–1777. *Apéndice a la educación popular,* 4 vols. Madrid: Antonio de Sancha.

————. 1776. "Discurso sobre la legislación gremial de los artesanos." In *Apéndice a la educación popular,* vol. III, lii–ccxl. Madrid: Sancha.

Canard, Nicolas-François. 1804. *Principios de economía política.* Madrid: Viuda de López e Hijos.

Cañedo, Ramón M. 1814. *Nociones de economía política.* Madrid: Miguel de Burgos.

Canga Argüelles, José. 1811. *Memoria sobre las rentas provinciales de Castilla y León.* Cádiz: Imprenta Real.

————. 1813. *Nociones de la economía política, y de la ciencia de la hacienda apoyadas en las leyes de la historia de España.* Palma: Miguel Domingo.

————. 1820. *Memoria sobre el crédito público que presenta a las Cortes Ordinarias de 1820 Don José Canga Argüelles.* Madrid: Imprenta que fue de García.

————. 1825. *Elementos de la ciencia de la hacienda.* London: A. Macintosh.

————. 1826–1827. *Diccionario de hacienda para el uso de los encargados de la suprema dirección de ella,* 5 vols. London: M. Calero.

Ceán Bermúdez, Agustín. 1814. *Memorias para la vida del Excmo. Señor D. Gaspar Melchor de Jovellanos.* Madrid: Fuentenebro.

Cistué, José Benito de. c.1804. *Elogio del Ilustrísimo Señor D. Juan Antonio Hernández Pérez de Larrea.* Zaragoza: Medardo Heras.

Colbert, Jean-Baptiste. 1801. *Proyecto de Mr. Colbert al rey Luis XIV de Francia sobre el comercio.* Madrid: Imprenta Real.

Condorcet, Marie-Jean-Antoine-Nicolas de, Marquis of. 1787. *Vie de Turgot,* 2 vols. London.

————. 1847 [1786]. "Vie de M. Turgot." In *Œuvres de Condorcet,* edited by Arthur O'Connor and François Arago, vol. V. Paris: Firmin Didot Frères.

————. 1847 [1792]. "De la nature des pouvoirs politiques dans une nation libre." In *Œuvres de Condorcet,* edited by Arthur O'Connor and François Arago, vol. X. Paris: Firmin Didot Frères.

Covarrubias, José de. 1783. *Memorias históricas de la última guerra con la Gran Bretaña desde el año 1774 hasta su conclusión.* Madrid: Andrés Ramírez.

Coyer, Gabriel François. 1768. *Chinki. Histoire Cochinchinoise.* London.

Crumpe, Samuel. 1793. *An Essay on the Best Means of Providing Employment for the People.* Dublin: Mercier and Co.

————. 1801. "Essai sur les meilleurs moyens de procurer de l'occupation au peuple." In *Recueil de mémoires sur l'établissemens d'humanité, traduits de l'allemand et de l'anglais,* edited by Adrien Dusquenoy, vol. X, no. XXIX. Paris: H. Agasse.

Danvila, Bernardo. 2008 [1779]. *Lecciones de economía civil, o de el comercio,* edited by Pablo Cervera. Zaragoza: IFC.

De las Heras Ibarra, Domingo. 1813. *Principios y sistemas de economía política, con relación a la situación de España.* Madrid: Fuentenebro.

*Diario de sesiones de las Cortes.* 1820–1823. https://app.congreso.es/est_sesiones/.

*Diarios de sesiones de las Cortes Generales y Extraordinarias.* 1810–1813. https://app.congreso.es/est_sesiones/.

*Dictamen y proyecto de Decreto sobre el arreglo general de la enseñanza pública.* 1814. Madrid: Cortes Generales and Comisión de Instrucción Pública.

Dou y Bassols, Ramón de. 1800–1803. *Instituciones del derecho público general de España,* 9 vols. Madrid: Benito García y Compañía.

————. 1829. *Conciliación económica y legal de pareceres opuestos en cuanto a laudemios y derechos enfitéuticos.* Cervera: José Cánovas.

————. 1831. *Pronta y fácil ejecución del proyecto sobre laudemios, fundada principalmente en una autoridad del Dr. Adam Smith.* Cervera: José Cánovas.

Duaso, José. 1814. *Vicios de la contribución directa decretada por las Cortes extraordinarias en 13 de septiembre de 1813.* Madrid: Ibarra.

Dusquenoy, Adrien. ed. 1798–1804. *Recueil de mémoires sur l'établissemens d'humanité, traduits de l'allemand et de l'anglais,* 18 vols. Paris: H. Agasse.

Dutot, Nicolas. 1738. *Réflexions politiques sur les finances et le commerce,* 2 vols. La Haye: Frères Vaillant and Nicolas Prevost.

*El emigrado observador.* 1828–1829. London: M. Calero.

Espinosa de los Monteros, José. 1831. *Tratado de economía política aplicada a España.* Madrid: Aguado.

Fernández de Navarrete, Martín. 1791. *Discurso sobre los progresos que puede adquirir la economía política con la aplicación de las ciencias exactas y naturales.* Madrid: Sancha.

Flórez Estrada, Álvaro. 1811. *Examen imparcial de las disensiones de la América con la España de los medios de su recíproco interés y de la utilidad de los aliados de la España.* London: R. Juigné.

————. 1812. *Examen imparcial* [...]. 2nd ed. Cádiz: Ximénez Carreño.

————. 1828. *Curso de economía política.* London: D. Manuel Calero.

————. 1831. *Curso* [...]. 2nd ed. 2 vols. Paris: Gaultier-Laguionie.

————. 1835. *Curso* [...]. 4th ed. 2 vols. Madrid: Miguel de Burgos.

————. 1839. *La cuestión social, o sea origen latitud y efectos del derecho de propiedad.* Madrid: Burgos.

————. 1840. *Contestación de D. Álvaro Flórez al artículo publicado en el número 194 de El Corresponsal, en que se impugna por el Sr. D. Ramón de la Sagra su escrito sobre la cuestión social.* Madrid: Burgos.

Foronda, Valentín de. 1994 [1788–1789]. *Cartas sobre los asuntos más exquisitos de la economía política y sobre las leyes criminales,* edited by José Manuel Barrenechea. Vitoria: Gobierno Vasco.

Franco Salazar, Pedro. 1812. *Restauración política, económica y militar de España.* Madrid: Sancha.

Gallard, Diego María. 1795. *Práctica de la administración y cobranza de las rentas reales,* 5 vols. Madrid: Antonio Ulloa.

Gallardo Fernández, Francisco. 1805–1807. *Origen, progresos y estado de las rentas de la Corona de España,* 7 vols. Madrid: Imprenta Real.

Garnier, Germain. 1807. *Breve exposición de la doctrina de Adam Smith comparada con la de los economistas franceses, y método para facilitar el estudio de su obra, intitulada Investigación de la naturaleza y causas de la Riqueza de las Naciones.* Valladolid: Viuda e hijos de Santander.

Gassó, Buenaventura. 1816. *España con industria, fuerte y rica.* Barcelona: Antonio Brusi.

*Gazeta de la Regencia de las Españas.* 6 January 1814, no. 3.

*Gazette nationale, ou le Moniteur universel.* 1847 [1789–1799]. Edited by Charles Joseph Panckoucke, vol. 8. Paris: Plon.

Genovesi, Antonio. 1765–1767. *Lezioni di comercio, o sia d'economia civile,* 2 vols. Naples.

Godoy, Manuel. 1836. *Cuenta dada de su vida política por Don Manuel Godoy, Príncipe de la Paz,* 3 vols. Madrid.

————. 1839. *Memorias de Don Manuel Godoy, Príncipe de la Paz.* Paris: Librería Americana de Lecointe y Lasserre.

Gómez Rombaud, Rafael. 1813. *Manifiesto documentado en respuesta a los hechos que se sientan en el papel del capitán de fragata Don José Luyando.* Cádiz: Diego García Campoy.

Gutiérrez, Manuel M. 1819. *Discurso inaugural y sucinta exposición de los principios de economía política demostrados por Mr. J. B. Say.* Málaga: Luis de Carreras.

———. 1837. *Impugnación a las cinco proposiciones de Pebrer sobre los grandes males que causa la ley de aranceles a la nación en general y a Cataluña en particular y a las fábricas catalanas.* Madrid: Don Marcelino Calero.

———. 1839. *Nuevas consideraciones sobre el comercio.* Madrid: Viuda de Marcelino Calero.

Herrenschwand, Jean D. 1800. *Principios de economía política.* Madrid: Vega y Compañía.

Hume, David. 1752. *Political Discourses.* Edinburgh.

———. 1789. *Discursos políticos del Señor David Hume.* Madrid.

*Informe de la Universidad de Salamanca sobre el Plan de Estudios.* 1820. Salamanca: Don Vicente Blasco.

Jaumeandreu, Eudaldo. 1816. *Rudimentos de economía política.* Barcelona: Antonio Bausí.

———. 1836. *Curso elemental de economía política con aplicación a la legislación económica de España.* Barcelona: De Gaspar.

———. 1988 [1816]. *Rudimentos de economía política.* Barcelona: Alta Fulla.

*Journal des révolutions de l'Europe en 1789 et 1790.* Vol. VII (1790). Neuwied sur le Rhin: Société Typographique; Strasbourg: J.G. Treutel Libraire.

Jovellanos, Gaspar Melchor de. 1789. *Elogio de Carlos Tercero.* Madrid: Viuda de Ibarra.

———. 1859. *Obras publicadas e inéditas,* edited by Cándido Nocedal. Madrid: BAE.

———. 1984. *Obras completas. T. 2: Correspondencia 1°, 1767-Junio de 1794.* Edited by José Miguel Caso. Oviedo: Centro de Estudios del Siglo XVIII.

———. 2000 [1796–1797]. "Introducción a un discurso sobre la economía civil y la instrucción pública." In Gaspar M. de Jovellanos, *Escritos económicos,* edited by Vicent Llombart, 535–53. Madrid: IEF and RACMP.

———. 2008a [1781]. "Discurso económico sobre los medios de promover la felicidad de Asturias dirigido a su Real Sociedad." In Gaspar M. de Jovellanos, *Obras completas. Vol. X. Escritos económicos,* edited by Vicent Llombart and Joaquín Ocampo, 267–304. Gijón: Ayuntamiento de Gijón, IFE and KRK.

———. 2008b [c.1784]. "Informe a la Junta General de Comercio y Moneda sobre la libertad de las artes." In Gaspar M. de Jovellanos, *Obras completas. Vol. X. Escritos económicos,* edited by Vicent Llombart and Joaquín Ocampo, 509–39. Gijón: Ayuntamiento de Gijón, IFE and KRK.

———. 2008c [1795]. "Informe de la Sociedad Económica de esta Corte al Real y Supremo Consejo de Castilla en el Expediente de Ley Agraria." In Gaspar M. de Jovellanos, *Obras completas. Vol. X. Escritos económicos,* edited by Vicent Llombart and Joaquín Ocampo, 693–824. Gijón: Ayuntamiento de Gijón, IFE and KRK.

———. 2008d [1783]. "Apuntes para una memoria sobre la libertad del comercio de granos". In Gaspar M. de Jovellanos, *Obras completes. Vol. X. Escritos económicos,* edited by Vicent Llombart and Joaquín Ocampo, 621–28. Gijón: Ayuntamiento de Gijón, IFE and KRK.

———. 2010 [1798]. "Apuntamientos para el plan de estudios, o discurso al Rey." In *Obras completas. Vol. XIII. Escritos pedagógicos,* edited by Olegario Negrín, 798–801. Oviedo: Ayuntamiento de Gijón, IFE and KRK.

Joyce, Jeremiah. 1797. *A Complete Analysis or Abridgement of Dr. Adam Smith's Inquiry into the Nature and Causes of the Wealth of Nations.* Cambridge: Benjamin Flower.

Lalande, Jérôme. 1796. "Notice historique sur la vie et les ouvrages de Condorcet." *Mercure français* 1796 (20 janvier): 141–62.

Larruga, Eugenio. 1789a. *Memorias políticas y económicas*, vol. IV. Madrid: Espinosa.

———. 1789b. *Memorias políticas y económicas*, vol.VI. Madrid: Espinosa.

López de Araujo, Manuel. 1813. *Informe del encargado interino de la Secretaría del Despacho de Hacienda*. Cádiz: Imprenta Nacional.

López de Lerena, Pedro, Count of. 1789. "Abusos que reinan generalmente en la administración de las principales rentas del real patrimonio, y explicación de varios medios prontos y eficaces para evitarlos." In Eugenio Larruga, *Memorias políticas y económicas*, vol. I, 283–99. Madrid: Espinosa.

———. 1834 [c.1790]. "Memoria sobre la naturaleza de las rentas públicas de España, número de empleados y sueldos que gozan." In José Canga Argüelles, *Diccionario de hacienda con aplicación a España*, vol. I, 129–39. Madrid.

———. 1990 [c.1788–1790]. *Memoria sobre las rentas públicas y balanza comercial de España (1789–1790)*, edited by Joaquín del Moral. Madrid: IEF.

López de Peñalver, Juan. 1812. *Reflexiones sobre la variación del precio del trigo*. Madrid: Sancha.

López Juana Pinilla, José. 1814a. *Proyecto de Real Hacienda que dedica al Rey nuestro Señor D. Fernando VII*. Madrid: Collado.

———. 1814b. *Exposición que el intendente de Guadalajara D. José López Juana Pinilla dirige al Augusto Congreso Nacional*. Madrid: Imprenta Nacional.

Luyando, José. 1813a. *Examen de las ventajas que producirá el desestanco del tabaco y ensayo de única contribución*. Cádiz: Imprenta patriótica.

———. 1813b. *Apéndice a el ensayo de única contribución*. Cádiz: Imprenta patriótica.

Macpherson, James. 1788. *Obras de Ossian poeta del siglo tercero en las montañas de Escocia traducidas del idioma y verso gálico-céltico al inglés por Jaime Macpherson y del inglés a la prosa y verso castellano por Joseph Alonso Ortiz, con la ilustración de varias notas históricas*, translated by José Alonso Ortiz, vol. I. Valladolid: Viuda e hijos de Santander.

Martínez de Irujo, Carlos. 1800. "Observations on the commerce of Spain with her America colonies in time of war." In *Communications Concerning the Agriculture and Commerce of America* [...] *Written by a Spanish Gentleman in Philadelphia* [...], edited by William Tatham. London: J. Ridgway.

Martínez de Montaos, Román. 1813. *Incompatibilidad de la Constitución española con el sistema de contribuciones indirectas que rige*. Cádiz: Vicente Lemos.

McCulloch, John R. 1825. *The Principles of Political Economy, with a Sketch of the Rise and Progress of the Science*. Edinburgh-London: Adam and Charles Black-Brown, Green and Longmans.

Melon, Jean-François. 1736 [1734]. *Essai politique sur le commerce*.

Mora, José. J. 1825. *Catecismo de economía política*. London: R. Ackermann, Strand y en su establecimiento, en Méjico.

———. 1828a. "Los sistemas de hacienda." In *El Mercurio Chileno*: 53–62.

———. 1828b. "De los bancos de descuento y circulación." In *El Mercurio Chileno*: 149–71.

———. 1828c. "Aduanas. Art.1°." In *El Mercurio Chileno*: 197–207.

———. 1828d. "Aduanas. Art.2°." In *El Mercurio Chileno*: 245–68.

———. 1829. "El comercio en el siglo XIX&C. Juicio de esta obra. Art.2°." In *El Mercurio Chileno*: 757–65.

———. 1843. *De la libertad de comercio*. Sevilla.

Morales, José Isidoro. 1789. *Discurso sobre la educación*. Madrid: Benito Cano.

Morant, Rafael. 1820. *Discurso sobre contribuciones*. Valencia: Benito Monfort.

Morellet, André. 1821. *Mémoires*, vol. I. Paris: De Ladvocat.

Mortimer, Thomas. 1772. *The Elements of Commerce, Politics and Finances*. London.

Necker, Jacques. 1775. *Sur la législation et le commerce des grains*. Paris: Pissot.

———. 1783. "Sobre la legislación y el comercio de granos." In *Memorias instructivas y curiosas*, edited by Miguel Suárez, vol. VIII, 1–260. Madrid: Pedro Marín.

———. 1784. *De l'administration des finances de la France*, 3 vols. Lausanne: J-P. Heubach.

Normante. Lorenzo. 1984 [1784]. *Discurso sobre la utilidad de los conocimientos económico-políticos*, edited by Antonio Peiró. Zaragoza: Diputación General de Aragón.

*Ocios de los españoles emigrados*. 1824–1827. London: A. Macintosh.

Orense, Casimiro. 1813. *Ideas económicas, políticas y morales*. Cádiz: Estado Mayor General.

Orléans, Joseph d´. 1693–1694. *Histoire des révolutions d'Angleterre, depuis le commencement de la Monarchie*, 4 vols. Paris: Chez Claude Barbin.

———. 1820. *Lección de economía política sobre población*. Madrid: Vega y Compañía.

Paso y Delgado, Nicolás. 1841. *Elementos de economía política y estadística*. Granada: Imprenta de Benavides.

Peñalver, Juan López de. 1812. *Reflexiones sobre la variación del precio del trigo*. Madrid Imprenta de Sancha.

Pita Pizarro, Pio. 1838. *Del crédito y los empréstitos públicos*. Madrid: Imprenta de Don Miguel de Burgos.

Plana, Antonio. 1820. *Agravios hechos en el repartimiento de la contribución directa de Aragón en especial y a toda la agricultura de España en general*. Zaragoza: Mariano Miedes.

Polo y Catalina, Juan. c.1804. "Informe sobre las fábricas e industria de España." In *Informe sobre las fábricas e industria de España (1804) y otros escritos*, edited by Alfonso Sánchez, 1–66. Zaragoza: PUZ.

Quintana, Manuel José. 2013 [1813]. "Informe de la Junta creada por la Regencia para proponer los medios de proceder al arreglo de los diversos ramos de instrucción pública." In Natividad Araque, *Manuel José Quintana y la instrucción pública*, 179–215. Madrid: Universidad Carlos III.

*Real Cédula de S.M. y Señores del Consejo por la cual se reduce el número de Universidades literarias del Reino*. 1807. Madrid: Imprenta Real.

RSEM (Real Sociedad Económica Matritense). 1780. *Memorias de la Sociedad Económica de Madrid*, vol. 1. Madrid: Antonio Sancha.

RSESAP (Real Sociedad Económica Segoviana de Amigos del País). 1785. *Actas y Memorias de la Real Sociedad Económica de Amigos del País de la provincia de Segovia*, vol. I. Segovia: Espinosa.

———. 1786. *Actas y Memorias […]*, vol. II. Segovia: Espinosa.

———. 1787. *Actas y Memorias […]*, vol. III. Segovia: Espinosa.

———. 1793. *Actas y Memorias […]*, vol. IV. Segovia: Espinosa.

———. 1799. *Extracto de las actas de la Sociedad de Segovia desde 1º de enero de 1792 hasta fin de julio de 1798*. Segovia: Espinosa.

Ruiz de Zelada, José. 1777. *Estado de la bolsa de Valladolid*. Valladolid.

Sagra, Ramón. 1839. "La propiedad." In *El Corresponsal*, 19 December.

Sempere y Guarinos, Juan. 1785–1789. *Ensayo de una biblioteca de los mejores escritores de Carlos III*, 6 vols. Madrid: Imprenta Real.

———. 1801. *Biblioteca española económico-política*, vol. 1. Madrid: Sancha.

Sixto de Espinosa, Manuel. 1787. "Memoria e informe sobre las ordenanzas para el gremio de sastres de esta Corte." In RSEM, *Memorias de la Sociedad Matritense*, vol. IV, 228–62. Madrid: Antonio de Sancha.

Terreros y Pando, Esteban de. 1786–1788 [1767]. *Diccionario castellano con las voces de ciencias y artes y sus correspondientes en las tres lenguas francesa, latina e italiana*, 3 vols. Madrid: Viuda de Ibarra, 3 vols.

Thiebault, Paul. 1811. *Informe general sobre la Universidad de Salamanca.* Salamanca: Celestino Manuel Rodríguez.

Torrente, Mariano. 1835. *Revista general de economía política,* 2 vols. La Habana: Jordan.

Uriortua, Francisco Javier. 1811. *Memoria sobre un nuevo plan, o sistema de rentas:* Imprenta de la Junta Superior.

Vadillo, José M. 1836. *Apuntes sobre los principales sucesos que han influido en el actual estado de la América del Sud,* 3rd ed. Cádiz: Feros.

———. 1844. *Discursos económico-políticos y sumario de la España económica de los siglos XVI y XVII, corregidos y aumentados.* Cádiz: Feros.

Valle Santoro, Francisco de Gregorio, Marquis of. 1830. *Memoria sobre la balanza de comercio y examen del estado actual de la riqueza de España.* Madrid: Ramón Verges.

———. 1840. "Impugnación a la cuestión social." In *Elementos de economía política con aplicación particular a España,* 3rd ed., 1–50. Madrid: Ramón Verges.

———. 1989 [1833]. *Elementos de economía política con aplicación particular a España,* edited by Manuel Martín. Madrid: IEF.

Veranio, Severo. 1807. *Datos sobre algunas leyes inglesas que han contribuido al poder de la Gran Bretaña en perjuicio de las demás naciones.* Madrid: Alban.

Ward, Bernardo. 1779. *Proyecto económico.* Madrid: Joaquín Ibarra.

Zuaznavar y Francia, José M. 1818. *Discurso sobre el comercio exterior de granos del reino de Navarra.* Pamplona: Paulino Longas.

## Secondary sources

Aguilar, Francisco. 1984. *La biblioteca de Jovellanos (1778).* Madrid: CSIC.

Almeida, Paulo Roberto de. 2018. "A Brazilian Adam Smith: Cairu as the Founding Father of Political Economy in Brazil at the Beginning of the 19th century." *MISES: Interdisciplinary Journal of Philosophy, Law and Economics* 6, no. 1: 1–14.

Almenar, Salvador. 1976. "Agrarismo y librecambio en la crisis del Antiguo Régimen. El primer modelo de crecimiento económico de Álvaro Flórez Estrada." *Moneda y Crédito* 517: 58–81.

———. 1997. "Los primeros economistas clásicos y la industrialización." In *Industrialización en España: entusiasmos, desencantos y rechazos,* 139–66. Madrid: Civitas.

———. 1980. "Estudio preliminar." In Álvaro Flórez Estrada, *Curso de economía política,* edited by Salvador Almenar, xxxi–cxxiii. Madrid: IEF.

———. 2000a. "El desarrollo del pensamiento económico clásico en España." In *Economía y economistas. Vol. IV. La economía clásica,* edited by Enrique Fuentes, 7–92. Barcelona: GG-CL.

———. 2000b. "Las aportaciones de Robert Sidney Smith (1904–1969) a la historia de las ideas e instituciones económicas españolas." In *Economía y economistas. Vol. IV. La economía clásica,* edited by Enrique Fuentes, 339–50. Barcelona: GG-CL.

———. 2003. "Economía política y liberalismo en España. De Jovellanos a La Gloriosa." In *Orígenes del liberalismo,* edited by Ricardo Robledo et al., 81–104. Salamanca: Universidad de Salamanca.

Almuiña, Celso. 1974. *Teatro y cultura en el Valladolid de la Ilustración.* Valladolid: Ayuntamiento de Valladolid.

———. 1978. "Estudio Preliminar." In *Diario Pinciano, primer periódico de Valladolid (1787–1788),* edited by Celso Almuiña, 5–74. Valladolid.

———. 1980. *La universidad de Valladolid.* Valladolid: Universidad de Valladolid.

Alonso, María Paz. 2012. *Salamanca, escuela de juristas.* Madrid: Universidad Carlos III.

Alonso, Narciso. c.1920. *Discurso leído por D. Narciso Alonso Cortés en la apertura del Curso 1919–1920. El primer traductor del falso Ossian y los vallisoletanos del siglo XVIII.* Valladolid: Castellana.

———. 1933. "Prólogo." In *Diario Pinciano, primer periódico de Valladolid (1787–1788),* edited by Narciso Alonso, v–xxxi. Valladolid: Castellana.

Álvarez, Joaquín. 1999. "El periodista en la España del siglo XVIII y la profesionalidad del escritor." *Estudios de Historia Social* 51–53: 29–39.

Álvarez de Miranda, Pedro. 1992. *Palabras e ideas: el léxico de la Ilustración temprana en España (1680–1760).* Madrid: RAE.

Amunátegui, Miguel Luis. 1888. *D. José Joaquín de Mora: apuntes biográficos.* Santiago de Chile: Nacional.

Araque, Natividad. 2013. *Manuel José Quintana y la instrucción pública.* Madrid: Universidad Carlos III.

Arenas-Dolz, Francisco. 2015. "Libertad sin moral: José Marchena y la elocuencia." In *Retórica. Fundamentos del estilo narrativo en la novela romántica,* edited by M. Asunción Sánchez, 165–98. Berlin: Logos.

Astigarraga, Jesús. 1998. "Necker y Jovellanos: un 'área *neckeriana*' en el *Informe de Ley Agraria.*" *Revista de historia económica* XVI: 559–70.

———. 2000. "Necker en España, 1780–1800." *Revista de Economía Aplicada* 23: 119–41.

———. 2003. *Los ilustrados vascos.* Barcelona: Crítica.

———. 2005a. "I traduttori spagnoli di Filangieri e il risveglio del dibattito costituzionale (1780–1839)." In *Diritti e Costituzione. L'opera di Gaetano Filangieri e la sua fortuna europea,* edited by Antonio Trampus, 231–90. Bologna: Il Mulino.

———. 2005b. "La fisiocracia en España: los *Principes de la législation universelle* (1776) de G.L. Schmid d'Avenstein." *Historia Agraria* 37: 545–71.

———. 2009. "André Morellet y la enseñanza de la economía en la Ilustración española." *Cuadernos de Historia Moderna* 35: 143–73.

———. 2010. "Hacienda pública y opinión pública: la reforma fiscal de 1785, sus publicistas y sus críticos." *Storia e Politica* II, no. 3: 563–91.

———. 2011a. *Luces y republicanismo.* Madrid: CEPC.

———. 2011b. "La traduction au service de la politique. Le succès de Jacques Necker dans les Lumières espagnoles." *Annales Historiques de la Révolution Française* 364: 3–27.

———. 2017. "Turgot et le débat sur la liberté du travail dans l'Espagne des Lumières (1776–1813)." *Mediterranea. Richerque storiche* 40: 343–72.

———. 2021. *A Unifying Enlightenment. Institutions of Political Economy in Eighteenth-Century Spain (1700–1808).* Leiden-Boston: Brill.

———. ed. 2015. *The Spanish Enlightenment Revisited.* Oxford: Voltaire Foundation.

Astigarraga, Jesús, and Javier Usoz. 2008–2009. "El pensamiento político ilustrado y las cátedras de la sociedad económica aragonesa." *Anuario de Historia del Derecho Español* 78–79: 423–46.

———. eds. 2013. *L'économie politique et la sphère publique dans le débat des Lumières.* Madrid: Casa de Velázquez.

Astigarraga, Jesús, and Juan Zabalza. 2007. "Los diccionarios de comercio y economía en el siglo XVIII español." *Revista de historia industrial* 35: 13–46.

———. 2017. "José Joaquín de Mora y la divulgación de la doctrina liberal en Latinoamérica en los inicios del siglo XIX." *Revista de historia industrial* 26, no. 67: 39–68.

Astigarraga, Jesús, Niccolò Guasti, and Juan Zabalza. 2015. "The Spanish Debate on Public Finances. A Privileged Laboratory for the Enlightened Reforms." In *The Spanish Enlightenment Revisited*, edited by Jesús Astigarraga, 169–91. Oxford: Voltaire Foundation.

Astigarraga, Jesús, Javier Usoz, and Juan Zabalza. 2020. "Entre la economía, la política y la opinión pública: el nacimiento de las reseñas económicas en España (1737–1805)." *Revista de Estudios Políticos* 190, no. 4: 259–88.

Astorgano, Antonio. 1998. "Aproximación al marco liberal del *Informe sobre la postura del vino* (1798) de Juan Meléndez Valdés." *Cuadernos aragoneses de economía* 8, no. 1: 91–104.

Augello, Massimo M., and Marco E.L. Guidi. eds. 2005. *Economists in Parliament in the Liberal Age (1848–1920)*. Aldershot: Ashgate.

Barrenechea, José Manuel. 1984. *Valentín de Foronda, reformador y economista ilustrado.* Vitoria: Diputación Foral de Álava.

Bee, Michele, and Maria Pia Paganelli. 2019. "Adam Smith, Anti-Stoic." *History of European Ideas* 45, no. 4: 572–84

Beerman, Eric. 1981. "Spanish Envoy to the United States (1796–1809): Marques de Casa Irujo and his Philadelphia Wife Sally McKean." *The Americas* 37, no. 4 (April): 445–56.

Beltrán, Lucas. 1961. *Historia de las doctrinas económicas*. Barcelona: Teide.

Bernácer, Germán. 1961. "Prefacio." In Adam Smith, *Indagación acerca de la naturaleza y causas de la Riqueza de las Naciones*, ix–xv. Madrid: Aguilar.

Berry, Christopher J. 2013. *The Idea of Commercial Society in the Scottish Enlightenment*. Edinburgh: Edinburgh University Press.

Besomi, Daniele. 2001. *Gli economisti e la scuola*. Bellinzona: Messaggi Brevi.

Blázquez, Carmen. 2002. "Los ministerios de Hacienda de Miguel Lerdo de Tejada." In *Los secretarios de Hacienda y sus Proyectos (1821–1933)*, coordinated by Leonor Ludlow, vol. I, 399–434. México: Universidad Nacional Autónoma de México and Instituto de Investigaciones Económicas.

Boissel, Thierry. 1988. *Sophie de Condorcet. Femme des Lumières (1764–1822)*. Paris: Presses de la Renaissance.

Breton, Yves. 1990. "Germain Garnier, l'économiste et l'homme politique." In *La pensée économique pendant la Révolution Française*, edited by Gilbert Faccarello and Phillippe Steiner, 141–50. Grenoble: PUG.

Briody, Michael. ed. 2015. *The Scots College in Spain: Memoirs of the Translation of the Scotch Collge from Madrid to Valladolid*. Salamanca: Universidad Pontificia de Salamanca.

Cabrillo, Francisco. 1978. "Traducciones al español de libros de economía política (1800–1880)." *Moneda y Crédito*, 147: 187–91.

Cáceres, Ingrid. 2004. *Historia de la traducción en la administración y en las relaciones internacionales en España (S. XVI–XIX)*. Vertere, Monográficos de la revista Hermeneus, no. 6. Soria: Diputación Provincial de Soria.

Calderón, Francisco. 1985. "El pensamiento económico de Lucas Alamán." *Historia Mexicana* 34, no. 3: 435–59.

Calderón, Reyes. 2000. "Difusión de la doctrina de la *Riqueza de las Naciones*. Nuevos apuntes acerca de la traducción de 1794 y de su traductor, José Alonso Ortiz. La hipótesis del funcionario ilustrado." *Revista Empresa y Humanismo* III: 75–100.

Cárdenas, John Jairo. 2020. *Los criollos. 1759–1810. Reflexión económica. Patriotismo neogranadino*. Bogotá: Academia Colombiana de Ciencias Económicas.

Carpenter, Kenneth E. 1995. "*Recherches sur la nature et les causes de la Richesse des Nations d´Adam Smith et politique culturelle en France.*" *Economies et Sociétés* 24: 5–30.

———. 2002. *The Dissemination of the "Wealth of Nations" in French and in France, 1776–1843.* New York: The Bibliographical Society of America.

Castro, Mariano. 2012. *El pensamiento económico en la Cátedra de economía política de la Universidad de Granada (1807–1842): personajes e ideas.* Doctoral thesis. Jaén: Universidad de Jaén.

Cervera, Pablo. 2003. *El pensamiento económico de la Ilustración valenciana.* Valencia: Generalitat Valenciana.

———. 2008. "Lecciones y lecturas de Bernardo Danvila." In Bernardo Danvila, *Lecciones de economía civil, o de el comercio*, edited by Pablo Cervera, 9–76. Zaragoza: IFC.

———. 2019. "Ciencia del comercio, economía política y economía civil en la Ilustración española (1714–1808)." *Cuadernos dieciochistas* 20: 97–158.

———. 2020. "Civil Economy and Physiocracy in the Royal Nobility Seminar of Madrid (1770–1808)." In *Percorsi di Storia del Pensiero Economico e del Pensiero Sociologico. Scritti in onore di Vitantonio Gioia*, edited by Simona Pisanelli and Giulio Forges Davanzati, 31–48. Macerata: Università di Macerata.

Chaparro, Germán, and Álvaro Gallardo. 2015. "El pensamiento económico de los primeros economistas colombianos." *Lecturas de Economía* 83: 229–53.

Clément, Jean Pierre. 1980. *Las lecturas de Jovellanos.* Oviedo: Instituto de Estudios Asturianos.

Coats, Alfred W. 1971. "Editor's Introduction." In *The Classical Economists and Economic Policy*, edited by Alfred W. Coats, 1–32. London: Methuen and Co.

Colmeiro, Manuel. 1863. *Historia de la economía política en España*, 2 vols. Madrid: Cipriano López.

Comín, Francisco. 2000a. "Los economistas clásicos y los políticos liberales ante los problemas de la economía española (1808–1874)." In *Economía y economistas. Vol. IV. La economia clásica*, edited by Enrique Fuentes, 621–703. Barcelona: GG-CL.

———. 2000b. "Canga Argüelles: un planteamiento realista de la hacienda liberal." In *Economía y economistas españoles. Vol. IV. La economía clásica*, edited by Enrique Fuentes, 413–39. Barcelona: GG-CL.

Coutinho, Mauricio. 2017. "Silva Lisboa on Free Trade and Slave Labor: the Fate of Liberalism in a Colonial Country." In *The Political Economy of Latin American Independence*, edited by Alexandre Mendes-Cunha and Eduardo Suprinyak, 58–80. London: Routledge.

Defourneaux, Marcelin. 1973. *Inquisición y censura de libros en la España del siglo XVIII.* Madrid: Taurus.

De Haro, Dionisio. 2013. "Papel para un Perú independiente: el pensamiento económico español y la creación del *Banco Auxiliar de Papel Moneda.*" *Revista Complutense de Historia de América* 39: 203–27.

De Solano, Francisco. 1981. "Reformismo y cultura intelectual: la biblioteca privada de José Gálvez, ministro de Indias." *Quinto Centenario* 2: 1–100.

Demerson, Jorge. 1969. *La Real Sociedad Económica de Valladolid (1784–1808).* Valladolid: Universidad de Valladolid.

Démier, Francis. 1990. "Les 'économistes de la nation' contre l´économie-monde du XVIIIᵉ siècle." In *La pensée économique pendant la Révolution Française*, edited by Gilbert Faccarello and Phillippe Steiner, 281–321. Grenoble: PUG.

DICTER. 2011. *Diccionario de la ciencia y de la técnica del Renacimiento*, directed by María Jesús Mancho. Salamanca: Universidad de Salamanca. http://dicter.usal.es.

Díez, Fernando 1980. *Prensa agraria en la España de la Ilustración*. Madrid: Ministerio de Agricultura.

Domergue, Lucienne. 1982. *Censure et Lumières dans l'Espagne de Charles III*. Paris: CNRS.

Dopico, Fausto. 2005. "Matemáticas, fiscalidad y crítica de la escuela clásica. El pensamiento liberal de José Alonso López." *Investigaciones de historia económica* 1, no. 1: 81–96.

Dubet, Anne, and Sergio Solbes. 2019. *El rey, el ministro y el tesorero*. Madrid: Marcial Pons.

Edwards, José. 2018. "Historia del pensamiento económico en Chile." In *Historia política de Chile 1810–2010. Tomo III, Problemas económicos*, edited by Iván Jaksic, Andrés Estefane and Claudio Robles, 369–95. Santiago de Chile: FCE.

Elorza, Antonio. 1970. *La ideología liberal en la Ilustración española*. Madrid: Taurus.

———. 2021. *Ilustración y liberalismo en España*. Madrid: Tecnos.

Enciso, Luis Miguel. 1958. *Prensa económica del XVIII*. Valladolid: Universidad de Valladolid.

———. 1975. "La Real Sociedad Económica de Valladolid a finales del siglo XVIII." In *Homenaje al Dr. D. Juan Reglá Campistol*, vol. II, 155–78. Valencia: Universidad de Valencia.

———. 1980. "La Valladolid ilustrada." In *Valladolid en el siglo XVIII*, 13–155. Valladolid: Ateneo de Valladolid.

———. 2010. *Las sociedades económicas en el siglo de las Luces*. Madrid: Real Academia de la Historia.

Escolar, Hipólito. 1993 [1926]. *Catálogo razonado de obras impresas en Valladolid, 1481–1800*. Valladolid: Junta de Castilla y León.

Estapé. Fabián. 1971. *Ensayos sobre historia del pensamiento económico*. Barcelona: Ariel.

Faccarello, Gilbert. 1989. "Troisième partie: Économie. Introduction." In *Condorcet: mathématicien, économiste, philosophe, homme politique*, edited by Pierre Crépel and Christian Gilain, 121–49. Paris: Minerve.

Faccarello, Gilbert, and Philippe Steiner. 2002. "The Diffusion of the Work of Adam Smith in the French Language: An Outline History." In *A Critical Bibliography of Adam Smith*, edited by Keith Tribe and Hiroshi Mizuta, 61–119. London: Pickering & Chatto.

Ferguson, Niall. 2017. *The Square and the Tower: Networks, Hierarchies and the Struggle for Global Power*. Harmondworth: Penguin.

Fernández, Francisco, and Pedro Schwartz. 1978. "El *Ensayo* de José Alonso Ortiz: monetarismo *smithiano* en la España de los vales reales." In *Dinero y Crédito (siglos XVI y XIX)*, edited by Alfonso Otazu, 393–435. Madrid: Moneda y Crédito.

Franco, Gabriel. 1958. "Estudio preliminar." In Adam Smith, *Investigación sobre la naturaleza y causas de la Riqueza de las Naciones*, vii–xxxii. México D.F.: FCE.

Fuentes, Enrique. 1999. "Ensayo introductorio." In *Economía y economistas españoles. Vol. I. Una introducción al pensamiento económico*, edited by Enrique Fuentes, 7–388. Barcelona: GG-CL.

———. 2000a. "Una aproximación al pensamiento económico de Jovellanos a través de las funciones del estado." In *Economía y economistas españoles. Vol. III. La Ilustración*, edited by Enrique Fuentes, 331–420. Barcelona: GG-CL.

———. ed. 2000b. *Economía y economistas españoles. Vol. IV. La economía clásica*. Barcelona: GG-CL.

Fuentes, Enrique, and Luis Perdices. 1996. "Introducción." In Adam Smith, *Investigación de la naturaleza y causas de la Riqueza de las Naciones*, edited by Enrique Fuentes and Luis Perdices, vol. I, xvii–cxiv. Salamanca: Junta de Castilla y León.

Galland-Seguela, Martine. 2004. "Las condiciones materiales de la vida privada de los ingenieros militares en España durante el siglo XVIII." *Scripta Nova* 8: 157–80. www.ub.es/geocrit/sn/sn-179.htm.

García, Juan Luis, and José Manuel Valles. 1989. *Catálogo de la biblioteca del Real Colegio de Artillería de Segovia. Vol. I. Fondos científicos.* Segovia: BCA.

Garriga, Cecilio. 1996. "Notas al léxico económico del siglo XVIII." In *Actas del III Congreso Internacional de Historia de la Lengua Española*, edited by A. Alonso, 1279–88. Madrid: Arco/Libros.

Garriga, Cecilio, M.L. Pascual, and M.B. Pedraza. eds. 2019. *Lengua de la ciencia y lenguajes de especialidad.* Coruña: Universidade da Coruña.

Gestido del Olmo, Rosario. 1993. *Una biblioteca ilustrada gaditana: los fondos bibliográficos humanísticos del Real Colegio de Cirugía de Cádiz.* Cádiz: Universidad de Cádiz.

Giacomin, Alberto. 2007. "Paper-Money: A Reassessment of Adam Smith's Views." In *Money and Markets*, edited by Alberto Giacomin and Maria Cristina Marcuzzo, 181–89. London-New York: Routledge.

Gioli, Gabriela. 1972. "Gli albori dello smithianesimo in Italia". *Rivista di Politica Economica* 62: 917–62.

Gislain, Jean-Jacques. 1995. "Jean Herrenschwand, un physiocrate suisse héterodoxe?" In *La diffusion internationale de la phisyocratie (XVIIIᵉ-XIXᵉ)*, edited by Bernard Delmas, Thierry Demals and Philippe Steiner, 195–208. Grenoble: PUG.

Goldie, Mark. 1991. "The Scottish Catholic Enlightenment." *Journal of British Studies* 30: 20–62.

Gómez de Enterría, Josefa. 1992. *El tratamiento de los préstamos técnicos en español: el vocabulario de la economía.* Madrid: Universidad Complutense de Madrid.

———. 1996. *Voces de la economía y el comercio en el español del siglo XVIII.* Alcalá de Henares: Universidad de Alcalá de Henares.

González, Francisco José, and María del Carmen Quevedo. 2011. "Cátalogo de las obras antiguas de la Biblioteca del Real Instituto y Observatorio de la Armada: (siglos XV al XVIII)." *Boletín ROA* 1: 1–209.

Goodwin, Craufurd D., Joseph J. Spengler and Robert S. Smith. 1969. "Robert Sidney Smith, 1904–1969: An Appreciation." *History of Political Economy* 1, no. 1: 4–7.

Grange, Henri. 1974. *Les idées de Necker.* Paris: C. Klincksieck.

Groenewegen, Peter. 2002. *Eighteenth Century Economics.* London-New York: Routledge.

Guasti, Niccolò. 2000. "'Más que catastro, 'catástrofe': il dibattito sull´imposizione diretta nella Spagna del Settecento." *Storia del pensiero económico* 40, 77–128.

———. 2013. "Campomanes' Civil Economy and the Emergence of the Public Sphere in Spanish *Ilustración*." In *L'économie politique et la sphère publique dans le débat des lumières*, edited by Jesús Astigarraga and Javier Usoz, 229–44. Madrid: Casa de Velázquez.

———. 2017. *Juan Andrés e la cultura del Settecento.* Milano: Mimesis.

Guidi, Marco E.L. 2002. "Note on Italian Editions." In *A Critical Bibliography of Adam Smith,* edited by Keith Tribe and Hiroshi Mizuta, 392–96. London: Pickering & Chatto.

Guinard, Paul-J. 1973. *La presse espagnole de 1737 à 1791.* Paris: Centre de recherches hispaniques.

Guzmán, Jesús. 2019. "Amando Lázaro Ros (1886–1962). Una reconstrucción bio-bibliográfica." *Lectura y signo. Revista de Literatura* 14: 7–33.

Hale, Charles Adams. 1972. *El liberalismo mexicano en la época de Mora, 1821–1853.* México: Siglo Veintiuno.

Hamnett, Brian. 2017. *The Enlightenment in Iberia and Ibero-America*. Cardiff: University of Wales Press.

Harley, Ryan and Maria Pia Paganelli. 2014. "Adam Smith on Money, Mercantilism, and the System of Natural Liberty." In *Money and Political Economy in the Enlightenment*, edited by D. Carey, 185–99. Oxford: Voltaire Foundation.

Hernández, Juan. 1972. "Evolución histórica de la contribución directa en España desde 1700 a 1814." *Revista de Economía Política* LXI: 3–90.

———. 1978. "Evolución histórica de la contribución directa en España desde 1700 a 1814." In *Historia Económica de España*, 121–83. Madrid: UNED.

———. 1993. "Vicente Alcalá-Galiano, los *frutos civiles* y la influencia *smithiana*." *Revista de historia económica* 11, no. 3: 647–54.

Hernando, María Pilar. 2002. "La Universidad de Valencia: del plan ilustrado de Blasco al plan de 1807." *Cuadernos del Instituto Antonio de Nebrija* 5: 295–330.

Herr, Richard. 1959. *The Eighteenth-Century Revolution in Spain*. Princeton, NJ: Princeton University Press.

———. 1964. *España y la revolución del siglo XVIII*. Madrid: Aguilar.

Hont, Istvan. 2005. *Jealousy of Trade*. Cambridge-London: Harvard University Press.

Hoyos, José Carlos de. 2016. "*Empresario*, noción económica a finales del siglo XVIII y principios del XIX: vías de consolidación neológica." In *La neología en las lenguas románicas,* edited by J. García Palacios et al., 155–67. Frankfurt am Main: Peter Lang.

———. 2018. *Léxico económico en la lengua española del siglo XIX. El 'Epítome' de Jean-Baptiste Say*. San Millán de la Cogolla: Cilengua.

Hurtado, Jimena. 2017. "Jean-Baptiste Say's Social Economics and the Construction of the 19th Century Liberal Republic in Colombia." In *The Political Economy of Latin American Independence*, edited by Alexandre Mendes-Cunha and Carlos Eduardo Suprinyak, 141–62, London: Routledge.

———. 2019. "Adam Smith in Hispanic America in the 19th Century." Working paper. Adam Smith Works. www.adamsmithworks.org/documents/adam-smith-in-hispanic-america-in-the-19th-century.

Hutchison, Terence W. 1955. "Insularity and Cosmopolitanism in Economic Ideas, 1870-1914". *The American Economic Review* 45-2: 1–16.

Ibarra, Laura. 2012. "Las ideas de Ignacio Ramírez, El Nigromante. Su significado en la historia del pensamiento mexicano." *Iztapalapa. Revista de Ciencias Sociales y Humanidades* 72: 153–78.

Israel, Johathan. 2002. *Radical Enlightenment. Philosophy and the Making of Modernity, 1650–1750*. Oxford: OUP.

Jaramillo, Jaime. 2001. *El pensamiento colombiano en el siglo XIX*. Bogotá: Alfa Omega.

Kaplan, Steve L., and Sophus A. Reinert. eds. 2019. *The Economic Turn. Recasting Political Economy in Enlightenment Europe*. London: Anthem Press.

Larrère, Catherine. 1992. *L'invention de l'économie au XVIIIᵉ siècle*. Paris: PUF.

———. 2008. "L'Encyclopédie méthodique: une économie très politique". In *L'Encyclopédie méthodique (1782–1832). Des Lumières au positivisme,* edited by Claude Blanckaert, Michel Porret and Fabrice Brandli, 215–40. Genève: Librairie Droz.

Larriba, Elisabel. 2012. "Las aspiraciones a la libertad de imprenta en la segunda mitad del siglo XVIII." In *El nacimiento de la libertad de imprenta*, edited by Elisabel Larriba and Fernando Durán, 19–41. Madrid: Sílex.

———. 2013. *El público de la prensa en España a finales del siglo XVIII (1781–1808)*. Zaragoza: PUZ.

Larriba, Elisabel, and Gérard Dufour. 1997. *El 'Semanario de agricultura y artes dirigido a los párrocos' (1797–1808)*. Valladolid: Ámbito.

Lasarte, Javier. 1975. "Adam Smith ante la Inquisición y la Academia de la Historia." *Hacienda Pública Española* 33: 201–42.

———. 1976. *Economía y hacienda al final del Antiguo Régimen. Dos estudios*. Madrid: Fábrica Nacional de Moneda y Timbre.

Llombart, Vicent. 1992. *Campomanes, economista y político de Carlos III*. Madrid: Alianza.

———. 1995. "Una nueva mirada al *Informe de Ley Agraria* de Jovellanos doscientos años después." *Revista de historia económica* XIII, no. 3, 553–89.

———. 1996. "El *Informe de Ley Agraria* y su autor, en la historia del pensamiento económico." In *Reformas y políticas agrarias en la historia de España*, edited by Ángel García and Jesús Sanz, 105–59. Madrid: Ministerio de Agricultura, Pesca y Alimentación.

———. 2000a. "El pensamiento económico de la Ilustración española." In *Economía y economistas españoles. Vol. III. La Ilustración,* edited by Enrique Fuentes, 7–89. Barcelona: GG-CL.

———. 2000b. "Jovellanos, economista de la ilustración tardía." In G.M. de Jovellanos, *Escritos económicos*, edited by Vicent Llombart, 3–177. Madrid: IEF and RACMP.

———. 2004. "Traducciones españolas de economía política (1700–1812): catálogo bibliográfico y una nueva perspectiva." *CROMOHS* 9: 1–80, www.cromohs.unifi.it/9.2004/llombart.html.

———. 2009. *Un programa patriótico escalonado de fomento económico y promoción del empleo en el reinado de Carlos III*. Gijón: IFE and KRK.

———. 2013. *Jovellanos y el otoño de las Luces*. Gijón: Ediciones Trea.

———. 2017. "Jovellanos y Adam Smith. Acerca del fenómeno de las influencias en la historia del pensamiento económico." *Iberian Journal of the History of Economic Thought* 4, no. 2: 147–56.

Llombart, Vicent, and Jesús Astigarraga. 2000. "Las primeras 'antorchas de la economía': las sociedades económicas de amigos del país en el siglo XVIII." In *Economía y economistas españoles. Vol. III. La Ilustración*, edited by Enrique Fuentes, 677–707. Barcelona: GG-CL.

Llorens, Vicente. 1979. *Liberales y románticos. Una emigración española en Inglaterra (1823–1833)*. Madrid: Castalia.

Lluch, Ernest. 1971–1972. "Guillermo Oliver: la política económica de la reforma burguesa." *Boletín Arqueológico* V, 113–120: 405–32.

———. 1973. *El pensament econòmic a Catalunya (1760–1840)*. Barcelona: Ediciones 62.

———. 1988. "Prólogo." In Eudaldo Jaumeandreu, *Rudimentos de economía política* (1816), edited by Ernest Lluch, 5–17. Barcelona: Alta Fulla.

———. 1989. "Condorcet et la diffusion de la *Richesse des nations* en Espagne." In *Condorcet: mathématicien, économiste, philosophe, homme politique*, edited by P. Agel and C. Gilain, 188–94. Paris: Minerve.

———. 1992. "Juan López de Peñalver en los orígenes de la economía matemática." In Juan López de Peñalver, *Escritos de López de Peñalver*, edited by Ernest Lluch, ix–cxxiv. Madrid: IEF.

———. 1996. "El cameralismo más allá del mundo germánico." *Revista de Economía Aplicada* 10, no. 4: 163–75.

———. 2001. "López de Peñalver´s *Reflexiones*: an economic and mathematical approach." *European Journal for the History of Economic Thought* 8, no. 2: 130–45.

Lluch, Ernest, and Salvador Almenar. 1992. "Difusión e influencia de los economistas clásicos en España (1776–1870)." In *Actas do Encontro Iberico sobre História do Pensamento Económico*, 91–155. Lisboa: CISEP.

———. 2000. "Difusión e influencia de los economistas clásicos en España (1776–1870)." In *Economía y economistas españoles. Vol. IV. La economía clásica,* edited by Enrique Fuentes, 93–170. Barcelona: GG-CL.

Lluch, Ernest, and Lluis Argemí. 1987. "La difusión en España de los trabajos económicos de Condorcet. y Lavoisier: dos científicos entre el enciclopedismo y la revolución." *Hacienda Pública Española* 108–109: 108–56.

Lluch, Ernest, Salvador Almenar, and Lluis Argemí. 1999. "Els industrialismes a Espanya: 1804–1850." In *La industrialització i el desenvolupament econòmic d'Espanya*, edited by Albert Carreras et al., vol. II, 1436–54. Barcelona: Universitat de Barcelona.

Longás, María Ángeles. 2015. *Historia de la biblioteca de la Universidad de Mallorca (1767–1829)*. Madrid: Universidad Carlos III.

López, Fernando. 1995. *Liberalismo económico y reforma fiscal. La contribución directa de 1813*. Granada: Universidad de Granada and Fundación Caja de Granada.

———. 1999. "Estudio preliminar." In Román Martínez de Montaos et al., *El pensamiento hacendístico liberal en las Cortes de Cádiz*, edited by Fernando López, xiii–cciv. Madrid: IEF.

———. 2000. "La *Lección de economía política sobre población* de Casimiro Orense." In *Economía y economistas españoles. Vol. IV. La economía clásica*, edited by Enrique Fuentes, 351–68. Barcelona: GG-CL.

———. 2005. "Economía política, administración y hacienda pública en Canga-Argüelles." *Revista Asturiana de Economía* 32: 145–75.

———. 2010. "Estudio introductorio." In José Duaso and Antonio Plana, *Vicios y agravios de la contribución directa*, edited by Fernando López, 9–61. Zaragoza, Diputación de Zaragoza and IFC.

López-Cordón, María Victoria. 2020. "El bien público y el sistema político de la Europa: autores, traductores, divulgadores." In *Bajo el velo del bien público*, edited by Jesús Astigarraga and Javier Usoz, 249–75. Zaragoza: IFC.

Lucas, Francisco D. 2017. *La hacienda española entre la transición del Antiguo Régimen y el estado liberal*. Doctoral thesis. Universidad Carlos III.

Martín, Manuel 1989. "La institucionalización de la economía política en la universidad española (1784–1857)." In Francisco de Gregorio, Marqués de Valle Santoro, *Elementos de economía política con aplicación particular a España* (1833), edited by Manuel Martín, ix–ccxxxvii. Madrid: IEF.

———. 2000. "La enseñanza de la economía en España hasta la ley Moyano." In *Economía y economistas españoles. Vol. IV. La economía clásica*, edited by Enrique Fuentes, 593–619. Barcelona: GG-CL.

———. 2008. "Noticia sobre una temprana traducción al español de la *Teoría de los sentimientos morales* de A. Smith." *Homenaje a Antonio Domínguez Ortiz*, edited by Juan Luis Castellano and Miguel Luis López-Guadalupe, vol. 3, 595–600. Granada: Universidad de Granada.

———. 2011. "Los estudios de economía en España. La cátedra de economía política de la Universidad de Sevilla, 1807–1936." *Historia de la educación* 30: 145–65.

———. 2012. *Historia del pensamiento económico en Andalucía*. Granada: Comares.

———. 2018. *Traducciones y traslaciones en economía*. Granada: Tleo.

———. 2019. "La biblioteca de economía de Manuel de Torres en la editorial Aguilar (1945–1960)." Working paper, DT-1.908. Asociación Española de Historia Económica.

Martín-Valdepeñas, María Elisa. 2015. *Ilustrados, afrancesados y liberales: La Real Sociedad Económica Matritense de Amigos del País durante la Guerra de la Independencia (1808–1814)*. Doctoral thesis. Madrid: UNED.

Martínez, Manuel. 1998. "Lecturas antiguas y lecturas ilustradas. Una aproximación a los primeros manuales jurídicos." *Cuadernos del Instituto Antonio de Nebrija* 1: 143–209.

Martínez, Pablo F. 2009. "El pensamiento agrario ilustrado en el Río de la Plata: un estudio del *Semanario de Agricultura, Industria y Comercio* (1802–1807)." *Mundo Agrario* 9, no. 18: 1–23.

Matos, Covadonga. 2012. *Las lecturas y los libros en Valladolid (siglo XVIII)*. Doctoral thesis. Valladolid: Universidad de Valladolid.

McRoberts, David. 1955, "Ambula Cora Deo: The Journal of Bishop Geddes for the Year 1790, Part One," *Innes Review* 6. no. 1: 46–68.

Meikle, Scott. 1995. "Adam Smith and the Spanish Inquisition." *New Blackfriars* 76, no. 890: 70–80.

Melón, Miguel Ángel. 2009. *Los tentáculos de la hidra*. Madrid-Cáceres: Sílex and Universidad de Extremadura.

Mendes-Cunha, Alexandre, and Carlos Eduardo Suprinyak. 2017. "Political Economy and Latin America Independence from the 19th Century to the 20th Century." In *The Political Economy of Latin American Independence*, edited by Alexandre Mendes-Cunha and Carlos Eduardo Suprinyak, 7–31. London: Routledge.

Menudo, José Manuel. 2005. "Revisión sensualista de la economía clásica." In *Gonzalo de Luna. Un vallisoletano en los albores de la ciencia económica*, edited by José Manuel Menudo, 13–57. Valladolid: Ayuntamiento de Valladolid.

———. 2007. "Agricultura y política monetaria en España (1814–1820). La crítica de Gonzalo de Luna." *Áreas* 26: 31–45.

———. 2013. "José Domingo Alonso Ortiz Rojo." In *Economía y economistas andaluces*, edited by Rocío Sánchez, 277–87. Madrid: Ecobook and Editorial del Economista.

———. 2016. "Cartas españolas de Jean-Baptiste Say: evidencias para el estudio de la circulación de ideas económicas." *Revista de historia económica* 34, no. 2: 323–48.

Menudo, José Manuel, and José María O'Kean. 2005. "La recepción de la obra de Jean-Baptiste Say en España: la teoría económica del empresario." *Revista de historia económica* 23, no. 1: 117–42.

———. 2019. "Ediciones, reimpresiones y traducciones en español del *Tratado de economía política* de Jean-Baptiste Say." *Revista de historia económica* 37, no. 1: 169–92.

Millares, Agustín. 1972. *Don José Beristain de Souza (1756–1817)*. Madrid-Barcelona: CSIC.

Molina, Miguel. 1991. "Ilustración y reforma: la biblioteca de Francisco de Saavedra, segundo intendente de Caracas." *Estudios de historia social y económica de América* 7: 1–21.

Montes, Leónidas. 2003. "*Das Adam Smith Problem*: Its Origins, the Stages of the Current Debate, and one Implication for our Understanding of Sympathy." *Journal of the History of Economic Thought* 25, no. 1: 63–90.

———. 2004. *Adam Smith in Context*. New York: Palgrave-Macmillan.

Moral, Enrique. 2015. "Influencia de Beccaria y Adam Smith en León de Arroyal." In *IX Encuentro de la Asociación Ibérica de Historia del Pensamiento Económico*. Draft. Valencia.

Moral, Joaquín del. 1990. "Estudio Preliminar." In Pedro López de Lerena, *Memoria sobre las rentas públicas y balanza comercial de España (1789–1790)*, edited by Joaquín del Moral. Madrid: IEF.

Nava, María Teresa. 1990. "Robertson, Juan Bautista Muñoz y la Academia de la Historia." *Boletín de la Real Academia de la Historia* 187, no. 3: 435–56.

Navarro, Juan. 2013. *Don Pedro Giannini o las matemáticas de los artilleros del siglo XVIII.* Segovia: BCA.

Nieli, Russell. 1986. "Spheres of Intimacy and the Adam Smith Problem." *Journal of the History of Ideas* 47, no. 4: 611–24.

NTLLE: RAE. 2001. *Nuevo tesoro lexicográfico de la lengua española.* Madrid: Espasa Calpe. www.rae.es.

O´Brien, Denis P. 1989. *Los economistas clásicos.* Madrid: Alianza.

———. 2017. *The Classical Economists Revisited.* Princeton, NJ: Princeton University Press.

Oncken, August. 1897. "The consistency of Adam Smith." *Economic Journal* 7, no. 3: 443–50.

Paganelli, Maria Pia. 2013. "Commercial Relations: From Adam Smith to Field Experiments." In *The Oxford Handbook of Adam Smith*, edited by Christopher Berry, Maria Pia Paganelli and Craig Smith, 333–51. Oxford. OUP.

———. 2014. "David Hume in Banking and Hoarding." *Southern Economic Journal* 80, no. 4: 968–80.

———. 2015. "Adam Smith and the History of Economic Thought: the case of Banking." In *Adam Smith. His life, thought, and legacy*, edited by Ryan Patrick Hanley, 247–61. Princeton, NJ: Princeton University Press.

Palomares, Jesús María. 1974. *Imprenta e impresores de Valladolid en el siglo XVIII.* Valladolid: Universidad de Valladolid.

Palyi, Melchior. 1966 [1928]. "The introduction of Adam Smith on the Continent." In *Adam Smith, 1776–1926*, edited by John Maurice Clark et. al., 180–233. New York: A.M. Kelley.

Parisi, Daniela. 1972. "Gli albori dello smithianesimo in Italia." *Rivista di Politica Economica* 62: 917–62.

Perdices, Luis. 1991. "*La Riqueza de las Naciones* y los economistas españoles." Working paper, no. 9101. Madrid: Universidad Complutense de Madrid, Facultad de Ciencias Económicas y Empresariales.

———. 2000a. "*La Riqueza de las Naciones* y los economistas españoles." In *Economía y economistas españoles. Vol. IV. La economía clásica,* edited by Enrique Fuentes, 269–303. Barcelona: GG-CL.

———. 2000b. "The *Wealth of Nations* and Spanish Economists." In *Adam Smith Across Nations. Translations and Receptions of The Wealh of Nations,* edited by Cheng-chung Lai, 347–76. Oxford: OUP.

Perdices, Luis, and John Reeder. 2003. "Smith (Adam) en España. La recepción de." In *Diccionario de pensamiento económico en España (1500–2000)*, edited by Luis Perdices and John Reeder, 762–66. Madrid: Síntesis.

Perdices, Luis, and José Luis Ramos. 2021. "La economía en las colecciones divulgativas del primer tercio de siglo XX: los manuales Labor." *Investigaciones de Historia Económica* 17, no. 1: 48–57.

Perpere, Álvaro. 2014. "Felicidad pública y civilidad en el pensamiento de Juan Hipólito Vieytes." *Revista Cultura Económica*, 87: 66–73.

─────.2020."La primera referencia directa a La 'Riqueza de las Naciones' en Buenos Aires: 1797, 22 de julio." Working paper. Adam Smith Works. www.adamsmithworks. org/documents/la-primera-referencia-directa-a-la-riqueza-de-las-naciones-en-buenos-aires-1797.

─────.2021. "De Escocia a Buenos Aires: A. Smith, J.H. Vieytes y la importancia del interés personal." 24 de marzo. Working paper. Adam Smith Works. www.adamsmithworks. org/documents/Alvaro-Perpere-Vi%C3%B1uales-smith-vieytes-espanol.

Perrot, Jean-Claude. 1992. *Une histoire intellectuelle de l'économie politique, XVII – XVIII Siècle*. Paris: École des hautes études en sciences sociales.

Peset, Mariano. 1995. "Catedráticos juristas: formación y carrera." *Bulletin Hispanique* 97, no. 1: 261–78.

Peset, Mariano, and José Luis Peset. 1974. *La universidad española (siglos XVIII y XIX)*. Madrid: Taurus.

Pinilla, Julia, and Brigitte Lépinette, eds. 2016. *Reconstruyendo el pasado de la traducción en España. A propósito de obras francesas especializadas, científicas y técnicas en sus versiones españolas*. Granada: Editorial Comares.

Pisanelli, Simona. 2018. *Condorcet et Adam Smith. Réformes économiques et progrès social au siècle des Lumières*. Paris: Classiques Garnier.

Planas, Antonio, and Rafael Ramis. 2011. *La Facultad de Leyes y Cánones de la Universidad Luliana y Literaria de Mallorca*. Madrid: Universidad Carlos III.

Plaza, Juan. 1957. "Estudios y documentos de economía española." *Revista de Economía Política* VIII, no. 3: 1199–214.

Polt, John H.R. 1971. *Gaspar Melchor de Jovellanos*. New York: Twayne Publishers Inc.

─────. 1978. "El pensamiento económico de Jovellanos y sus fuentes inglesas." *Información Comercial Española* 512: 23–56.

Pradells, Jesús. 1990. "Juan Bautista Virio (1753–1837): experiencia europea y reformismo económico en la España ilustrada." *Revista de historia moderna* 8–9: 233–72.

Prado, Ángel de. 1996. *Las hogueras de la intolerancia*. Valladolid: Junta de Castilla y León.

Prats, Joaquim. 1993. *La Universitat de Cervera i el reformisme borbònic*. Lleida: Pagès.

Prieto, Enrique, and Dionisio De Haro. 2012. "La reforma monetaria en el Trienio liberal en España, 1820–1823. Modernización y límites." *América Latina en la historia económica* 2: 131–61.

Rae, John. 1895. *Life of Adam Smith*. London: McMillan and Co.

RAE (Real Academia Española). 1984 [1726–1739]. *Diccionario de Autoridades*, 6 vols. Madrid: Gredos. www.rae.es.

─────. 1780–2014. *Diccionario de la lengua española*. Madrid: NTLLE. www.rae.es.

Raphael, Davis Daiches. 1985. *Adam Smith*. Oxford: OUP.

Redondo, Alba de la Cruz. 2014. *Las prensas del Rey*. Doctoral thesis. Madrid: Universidad Complutense.

Reeder, John. 1973. "Bibliografía de traducciones, al castellano y al catalán, durante el siglo XVIII, de obras de pensamiento económico." *Moneda y Crédito* CXXVI: 51–86.

─────. 1978. "Economía e Ilustración en España: traducciones y traductores 1717–1800." *Moneda y crédito* 147, 47–71.

Reeder, John, and Jose Luis Cardoso. 2002. "Adam Smith in the Spanish and Portuguese-speaking World." In *A Critical Bibliography of Adam Smith*, edited by Keith Tribe and Hiroshi Mizuta, 184–97. London: Pickering & Chatto.

Reinert, Sophus A. 2011. *Translating Empire*. Cambridge-London: Harvard University Press.

Reyes, Jesús. 2002. *El liberalismo mexicano*, 3 vol. México: FCE.

Robertson, John. 1983. "Scottish Political Economy Beyond the Civic Tradition: Government and Economic Development in the *Wealth of Nations.*" *History of Political Thought* IV, no. 3: 451–82.

Robbins, Lionel. 1961. *The Theory of Economic Policy.* London: McMillan and Company Ltd.

Robledo, Ricardo. 2014. *La universidad española: de Ramón Salas a la Guerra Civil.* Valladolid: Junta de Castilla y León.

Rockoff, Hugh. 2013. "Adam Smith on Money, Banking and the Price Level." In *The Oxford Handbook of Adam Smith*, edited by Christopher Berry, Maria Pia Paganelli and Craig Smith, 307–32. Oxford: OUP.

Rodríguez-Braun, Carlos. 1994. "Estudio preliminar." In Adam Smith, *La Riqueza de las Naciones,* 7–24. Madrid: Alianza.

———. 1997. "Early Smithian Economics in the Spanish Empire: J.H. Vieytes and colonial policy." *Journal of the History of Economic Thought* 4, no. 3: 444–54.

Rodríguez Domínguez, Sandalio. 1979. *Renacimiento universitario salmantino a finales del siglo XVIII. Ideología liberal del Dr. Ramón de Salas y Cortés.* Salamanca: Universidad de Salamanca.

Ross, Ian Simpson. 2010. *The Life of Adam Smith.* Oxford: OUP.

Rothschild, Emma. 2001. *Economic Sentiments. Adam Smith, Condorcet, and the Enlightenment.* Cambridge, MA: Harvard University Press.

Ruiz, Joaquín. ed. 1982. *Floridablanca: escritos políticos.* Murcia: Academia Alfonso X el Sabio.

San Julián, Javier. 2000. *José María Zuaznavar y Francia y el debate sobre el comercio de granos en Navarra a principios del siglo XIX.* Bachelor´s Thesis. Barcelona: Universitat de Barcelona.

———. 2013. "Los avatares de la primera traducción de *La Riqueza de las Naciones* al español." EE-T Project Research Papers. http://eet.pixel-online.org/files/research_papers.

Sánchez, Alfonso. 2003. *Don Juan Antonio Hernández y Pérez de Larrea.* Zaragoza: Real Sociedad Aragonesa de Amigos del País.

———. 2005. "*Smithianismo* e industrialismo en la España de Carlos IV." In Juan Polo y Catalina, *Informe sobre las fábricas e industria de España (1804) y otros escritos*, edited by Alfonso Sánchez, xxi–cxxiii. Zaragoza: PUZ.

———. 2006. "Los *ideólogos*, el pensamiento económico y los ecos de la revolución francesa en España, 1800–1808." In *En la estela de Ernest Lluch*, edited by Alfonso Sánchez, 83–104. Zaragoza: Gobierno de Aragón.

———. 2018. "Adam Smith and the Neophysiocrats: War of Ideas in Spain (1800–4)." In *Classical Economics Today. Essays in Honour of Alessandro Roncaglia*, edited by Marcella Corsi, Jan Kregel and Carlo D´Ippoliti, 223–42. London: Anthem Press.

Sánchez, Alfonso, José Luis Malo and Luis Blanco. 2003. *La cátedra de economía civil y de comercio de la Real Sociedad Económica Aragonesa de los Amigos del País (1784–1846).* Zaragoza: Ibercaja.

Sánchez Agesta, Luis. 1981. "Introducción." In Agustín de Argüelles, *Discurso preliminar a la Constitución de 1812*, edited by Luis Sánchez Agesta, 7–64. Madrid: CEPC.

Sánchez-Blanco, Francisco. 2002. *El Absolutismo y las Luces en el reinado de Carlos III.* Madrid: Marcial Pons.

Sánchez Sarto, Manuel. 1959. "Adam Smith, en el Fondo de Cultura Económica." *El Trimestre Económico* 26, no. 1: 141–50.

Sarrailh, Jean. 1954. *L'Espagne éclairée de la seconde moitié du XVIII<sup>e</sup> siècle*. Paris: Imprimerie nationale.

———. 1957. *La España ilustrada de la segunda mitad del siglo XVIII*. México-Madrid-Buenos Aires: FCE.

Schumpeter, Josep Alois. 1954. *History of Economic Analysis*. Oxford: OUP.

Schwartz, Pedro. 1990. "La recepción inicial de *La Riqueza de las Naciones* en España." Working paper, no. 9034. Madrid: Universidad Complutense de Madrid, Facultad de Ciencias Económicas y Empresariales.

———. 1999. "Estudio Preliminar". In José Joaquín de Mora, *De la libertad de comercio*, edited by Pedro Schwartz, 8–49. Madrid: IEF.

———. 2000. "La recepción inicial de *La Riqueza de las Naciones* en España." In *Economía y economistas españoles. Vol. IV. La economía clásica*, edited by Enrique Fuentes, 171–238. Barcelona: GG-CL.

———. 2001. "The *Wealth of Nations* Censored: Early Translations in Spain." In *Contributions to the History of Economic Thought,* edited by A.E. Murphy and P. Prendergast, 119–31. Abingdon: Routledge.

———. 2006. "José Alonso Ortiz". In *Diccionario biográfico de la Real Academia de la Historia*. http://dbe.rah.es/biografias/9064.

Schwartz, Pedro, and Francisco Fernández. 1999. "Estudio Preliminar." In José Alonso Ortiz, *Ensayo económico sobre el sistema de la moneda papel y sobre el crédito público*, edited by Pedro Schwartz and Francisco Fernández, ix–lxvii. Madrid: IEF and Ministerio de Economía y Hacienda.

Scurr, Ruth. 2009. "Inequality and political stability from Ancien Régime to revolution: The reception of Adam Smith's *Theory of Moral Sentiments* in France." *History of European Ideas* 35: 441–49.

Sen, Amartya K. 2013. "The Contemporary Relevance of Adam Smith." In *The Oxford Handbook of Adam Smith*, edited by Christopher Berry, Maria Pia Paganelli and Craig Smith, 581–91. Oxford: OUP.

Serrano, José M. 2012a. "Estudio introductorio." In Francisco de Gregorio, Marqués de Valle Santoro, *Hacienda Pública-Balanza del comercio,* edited by José M. Serrano, 11-54. Zaragoza: IFC.

———. 2012b. "Librecambio y protección en la España liberal." *Historia Contemporánea* 43: 623–52.

Sher, Richard. 2002. "Early Editions of Adam Smith's Books in Britain and Ireland, 1759–1804." In *A Critical Bibliography of Adam Smith*, edited by Keith Tribe and Hiroshi Mizuta, 13–26. London: Pickering & Chatto.

Silva Herzog, Jesús. 1967. *El pensamiento económico, social y político de México 1810–1864*. México: Instituto Mexicano de Investigaciones Económicas.

Simal, Juan L. 2012. *Emigrados. España y el exilio internacional 1814–1834*. Madrid: CEPC.

Skinner, Andrew. 1975. "Adam Smith. An Economic Interpretation of History." In *Essays on Adam Smith*, edited by Andrew Skinner and Thomas Wilson, 154–78. Oxford: Clarendon Press.

———. 1995. "Adam Smith et le 'système agricole'." In *La diffusion internationale de la Phisyocratie (XVIII<sup>e</sup>–XIX<sup>e</sup>)*, edited by Bernard Delmas, Thierry Demals and Philippe Steiner, 33–57. Grenoble: PUG.

———. 1997. "Adam Smith: The French Connection." Working paper, no. 9703. Glasgow: University of Glasgow, Department of Economics.

Smith, Robert Sidney. 1955. "Economists and the Enlightenment, 1750–1800." *Journal of Political Economy* 63, no. 4: 345–48.

————. 1957a. "*The Wealth of Nations* in Spain and Latin America, 1780–1830." *Journal of Political Economy* LXV: 104–25.

————. 1957b. "*La Riqueza de las Naciones* en España e Hispanoamérica, 1780–1830." *Revista de Economía Política* VIII, no. 3: 1215–53.

————. 1959. "Manuel Ortiz de la Torre, economista olvidado." *Revista de Historia de Ámérica* 48: 505–16.

————. 1961. "Notas sobre las ediciones de *La Riqueza de las Naciones* de Adam Smith." *Revista de la Facultad de Ciencias Económicas de la Universidad de Cuyo* 38, no. 2, 40–48.

————. 1967. "The first Spanish edition of the *Wealth of Nations*." *South African Journal of Economics* XXXV, no. 3, 265–68.

————. 1968a. "English economic thought in Spain, 1776–1848." *South Atlantic Quarterly* LXVII, no. 2: 306–37.

————. 1968b. "English Economic Thought in Spain 1776–1848." In *The transfer of Ideas,* edited by Craufurd D.W. Goodwin and Irving B. Halley, 106–37. Durham, NC: Duke University Press.

————. 2000. "El pensamiento económico inglés en España (1776–1848)." In *Economía y economistas españoles. Vol. IV. La economía clásica*, edited by Enrique Fuentes, 305–38. Barcelona: GG-CL.

Sonenscher, Michael. 2007. *Before the Deluge.* Princeton, NJ: Princeton University Press.

Steiner, Philippe. 1995. "Quelques principes pour l'économie politique? Charles Ganilh, Germain Garnier, Jean Baptiste Say et la critique de la Physiocratie." In *La diffusion internationale de la Physiocratie*, edited by Bernard Delmas, Thierry Demals and Philippe Steiner, 209–30: Grenoble: PUG.

Stone, John. 2014. "The Case for English as a Language of Culture in Eighteenth-Century Spain: The English Libraries of the Conde de Fernán Núñez and John Hunter." *Cuadernos Jovellanistas* 8: 75–112.

Subercaseaux, Bernardo. 2016. "Juan Bautista Alberdi: modernidad y modernizaciones en el siglo XIX." *Revista Estudios Avanzados* 25: 1–19.

Tallada, José María. 1933–1934. "Prólogo." In *Investigación de la naturaleza y causas de la Riqueza de las Naciones*, 5–25. Barcelona: España Bancaria and Bosch.

Taylor, Maurice. 1971. *The Scots College in Spain.* Valladolid: Royal Scots College.

Tedde de Lorca, Pedro. 2000. "Comercio, dinero y banca en los escritos de Cabarrús." In *Economía y economistas españoles. Vol. III. La Ilustración*, edited by Enrique Fuentes, 487–528. Barcelona: GG-CL.

Toboso, Isabel. 1996. "La Junta del Crédito Público en el Trienio Liberal." *Revista de Estudios Políticos* 93: 401–13.

Torremocha, Margarita. 1986. "La matriculación estudiantil durante el siglo XVIII en la Universidad de Valladolid." *Investigaciones históricas* 6, 39–74.

————. 1991. *Ser estudiante en el siglo XVIII. La Universidad vallisoletana de la Ilustración.* Valladolid: Junta de Castilla y León.

Torres, Rafael. 2012. *La llave de todos los tesoros.* Madrid: Sílex.

————. 2013. *El precio de la guerra.* Madrid: Marcial Pons.

Tribe, Keith. 1988. *Governing Economy.* Cambridge: CUP.

————. 2002a. "General Introduction." In *A Critical Bibliography of Adam Smith*, edited by Keith Tribe and Hiroshi Mizuta, 1–11. London: Pickering & Chatto.

————. 2002b. "The German Reception of Adam Smith." In *A Critical Bibliography of Adam Smith*, edited by Keith Tribe and Hiroshi Mizuta, 120–51. London: Pickering & Chatto.

————. 2002c. "Adam Smith in English: From Playfair to Cannan." In *A Critical Bibliography of Adam Smith,* edited by Keith Tribe and Hiroshi Mizuta, 27–49. London: Pickering & Chatto.

————. 2002d. "The German Reception of Adam Smith." In *A Critical Bibliography of Adam Smith,* edited by Keith Tribe and Hiroshi Mizuta, 120–52. London: Pickering & Chatto.

————. 2008. "'Das Adam Smith Problem' and the origins of modern Smith scholarship." *History of European Ideas* 34: 514–25.

Tribe, Keith, and Hiroshi Mizuta. eds. 2002. *A Critical Bibliography of Adam Smith.* London: Pickering & Chatto.

Trincado, Estrella. 2014. "The translation into Spanish of the *Theory of Moral Sentiments* by Adam Smith." *The Adam Smith Review* 8, 37–52.

Urzainqui, Inmaculada. 1990. "Los redactores del *Memorial literario* (1784–1808)." *Estudios de Historia Social* 52–53: 501–16.

————. 1995. "Un nuevo instrumento cultural: la prensa periódica." In *La República de las Letras en la España del Siglo XVIII*, edited by Joaquín Álvarez, François Lopez and Inmaculada Urzainqui, 125–216. Madrid: CSIC.

Usoz, Javier. 2000. "El pensamiento económico de la ilustración aragonesa." In *Economía y economistas españoles. Vol. III. La Ilustración*, edited by Enrique Fuentes, 583–606. Barcelona: GG-CL.

————. 2011. "La 'nueva política' ilustrada y la esfera pública: las introducciones a la economía en el siglo XVIII español." *Revista de estudios políticos* 153: 11–46.

————. 2015. "Political Economy and the Creation of the Public Sphere during the Spanish Enlightenment." In *The Spanish Enlightenment Revisited*, edited by Jesús Astigarraga, 105–27. Oxford: Voltaire Foundation.

Vallejo, Irene. 1984. "Ambiente cultural y literario en Valladolid durante el siglo XVIII." In *Valladolid en el siglo XVIII*, 373–405. Valladolid: Ateneo de Valladolid.

Vallejo, Rafael. 1999. "Actores y naturaleza de la reforma tributaria de 1845," *Revista de Economía Aplicada* 21, no. 8: 5-28.

Valles, José Manuel. 1992. "Estudio Preliminar." In Vicente Alcalá-Galiano, *Sobre la economía política y los impuestos,* edited by José Manuel Valles, 13–148. Segovia: Academia de Artillería.

————. 2008. *Ciencia, economía política e Ilustración en Vicente Alcalá-Galiano.* Madrid: CEPC.

Varela, Javier. 1988. *Jovellanos.* Madrid: Alianza.

Varela, Joaquín. 2020. *Historia constitucional de España*, edited by Ignacio Fernández. Madrid: Marcial Pons.

Velasco, Eva. 2000. *La Real Academia de la Historia en el siglo XVIII.* Madrid: CEPC.

Viner, Jacob. 1927. "Adam Smith and *laissez-faire*." *Journal of Political Economy* 35, no. 2: 198–232.

————. 1958 [1926]. "Adam Smith and *Laissez Faire*." In *The Long View and the Short*, 213–45. Glencoe, IL: The Free Press.

White, Eugene N. 1987. "¿Fueron inflacionarias las finanzas estatales en el siglo XVIII? Una nueva interpretación de los vales reales." *Revista de historia económica* 5, no. 3: 509–26.

Winch, Donald. 1978. *Adam Smith's Politics*. London: CUP.

Yñíguez, Rocío. 2000. *Los estudios de economía y hacienda en la Universidad de Sevilla.* Doctoral thesis. Sevilla: Universidad de Sevilla.

Zapatero, Juan Carlos. 1975. "El caso español en *La Riqueza de las naciones.*" *Revista española de economía* II: 205–12.

Zylberger, Michel. 1993. *Une si douce domination*. Paris: Comité pour l'Histoire Économique et Financière and Imprimerie Nationale.

# Index

Absolutism 121, 180, 205–6
Academy of Geography and History
  (Valladolid) 80–1; of Law and Forensic
  Practice (Salamanca), 139, 178; of
  Mathematics and Noble Arts (Valladolid),
  80–81; of Medicine and Surgery
  (Valladolid), 80–1; of Midshipmen
  (Cádiz), 24; of Political Economy
  (Majorca), 139, 176; of San Carlos of
  National Jurisprudence (Valladolid), 80
Accarias de Serionne J. 90, 129, 174
Ackermann, R. 211
Aguirre, M. de 113, 157
Aguirre, P. A. 199
Ailmer, R. 24
Alamán, L. 219
Albani, A. 14
Alcalá-Galiano, A. 33, 122, 125, 131–2,
  189
Alcalá-Galiano, V. 4–5, 28–37, 87, 92–3, 103,
  106–9, 122, 125, 131, 133, 188–9, 222
*Alcabalas*, see *Rentas provinciales*
Almici, G. 179
Alonso, J.V. 180
Alonso Ortiz, J. 4–5, 12, 13, 15–22, 31–2,
  41, 54, 57–76, 79–98, 103, 109–112, 114,
  116, 122, 123–6, 129, 143, 147, 149, 153,
  159–160, 165, 180–1, 216, 218, 222–3,
  225–7
Ancien Régime 3, 52, 119, 121, 135, 172,
  181, 186–8, 193, 195, 213
Álvarez Guerra, J. 106, 127
Álvarez Osorio, M. 106
Andrés, J. 85
Aner, F. 190–1, 195, 197, 199
Anquetil, M. 168
Antillón, I. 131–3, 178, 193
Anti-Physiocracy 189
Antuñano, E. de 219

Aranda, P. P. Abarca de Bolea, Count of
  87, 174–5
Arango y Parreño, F. 216
Aragonese (or military) party 174
Aribau, B. C. 131
Arnoud, A. H. 167
Argüelles, A. 190, 193, 195–6, 199–200
Arriaga, J. de 23
Arriquíbar. N. de 29, 104, 106, 127, 130,
  133, 173
Arróspide, M. 125
Arroyal, L. 106, 157
Arteta de Monteseguro, A. 104, 175
Ayala, M. J. de 23
Azanza, M. J. de 32

Balance of trade office (or *secretaría*) 31,
  94, 109
Bank, of Amsterdam 42, 45, 54; of San
  Carlos, 45, 65, 89, 92, 97, 118
Banqueri, J. J. 87, 121
Barberi, M. A. 158
Bastiat, F. 4, 138, 217
Baudeau, N. 114
Beattie, J. 24
Beawes, W. 94–5
Beladiez, J. M. de 193
Belgrano, M. 216–7
Benavente, D. J. 218
Bentham, J. 118, 127, 130, 163, 218–9
Beristain, J. M. 81–2, 84–6, 90
Bethancourt, A. 166
Bielfeld, J. F. von 175–6
Bigot de Saint-Croix, C. 104
Blasco, V. 17
Blavet, J.-L. 87, 89, 95, 116
Board of trade, Spanish 105, 114–5, 192;
  of Barcelona 104, 124, 130, 176
Bonaparte, J. 32, 179, 181, 186, 206

Borrelly, J.-A. 95
Borrull, F. J. 191
Butel Dumont, G.-M. 174
Butler, A. 20, 57, 85–6

Caamaño, J. 106
Caballero university plan 97, 140, 160,
    179–180
Cabarrús, F. 32, 45, 87, 89, 106, 118,
    133, 157
Cadalso, J. 23
Cadastre (*catastro*) 92
Cagigal, F. 24
Calatrava, J. M. 193
Calatrava, R. 146
Calomarde, F. T. 127
Camacho, S. 218
Cambronero, M. M. 127
Cameralism 129, 175–6
Cameron, A. (RSC's 2nd rector) 14
Cameron, A. 11, 14
Campomanes, Pedro Rodríguez de 2, 4–5,
    11, 14–5, 20–1, 23–4, 29, 33, 85, 88,
    91–2, 95, 103–5, 115–6, 118, 127–130,
    160, 173–5, 178, 188, 194, 210
Campos, R. de 97, 112–3, 222
Cana, A. de la 104
Canard, N.-F. 126, 129–130, 133, 176
Canga Argüelles, J. 109, 128, 131–2, 138,
    146, 188, 196, 206–213, 220
Cantillon, R. 116, 126, 140, 142, 176,
    214, 224
Cantos Benítez, P. de 89
Cañedo, R. 127, 133
Capmany, A. 104, 194
Carlos III, King of Spain 28, 91
Carlos IV, King of Spain 32
Casa Santander (Valladolid) 79–80, 82–7,
    90, 94, 96–8
Castelli, G. 17
Castelló, J. J. 194
Castillo, F. del 195–196
Castro, M. 181
Catholicism, see Church, Inquisition; 1–2,
    12, 17, 22, 65–6, 69, 73, 86, 89–90, 97,
    109, 174, 178, 199
Censorship (and auto-censorship), see
    Inquisition 3, 5, 23, 42, 74, 85, 87, 89, 90,
    94, 97, 121, 157–8
Cerdá y Rico, F. 17, 22, 24
Chairs in political economy 7, 80, 122,
    127, 130, 134, 138–140, 143, 172–173,
    175–188, 219

Chamberlayne, J. 174
Chancery (Valladolid) 79–80, 85
Church, see Catholicism, Protestantism,
    Inquisition; Roman Catholic 50, 69, 73,
    89–90, 96, 158, 172, 174, 188, 199, 209;
    Scottish Catholic 11, 16, 21
Chaptal, J. A. 129–130, 148
Cía, J. 178, 181
Cistué, J. B. de 127, 176, 181
Civil economy 114, 139, 172, 174–5,
    177–180, 217
Cladera, C. 157, 159, 161
Classical school (or economists) 4–5, 126,
    129–130, 138, 141, 144–6, 169–170, 197,
    206–8, 210–1, 213–7, 220, 223
Clicquot de Blervache, S. 104
Colbertism 121, 165
Colegio de Santa Cruz (Valladolid) 79
College of Nobles (Madrid) 139
Colonies 47–8, 65–72, 83, 89, 91, 98, 123,
    130, 146, 163, 167, 220
Columbus 66
Commercial society 93, 161
Concordat of 1737 90
Condado, M. J. del 178
Condillac, E.-B. de 84, 90, 116–7, 126,
    130–1, 140, 178
Condorcet, M.-J.-A. Nicolas de Caritat,
    Marquis de 31–2, 41, 52–5, 59, 113,
    116–7, 123, 126–7, 140, 161, 174, 176,
    180, 216–7, 222, 225
Congress of Viena 205
Conjectural history 86
Conservatory of Arts and Crafts 129
Constant, B. 219
Constitution, of Bayonne 32, 186; of
    Cádiz, 121, 131–2, 186–8, 190, 196–200,
    205, 207
Consulates of trade 31, 139; of Malaga,
    134, 177
Cortes, of Cádiz 7, 32, 121, 132–3, 147,
    149, 157, 186–201; of Navarre, 127–8
Council of Castile 33, 57, 80, 85, 87–8, 91,
    103–4, 112, 116, 157, 160, 205
Courcelle-Seneuil J. G. 218
Covarrubias, J. de 32, 93, 107–9
Coyer, G.-F. 104
Creus, J. 194–5, 199
Crumpe, S. 162–5
Cruzado, A. 159

*Damnun emergens* 124
Danvila, B. 97, 104, 140, 173–8

*Das Adam Smith Problem* 53, 96, 225
Davenant, Ch. 163
De Paw, C. 90
De Weltz, G. 146
Destutt de Tracy A.-L.-C., 134, 145, 177, 213
Deza y Goyri J. 95
Díaz Caneja J. 196
Díaz de Yabarrena J. 177
Diderot, D. 29
Dou y de Bassols, R. L. 4, 123–6, 149–50, 190, 193–5, 198–9, 222, 226
Droz, J. 140
Duaso, J. 133
Dusquenoy, A. 162–3
Dutot, Ch. 111
Dyannière, A. 129

Economic Society, of Aragon, 80, 127, 139, 176, 178; of Asturias, 114; of the Basque Country (Bascongada), 81, 113, 139; of Madrid (Matritense), 29, 80, 103–5, 114, 117, 139, 163, 174, 176–7; of Majorca, 139, 176; of Segovia, 28–30, 33, 36; of Seville, 114, 148, 177; of Valladolid, 80–2
Economists of the nation 129, 134, 170
Eden, W. 107
Egaña, J. 217
El Escorial, library 81
Emphyteusis 124, 141, 149–150
Ensenada, Z. de S. 92
*Essays on Philosophical Subjects* 159
Escartín, F. 159
Escartín, J. 159
Espinosa de los Monteros, J. 143
Exile 23, 85, 145, 148, 205–6, 210–3, 220, 224
*Expediente de Ley Agraria* 91, 116, 168
Ezquerra, J. 157, 159–160

Fernán Núñez, Count of 11
Fernando VII, King of Spain 32, 42, 121–2, 186, 205
Ferguson, A. 12, 24, 116
Figuerola, L. 147
Filangieri, G. 122, 125–6, 128, 178, 219
Fiscal–military system 109
Five Major Guilds 89
Floranes, R. 80, 82–3
Flórez Calderón, M. 177
Flórez Estrada, A. 128, 138, 140–2, 144–6, 151–2, 177, 206, 210–1, 213, 216, 220

Floridablanca, J. M. 23, 30, 36–7, 80, 85, 103, 105, 108, 157, 174, 194
Forbonnais, F. V. de 146
Foronda, V. de 4, 81, 104, 106, 113–4, 128, 130–1, 140, 157, 166
Franco Salazar, P. 122
Franklin, B. 163
Freedom, of expression 81, 157, 200; of work see guilds.
French revolution 45, 52–3, 87, 139, 181
Freire, J. J. 210
*Frutos civiles* (civil fruits) 30, 33–5, 92, 105–6

Galiani, F. 116–7, 128
Gallard, D. 30, 106–7, 109, 168
Gallardo, F. 109
Gándara, M. A. de la 157
Ganilh, Ch. 130, 134–5, 148, 177
Garay, M. de 126
Garcés, F. 190
García Cañuelo, L. 157
García de la Madrid, M. 177
García Herreros, M. 191, 193, 195, 199
Gardoqui, D. 32, 94–5, 109–10, 112
Garnier, G. 96–8, 123, 126, 129–130, 134–5, 143–4, 159, 160, 176, 179, 209, 212
Garoz, M. B. 195
Gassó, B. 130
Genovesi, A. 59, 90, 97, 111, 116, 122, 127, 134, 140, 146, 172, 174–5, 177–8, 181, 217
Giannini, P. 29
Gilbert, Th. 11
Gioja, M. 143
Godoy, M. 32, 42, 57, 87–8, 95–6, 112, 121, 174, 180
Gómez-Farías, V. 219
Gómez Rombaud, R. 131
Gordoa, J. M. 190–2
Graef, J. E. 158
Grain trade 5, 84, 91, 114–5, 128, 136, 168, 190–1, 197; 1765 *Pragmática* and 91, 115, 190
Grenville, G. 174
Grivel, G. 105
Grotius, H. 86, 179
Grouchy, S. de 52, 159
Gueddes, J. 11–25, 103
Guevara, R. 17, 23–4
Guilds 5, 31–32, 91, 103–5, 115, 117, 119, 130, 136, 164, 169, 192
Guiraudet, Ch.-Ph.-T. 133, 162, 168, 189

Gutiérrez, M. M. 134–5, 149, 177, 181
Gutiérrez de la Huerta, F. 190, 195

Habsburgs 90–91
Heinetius, J. G. 82, 177, 179, 181
Heras Ibarra, D. de las 122
Herbert, J.-C. 69, 115, 117
Henríquez, C. 217–8
Hernández Pérez de Larrea, J. A. 80,
    175–6, 181
Herrenschwand, J. D. 126–7, 129, 142,
    176, 178
Hispanic America 2, 6–7, 205–6, 210–1,
    213–4, 216–220, 224–6
Holy Office, see Inquisition
Howard, J. 11
Hume, D. 24, 110–1, 126, 128, 163–4
Huskisson, W. 210
Hutcheson, F. 24, 116, 177–8

Inquisition 3, 5, 11, 24, 45–7, 52, 79, 81–3,
    85, 87, 89, 90, 96, 98, 139, 175, 179
Invisible hand 35, 119, 192
Iriarte, T. 17, 24

Jaumeandreu, E. 4, 124, 128, 130, 134–5,
    138, 141–3, 152, 176
Jesuits 21–2, 82, 85, 177
Jones, R. 143
Jovellanos, G. M. de 2, 4, 88, 105–6, 114–8,
    127–8, 130, 133, 168, 173, 179, 180,
    187–8, 191, 194, 200, 210, 216
Joyce, J. 113

Kindelán, B. 24
King's College (Aberdeen) 23

La Rochefoucauld, F. 163
Ladies' Board 80
Lardizábal, M. de 81
Larruga, E. 30–1
Laso, N. 24
Le Maur, C. 82
Le Trosne, G.-F. 114
Lerena, P. de 30, 32–3, 35–6, 87, 92, 94,
    105–108, 118, 131
Lerdo de Tejada, M. 219
Lesperat, M. 166
Liberal Triennium 7, 121, 135, 140, 172,
    186, 205–6, 211, 213, 220
Linguet, S.-N.-H. 114
Locke, J. 178
López, A. 193

López Ballesteros, J. 131, 147
López de Peñalver, J. 129
López Juana Pinilla, J. 131, 133, 146
López Momediano, A. 31–2
López Pelegrín F. 193, 195
Lora, P. de 177
Loynaz, M. de 92
*Lucrits cessans* 124
Lueder, A. F. 145
Luján, M. 188, 190
Luna, G. de 125–6, 135, 138, 222
Luxury 34, 82, 110, 126, 133, 197, 200
Luyando, J. 131–2

M'Farlan, J. 24
Mably, G.-B. de 32, 83
McCulloch, J. R. 145–6, 148, 213–5, 220
Macpherson, J. 20, 57, 82, 85–6
Madoz, P. 147
Magallón, J. M. 95
Malthus, Th. R. 143
Mantecón de Arce, V. 30–1, 106
Mariana, J. de 125
Marmilla, Count of 24
Marmotel, J.-F. 82
Martín de Miravall, F. 24
Martín y de Magarola, C. de 24
Martínez de Irujo, C. 5–6, 31–2, 41–55,
    87–8, 93, 97, 103, 113, 116, 123, 149,
    159–160, 217, 222, 226
Martínez de Mata, F. 88, 106, 130
Martínez de Montaos, R. 131–2, 188
Marx, K. 223–4
Masson de Morviliers, N. 81, 84
May, G. 23
Mayans, G. 81, 178
Meléndez Valdés J. 80, 83
Meléndez Vidal, J. 23
Melón, J. A. 163
Melon, J.-F. 111, 128, 146, 175–6
Mendizábal, J. A. de 151
Mercantilism 51, 174–6, 182, 211–2, 215
Mercantile system 4, 36, 93–4, 107, 110,
    124, 129–130, 161, 164–5, 167, 217, 220
Mercier de la Rivière, P.-P. 114, 117
Mill, J. 145, 213, 218, 224
Mill, J. S. 148, 224
Mirabeau, V.-R. de 59, 82, 114, 116, 127,
    129, 133
Mon de Velarde, J. A. 80, 176
Moncada, S. de 88, 106
Montegón, P. 81

Mora, J. J. de 148–149, 211–217, 219, 221
Moral philosophy 95, 139, 177–9
Morales, J. I. 113
Morales Gallego, J. L. 193
Morant, R. 133–4
Morellet, A. 163, 168
Montesquieu, Ch.-L. de Secondat, Baron de 29, 122, 127, 133, 178, 194
Moreno, M. 217
Moreno, M. L. 181
Moreno-Guerra, J. M. 210
Mortimer, Th. 95, 111
Mun, Th. 224
Munárriz, J. M. 31
Múzquiz, M. de 105, 107

Nadal Crespí, B. 198
Navarro, F. B. 180
Natural freedom 84, 94, 103, 117–8
Navigation Acts 115, 122, 131, 164, 168
Necker, J. 106–7, 109, 114, 116–7, 122, 128, 132–3, 146, 189, 207
Negrete, J. J. 178
Neo-Mercantilism 217–8
Neo-Physiocracy 126, 174, 176
Newton, I. 123
Nifo, F. M. 158
Normante, L. 104, 139, 173, 175–6

Ochoa, S. de 208
Ogilvie, W. 23
Olavide, P. 11, 118, 173, 178
Olive, J. F. 177
Oliver, G. 209
Oliveros, A. 192
*Ordnungspolitik* 118–9
Orense, C. 127, 134–5, 141, 177, 181
Orléans, J. d' 57, 85, 87
Ortiz de la Torre, M. 219
Ossian 20, 85–6
Osteret, A. 177
Osuna, Duke of 24

Panckoucke, Ch.-J. 29, 116
Paper money 109–111, 119
Pastor, L. M. 138
Pechenet, J. 104
Peñalver, J. López de 129
Pereira, L. M. 118
Peuchet, J. 126, 134
Philippine Company 89

Physiocracy 33, 36–7, 84, 104–7, 114–6, 118, 122–3, 126–9, 132–4, 141, 160, 162, 165, 168, 178–9, 194, 197
Pinto, F. A. 214
Pita Pizarro, P. 146–7
Plana, A. 133
Plano, J. F. del 80
Playfair, J. 166
Plumard de Dangeul, L.-J. 104, 174
Political arithmetic 30, 129, 135
Polo de Alcocer, P. M. 131
Polo y Catalina, J. 129–130, 176, 190, 193, 195, 199
Paso y Delgado, N. 143
Ponzoa, J. A. 177
Poor laws, see poverty
Poverty 11, 24, 33, 103–104, 119
Porcel, A. 132-2
Preber, P. 149
Press, Spanish 157–169; see censorship, freedom of expression and "Republic of letters"; "public writers" and 157; reviews on political economy and 158–9; the "Golden Age" and 157; *Correo mercantil* (Madrid) 158–160, 162, 165–6, 168, 170; *Diario pinciano* (Valladolid) 81–2, 84; *Espíritu de los mejores diarios literarios que se publican en Europa* (Madrid) 158–9, 161, 165–6; *Memorial literario* (Madrid), 158–9, 165–6; *Miscelánea instructiva, curiosa y agradable* (Madrid) 159, 161–2
Prevost, P. 159
Priestley, J. 166
Protectionism 4, 36, 46, 93, 107, 117, 123, 129–130, 132, 136, 141, 147–9, 153, 164, 167, 169–170, 190, 197, 210, 222
Protestantism, see Church 2, 86
Proudhon, P. J. 223
Proust, L. J. 29, 31
Public debt 105–6, 110–1, 119, 129, 143, 146–7, 194, 197, 205, 207–9, 213, 220
Public opinion 35, 89, 93, 106, 108–9, 111, 118, 158, 168, 197
Pufendorf, S. von 179

Quesnay, F. 59, 114, 125, 143, 165, 177, 218
Quintana, M. J. 180

Radical Enlightenment 86
Ramírez, I. 219
Ramos, E. 104, 140
Ramos Arizpe, M. 199
Ranz, A. 131

Rau, K. H. 143
Raynal, G.-Th. 90, 114, 163
Rayneval, J.-M. 107
Rech, J. 192
Regas, A. 176
Regional Enlightenments 4
Reid, Th. 24
*Rentas provinciales* (provincial revenues) 30,
    32, 34, 37, 92, 105–6, 131, 189, 208
Republic of letters 157
Ricardo, D. 130, 143–5, 148, 197, 211, 213,
    218, 223–4
Ricci, L. 143
Riego, R. del 205
Ripia, J. de la 109
Robertson, W. 23, 103
Rodríguez Aldea, A. 218
Romà, F. 104
Román, B. 159
Romero Alpuente, J. 210
Rossi, P. 140
Roucher, J.-A. 32, 45, 52–5, 89, 143,
    159, 161
Rousseau, J.-J. 29, 32, 82, 163
Royal Academy of Artillery (Segovia)
    28–9, 106
Royal Academy of History (Madrid) 24, 85,
    87, 114
Royal Irish Academy 163
Royal Institute and Observatory of the
    Navy (Cádiz) 24
Royal Scots College 11–5, 17–9, 21–2, 24
Royal Surgery College (Cádiz) 24
Royalist (*regalista*) 87, 92, 104, 108, 157
Rozier, F. 59
Ruiz de Zelada, J. 84
Rumford, B. Thompson, Count of 163, 167

Saa, D. A. 181
Saavedra, F. (Caracas' *Intendente*) 23
Saavedra, F. (Finance Minister) 23, 131
Saavedra Fajardo, D. 125
Sagra, R. de la 151–2
Saint-Aubin, M. 168
Salas, M. de 217
Salas y Cortés, R. de 106, 178–9, 217
San Isidro Royal Studios 112
San Martín, J. de 218
San Millán, J. 146
Samaniego, F. de 23
Samper, M. 219
Sánchez, A. 104
Sánchez Rivera, J. 143

Santander, M. 82, 98
Santander, R. 82, 98
Santander, T. 82–3
Santillán, R. de 131
Santiváñez, V. M. de 80, 82
Saura, J. P. 158
Say, J.-B. 2, 4, 18, 97, 125, 127–130, 132–5,
    138, 144, 147–150, 152–3, 158, 162,
    172–182, 211, 217–9
Schmid d'Avenstein, G. L. 122
Seminaries, for the Nobility (Madrid) 177;
    of Vergara 80
Scholasticism 172, 178
Scottish Catholic College 22
Scottish Enlightenment 1, 24, 76, 86
Sempere y Guarinos, J. 173
Serna, F. de 193
Sierra Pambley, F. 207–8
Silva, B. 219
Silvela, M. 80
Silves, P. 188
Sinclair, J. 166
Sismonde de Sismondi J.-Ch.-L. 127,
    142–3, 145, 168, 213, 215
Sisternes, M. 118
Sixto de Espinosa, M. 104–5
Slavery 20, 48, 91, 117, 198, 219
Smith, A. see censhorship, *Das Adam
    Smith problem, Essays on Philosophical
    Subjects*, Inquisition, *The Theory of Moral
    Sentiments, The Wealth of Nations*; citations
    in the Spanish press and 165–9; Geddes
    and 12–21; in chairs of political economy
    139–140, 175–181; in Hispanic America
    213–220; in the Cortes of Cádiz
    186–201; in the Liberal Trienium
    206–210; in reviews and bibliographical
    information in the Spanish press
    158–162; Jovellanos and 114–8; Spanish
    public finance and 105, 112, 131–4,
    146–7, 188–9; "Spanish Smith" 1–7;
    Spanish strategies of development and
    126–131, 147–150; the social question
    and 151–2; the Spanish exile and 210–3
Social question 146, 151–2
Society of Jesus, see Jesuits
Sorá, J. 181
Southwell, Th. 23
Spanish Law Society (Madrid) 108
Spanish Royal Academy 20, 60
Spirit of conquest 90
Stauton, G. L. 167–8
Steuart, J. 112, 129, 133–4, 140, 146, 163

Stewart, D. 159
Storch, M. F. 148, 211, 213
Sumptuary laws, see Luxury
Supreme Central Board of the Kingdom
    32, 186
Surrá, P. 146
Swing, M. 24

Tariff, see protectionism; of 1778-1782 93,
    107; of 1825 147; of 1849 147
Tariff Board 147, 209
Terreros y Pando, E. 20, 61
*Theory of Moral Sentiments, The* (TMS) 1, 53,
    88, 95–6, 159, 224–5
TMS, see *The Theory of Moral Sentiments*
Toreno, J. M. Queipo de Llano, Count of
    131, 133, 189, 191–5, 199, 208–10
Torre, D. de la 106
Torrente, M. 140, 143
Treaties, of Amiens 212; of Eden-Rayneval
    107, 129
Turgot, A.-R.-J. 55, 59, 90, 104–5, 115–6,
    126–7, 130, 132

Uriortua, F. X. 131
Uztáriz, J. de 92, 123, 130, 163, 174
Ulloa, A. de 82, 159
Ulloa, B. de 106, 123, 174
*Única contribución* (single tax) 92, 106, 124,
    132–3, 141
Universities, of Aberdeen 11; of Alcalá de
    Henares 79, 180; of Cervera 125; of
    Granada 57, 79, 143, 180; of Glasgow
    1; of Majorca 176; of Oxford 49; of
    Salamanca 79, 83, 98, 128, 139, 178–80;
    217; of Valencia 80–1; of Valladolid 79–83,
    85, 90, 98, 177
Uría Nafarrondo, J. M. de 90
Usury 65, 89–90, 124

Vadillo, J. M. 147–8, 210
*Vales reales* (royal bonds) 92, 105, 106,
    109–110, 197
Valle, J. 209

Valle Santoro, F. de Gregorio, Marquis of
    140, 143, 146–7
Vargas, F. P. 218
Vattel, E. de 82
Vaughan, B. 165
Veranio, S. 122, 168
Verri, P. 116, 134
Vicent de Gournay, J.-C.-M. 104–5, 174
Vicuña, P. F. 218
Viegas, S. de 179
Vieytes, H. 217
Villanueva, J. L. 196
Villava, V. de 178, 216
Virio, J. B. 36

Wars, of Convention (1793-1796) 92, 109;
    Anglo-Spanish (1796-1802) 109; of
    Independence (1808-1812) 121, 123,
    135, 186
Ward, B. 88, 122, 125, 127, 129, 133,
    166
*Wealth of Nations, The*, see Smith; *Breve
    exposición de la doctrina de Adam Smith*
    and 98; early Spanish translations
    11–25; Alonso Ortiz *Ensayo* and
    109–112; beyond the Enlightenment
    222–8; Covarrubias' *Código* and 107–9;
    Crumpe's *Essay* and 162–5; translation
    by Alcalá-Galiano 33–7; translation by
    Alonso Ortiz (1st ed.) 87–94 (2nd ed.)
    94–8; (philological analysis) 61–76;
    translation by Martínez de Irujo, 42–55;
    version by Campos 112–3; version by
    Dou 123–5; version by Luna 125–6; WN
    see *The Wealth of Nations*

Yberri, F. P. 181
Young, A. 126, 166–8

Zarco, J. F. 219
Zavala, M. de 89–90, 92, 106, 127–8,
    132, 219
Zorraquín, J. 191
Zuaznabar, J. M. 128

Printed in the United States
by Baker & Taylor Publisher Services